Elusive Refuge

Elusive Refuge

CHINESE MIGRANTS IN THE COLD WAR

LAURA MADOKORO

HARVARD UNIVERSITY PRESS

Cambridge, Massachusetts

London, England

2016

Library of Congress Cataloging-in-Publication Data

Names: Madokoro, Laura, author.
Title: Elusive refuge : Chinese migrants in the Cold War / Laura Madokoro.
Description: Cambridge, Massachusetts : Harvard University Press, 2016. | Includes
    bibliographical references and index.
Identifiers: LCCN 2016021043 | ISBN 9780674971516
Subjects: LCSH: China—Emigration and immigration—Political aspects. | China—
    Emigration and immigration—History—20th century. | Political refugees—China. |
    Cold War. | Chinese—Foreign countries. | Humanitarian assistance—Political aspects.
Classification: LCC JV8701 .M34 2016 | DDC 305.895/10086914—dc23
LC record available at https://lccn.loc.gov/2016021043

For Tom

CONTENTS

ABBREVIATIONS

AFSC	American Friends Service Committee
ARCI	Aid Refugee Chinese Intellectuals
CCC	Canadian Council of Churches
CORSO	Council of Organizations for Relief Services Overseas
CPA	Comprehensive Plan of Action
ECOSOC	United Nations Economic and Social Council
FCRA	Free China Relief Association
FERP	Far Eastern Refugee Program
ICEM	Intergovernmental Committee for European Migration
INS	United States Immigration and Naturalization Service
IRO	International Refugee Organization
ISS	International Social Service
MCC	Mennonite Central Committee
NCC	National Council of Churches in New Zealand
PRC	People's Republic of China
RCMP	Royal Canadian Mounted Police
ROC	Republic of China
RSAC	Refugee Status Advisory Committee
UN	United Nations

UNESCO	United Nations Educational, Scientific and Cultural Organization
UNHCR	Office of the United Nations High Commissioner for Refugees
UNKRA	United Nations Korean Reconstruction Agency
UNRRA	United Nations Relief and Rehabilitation Agency
WCC	World Council of Churches
WRRA	Wartime Refugees Removals Act

Elusive Refuge

INTRODUCTION

IN MARCH 1961, a special subcommittee of the US House of Representatives Committee on the Judiciary was convened to make an "on-the-spot" investigation of the situation of migrants in Hong Kong. The subcommittee was tasked with determining whether or not the people who had left the People's Republic of China (PRC) for the British colony after the establishment of a communist regime in 1949 could, and should, be considered refugees. Committee members included Representatives Arch A. Moore Jr. and Basil L. Whitener, as well as William H. Crabtree, associate counsel. In the opening pages of their final report, the members noted:

> There are in excess of an estimated 1 million refugees in Hong Kong out of a total population of 3,128,044. The exact number of refugees cannot be calculated. It is misleading to classify all of these persons as refugees in the political sense. There are no reliable statistics on the number who have fled Red China because of political persecution and those who simply got "fed up" with conditions in China and migrated to Hong Kong in order to improve their "lot in life." The latter group, in fact, are [sic] commonly referred to as "rice refugees" and not as political escapees.[1]

In this brief excerpt from the subcommittee's final report, we find all the elements that defined the response of the United States, as well as other white settler societies such as Canada, Australia, New Zealand, and South Africa, to hundreds of thousands of migrants who moved from the PRC to Hong Kong during the Cold War. Most notably, Moore, Whitener, and Crabtree underscored the difficulty in determining the exact number of refugees in Hong Kong, owing to definitional ambiguities. In doing so, they drew attention to the imprecise line between migrants who wanted to improve their conditions and so-called political refugees who moved because of ideological persecution.

In using the use of the term *rice refugee* to describe the character of the migrant population in Hong Kong, the subcommittee called into question the authenticity of the refugee experience in the colony, as well as any sense of obligation to provide assistance. The term *rice refugee* was a derogatory one that echoed earlier missionary references to "rice Christians," a phrase used to describe people who converted to Christianity in the hopes of obtaining material benefits, rather than spiritual ones.[2] The subcommittee's acknowledgement of the term *rice refugee* was a deliberate effort to deflect any seeming responsibility for assisting people in Hong Kong, especially through resettlement programs that would have seen the migration of people historically excluded from permanent settlement in the United States and elsewhere. The subcommittee's report therefore reflected the spirit of the response amongst white settler societies that attended the movement of people out of the PRC after 1949.

Caught up in the political turmoil of the Cold War, those who made their way to the British colony of Hong Kong became the subjects of intense international debate, one that transformed notions of humanitarian responsibility and refugee protection in the postwar period. The decades-long dispute over the refugee qualities of the migrants in Hong Kong was a product of the intensely subjective nature of the refugee experience and the manner in which this existence was mediated by migrants, humanitarians, local and national governments and the international community. Hong Kong—a historic meeting place between East and West—became a pivotal site for encounters between Western humanitarians and Chinese migrants during the Cold War. As the Anglican Bishop of Hong Kong, Ronald Hall, observed, "Hong Kong has traditionally faced in two directions—towards China and out towards the world."[3] Throughout the Cold War, developments in Hong Kong had a profound impact on how refugees were conceptualized and how notions of refugee protection evolved globally.

The very concept of a refugee has changed radically over time. Today, a refugee is typically understood as "A person who has been forced to leave his or her home and seek refuge elsewhere, especially in a foreign country, from war, religious persecution, political troubles, the effects of a natural disaster, etc."[4] Derived in part from the Middle French *réfugié*, the term has biblical origins, strongly associated with the experience of the Jewish people, the loss of homeland, and the flight to safety.[5] The term *refugee* was first used in modern times in 1685 to describe the departure of the Protestant Huguenot population from France, in the face of forced religious conversion. However, it was only in the twentieth century with the fall of empires, the establishment of nation-states, and the drawing of national borders that the term *refugee* came into common parlance.

The creation of new states redrew the borders of traditional homelands. Those displaced by these processes were understood to be stateless people, or refugees and solutions were envisioned accordingly. This was the case for Armenians persecuted after the fall of the Ottoman Empire as well as Russians fleeing their revolutionary state in the 1920s. After the Second World War, the definition of a refugee underwent a dramatic transformation as observers confronted the devastating effects of the Holocaust and the specter of millions of displaced persons living in makeshift camps and temporary accommodations across the European continent. Animating concerns shifted from the legal implications of statelessness to questions of appropriate relief and protection. These two issues assumed even greater urgency as the politics of the Cold War thickened. Western nations began to think of refugees as people fleeing communist protection who needed assistance as well as individuals who could play an important symbolic role in the emerging propaganda war as the recipients of Western aid and protection.

In 1951, at a time of heightened Cold War tensions characterized by the conflict over Korea, the United Nations adopted the Convention Relating to the Status of Refugees, which defined a refugee on the basis of individual persecution.[6] The notion of a political refugee or, more specifically, an individual persecuted, or fearing persecution, because of their political beliefs was a product of Cold War confrontations between East and West. Western governments considered political refugees to be in need of assistance and protection, distinct from other migrants who moved for seemingly less coerced reasons. The narrow convention definition became the cornerstone of how signatories, and nonsignatories alike, understood their obligations to refugees.

Despite its limitations, the convention definition became central to how secular and religious humanitarians—including missionaries, NGOs, and voluntary organizations—advocated for refugee protection and assistance. Secular and religious humanitarians recognized that the convention's limited legal definition failed to capture the variety of experiences that might be considered refugee-like. As a result, advocates consistently campaigned on behalf of refugees using the language of hardship, fear, and desperation, in addition to that of persecution. In popular culture therefore, refugees continued to be thought of in broad terms as people in flight, and in need. Western humanitarians applied their expansive vision of refugeehood to the populace in Hong Kong, which swelled and contracted in tandem with conditions on the mainland.

There was a history of open movement between China and Hong Kong. For centuries people had moved back and forth between the two spaces in times of conflict. This continued after the transfer of Hong Kong to British control in 1842. People fled China during the Taiping Rebellion in 1854 and left Hong Kong during the Japanese occupation in 1941. In 1927, civil war broke out on the mainland and continued intermittently for the next two decades. At the end of the confrontation, the Chinese Communist Party emerged victorious, and the Guomindang, under the leadership of General Chiang Kai Shek, fled to Taiwan, establishing the Republic of China (ROC) and advancing claims to being the legitimate government of China. An estimated two million supporters and former soldiers followed.[7] Hundreds of thousands of others moved southwestward towards Burma and hundreds of thousands more relocated to Hong Kong.[8]

Devastated by four years of Japanese occupation, Hong Kong was in a ruinous state when the British resumed control of the colony in 1945. Its infrastructure was almost nonexistent and many of its inhabitants were deeply scarred by wartime events.[9] Despite the colony's terrible state, an estimated 700,000 people made their way to Hong Kong from the PRC between 1949 and 1951, resulting in difficult, overcrowded conditions in an environment where people were struggling to rebuild. The continuous movement of people into the British colony after the initial influx compounded this situation. An estimated 40,000 people moved to Hong Kong annually throughout the 1950s. This number dropped to about 10,000 a year in the 1960s, with the exception of the tumultuous events in the spring of 1962, which saw a sudden rise in numbers.[10] Arrivals consistently outnumbered departures in the colony throughout the postwar period.

Attuned to the politics of Cold War migration, the ROC government campaigned aggressively to convince the international community that migrants leaving the Chinese mainland were victims of communist oppression. Authorities in Hong Kong, however, were determined to maintain a neutral stance in the standoff between East and West.[11] Neutrality was considered a question of survival. To choose sides would be to risk the animosity of the communist regime in Beijing and the economic survival of the colony.[12] This commitment to neutrality had important implications for the movement of people from the PRC as the colonial government refused to participate in the propaganda exercises around Cold War refugees. In fact, local authorities regularly sought to deter movement into the colony given Hong Kong's overcrowded conditions and fragile infrastructure.

In the face of the ambiguous response from colonial officials about the fate of migrants from the PRC, secular and religious humanitarians on the ground in Hong Kong made a determined effort to secure international support for people they believed to be refugees. A number of Western missionaries and humanitarian organizations relocated from the PRC to Hong Kong in the early 1950s after conditions became decidedly hostile under the communist regime. They proceeded to develop a vested interest in the plight of the migrant population in the colony.[13] Some refugee advocates instrumentalized the idea of being humanitarian to convince prospective supporters of the value of their cause. Others understood humanitarian work as a vocation, operating on the ground in Hong Kong to provide immediate relief in the form of food, clothing, and shelter. These various strands of humanitarianism evolved over the course of the Cold War, leading to an array of proposed solutions to address the needs of Chinese migrants in the colony. Humanitarians in Hong Kong would be the first, and the most insistent, to propose that resettlement abroad was a viable option to alleviate population pressures in the colony. Confronted with a generally indifferent international community, they would also be the most determined to convince potential donors and supporters that the people in Hong Kong were indeed refugees.[14]

Somewhat ironically, given the energy Western humanitarians invested in their plight, migrants in Hong Kong after 1949 projected ambivalence about the term *refugee*. Some were prepared to self-identify as refugees, particularly if it meant that they could secure tangible benefits, but for others the notion of being a refugee was an alien concept. In following the tradition of open movement between the mainland and Hong Kong, migrants did not necessarily see themselves as desperate individuals in need of Western assistance. Rather, many people simply followed family and neighbors, with the support of clan and village associations, to safety. The expectation was that they would eventually return home. For migrants, therefore, the interplay between the contest over who, exactly, was a refugee and what kinds of humanitarian assistance they deserved had mixed effects. For those who conformed to Western expectations of what a refugee should look or act like, there was the promise and hope of some kind of assistance. For those who did not, their options were more limited. If they decided to seek assistance from Western parties, their position became highly tenuous, dependent on the inclination of humanitarian advocates and potential countries of assistance as well as those of resettlement. Migrants read and deciphered the landscape of possibilities available to them. This included making decisions about whether to actively claim the refugee label for themselves.

Prior to the development of refugee status as an official, if limited, designation in the 1950s, migrants, including refugees, moved however possible, navigating discretionary humanitarianism and a web of rules and regulations in order to do so.[15] The presence of a new, and narrow, legal definition of refugees after 1951 did not change this traditional practice. Nor did it remove the capacity for humanitarian discretion on the part of governments. Migrants continued to move for a variety of reasons, some more coerced than others, but they also continued to make decisions about movement, including whether or not to accept the label, and the potential benefits, of being a refugee. Being a refugee was not the result of some essential trait. Rather it resulted from a "refugeeing process" whereby certain migrants were labeled or embraced as refugees or where migrants themselves made the decision to self-identify as refugees.[16]

The idea of a refugeeing process complicates any historical account of a migrant population that starts from the premise that certain people were essentially refugees. Such an approach ignores the contests at the heart of the very term *refugee* and assumes a preexisting identity when, in fact, the very notion of being a refugee was, and continues to be, highly subjective and at the mercy of social, economic, political, as well as historical contingencies.[17] Still, there are a number of strategies for working through how the refugee label has been alternately imposed, embraced, and negotiated by the people to whom it has been applied.[18] Some advocate embracing the term *refugee* to do this work so that humanitarian need becomes the baseline of experience. Others suggest a different vocabulary for every experience, hence the evolution of terms such as forced migrants and internally displaced persons.[19] A more effective strategy, however, is to return refugees to the world of the migrant and describe the people in motion as migrants. Using the term *migrant*, while attending to the occasions when observers, interested parties, and migrants used the term *refugee* to describe themselves and their situation, highlights the shared experiences of people moving across national borders even as they were, and continue to be, distinguished by historical contingencies, perceived need and various forms of self-representation and identity.[20]

Using *migrants* as a descriptor, rather than *refugees*, in no way suggests that people did not move under difficult, and in many cases coerced and dangerous, circumstances. They did. Moreover, the decision to move was always a complicated one, based on a myriad of factors. It is precisely because of the complexities involved that it is impossible to capture all of the contingencies and processes by adopting the singular, flattening frame suggested by the word *refugee*. The term *migrant*, by contrast, leaves room to investigate how and why someone might be called a *refugee*. In this sense, the inadequacy of language to capture a complicated process is actually a gift. Language itself becomes an opening through which to explore the history of people in motion. It is also central to understanding the opposition that humanitarian appeals on behalf of refugees in Asia engendered and the nature of the contest over who could, and should, be considered a refugee. Words, rhetoric and innuendo were critical to efforts to minimize responsibility for the care of migrants in Asia.

The indifference, and sheer disregard, that characterized the international response to migrants in Hong Kong in the early Cold War was markedly different from the treatment that attended migrants in Europe in the same period. In the aftermath of the Second World War, there were millions of people sheltered in camps and temporary accommodations across the European continent. Their uncertain futures added to the tragedy of the millions who perished in the Holocaust, in attacks on civilian populations and on the battlefield. Yet the question of what to do was fraught, particularly as the situation in Europe was absorbed into the emerging fault lines of the global Cold War, with the United States and its allies confronting the Soviet Union over the heated subject of repatriation and resettlement.[21] Almost seven million people were repatriated between the spring and fall of 1945. This left 1.2 million homeless, the so-called "last million", many of whom refused to return to the Soviet Union.[22] In response, the idea of resettling people to new countries gained currency as a way of closing the camps, meeting labor market needs of potential countries of resettlement and advancing Cold War political objectives.[23] Under the auspices of the International Refugee Organization, hundreds of thousands of people were resettled from Europe to the United States and other white settler societies over the following decade.

To ease admissions, governments interpreted normally rigid selection criteria in self-described "humanitarian" ways, with a view to facilitating the movement of potential laborers and the reunification of families. The United States resettled 329,000 people. 182,000 went to Australia, 132,000 to Israel, 123,000 to Canada, 2,000 to New Zealand, and 170,000 to various European states.[24] This resettlement represented "an unprecedented instance of planned population redistribution" and one that had significant political implications.[25] Western governments used newly arrived migrants to suggest that individuals were choosing a liberal democratic way of life over the communist alternative. This narrative played out in news stories and radio broadcasts throughout the early postwar period, and governments elaborated on this public performance in subsequent years. The 200,000 European refugees resettled after the violent Soviet suppression of the 1956 Hungarian Revolution and the 1968 Prague Spring were depicted as "freedom fighters" and celebrated for "voting with their feet."[26]

The focus on migrants in Europe deliberately precluded attention from those in other parts of the world, marginalizing the experience of people outside of the continent who also made claims to refugee status and protection.[27] Alongside the millions of persons who moved across the European continent, for instance, there were millions of people in Asia who left established homes and families in the face of military aggression during the Second World War and its aftermath. In addition to the upheaval caused by the violence and turmoil of the protracted Chinese Civil War, the aggressive march of the Japanese empire, first into Manchuria in 1937 and then into Southeast Asia beginning in 1941, led to the deaths of thousands and the flight of millions.[28] Japan's defeat four years later triggered further upheavals as competing factions sought to occupy power vacuums in the Dutch East Indies, the Philippines, and Malaya. So too did the Korean War (1950–1953), which witnessed the movement of thousands of people as a result of the invasion of South Korea by Soviet and PRC-backed North Korean forces in 1950. The French War (1945–1954) and later the American War in Indochina (1954–1975) also created tremendous population upheavals internally. French authorities returned to Indochina following the fall of the Japanese empire. In response, the Viet Minh led by Ho Chi Minh and Vo Nguyen Giap launched a rebellion against the recolonizers. The conflict lasted from 1946 to 1954, and when a cease-fire divided the country, 140,000 people moved to the North and 860,000 moved to the South. The internal displacement continued with the onset of the American War in 1954. When the conflict ended in 1975, thousands tried to escape the oppressive policies of the newly established communist regime. Further political turmoil ensued in Cambodia and Laos. Over three million people subsequently sought refuge by making perilous sea voyages across the South China Sea and the Gulf of Thailand. Although the international community was slow to respond, two million refugees from Indochina were ultimately resettled abroad, including to many white settler societies. The case of the Indochinese refugees proved to be an exception to the long-standing policies of exclusion that characterized white settler society responses to migrants in Asia during the Cold War.

Given that migrants in Cold War Europe benefited from relaxed immigration criteria and received praise and acclaim when they left the Soviet bloc for the West while migrants in Asia generally did not, the question arises about differences in treatment between people escaping communism in Europe and those fleeing communism in Asia. Why would some migrants from communist oppression be celebrated and welcomed as "freedom fighters" while others were simultaneously derided as "rice refugees"? The geopolitics of the Cold War, where Europe was seen as the main theatre, certainly played a part.[29] However, the most compelling reason lies in the racial differences between migrants from Europe and Asia. The long history of Chinese exclusion in the West defined the politics around humanitarian assistance and settlement programs for people from "Red China."[30]

The people who left violent conditions and economic turmoil in the People's Republic of China traveled along well-trod migration routes and circuits established by the *huáqiáo* (overseas Chinese), and the reception to their movements amongst white settler societies was shaped by decades of animosity and racial prejudice. Wars, imperial expansion, the spread of capitalism, uneven economic development, and environmental factors inspired generations of Chinese migrants to move near and far.[31] The arrival of European imperial powers in the eighteenth century and the forced opening up of China resulted in a number of changes, none more significant than the indentured labor schemes introduced following the end of the African slave trade. The indentured labor of men and women from across Asia formed a bridge "between slavery and modern forms of contract labor" and resulted in the first significant population flows across the Pacific and Indian Oceans.[32] From 1800 to 1914, approximately 2.5 million Chinese migrants moved within Asia and another 700,000 moved overseas.[33] Those moving within Asia went to Burma, Malaya, the Dutch East Indies, Siam, French Indochina, the Philippines, and the Pacific Islands. Of those going overseas, 330,000 went to North America, 270,000 to Cuba, Peru, and Latin America, and 100,000 to Australia.[34] The discovery of gold in the United States, Canada, Australia, New Zealand, and South Africa beginning in the 1840s led to further migration as Chinese miners sought their fortunes in *gam saan* (Gold Mountain). Although much of this early migration was temporary, based on the concept of sojourning until one amassed sufficient resources to return home, it did lead to established communities, despite efforts by white settler societies to exclude Chinese migrants from permanent settlement.[35]

Neither the Chinese migrants recruited through indentured labor schemes in the mid-1800s nor the later generations who moved to *gam saan* were desired as citizens by governing officials. Their labor was valued but their permanent membership in white settler societies was not. Male Chinese laborers, for instance, were rejected as settlers on the basis of racial differences, manifested in perceived crowded and unsanitary living conditions and their apparent membership in an outwardly unassimilable, bachelor society.[36] As a result of concerns about the assimilability of Chinese laborers, governments introduced exclusionary legislation. New Zealand introduced a poll tax in 1881, the United States banned large-scale immigration in 1882, Canada introduced a head tax in 1885, Australia introduced a dictation test in 1901, and South Africa limited Chinese migration in 1902. Looking to one another for reassurance in establishing discriminatory precedents, these settler societies constructed "great white walls," developing exclusionary practices that shaped, and linked, their nation-building trajectories.[37]

In excluding Chinese migrants on the basis of perceived racial difference, white settler societies evidenced a particular strand of what political philosopher Hannah Arendt described as "race-thinking".[38] Race-thinking was, and remains, a way of seeing the world on the basis of racial difference. In the context of immigration issues, it operated historically by dividing people into categories of desirability, privileging only certain migrants as permanent citizens.[39] Race-thinking endured in the postwar period, evidenced in discussions around refugee assistance and resettlement, where the rhetoric of humanitarian generosity was confronted by the reality of having "outsiders" within.

The fear and anxiety Chinese migrants engendered amongst citizens of white settler societies in the nineteenth and early twentieth centuries haunted migrants in Cold War Asia and shaped the contours of their experience.[40] In the early Cold War, when the issue of refugees from the People's Republic of China was proving to be an ongoing concern, there were 32,355 Chinese in Canada, 13,174 in Australia, 7,000 in New Zealand, and 4,179 in South Africa. Despite these relatively insignificant numbers (there were 3,690,000 *huáqiáo* in Thailand, 893,400 in Singapore, and 2,452,128 in Malaysia in the same period), the presence of Chinese migrants in white settler societies and the possibility of "thousands of refugees from Red China" fostered an extraordinary sense of insecurity.[41] As a result, throughout much of the Cold War, white settler societies resisted campaigns to assist migrants in Asia as a result race-thinking and a persistent settler colonial mentality that perpetuated fears of the "yellow peril".

Settler colonialism is a distinct form of colonialism that relies on the settlement of select individuals for the express purpose of securing control over people and territory.[42] White settler societies were built on indigenous displacement and the permanent settlement of migrants who fit the racialized and classed notions of desirability envisioned under the conquering norms of nineteenth-century British imperialism.[43] Combined in practice with circuits of race-thinking across the British Empire, the settler colonial mentality meant that people were excluded on the basis of race as well as classist notions about what constituted civilized behavior.[44] This meant that British imperialists relied on the movement of people from Britain, Scotland, and Ireland to secure colonial holdings abroad, perpetuating a project of imperial whiteness notwithstanding the raced and classed preferences within this mass settler migration.[45] Chinese migrants, by contrast, were only ever desired as temporary sojourners.

To date, much of the research on settler colonialism has rightly focused on Indigenous-settler relations. However, it is important to consider how the selection of some migrant groups, and the exclusion of others, perpetuated the aspirations underpinning the initial settler colonial project even as it became politically unpalatable to exclude migrants on the basis of race.[46] Considering the relationship between migrants, settlers and Indigenous persons is also critical because the exclusionary practices and trajectories that white settler societies pursued were only ever aspirational. White settler societies were never really white, even in their most extreme political incarnations as in apartheid South Africa. As such, at their core, white settler societies were profoundly vulnerable, marked by deep political and psychological vulnerabilities.[47]

For much of the postwar period, Chinese migrants, and especially those from the PRC, remained "quintessential outsiders."[48] Governments continued to be unsure about the desirability of permanent Chinese migration, and legal and regulatory frameworks reflected this unease. Cracks in the foundation of the White Australia policy, for instance, emerged in the 1950s, but it wasn't until 1973 that the policy was formally abandoned. Reservations about the admission of Chinese migrants for permanent settlement were compounded by the politics of the Cold War and the fear engendered by the communist regime in Beijing. Still, white settler societies proved reluctant to acknowledge their reservations explicitly. Critically, the race-thinking that informed the very character and development of white settler societies did not disappear after the horrors of the Second World War or in the face of progressively pointed civil rights campaigns—it evolved.[49]

The suggestion that settler colonialism "is a structure, not an event" is of paramount importance in exploring how white settler societies responded to refugees in Asia during the Cold War.[50] Unwilling to acknowledge continued racial biases in the postwar period, white settler societies consistently invested energy instead in contesting the authenticity of the refugee experience claimed, or attributed, to migrants leaving the PRC. Authorities in white settler societies consistently refused to countenance evidence of political oppression in their assessment of the migrant condition in Hong Kong.

In the 1950s, secular and religious humanitarians in Hong Kong shifted their focus from campaigns for material and financial support to refugee resettlement issues. In doing so, they issued a direct challenge to the ideological underpinnings that animated the immigration preferences of white settler societies. Authorities reacted with alarm to these new campaigns, concerned about the implications of accepting racially undesirable migrants for permanent admission. However, rather than making public pronouncements about their reservations regarding racial difference, governments used more obscure language to rebuff humanitarian appeals, referring to their countries' limited "absorptive capacity," which had both economic and social dimensions, or dismissing the alleged refugee qualities of the migrants.[51] This rhetorical strategy ultimately affected how governments, the general public, and concerned observers conceptualized refugee populations. "Genuine refugees" were celebrated for their heroism.[52] Undesirables were labeled as "economic migrants" or "rice refugees" and their motives for moving were called into question in public forums.

Still, as the intensity of humanitarian advocacy increased, white settler societies found themselves caught up in their own Cold War rhetoric, particularly their claims to freedom, liberty, democracy, and justice.[53]

This tangled web of words forced governments to deal with humanitarian advocacy in Hong Kong, even as they remained wary of it—especially on the question of resettlement. This phenomenon was most pronounced in the United States, which strongly desired to use rhetoric about refugees in all parts of the world for political advantages, and ultimately did so—to a limited extent.

Beneath the bluster of America's Cold War rhetoric, there lived many of the same concerns shared by other white settler societies about the desirability of providing assistance through resettlement programs. It wasn't until the 1970s, with the end of the American War in Vietnam, that the United States offered migrants in Asia significant resettlement opportunities. Still, as early as 1950, US leaders recognized that they had to do something for refugees in Asia, even nominally, to affirm their rhetorical positions and avoid charges of racism and discrimination of the sort that animated communist critiques of America's civil rights situation domestically.[54] Although American political and civic leaders regularly revealed an imperial outlook by suggesting the resettlement of refugees not to the United States but to other territories in the Pacific, President Eisenhower and others ultimately came to believe that there were political and strategic benefits to providing humanitarian relief, including resettlement to the United States, to people in Asia.[55] The lobbying of a variety of religious and secular humanitarians laid the groundwork for this to happen.

To convince white settler societies of the merit of offering aid to people from "Red China," humanitarians had to demonstrate that the individuals in question were not only in need, but also deserving of assistance and protection. This was a complicated undertaking with perverse, contradictory effects. In order to distinguish refugees as people in need, advocates depicted them as destitute, impoverished, desperate, and helpless in contrast to migrants, who were understood to be entrepreneurial and filled with self-starting initiative. This had the accidental effect of underscoring the seemingly alien nature of the refugee populace. Moreover, humanitarian campaigns often exacerbated the differences between would-be donors and the people they sought to assist, leading to critiques about the expected burden of gratitude that accompanied the bestowal of humanitarian gifts.[56] In other words, humanitarian campaigns often rendered their subjects even more foreign to their target audiences while simultaneously placing a powerful psychological burden on the very people they were trying to assist.

Perhaps not surprisingly therefore, humanitarian efforts on behalf of refugees in Asia were only intermittently successful. This was due in part to the complicated messaging but it was also the result of the close ties that bonded white settler societies to one another.[57] As with previous efforts at exclusion, white settler societies benefited from looking to one another to develop their strategies for restricting entry and undermining humanitarian campaigns, including denouncing Chinese migrants as illegal. They also looked to one another for affirmation about the policies they were pursuing, such as ignoring humanitarian appeals from missionaries and NGO workers in Hong Kong.

Although immigration and refugee policies have long been understood as the prerogative of individual nations, in reality they are the result of shared communications and outlooks that work to normalize the acceptance of some migrants and not others.[58] White settler societies addressed the plight of refugees from communist China by relying on shared practices and knowledge in order to moderate humanitarian advocacy and the aspirations of the migrants themselves. Each nation authored its own policies of exclusion, but every nation's policies were reinforced by the knowledge that others, with shared histories, were promoting similar barriers to entry. Whiteness was a fragile project and officials relied on their counterparts in other countries to legitimize their pursuit of this ideal through their national immigration programs.[59] Even when white settler societies began to move away from formal policies of exclusion in favor of an instrumental humanitarian agenda, they did so by looking to one another for precedent and reassurance.

Over the course of the postwar period, humanitarian lobbying that embraced the language of human rights, justice and equality, caused white settler societies—with the exception of South Africa—to distance themselves from their history of exclusion. As a result of the transnational lobbying by NGOs and church groups, by the 1960s humanitarianism had become the marker of enlightened, liberal nations that were "good, prosperous and generous."[60] For white settler societies, this was an identity firmly bound up with the idea of being softer, gentler nations vis-à-vis the oppression they used to characterize life under communism. It was also an identity that enabled white settler societies to protect their selective immigration programs while making carefully managed gestures towards refugee assistance and protection.

The degree to which nations embraced the humanitarian mantle as a strategy of exclusion differed among white settler societies. Apartheid South Africa represented one extreme in the politics of exclusion after the Second World War. In the eyes of many scholars and contemporaries, the election of the National Party in 1948 and the deliberate pursuit of a policy of apartheid set South Africa on a different path from those of other white settler societies.[61] Yet although it often appears as an anomaly in the history of white settler societies, by including South Africa in the interconnected response of white settler societies to the plight of Chinese migrants from the communist mainland, it becomes clear that South Africa simply occupied one end of the spectrum of exclusion. When the apartheid government banned Chinese migration entirely after 1953, it learned from the experience of other white settler societies about how to do this.[62] Moreover, the manner in which the United States, Canada, Australia, and New Zealand approached the question of refugees in Asia was animated by the same worldview that molded the South African government's determination to privilege only certain migrants for admission, assistance, or resettlement. Only in apartheid South Africa was the government able to say outright that it wanted nothing to do with providing assistance or resettling refugees from Asia. As a result, unlike other white settler societies, South Africa rejected humanitarianism as a national ideal.[63] Committed to the apartheid project, National Party officials saw no reason to project an image of liberal humanitarianism in the face of pressure to provide assistance to the world's refugees. Authorities in other white settler societies, by contrast, instrumentalized the notion of being a humanitarian nation to protect ongoing structures of exclusion and privilege.[64]

Four years after the work of the special subcommittee that investigated the condition of Chinese refugees in Hong Kong, President Johnson signed the 1965 Immigration and Nationality Act at the base of the Statue of Liberty, underscoring how the new legislation, which removed the longstanding racialized immigration quotas in the United States, would "repair a very deep and painful flaw in the fabric of American justice."[65] In the same speech, Johnson drew attention to what he saw as the important work of assisting Cuban refugees from communism. Unlike its approach to migrants from Red China, the American government fêted migrants from Cuba as refugees after the revolution in 1958. In the years that followed Fidel Castro's rise to power, 100,000 arrived in the United States from the Caribbean island.[66] In his speech, Johnson declared, "to the people of Cuba . . . those who seek refuge here in America will find it. The dedication of America to our traditions as an asylum for the oppressed is going to be upheld." He continued,

> And so we Americans will welcome these Cuban people. For the tides of history run strong, and in another day they can return to their homeland to find it cleansed of terror and free from fear.[67]

With these remarks, Johnson married the formal end of exclusion on racial grounds with America's commitment to Cold War refugees, positioning the nation as a welcoming, humanitarian beacon of hope. Still, these were aspirational words, they did not reflect the country's historic approach to refugees, especially those in Asia.[68]

Only in the late 1970s did white settler societies provide significant resettlement opportunities to refugees in Asia in the face of millions of people in Indochina taking to treacherous sea conditions to secure their futures. Throughout the postwar period, citizens, churches, and NGOs provided material and financial support, but governments made only modest efforts at resettlement; the US government paroled 5,000 people from Hong Kong in 1962, and in the same year the Canadian government accepted 100 families while the government of New Zealand facilitated the adoption of fifty orphans. Until the 1970s, this was the extent of resettlement assistance provided to Chinese migrants. The reluctant engagement on the part of white settler societies with people from "Red China," in contrast to refugees from Europe, Cuba, and the Soviet bloc, undermines the narrative advanced in Johnson's remarks in 1965. It also serves as a reminder that the embrace of global humanitarianism disguised, rather than replaced, ongoing reservations about the desirability of certain migrants as citizens.

The effects of this disguise are very much apparent today. The groups that have inherited the legacy of earlier refugee advocacy—today's asylum seekers, "illegal immigrants", displaced persons, and refugees—are the groups who illustrate most clearly the ongoing reluctance of countries around the world to open their doors to people they do not considerable desirable. Over the course of researching this book, the Abbott govern-ment in Australia persisted with its "Pacific Solution," which prevented people from making refugee claims by redefining the nation's territorial frontiers; New Zealand was criticized for its low number of refugee admis-sions; the Conservative government in Canada denied health coverage to various categories of refugee claimants in the hopes of deterring future arrivals; and the United States Congress wrestled with reforming its im-migration system to address the millions of undocumented migrants in the country, including many victims of violence and persecution.

At the time of writing, there were an estimated four million refugees from Syria living in the neighboring countries of Iraq, Lebanon, Egypt, Turkey, and Jordan. 150,000 had made asylum claims in Europe. Most, an estimated 6.6 million, had left their homes but remained within Syria's borders. In the post-9/11 world, Syrian refugees, and especially those of the Muslim faith, have experienced neglect and disregard amongst poten-tial countries of resettlement that mirrors the animus that once shaped public perceptions of refugees in Asia. In 2015 alone, an estimated 300,000 Syrian migrants undertook perilous boat crossings across the Mediterra-nean Sea to Europe. The treacherous conditions resulted in the death of an estimated 2,500 people. In the face of this growing movement, critics began to insist that the people leaving Syria weren't "real refugees" but rather were economic migrants, seeking opportunity in Europe.[69] The in-ternational community did not begin to engage in serious resettlement efforts until the images of children drowned at sea and families desperate-ly seeking a future for their young ones began to circulate on social media and amongst conventional media outlets.[70] The government of Australia announced an opening for 12,000 people in September 2015. The Obama Administration committed to 10,000. The government of New Zealand offered admission to 750 while the Liberal Party of Canada, in the midst of an election campaign, promised—and later facilitated—the admission of 25,000 people. Then came the terror attacks in Paris in November 2015 and Brussels in March 2016, which spawned a backlash against refugees and plans for resettlement due to fears about the possible admission of terrorists. In the wake of the attacks, critics transformed a heterogeneous population into a homogeneous, racialized threat. This transformation revealed the workings of blatant discrimination, echoing earlier racialized agitation about the movement of migrants across borders.

1

WRITTEN OUT

The 1951 Convention and Refugees in Asia

IN THE LEAD UP to the establishment of the People's Republic of China in October 1949 and in the two years that followed, hundreds of thousands of people moved to Hong Kong. Their motives were complex and varied. Some were returning home after the wartime Japanese occupation, while others were seeking a place of refuge as they awaited the outcome of the communist experiment. With their movements, the migrants followed in the steps of millions of people who had previously moved across Asia as a result of war and economic turmoil, many in the mid-twentieth century. The rise and fall of the Japanese empire, the retreats of the French and British empires, and the subsequent creation of India, Pakistan, Burma, Indonesia, Ceylon, and the Republic of the Philippines all generated massive movements of people.[1] Yet unlike the many people displaced in Europe during the Second World War and left homeless in its aftermath, the international community largely ignored large-scale migrations in Asia. This was not an accident of history.

After the Second World War, momentum for an international legal instrument to address the issue of refugees and displaced persons grew. As pressure for such a legal instrument intensified, so too did the desire to restrict its application. At the forefront of these concerns was the fearful prospect of having to admit, and protect, millions of people in Asia. This shaped the creation and application of the principle legal instrument of the postwar international refugee regime, the 1951 Convention Relating to the Status of Refugees. Race-based prejudice meant that although refugees in Asia were discussed during preparatory discussions for the convention, they were written out of the scope of protection enshrined in the postwar international refugee regime.[2]

The term international refugee regime refers to the principles, standards, rules, and formal institutions developed to protect and assist refugees over time. The origins of the postwar, and still current, regime date to the League of Nations, which confronted the problem of how to provide for the admission and settlement of people who had been rendered stateless.[3] As a result of strong exclusionist sentiments in the United States and other countries, the League's efforts were piecemeal and far from comprehensive.[4] Its primary focus was on those displaced by the violence that marked the crumbling Ottoman Empire and people rendered stateless following the 1917 Russian Revolution.[5] In response to these situations, the first High Commissioner for Refugees, Fridtjof Nansen, proposed the idea of a document that refugees could carry to secure entry into countries that would otherwise have refused them entry because of their stateless status.[6] In this manner, 450,000 people were assisted.[7] Other League efforts, including attempts to secure protection for Jewish refugees fleeing Nazi Germany, proved less effective, as evidenced by the failure of the 1938 Evian Conference.[8] As a result, Jewish refugees were often turned away from potential places of refuge. The tragic voyage of the *St. Louis* in 1939 reflected this all-too-frequent occurrence. Refused entry in Cuba, the United States, and Canada on the grounds that a "line" had to "be drawn somewhere," the boat carrying 620 passengers, many of them German Jews, was forced back to Europe.[9] Of these passengers, 532 returned to Germany, where over half perished in the Holocaust. Racial prejudice, reflected in restrictive immigration quotas, precluded attempts by the *St. Louis's* passengers to secure humanitarian protection. Similar biases would later characterize the international community's response to refugees in Asia.

Despite this checkered history, the League of Nations changed how people conceived of international protection as it moved from addressing refugees in terms of statelessness to thinking of refugees as individuals in need of protection.[10] These antecedents formed the basis for refugee relief work after the Second World War when the international refugee regime became more formalized and permanent. Notions of humanitarian protection also developed along more elaborate lines. This was partly in response to the horrors of the Holocaust and the massive displacement of millions of people across the European continent, including eight million in Germany alone.[11] It was also the product of how ideas about the international community's responsibility for providing humanitarian assistance evolved in the context of the emerging fault lines of the global Cold War.[12]

There were two key organizations involved in refugee work in the immediate postwar period. The first was the United Nations Relief and Rehabilitation Agency (UNRRA) and the second was the International Refugee Organization (IRO). Established in 1943, UNRRA was mandated to "plan, co-ordinate, administer or arrange for the administration of measures for the relief of victims of war in any area under the control of any of the United Nations through the provision of food, fuel, clothing, shelter and other basic necessities, medical and other essential services."[13] In practice, it facilitated repatriation rather than resettlement to new countries. With a membership of forty-four countries and largely funded by the United States, UNRRA provided billions of dollars to relief organizations working on the ground in Europe. By 1945, it had repatriated seven million people, including five million to Soviet territories.[14] When the Cold War intensified, the United States withdrew from UNRRA, believing it "too willing to accede to Soviet interests," and shifted its energies to funding the Marshall Plan in Europe.[15]

At the time of the US withdrawal in 1946, UNRRA was supervising over 700 camps across Europe.[16] To address ongoing needs on the continent, the IRO was established to assume UNRRA's responsibilities in the area of refugee relief.[17] In contrast to UNRRA, the IRO's primary purpose "was not to repatriate European refugees but to enable them to find new homes beyond Stalin's reach."[18] Not surprisingly, the Soviet Union refused to join the organization. The IRO focused on Germany, Austria, and Italy, where it was responsible for victims of Nazism and Fascism, Spanish Republicans and "other pre-war exiles," and the more than one million people who were "unable to return (home) as a result of events subsequent to the outbreak of war."[19] It also had some responsibilities in the Far East, helping 6,265 Chinese return to their prewar homes in Burma, Malaya, and the East Indies.[20]

During the four years it operated, the IRO resettled more than a million refugees in collaboration with sixty voluntary agencies.[21] Refugees were selected and resettled on the basis of their employability, even though the focus on moving laborers seemed to many to undermine the unspoken purpose of the organization, that of "being the moral voice of the democratic world."[22] Despite the benefits countries derived from the IRO's work, by the end of the 1940s, the appetite for intensive, large-scale resettlement work was shrinking. Western governments therefore suggested that a small successor agency with a limited mandate address the residual needs in Europe through a combination of local integration and resettlement programs.[23]

In discussing what would replace the IRO, most UN members wanted to curtail their commitments to refugee protection and assistance; the British and French governments were the most vocal in advocating a more expansive solution. As a compromise, the UN's Economic and Social Council (ECOSOC) created the small Office of the United Nations High Commissioner for Refugees (UNHCR) to seek "permanent solutions" for refugee problems. In 1949, the General Assembly of the United Nations approved the appointment of a High Commissioner for Refugees to begin work on 1 January 1951. At first, the authority of the office extended to refugees and displaced persons as defined in the IRO's constitution, with the possibility of extending this mandate to certain classes of people at any given time.[24] The development of the Convention Relating to the Status of Refugees changed the scope and character of postwar refugee work significantly.[25]

The idea for a convention emerged from a 1947 resolution passed by the UN Human Rights Commission. Chaired by Eleanor Roosevelt, the commission initiated the resolution in order to draw attention to the issue of statelessness and to request that the United Nations give the matter further study. The resulting "Study of Statelessness" led to the drafting of a refugee convention, with the idea that a binding convention was the best way to protect people seeking refuge and also guarantee certain economic and social rights.[26] The convention that resulted ultimately expanded the notion of persecution as the basis for refugeehood and elaborated the relationship between citizen and state that informed refugee relief work in the Nansen era, affirming that governments were responsible for the protection of individuals.

Displaced populations in Asia were integral to how drafters of, and signatories to, the 1951 Convention conceptualized refugees and state responsibilities towards people in need, even as they were written out of the convention's final terms. The existence of major population movements in Asia encouraged the inclination amongst most policymakers to design a narrow definition for refugees and to create a convention that was limited in scope. In this way, refugees in Asia were present at the creation of the 1951 Convention, even as they were marginalized in the central legal instrument of the postwar international refugee regime. Once they were written out of the convention, refugees in Asia were also written out of the historical record, as population movements in Cold War Europe came to embody the very notion of what it meant to be a refugee.[27] This, despite the millions of people in Asia who were displaced following the violent expansion and then retreat of Japanese and European imperial powers.[28]

In 1947, the British government decided to withdraw from India. The ensuing partition of the subcontinent created India and Pakistan (which was later divided into Pakistan and Bangladesh) by redrawing the borders between Bengal and Punjab. It was a brutal and tumultuous process. The split created chaos on the ground and resulted in vast human suffering. Partition resulted in one of the largest and most violent population displacements in the twentieth century, "remembered for its carnage, both for its scale—which may have involved the deaths of half a million to one million men, women and children—and for its seemingly indiscriminate callousness."[29] By the end of 1947, 7.3 million people had crossed newly created borders. Many of these were minority populations who were the target of vicious attacks, which were followed by brutal counterattacks. An estimated one million people died during the violence. There were an estimated 14.5 million refugees across the subcontinent in 1951, yet their situation failed to inspire international concern.[30] Drafters in New York and Geneva, hard at work on the 1951 Convention, considered the refugees in India and Pakistan to be "national refugees" who did not need the protection of the international community.[31] Drafters similarly disregarded the movement of people out of the Chinese mainland following the victory of the Chinese Communist Party in the country's civil war.

Uniquely, the population movements created by the Korean War (1950–1953) engaged the attention of policymakers at the United Nations, if not the drafters of the 1951 Convention. Following Japan's defeat in the Second World War, the allied powers carved up Korea along the 38th parallel and established a shared trusteeship with American responsibility for the south and Soviet responsibility for the north. It was an uneasy peace and tensions soon mounted. In 1950, the north (with support from the Soviet Union and the PRC) invaded the south, and the United Nations Security Council, without the Soviet delegate in attendance due to a boycott, authorized military intervention. The war that ensued lasted three years and created millions of refugees. By 1951, there were an estimated 5.3 million refugees in South Korea alone and additional unknown numbers in the north.[32] A number of American voluntary agencies, including American Relief for Korea, the American Friends Service Committee, Church World Service, Lutheran World Federation, the Mennonite Central Committee, Save the Children Federation, and National Catholic Welfare Conference's War Relief Services, provided relief on the ground.

For American military forces in Korea, refugees presented a potential security threat and, as a result, concerns advanced by religious and secular humanitarians regularly took second place to military ones.[33] The killing of hundreds of refugees leaving the village of No Gun Ri in July 1950 on suspicion that there were enemy infiltrators amongst them, for example, was sad evidence to observers of the extent to which refugees in Korea were considered a problem by US military forces.[34] Despite the primacy of the military campaign, the United Nations did make some effort to address the refugee situation in Korea as part of reconstruction efforts in the south. A Security Council resolution in July 1950 provided the framework for the relief operations of the United Nations Command. Pointing to the "hardships and privations to which the people of Korea [were] being subjected as a result of the continued prosecution by the North Korean forces of their unlawful attack," the Council called on the UN and nongovernmental organizations to "provide such assistance as the Unified Command may request for the relief and support of the civilian population of Korea, and as appropriate in connection with the responsibilities being carried out by the Unified Command on behalf of the Security Council."[35] Later that year, the United Nations Korean

Reconstruction Agency (UNKRA) was established to provide relief to refugees and those rendered homeless by the war.

UNKRA's work was entirely focused on providing relief within Korea, and there was little thought given to the protection of refugees who crossed international borders—an issue that was being concurrently discussed at the drafting sessions for the new refugee Convention. Delegates to the drafting conference dismissed the question of whether or not Korean refugees, as well as Palestinian Refugees (who were being assisted by the United Nations Relief and Works Agency for Palestine Refugees in the Near East), should be included in the scope of the Convention's application. They simply considered their situations "quite a different matter from the one under consideration."[36]

Refugees in Korea and other parts of Asia were considered a "different matter" in part because of the presence of distinct, if disrupted, commercial and personal migration networks that had historically facilitated the movement of people in Asia.[37] The routes people followed in the mid-twentieth century emerged from earlier patterns of circulation: along the Silk Road, and across the Indian Ocean and the South China Sea.[38] People had been moving across, within, to, and from Asia for centuries by the time the drafters sat down to pen the 1951 Convention. Wars, imperial expansion, the spread of capitalism, uneven economic development, and environmental factors inspired generations of people to move near and far.[39]

Perhaps even more importantly, refugees in Asia were considered a "different matter" because countries did not want to be legally obligated to accept refugees from Asia within their borders. The underlying premise of the discussions in New York and Geneva was that refugees and displaced persons were a problem and that if countries were asked to assist people from beyond Europe, namely Asia, Africa, and the Middle East, it would be asking too much. As a result, the situation of refugees in Asia, and those of other groups outside of Europe, was deliberately excluded from the scope of the 1951 Convention to make the legal instrument more palatable to potential signatories, particularly the United States and other white settler societies, which jealously guarded their sovereignty in order to restrict the admission of migrants considered racially undesirable.

These assumptions shaped the general scope and character of the convention from the outset. Nevertheless, the document presented to the General Assembly for approval in 1951 was the product of much writing and rewriting. It was first prepared by a committee of five countries, revised by the Secretary General's Secretariat, and then submitted to the Ad Hoc Committee on Statelessness and Related Problems for revision. Members of the committee included: Belgium, Brazil, Canada, China, Denmark, France, Israel, Poland, Turkey, the Soviet Union, the United Kingdom, the United States, and Venezuela. Members were invited on the basis of their experience in receiving refugees. China, for instance, was represented because of the estimated 200,000 White Russian and 18,000 Jewish refugees who had sought shelter in China beginning in the 1920s.[40] Shanghai was the last open port where people could disembark without a passport and, as a result, many Jewish refugees fled there in the 1930s. However, because the Chinese representative was from the ROC and not the PRC (the General Assembly did not give the "China seat" at the United Nations to the People's Republic of China until 1971), the Polish and Soviet delegations refused to participate in the committee's meetings.[41] As a result, there was ample room for Western nations to advance their Cold War interests in the discussions.

Leslie Chance, the Canadian representative, was elected chairman of the Ad Hoc Committee. He faced the thankless task of mediating discussions about the scope of the proposed convention and the particularly contentious issue of how refugees should be defined.[42] Chance's first reaction to the draft convention, which was prepared with "surprising speed," was somewhat dispirited. He wrote, "As it stands this is obviously not a very good draft. It contains I fear the sort of illiteracies which seem to emerge from the efforts of five people with differing points of view."[43] The greatest point of contention during the revision process was the question of the convention's scope; there was debate over how to define refugees and further conflict over whether or not to include geographic and temporal limits.

The French delegation, initially the leader of the "universalists"—who stood in opposition to the "Europeanists" led by the United States—pressed for a broad refugee definition based on the principle of asylum. The French argued that a "dynamic" definition should "cover not only all the refugees who existed at present, but also all those who would come after them."[44] The United States, meanwhile, advanced a narrow, categorical definition of the sort that typified the League of Nations approach to refugees. The ROC government supported the American position. Delegate Cha stated, "The different categories of refugees to which the proposed convention should apply must be clearly indicated." He insisted that "it would be difficult for the Governments to ratify a convention which otherwise would amount to a kind of document signed in blank to which could be subsequently added new categories of beneficiaries without number."[45] Presciently, the French delegate at the time, Mr. Rain, suggested, "the Chinese representative should consider the inadequacy of the solution he had championed." Rain noted that only providing for the protection of designated categories of refugees would mean that "any new groups of refugees, such as those which might conceivably be created as a result of the situation in China, would have to await a session of the General Assembly and a decision by that body before they could enjoy the benefits of the convention."[46]

Somewhat surprisingly, Delegate Cha did not advance the Guomindang's position that the People's Republic of China was a refugee-producing country. He only thought of his own country's limited capacity for receiving refugees. His interventions at the meeting were purely from the perspective of a state that might be asked to accept refugees. During discussions of the geographic scope of the convention, for instance, Cha expressed caution about suggested wording that emphasized the "necessity for international cooperation to help to distribute refugees throughout the world." Cha insisted that the "Chinese Government was not in a position to accept refugees from other countries, though in the past China had played its full part by giving asylum, particularly to White Russians and Jews."[47]

It took eighteen months to modify the original draft and submit a revised convention to a conference of twenty-six plenipotentiaries. The proposed definition of a refugee was very reminiscent of the preamble to the IRO's constitution, emphasizing the persecuted nature of refugees. Crucially, the Ad Hoc Committee ultimately proposed to limit the scope of the convention's application to people in Europe who met the definition of a refugee.[48] This decision provoked further debate at the Conference of Plenipotentiaries, which met in July 1951 to discuss the draft convention.[49]

At the conference, the French government sent a new delegate, Robert Rochefort, who immediately shifted his country's support towards a more limited definition for refugees. Only the British delegation, with the support of the Nordic countries, continued to argue for a generous conception of refugee status.[50] The British delegate, Sir Samuel Hoare, descended from Quakers, considered "that a refugee was a refugee wherever he was, and that the convention should provide that Contracting States should grant him minimum rights and benefits." [51] However, Rochefort, who apparently had designs on being the Assistant High Commissioner for Refugees (he assumed that the head of the organization would be American), described the need to separate "the wheat from the chaff."[52] He insisted that the scope of the convention should apply to events "in Europe" and padded his position by hinting at the danger of negative pushback if too broad a definition was adopted. Rochefort was adamant that governments had to be selective; otherwise, the admission of "undesirable elements" would risk "a wave of xenophobia prejudicial to the mass of refugees as a whole."[53] Significantly, white settler societies used this very same argument when confronted with calls to admit greater numbers of migrants from Asia. Four years prior, for instance, the prime minister of Canada declared in the House of Commons with regard to continued restrictions on the admission of Asian migrants that "the people of Canada do not wish as a result of mass immigration to make a fundamental alteration in the character of our population." His rationale was that immigration should "foster the growth of the population of Canada," that people should be "advantageously absorbed in our national economy," and that social costs, including potential racial tensions, "should be minimized."[54]

Robert Rochefort similarly insisted that the scope of the proposed convention be limited to refugees in Europe because "neither the total number of refugees, nor their distribution by nationality of origin, was yet known." In his view, this "raised a whole series of problems," especially because "immigration countries" had laws that did not "provide for the immigration of refugees from countries outside Europe."[55] The white settler societies of the United States, Canada, Australia, New Zealand, and South Africa were all so-called "immigration countries." Italy supported the French position and echoed Rochefort's concerns about the impact of the convention on Western countries, saving white settler societies from having to vocalize their hesitations explicitly. "The western countries," said delegate del Drago, were "the only ones which would assume a specific obligation by signing the Convention." What would happen, del Drago asked, if they "were obliged to admit the victims of national movements such as those which had recently occurred in India and the Middle East"? He suggested, "They would be faced with very serious problems, and would be quite unable to meet the commitment which the application of the convention in its present form would entail."[56]

George L. Warren of the United States, who had advised the US delegation at the 1938 Evian Conference on Jewish refugees, likewise argued that too little was known about the condition of refugees outside of Europe to warrant their inclusion in the scope of the convention. He believed, "the situation with regard to refugees in the Far East was still obscure, and very little was known of those from continental China in particular." As such, he considered it "unrealistic for the Conference to attempt to legislate for refugees in the Far East."[57] The Israeli delegate, Jacob Robinson, an international jurist, insisted that the convention should focus on political refugees, as opposed to refugees from natural or environmental disasters, so that it would only apply to Europe. Taking the example of refugees from the PRC, Robinson described their situation as "unique in history" observing that "they had a Government of their own, still recognized by many States, with a seat in the United Nations, and able to provide refuge in Formosa [Taiwan] to those who sought asylum there."[58]

The existence of the Republic of China and its claims to being the legitimate government of China complicated discussions of refugee protection at the United Nations. The "two China" problem plagued the work of the United Nations and its relief agencies for much of the postwar period. The presence of "two Chinas" meant that the legal status of the people leaving the PRC was confused. Did they have a place of refuge if the Republic of China, and not the People's Republic of China, was the legitimate Chinese state? This question, like the answers advanced in response to it, was highly contentious. The fractious issue of recognizing the legitimate Chinese state therefore proved to be an additional imperative to the general inclination to ignore the refugees from the Chinese mainland rather than attempting to incorporate their situation into the convention's definition of a refugee or its scope of application.

Robinson, for instance, observed that refugees from the PRC did not meet one of the convention's conditions for refugee status—that of being stateless—since in theory they could go to the ROC. He believed them to be automatically excluded as a result. The Israeli delegate concluded that for "the purposes of the Convention, there were practically no refugees in the world other than those coming from Europe."[59]

There was no Chinese delegate at the conference of plenipotentiaries, yet it is clear from Robinson's comments and those of other delegations that the movement of Chinese nationals figured into the drafters' thinking, especially in terms of the imagined pitfalls if the scope of the convention was extended too broadly.[60] In discussions over whether refugee status should apply to people who entered countries of potential asylum illegally, for instance, the Australian delegate, Patrick Shaw, insisted that such an allowance would lead to undesirable migration. He explained that "during the war many thousands of such immigrants had fled from their countries of origin, which had then been under Japanese occupation, including Indonesia, the Pacific Islands, New Guinea, China and the Malay Peninsula, and had landed illegally on Australian territory, where they had been considered as refugees fleeing from a common enemy." He claimed, "they had been given the same rations and treatment as Australian nationals." The issue for the government of Australia was that after the war, many had insisted on staying, and so the country was confronted with the problem of "illegal immigrants claiming refugee status."[61]

Instructions from Tasman Heyes, the Minister of Immigration, made it clear that allowing such people to stay was incompatible with the governing principles of the White Australia Policy. Heyes wrote,

> There are thousands of non-European refugees, and acceptance by Australia of a convention which provides that such a class of persons should not be discriminated against and should not be subjected to any penalty for illegal entry, would be a direct negation of the immigration policy followed by all Australian Governments since Federation.[62]

The countries who participated in the drafting and revising of the Convention Relating to the Status of Refugees throughout 1950 and

1951 did so to protect their vested interests as countries who had received refugees or who might be called upon to receive refugees in the future. The climate in which the 1951 Convention was drafted was conservative, cautious, and inclined to limitations and restrictions rather than expansive thinking about how to define and assist refugees. France and the United Kingdom were alone in advocating, in a committed fashion, for a broad conception of refugees. Yet when the revolving door of French delegates was replaced by the authoritative and self-interested voice of Robert Rochefort, the French vision also narrowed. Rochefort considered it preposterous to create a convention with terms so broad it would be rendered useless. Only Europe, he insisted, "was ripe for the treatment of the refugee problem on an international scale." The French delegate believed that creating a convention that would cover refugees around the globe would "risk jeopardizing what could certainly be done for the sake of something which could not perhaps be achieved."[63]

The resulting 1951 Convention has been described as adopting the "most restrictive conception of refugee in modern times."[64] The convention defines a refugee as someone who:

> owing to well-founded fear of being persecuted for reasons of race, religion, nationality, membership of a particular social group or political opinion, is outside the country of his nationality and is unable or, owing to such fear, is unwilling to avail himself of the protection of that country; or who, not having a nationality and being outside the country of his former habitual residence as a result of such events, is unable or, owing to such fear, is unwilling to return to it.

While the definition was—and remains—a narrow one, the convention eroded, ever so slightly, the jealously guarded notion of state sovereignty on admissions. Article 33 enshrined the principle of *non-refoulement*, preventing states from returning refugees to situations where they might face harm. Article 33 impinged on the capacity of governments to unilaterally determine admissions, as it required states to explore whether or not refugees faced a genuine fear of persecution if they were returned. If they did, then admission had to be granted. It was a very tiny crack in the armor of national sovereignty, and it was one that states sought to close through a variety of means. One strategy was to allow signatories to limit the scope of the convention's application geographically and temporally, as suggested by the Swiss delegation and supported by the Vatican City. This proposal was ultimately adopted. As a result, Section B of the final convention gave signatories the option of applying the convention only to refugees in Europe whose "situations arose from events proceeding" or "as a result of events occurring before 1 January 1951" or of applying the convention to all persons who met its definition of a refugee, in all parts of the world. All of the initial signatories chose the more limited option, meaning that refugees in Asia were removed from the scope of the convention's coverage.

Notions of racial superiority separated, and elevated, refugees in Europe over other displaced populations. Members of the Ad Hoc Committee on Statelessness were predisposed to think about the refugee situation as a European one, given that the draft convention they contemplated was a direct product of previous efforts to address the plight of refugees on the continent. Nevertheless, this inclination towards linear thinking only became firmly embedded after governments began to consider the potential implications of a refugee convention and what it might mean for their ability to control admissions to their territories. This was true of white settler societies as well as other countries invested in safeguarding their sovereign right to control admissions. The government of the ROC, thinking in terms of a receiving country, was explicit about not wanting to accept persons it considered undesirable.

The specter of possible undesirables hovered over the proceedings that led to the 1951 Convention. These silent, but present, shadows meant that refugees outside of Europe were central to the character of the international refugee regime, even as they were written out of the scope of the final convention. None of the original signatories chose to apply the original convention to refugee situations outside of Europe. Instead, over subsequent decades, efforts to reform the convention led to the development of an associated protocol, introduced in 1967. The amending protocol removed the convention's geographic and temporal limitations but it did not alter the original definition of a refugee. The convention's definition, with its focus on individual persecution, has endured. This definition was the product of decades of activity on behalf of refugees in Europe, the political dynamics of the Cold War, and an early postwar interest in limiting the scope of the convention as much as possible. As a result, suspicions about the authenticity of refugee claims from other parts of the world, which required the adoption of a particularly European vocabulary of persecution, became a marked characteristic of the postwar period. Migrants and humanitarians subsequently worked to reconcile the gulf between expectations about what a refugee should look and act like with the amorphous nature of global migration.

The story of the migrants who left the PRC after 1949 for Hong Kong is bound up with the notion of refugees as a European phenomenon, a notion that was amplified in the immediate aftermath of the Second World War. Although the British government was one of the first to ratify the 1951 Convention Relating to the Status of Refugees, and had originally been one of the most vocal advocates for a generous refugee definition, it reserved application of the 1951 Convention to its colonies. This meant that Hong Kong was removed from the scope of the convention's application. In theory, therefore, the colonial government could address population flows into its territories without attending to the convention's legal requirements about who was a refugee or the principle of *non-refoulement* as outlined in Article 33. However, in practice, the moral weight of the convention could, on occasion, hinder the pursuit of unilateral action. The colonial government subsequently confronted the challenge of managing population pressures as well as growing interest in refugee rights and protection issues outside of Europe.

2

BORDER CROSSINGS

Migrants and the Refugee Label

IN 1956, Douglas Lam arrived in Hong Kong. He was eight years old. He traveled from the People's Republic of China with his grandmother and a young aunt, whose laborer husband sojourned in Cuba, under the guise that his grandmother needed medical treatment. They all obtained two-way permits from the local authorities, but everyone in their home village of Antang (On Tong) knew they weren't coming back. The "visit" to Hong Kong was an opportunity to escape difficult living conditions and uncertain prospects on the mainland. Douglas stayed in Hong Kong for five years. He struggled initially because he did not speak Cantonese. His family's first accommodation, in Mong Kok, was with a relative who lived in a building that had no water closet. Human waste was emptied by hand daily. It was so crowded that Douglas remembers literally sleeping on top of a sewing machine. After his grandmother passed away, Douglas moved in with another aunt and her children to a low-rise building where they slept three to a bed and cooked in the same room. When Douglas's uncle died suddenly, his widowed aunt was left to care for four young children. She could no longer provide for Douglas and he was left with nowhere to live. Douglas eventually moved to Australia, sponsored by yet another aunt and an uncle who lived in Sydney. Although he had never imagined that he would end up in Australia's largest city (where he now drives a commuter bus), Douglas reflects, "It was that or an uncertain future in Hong Kong."[1]

Douglas Lam's story is similar to that of thousands of migrants who moved into the British colony of Hong Kong following the establishment of a communist regime in Beijing. Douglas joined relatives previously established in the colony and experienced the crowded and makeshift housing conditions that characterized life for many in postwar Hong Kong. The population pressures created by large numbers from the Chinese mainland in the dying days of the Chinese Civil War and its aftermath produced large squatter settlements and raised fears about potential political and social instability. The colonial government began to address this situation in the 1950s, which meant that Douglas and his family arrived at a time when authorities were working to actively redefine what it meant to be a migrant in the colony by creating a new language of belonging. As for most migrants, this rhetorical transformation had a peripheral impact on Douglas' experience, yet it had a profound impact on how the politics of refugee assistance evolved globally. Over the course of a few short years, casual references to refugee populations became politically and symbolically charged, infused by the politics of the global Cold War.

It was clear from the earliest days of the Cold War in Asia that Hong Kong, a traditional meeting point between East and West, would be instrumental in shaping various kinds of Western engagement with political and social developments in the region. It would also be critical to how notions of refugeehood were conceptualized globally. By the mid-1950s, colonial officials and secular and religious humanitarians had begun to use the term *refugee* in deliberately provocative, and contradictory ways. As a result of local dynamics and the colonial government's governance practices, the term *refugee* was transformed in Hong Kong and it subsequently shaped the development of the international refugee regime.[2]

Hong Kong, which was transferred to British control in 1842 under the Treaty of Nanking, was characterized by a history of open movement, with people traveling casually between the Chinese mainland, the New Territories, Kowloon, and Hong Kong Island. The arrival and, in some cases, return of a million people after the end of the Japanese occupation in 1945, and another million in the decade following the rise to power of the Chinese Communist Party, created severe population pressures in the colony.[3] Impoverished squatter settlements dotted the landscape, inspiring descriptions of "teeming refugee masses."[4] The crowded living conditions, which officials feared would lead to health and security issues, prompted the colonial government to introduce restrictive migration policies in the early 1950s. Yet border controls ran counter to humanitarian efforts to assist people leaving "Red China." As a result, the borders between the Chinese mainland and the British colony of Hong Kong became contested sites where the politics and implications of particular migrant labels were brought into stark relief. Contests about the appropriateness of border controls shaped debates amongst Western humanitarians on the ground in Hong Kong, outside political interests, and the colonial government about who should be responsible for the welfare of the colony's residents and what kind of assistance should be provided. Defining people as residents, squatters, or refugees was central to these debates.

According to the colonial government in Hong Kong, in the final year of the Chinese Civil War, 210,423 people "poured into the colony."[5] Some returned, leaving lives they had established on the mainland during the Japanese occupation, while others made their way to Hong Kong for the first time.[6] The colonial government paid little notice to the motives that prompted the influx and referred broadly to all the migrants as "refugees." The term reflected the assumed temporary nature of the migrants' stay in the colony. This assumption resulted from the nature of historic refugee flows into the colony, following the Taiping Rebellion in the 1850s and the Japanese invasion of Manchuria in 1937. On both these occasions, the population influx to Hong Kong lasted only a short while and people returned to the mainland as soon as their sense of danger had passed.[7]

As many residents in Hong Kong and the neighboring province of Guangdong on the mainland shared a common language and ethnicity, it was widely understood that the people moving back and forth simply viewed the British colony, despite its imperial trappings, as part of a larger Chinese canvas.[8] As one British Foreign Office publication observed:

> Like a sponge Hong Kong draws in population and squeezes it out, and the hand that does the squeezing is China's. If conditions are good in China, people stay there, if they are uncomfortable they rush to Hong Kong.[9]

With the establishment of the People's Republic of China, people began to settle in Hong Kong on a more permanent basis. They moved for longer and longer periods of time, waiting and watching to determine what life was like under the new communist regime.[10] Between 1949 and 1950, 700,000 migrants arrived, increasing the colony's population to over two million people. There was a severe housing shortage. Squatter settlements had begun to appear in Hong Kong in 1946, following the Japanese occupation, but the situation worsened over the following three years. Squatters could be "found on the roofs of houses, in derelict buildings, in catacombs excavated below basements, in alleys and conduits [and] under bridges."[11] Others slept in the open air or in "squalid huts, made of scrounged wood, oil cans flattened out, bits of cloth etc.—whatever can be found that will hold together."[12] Most of the squatters were concentrated in the colony's urban areas, straining Hong Kong's scarce physical and social resources. Water shortages were frequent and desperate living conditions in the settlements made them appear to be "harboring places for criminals and vice-peddlers of all kinds."[13] By 1950, the squatter population was estimated at 330,000 and was attributed to the presence of a large refugee population in the colony.[14] The whole of Hong Kong was described as "one vast camp."[15] One British observer declared:

> Never in my life, in Africa, in Europe, in Arabia, had I seen slums worse than this, but never had I met slum-dwellers who looked so clean and tidy, so cheerful and welcoming, in such conditions. The Chinese seem able to rise above the drabbest surroundings.[16]

This last sentence is striking but not atypical. British observers regularly downplayed any responsibility the colonial government might have for the housing situation while celebrating the so-called Chinese character, whose positive traits, they implied, were flourishing in the colonial context.[17]

To address the growing population pressures in the colony's urban areas, the colonial government introduced two pieces of legislation to limit and control the number of people entering Hong Kong. Neither had any direct impact on the worsening squatter problem as people continued to occupy whatever makeshift housing they could find or create. Still, the legislation marked an escalation in the government's concerns about continued migration from the mainland and introduced a new, contested element into relations with the People's Republic of China. The Registration of Persons Ordinance required everyone in the colony to register for, and carry, a Hong Kong identity card, which indicated whether the holder was a British subject.[18] The psychological ties created by the requirement to register marked the beginning of a separation between the residents of Hong Kong and the Chinese mainland that would become thicker with time.[19] The second piece of legislation directed at controlling the swollen population numbers was the Immigrant Controls Ordinance, introduced in the spring of 1949 and placed under the administration of the Hong Kong Police Force. The Immigrant Controls Ordinance required everyone arriving in the colony to apply for, and carry, an entry permit. The colonial government believed that by imposing documentation requirements, people would be deterred from seeking shelter in the colony.[20]

Due to the tradition of open movement between Hong Kong and China and fears about upsetting authorities on the mainland, Chinese migrants entering or leaving the colony for a destination on the mainland and Macao were initially exempt from this clause.[21] Meanwhile, the colonial government continued to investigate a number of alternative options for reducing the population numbers, including possible resettlement to Southeast Asia.[22] None of these proved feasible. Still, the colonial government remained reluctant to move aggressively on the immigration control issue. Border controls were considered analogous to markers of sovereignty, and claims to that effect had the potential to upset communist authorities on the mainland at a time when the colonial government was attempting to establish a neutral position in the Cold War.

At the same time, the colonial government remained determined to reduce the numbers of migrants entering the colony. When the government observed a "sharp upswing" in the number of arrivals over departures at the end of March 1950, officials concluded that they were at a point where it was "necessary to consider tightening up all immigration control to cover Chinese travelers to and from the mainland."[23] On 28 April 1950, the government of Hong Kong introduced a quota system for people from the People's Republic of China. The novel controls led to the construction of fencing, the permanent presence of border guards, and a whole new philosophy about what Hong Kong's border signified.

People continued to move, as they had previously, but the character of their movements was seemingly transformed.[24]

Hong Kong's borders became demarcations of legality and illegality as the associated quota and permit systems established the "legitimate means of movement."[25] These systems amounted to processes for classifying migrants and ordering society "by marking off limits, assigning positions, and policing boundaries."[26] The system introduced in Hong Kong distinguished the residents of nearby Guangdong from Chinese "foreigners." Cantonese migrants wanting to cross into Hong Kong were required to possess either a Chinese-issued reentry permit or a Hong Kong identity card, and their entry was subject to a quota of fifty people per day. By contrast, non-Cantonese had to obtain an entry permit or a reentry visa issued by the Hong Kong Immigration Office or the British authorities in Beijing or Shanghai. Permit-holders were not subject to the quota, but the policy governing the issuance of these permits "was extremely restrictive."[27] The informal target, never announced publicly, was to have five departures from the colony for every four arrivals.[28]

Colonial officials initiated and pressed for these unprecedented controls.[29] By contrast, staff in the Foreign Office in London opposed these efforts, highlighting the potentially harmful repercussions of such policy initiatives on Britain's shaky relationship with the People's Republic of China. Diplomatic recognition had been established, with some difficulties, in January 1950. Despite the tenuous situation that existed, officials in the Colonial Office were ultimately convinced by Governor Grantham's insistence on the need for border controls to prevent the unimpeded entry of migrants.[30] The governor was concerned about controlling the population in the colony, but he was also aware that border controls heightened the apparent legitimacy and authority of the colonial government by impairing the PRC government's ability to claim an unbroken lineage between people in the two territories. Its political and territorial claims to Hong Kong were undermined as a result. Authorities in Beijing objected to the introduction of the permit system calling the controls "unreasonable and unfriendly." Communist officials declared:

For more than one hundred years, Chinese nationals entering or leaving Hong Kong have never been treated as foreign immigrants, nor have the British authorities in Hong Kong any justification whatsoever to treat Chinese nationals in the same way as other foreign immigrants.[31]

The introduction of restrictions on mobility produced a fundamental transformation in the historically open relationship between Hong Kong and mainland China and the manner in which authorities, on both sides, viewed migrants.[32] After the introduction of quota and permit systems, migrants from the Chinese mainland were no longer free to move as they wished; only state-sanctioned entries were permitted. The new border controls introduced the possibility of a migrant from the mainland being marked as illegal. They were indispensable in enabling the government of Hong Kong to manage movement by reducing people "to schematic categories."[33] The controls also proved beneficial to authorities in Beijing.

Contrary to what was suggested by the PRC government's public protests, Hong Kong's border controls coincided with the communist regime's growing interest in preventing departures from the mainland. Emigration was banned in 1951 and entries were severely restricted. These bans remained officially in place until 1978. After 1951, anyone wanting to enter or leave the PRC had to carry a permit issued by the Public Security Authorities. These permits were issued in limited numbers and applicants were subject to lengthy interrogation.[34] The effect of these Chinese regulations was uneven. When migrants couldn't obtain a permit, they moved to Hong Kong by bribing their way into the colony or by leaving under false pretenses. They took "shopping trips" or "medical visits" such as the one undertaken by Douglas Lam and his aunt and grandmother.[35] Others paid people to help them. One gentleman who arrived in 1950 explained:

> I paid $1,200 for my passage. Some of the others paid as much as $3,000—it all went to the younger brother of my relative, who operated the junk . . . Several of us borrowed it from relatives in Hong Kong, and some of the others had their savings with them in gold. They were rich people in the old days and must have carefully hidden their treasure for such an emergency as this.[36]

Significantly, the PRC's ban on emigration and its determined enforcement of rigid border controls meant that the government of Hong Kong could relax its vigilance over the quota and permit systems, which fell into abeyance by 1952—only a few short months after they were first introduced.[37] The squatter situation however, which had been used to justify the initial efforts to limit migration, remained.[38]

In 1952, the Hong Kong Police observed, "the determination of the Chinese not to return to China on any account has crystallized the squatter problem. The population which regarded itself as refugee and transient is now putting down roots."[39] The colonial government attributed this new rootedness to deteriorating conditions on the mainland as well as the work of humanitarians in the colony who relocated from the PRC following expulsion orders and barriers to entry in 1951. British colonial officials did not appreciate the enthusiasm of newly arrived Western missionaries whom they believed "were seeking to justify their existence."[40] Authorities held that providing large-scale relief in Hong Kong simply compounded the squatter situation by encouraging the population to become more established and stimulating additional movement from the Chinese mainland. In 1950, the Lutheran World Service—founded in Lund, Sweden in 1947 to coordinate the international work of various Lutheran organizations—proposed to distribute large amounts of relief to "political refugees" in the colony using goods originally intended for China. Governor Alexander Grantham, a highly respected administrator, rejected this suggestion, declaring that most of the people who would receive support were not "genuine political refugees." He claimed:

> The majority have come here purely for economic motives hoping for work and better pay than they would get in China. They are responsible for unhealthy squatter colonies which have grown up. If relief is given here we will never get rid of these people and we will merely attract more from all over South China.

In his view, there was "no reason for turning Hong Kong into a glorified soup kitchen for refugees from all over China." In fact, what the Governor wanted to do was send food into China, giving people incentive to stay there rather than seek out "food and work in Hong Kong."[41] It is not clear from the archival record if the Governor ever followed through with this plan, but it is evident that, in subsequent years, the activities of humanitarians in the colony, including those of Chinese clan and community associations as well as Western missionaries and NGOs, grew rather than diminished.

When the British colonial government set about rebuilding the colony after the Japanese occupation, it did so with the assistance of a number voluntary organizations including *kaifong* (traditional Chinese mutual aid organizations) and increasingly numerous international organizations and Western missionaries, who addressed the immediate, emergency needs of the colony's residents.[42] Robin Black, a colonial administrator in the 1950s who later became Governor of Singapore and then Hong Kong (1958-1964), describes the early postwar years as follows:

> There was a great voluntary effort under way, coping as well as possible with the problems created during the period of reconstruction after the war, aggravated, after 1949, by the large influx of refugees. The prospect was horrendous. We had to define a social policy; we had to find money; we had to engage and train staff for a prolonged commitment.[43]

Despite the demonstrated need for relief efforts in Hong Kong, the colonial government was itself unwilling to provide much in the way of social welfare, hoping instead that inhospitable conditions would encourage people to return to the mainland. When David Trench, who like Robin Black later became Governor of Hong Kong (1964-1971), first arrived in Hong Kong as a colonial officer, he was informed that the government's strategy was to ensure that social conditions in Hong Kong were not "so much better than they were in China so that all you did was drag in immigrants."[44] As a result until the 1960s, social welfare provision in Hong Kong was piecemeal and largely unplanned. Humanitarians in the colony found the situation deplorable and worked to alleviate the plight of refugees and squatters, unearthing "pockets of misery on rooftops and in alleyways of the kind the authorities were loath to admit existed."[45] Housing conditions were indeed appalling and, on occasion, outright dangerous.

From 1950 to 1954, 100,000 people lost their homes to fire.[46] The crowded conditions and the flimsy construction of the huts made squatter settlements vulnerable to the large-scale destruction that fire and other sorts of disasters could unleash. The government of Hong Kong was rarely prepared for such tragedies and often failed to provide adequate social support to the victims. If a squatter settlement was devastated by fire or typhoon (a regular occurrence during the rainy season), victims were required to register with the Social Welfare Department to obtain relief. Yet in reality, substantive support came from local *kaifong* as well as Western humanitarians who were kept busy attending to all of the emergencies that arose. As one missionary quipped, "Hong Kong can pretty well count on having emergencies every year of violent proportions, either from fire, water, or typhoon!"[47] The activities of the Lutheran World Service alone included "clothing distribution, vocational training for teenagers, roof-top schools, medical care, flood relief, and community services for the inhabitants of the new refugee apartment blocks."[48] The American-based organization, CARE—established in 1942 to facilitate the distribution of relief packages to refugees in Europe—opened a permanent office in Hong Kong in 1954. Its stated purpose was "to aid the thousands of Chinese refugees from the Red mainland."[49] It dedicated itself to distributing food packages—consisting first of powdered milk and rice and later dried cabbage, salted fish, and soybeans—with the assistance of local *kaifong*.[50] Much of this distribution took place following disastrous fires in the colony. As in Europe, CARE was careful to label packages of donations so that recipients would know that the gift was from the United States, which was making food surplus stocks "available to the needy throughout the free world."[51] The labels read:

Dear Friend, This gift for you is from some American friends—farmers, fishermen, students and others. We remember that our ancestors suffered hunger and disaster and they were helped in the time of their difficulties by friends overseas. We have had a good harvest this year. We thank God, and wish to share our happiness with you. This is a little remembrance from us, and we hope you will accept it.[52]

The Chinese characters on the label for America signified "beautiful land." This labeling was meant to communicate the bounty in the United States as well as Americans' generous spirits.

While colonial authorities appreciated, to a certain extent, the humanitarian work undertaken by CARE and other Western organizations, they were distressed by the associated propaganda, which they feared might provoke the ire of the communist regime in Beijing.[53] The colonial government also believed that relief efforts undertaken by Western humanitarians hampered its efforts to dissuade people from moving into the colony. By providing substantial relief, the government argued, voluntary organizations were drawing migrants into Hong Kong. Yet Western humanitarians insisted that there was a real need for relief efforts and that the government, in particular, should do more. The problem was that the casual manner in which officials and observers had described people moving into the colony as refugees, especially after 1949, had informed the way Western observers understood and responded to the squatter problem. The term *refugee* denoted a specific kind of need, one that many humanitarians—with the exception of the American Friends Service Committee, a Quaker organization that sought to remain above the fray of Cold War politics—conflated with communism in China.[54] As a result, Western humanitarians did not just see a housing problem, or a social welfare problem; they saw problems involving a particular group of oppressed people. The resulting Western humanitarian interest in the refugee population, which combined a mix of religious and secular motives, complicated the colonial government's efforts to curb population flows and address the related issue of widespread squatter settlements.

In addressing the housing situation, the colonial government initially used the term *refugee* to describe the targeted squatter population and to justify its rather draconian clearance policies despite the fact that squatter settlements were often populated by residents who were being dislocated by arriving migrants.[55] Squatters were treated as refugees rather than as permanent residents of Hong Kong. Colonial authorities therefore insisted that refugees were temporary residents to whom they had no obligation. In developing a public housing policy, the government conflated refugees with squatters to establish the grounds for policies intended to eliminate settlements and coerce the departures of undesirable residents. "Refugees" became the justification for clearance policies and, in turn, the destruction of the squatter settlements ensured that associations with the term "refugee" became progressively more negative. From 1950 to 1951, nearly twenty thousand squatter huts were destroyed, resulting in the dispossession of approximately one hundred and twenty thousand people.[56] Any attempt by squatters to resettle was "vigorously repressed." All property found on an "illegally occupied site" was confiscated after a twenty-four hours notice.[57] People were forced to find shelter elsewhere. In the drive to resettle and organize the colony's population, the government also sought to remove some of the colony's most politically active residents: the soldiers and supporters of the Guomindang. This, too, created troubling associations between conceptions of squatters and refugees.

Amongst the hierarchy of undesirables, ex-Guomindang soldiers, referred to as "refugee soldiers" or "Nationalist refugees," probably ranked highest in Hong Kong.[58] In October 1949, Governor Alexander Grantham identified "deserting or defeated Nationalist soldiers" as the greatest danger to the colony.[59] Many were blind or disabled. Most were totally impoverished. Although the government tried to push them "back over the frontier as quickly as possible," the 1950 Expulsion of Undesirables Ordinance—passed in response to the growing number of migrants—proved rather ineffective to this end.[60] As the name suggests, the Expulsion of Undesirables Ordinance gave the colonial government the power to expel "undesirables from the colony." The term "undesirables" was very loosely defined and was therefore widely applied. Immediately following the introduction of the Expulsion of Undesirables Ordinance, the number of expulsions rose from 3,046 in 1949 to 4,431 in 1950. Yet removing people proved to be a sensitive political issue as the political appeal of sheltering refugees from communism grew in the West. In 1953, American authorities protested after fourteen people were deported for distributing anticommunist propaganda. In the United States, the action appeared "somewhat undemocratic and to American eyes, out of line with Western resistance to Communism." The Governor of Hong Kong, however, believed the material the individuals were disseminating was "provocative and disruptive."[61] The solution that ultimately emerged as a result of the squatter clearance schemes was to create a separate space for undesirable elements within Hong Kong.[62]

In 1950, the Social Welfare Department founded Rennie's Mill Camp in the Sai Kung District next to Junk Bay. Officers proceeded to resettle almost 7,000 Nationalist refugees who were squatting in the Mount Davis area. The government provided the camp's residents with basic rations but little else. The intent was to "segregate" ex-Nationalist soldiers and their families from the rest of Hong Kong society in the hope that with a little bit of intimidation, they would leave the colony of their own volition.[63] At first the camp was extremely isolated, accessible only by boat-launch or footpath. Soon, however, the camp was "inundated with missionaries and professional do-gooders."[64] These included Western organizations as well as humanitarians from Taiwan, specifically the Free China Relief Association (FCRA), which had a distinctly cold war political agenda.

The FCRA was established by the ROC government in 1950 to assist famine victims in China and garner support for the Nationalist regime in Taipei amongst the *huáqiáo*. It also undertook important political campaigns. Although it presented itself as a "civil charity organization," the FCRA received financial support from the Guomindang and American governments.[65] Through the FCRA, Guomindang authorities used the refugee issue in Hong Kong to advance their claims to being the legitimate government of China, particularly at the United Nations, where the question of which government should occupy the China seat was a perennial test of where the communist regime and the Guomindang government stood in the eyes of the international community.[66] For the Guomindang government, the refugee issue in Hong Kong was a critical platform upon which to expand its case for legitimacy.

In Hong Kong, the FCRA operated as the Rennie's Mill Camp Refugees Relief Committee. The committee was responsible for the "resettlement of refugees in Taiwan and [the] provision of funds, rice and education to the residents in the Camp."[67] The committee also became a vocal advocate for the particular case of the Nationalist soldiers in Hong Kong, making frequent representations to the United Nations and the UNHCR on their behalf. The archival files of the FCRA and the Relief Committee organizations are replete with requests for aid, as well as complaints from the Relief Committee about the Hong Kong government's treatment of residents in Rennie's Mill Camp. Although the Relief Committee's stated mandate included the resettlement of refugees to Taiwan, the committee worked mostly to develop Rennie's Mill as a permanent enclave, providing both political and financial support to sustain the residents. It discouraged residents from attempting to move to Taiwan, which had its own population pressures to contend with.[68] As the camp became more prosperous, many people who observed the deteriorating conditions in Taiwan chose to stay in Rennie's Mill.[69] The camp quickly developed into a "state within a state."[70]

In response to this increasingly permanent presence, the government of Hong Kong set about trying to eliminate the very situation it had created, worrying about the camp's growing potential to become a magnet for "Guomindang disaffection."[71] On occasion, the government attempted to coerce the residents of Rennie's Mill into leaving by cutting off electricity and water supplies. External support hindered these efforts. Most famously, in 1953 residents sabotaged government efforts to withdraw free rations for one quarter of the camp's residents. Although a one-day hunger strike staged by 6,000 of the camp's 10,000 residents failed to reverse the government's decision, Western missionaries and local NGOs stepped in to provide a week's supply of rice to the residents.[72] When these same organizations refused to shoulder the long-term burden of feeding so many people, other agencies, including the Red Cross and the American-based Aid Refugee Chinese Intellectuals Inc. (ARCI), provided funds for the immediate and ongoing operations of the camp.[73] In an important propaganda coup, the Mainland Refugee General Relief Association of Taiwan sent $300,000 for direct distribution to residents.[74] The government of Hong Kong's efforts to use squatter clearance programs to simultaneously eliminate squatter settlements and coerce the departure of certain undesirables from the colony were hindered by humanitarian sentiments aroused by particular sensitivities attached to the notion of a refugee population. Rennie's Mill Camp remained in place until it was cleared in 1996 in advance of the handover of the colony to the People's Republic of China.

The government of Hong Kong's efforts to manage the population in the colony were complicated by the fact that people had few options once they were removed from one of the colony's squatter settlements. The ROC government refused to accept refugees in any significant numbers after 1950, and hardly any of the squatters desired to return to the Chinese mainland.[75] The World Council of Churches hoped that with their relief efforts in the colony, refugees might "have a chance for a new life in Hong Kong or elsewhere."[76] A few British parliamentarians supported the idea of "elsewhere," hoping the squatters might go overseas, but the Colonial Office knew that few countries were willing to open their doors to significant Chinese migration.[77] Countries such as Malaysia, where British authorities had battled the Communist Malayan National Liberation Army for over a decade, "didn't want any decanting of surplus population from Hong Kong."[78] Resettlement to former British Dominions, namely the white settler societies of Canada, Australia, New Zealand, and South Africa, barely registered as an option, for this would have risked similar demands for resettlement to the United Kingdom; a nonstarter as far as many in the Colonial Office were concerned.[79] Ogden Meeker, head of CARE's Hong Kong office, as well as other humanitarians, feared that Hong Kong was the "last stop" for many.[80]

Instead of leaving, squatters competed for settlement options internally. The initial clearance program therefore failed to reduce the population numbers in the colony, forcing the government to become progressively more involved in the provision of public housing and in population management generally. In 1952, the government introduced an expanded resettlement program that moved beyond early efforts at simply clearing squatter settlements.[81] The resettlement program extended at such a rapid pace that by 1954 the government was running out of land on which to resettle the squatter population. Discussions soon turned to the possibility of offering more permanent housing. A massive fire that broke out at the Shek Kip Mei squatter settlement in December 1953, which left more than 53,000 people homeless, cemented this shift. In response to the fire, the government of Hong Kong spent almost $16 million (HK dollars) in emergency relief alone.[82] Government efforts overshadowed those of the regular army of missionaries and voluntary organizations who attended to fire victims in the squatter settlements.

The fire at Shek Kip Mei practically eliminated the use of the term *refugee* in public discussions of population issues in Hong Kong. Robin Black recalled that after the Shek Kip Mei fire, he tried "to dodge the use of the word refugee to men and women who were becoming part of the population, and, instead, admit that we were giving rehabilitation to immigrants."[83] The fire confirmed to colonial authorities that it was no longer possible, and that it was even politically dangerous, to persist with the false distinction between refugees, migrants, residents, and squatters.

After the fire, when people could see the physical devastation, akin to what Black called a "great burned out space," they became more supportive of public housing initiatives. The colonial government demonstrated that it, too, was more willing to invest in public housing for all residents.[84] Authorities were also acutely aware of growing international interest in the refugee population as a result of the humanitarian activity in the colony.[85] Part of the government's strategy in abandoning its use of the term *refugee* had to do with dissuading organizations such as the UNHCR from singling out a "particular immigrant group and [assigning] them privileged status and treatment as 'refugees.'"[86] This was central to larger British efforts to keep up appearances of official neutrality in Hong Kong in the face of ongoing debates over which entity, the communist regime in Beijing or the Guomindang in Taiwan, represented the legitimate government of China. Importantly, the colonial government's endeavors to reframe understandings of Hong Kong's residents did not go unnoticed. Ogden Meeker of CARE observed in 1956:

> with the growth of humanitarianism and the conviction in our times that we are indeed our brothers' keeper, there has been increasing British concern for the refugees—complicated by the need for trade, an inclination to circumspection, and deep desire not to irritate the Chinese dragon next door. So quietly, the British government does everything it can to distract attention from the refugees. It does not call them refugees, but prefers "squatters" as being less controversial.[87]

The ongoing "two Chinas" debate, along with the burgeoning global humanitarian agenda, taught the colonial government that the swollen population in Hong Kong was a magnet for outside parties, including Western humanitarians as well as the leadership in Beijing and Taipiei, most of whom were interested in pursuing political objectives through the provision of material assistance.

Authorities in Taipei and Beijing discerned considerable political advantage from involving themselves in the social welfare of the colony's residents. They believed that offers of humanitarian relief could be used to strategic ends in the ongoing contest over who represented the legitimate government of China. Despite efforts by the colonial government to prevent the flow of aid into Hong Kong, Guomindang authorities directed their assistance to the residents of Rennie's Mill Camp while the communist government in Beijing offered aid more broadly. The communist regime believed that offers of aid could sow confusion about the source of authority and comfort in Hong Kong and undermine the colonial government's influence over the local populace. For instance, when a devastating fire broke out in Pak Tin village—one of the largest squatter settlements on the island—communist authorities sent money and rice, using the aid as a cover for political objectives. Although the government of Hong Kong monitored the Federation of Trade Unions—a front for the Chinese Communist Party—closely to ensure that relief was distributed only to those registered by the Social Welfare Department, the federation nevertheless issued special registration tickets, contributing to confusion about the source of relief in the colony.[88] The left-wing press in the colony praised the People's Republic of China for "giving so much when the country is undertaking major reconstruction works."[89] Meanwhile, the Guomindang press published letters from fire victims saying they would not accept blood money from the communist regime.

The political contest in Hong Kong intensified in the mid-1950s. Following the Soviets' violent suppression of the Hungarian Revolution, Mao's suspicion of the Kremlin's global ambitions grew. He therefore determined to strike a more independent path from the Soviet Union. The result was an increasingly radicalized modernization program, which manifested itself in a series of political and economic reforms known as the Great Leap Forward (1958-1960).[90] The reforms were an ambitious, and ultimately disastrous, effort to rapidly modernize the PRC's economy. They resulted in widespread famine and economic deprivation. Efforts at independence from the Soviet Union, also led Mao to seek warmer relations with authorities in Hong Kong. Colonial officials were receptive to these overtures, and in February 1956, the PRC and Hong Kong governments coordinated the lifting of quota restrictions for three weeks so that people could celebrate the Chinese New Year with their families, either in Guangdong or Hong Kong. When the government in Beijing requested an extension of the suspension beyond the holiday celebrations, the government of Hong Kong agreed. Cooperating on border issues seemed like a strategic way to maintain good relations with the authorities in the PRC. However, the colonial government warned Chinese officials that if "a fair proportion" of the new entrants did not return to the mainland upon the expiry of their permits, "quota restrictions would be re-imposed in the interests of the Colony."[91]

The effect of the extended suspension, as far as authorities in Hong Kong were concerned, was disastrous. Of the Chinese travelers who entered Hong Kong over the following eight months, 81% failed to return home after their permits expired. By the summer of 1956, Hong Kong had a net population gain of 55,000 people.[92] Douglas Lam and his family, a small group of three, represented a fraction of the total population flow to Hong Kong in the spring and summer of 1956. The squatter population jumped to 450,000, and the housing situation was understated as "gloomy."[93] The bitter pill for Hong Kong authorities was that officials in the People's Republic of China appeared to have purposely increased the number of exit permits being issued during these critical months. British colonial officials deduced that the government in Beijing had deliberately attempted to sabotage the security of the colony by letting large numbers of migrants leave the mainland, leading to population pressures and serious health concerns in the colony.[94] In July 1956, CARE staff observed,

> the rate of [population] increase is greater than that of the low-cost housing which the government is valiantly throwing up as fast as it can. Hence the ever-growing army of bodies sleeping in the streets, the spreading hillside shantytowns and the rooftop slums.[95]

When Beijing authorities refused to reintroduce controls on their side, the government of Hong Kong re-imposed the quota system that had lain dormant for almost four years. Restrictions were reintroduced at the border just a few short weeks before violent riots broke out in Kowloon.

Guomindang supporters celebrated October 10 as China's national day while communist loyalists commemorated October 4 as the founding of the PRC. In the fall of 1956, the British colonial government banned Guomindang supporters from displaying their flags during Double Ten Day celebrations, which were always a time of heightened tension in the colony. In anger, Guomindang supporters attacked known communist sympathizers. The government was slow to respond and the violence spread at an alarming rate. In the ensuing riots, sixty people were killed, including the wife of the Swiss consul, and five hundred people were injured. The government imposed curfews and used the police and military police to curb the violence. The PRC government was angered by the manner in which the colonial government dealt with the rioters, believing that colonial officials had not acted swiftly or zealously enough. Zhou Enlai, the Minister for Foreign Affairs, accused authorities in Hong Kong of acting irresponsibly and implied that they were not fit to govern, declaring that the residents of Kowloon had a right to self-defense and that the PRC could not tolerate such outrages on its doorstep.[96]

In addition to protesting the violence in Kowloon, the government in Beijing challenged the decision by authorities in Hong Kong to unilaterally impose immigration quota measures or to claim any kind of relationship with the Chinese populace. The PRC government featured Hong Kong's immigration controls in its colorful propaganda, which reflected the increased radicalism of the period. The regime in Beijing broadcast films and recordings of devastated people, including weeping women and children, who explained that they only wanted to cross into Hong Kong to see family and friends.[97] There was clear value in drawing attention to the border controls in order to suggest openness on the part of the PRC. Yet it was a strange game. While the movement of large numbers of people threatened the social and political stability of Hong Kong and created strategic advances for the government in Beijing, it also presented a propaganda risk for the communist regime. The government of Hong Kong was keenly aware of the potential value of the rhetoric about people voting with their feet; however, it chose to preserve its neutral stance and never exploited the migration of people from the PRC.[98]

For colonial officials in Hong Kong, the primary imperative was to manage the population in the colony while fostering political, social, and economic stability. The malleable nature of the refugee label was essential for this insulating purpose.[99] The government used the refugee label to justify border controls and quota systems, as well as regulations that permitted the categorization of people and facilitated deportations. Confronted with a persistent housing crisis, the refugee label disappeared from public discourse, replaced by more neutral sounding terms such as immigrants, residents and, simply, squatters. The government also instrumentalized its border control policies to collapse distinctions between different groups in the colony and gain support for public housing projects and squatter clearance programs.

By rejecting the refugee label as a descriptor for arriving migrants in the colony, and many of the destitute populace, the colonial government avoided suggestions of any implicit humanitarian obligations and proceeded instead with massive internal resettlement programs and social welfare projects that subsumed previous distinctions made between residents and refugees. This strategy was intended to manage population pressures in the colony as well as depoliticize the burgeoning humanitarian agenda.

Refugees were not considered a problem in Hong Kong for most of the nineteenth and early twentieth centuries, although so-called refugee movements were common. As the majority of the people who moved between the Chinese mainland and the British colony shared a common language and ethnicity, their free movement was accepted as the norm. All this changed with the advent of a larger and more permanent population in the colony after 1949. The size and permanency of the population in Hong Kong, the dispute over which regime represented the legitimate government of China, and the emerging Cold War in Asia altered how refugees were discussed in Hong Kong and how the population was managed. The refugee discourse produced by authorities in Hong Kong after the victory of the Chinese Civil War was a highly localized one, born of anxieties about relations with the newly established communist regime in Beijing and the Guomindang in Taiwan, and threats to the internal stability of the colony posed by unstable, dangerous living conditions.

After 1949, colonial authorities increasingly conceptualized of refugees as a problem because people were becoming established in the colony and there was an emerging political agenda around so-called refugee populations. Observing the large numbers of migrants leaving the mainland, the government had initially discussed refugees in a rather cavalier manner. Within a few years, however, the colonial government's refugee discourse was complicated by the growing number of humanitarians and outside interests who sought to provide relief to the colony's residents. Importantly, the refugee label in Hong Kong was one that intersected, and resonated, with discussions about refugees globally.

In the face of considerable outside interest, the colonial government began to evolve the way it spoke about, and managed, the population in Hong Kong. Although officials referred to refugees in the initial process of clearing and resettling squatters, this refugee discourse ultimately dissipated, replaced by discussions about "squatters" and "residents." The refugee population the government had once considered a temporary presence was reconstructed as a permanent population that required stable and secure housing. The refugee label evolved concurrently. The nature of this change reinforced the unique and specific genealogies, born of a history of open migration between China and Hong Kong and the political context of the Cold War in Asia, that shaped the refugee label in the British colony. Crucially, the refugee label that evolved was largely divorced from the lived experience of migrants crossing the border from the Chinese mainland. Douglas Lam, who moved with his family to Hong Kong in 1956, never thought of himself as a refugee. Although the term, and the way it was used, was increasingly important to British officials charged with managing the colony's affairs, it had little to do with how the people from the mainland identified themselves.

By the mid-1950s, official use of the term refugee in Hong Kong diverged from evolving ideas about refugeehood and responsibilities enshrined in the 1951 Convention Relating to the Status of Refugees and advocated by the UNHCR. Yet as Western humanitarians became progressively more interested in the refugee situation in the colony, the local contingencies that shaped Hong Kong's unique refugee discourse were absorbed into refugee discussions born of the postwar situation in Europe.

3

PROMOTING REFUGEES

Western Humanitarians in Hong Kong

IN APRIL 1960, Walter Judd of Aid Refugee Chinese Intellectuals Inc. (ARCI)—an American humanitarian organization motivated by strong anticommunist sentiments—advised a correspondent about the work of the Lutheran World Federation in Hong Kong,

> Its program of medical care, basic education, loans to persons to get established in simple businesses that will enable them to sustain themselves, vocational training, as well as food and clothing for the utterly destitute, is well-balanced and efficient. I am not a Lutheran myself, but this is an honest appraisal of the merit of this effort.[1]

Such praise disguised the fault lines that ran between the work of many Western humanitarian organizations in the colony in the early 1950s. They were connected by their interest in relieving the social and welfare pressures created by the crowded conditions in the colony, but they were divided between those interested in direct relief efforts, as in the case of the Lutheran World Service; those interested in long-term development projects, such as the American Friends Service Committee (AFSC); and those, such as ARCI, which were interested in the situation in Hong Kong for primarily political objectives. There were fundamental differences in how Western humanitarians perceived need, relief, and responsibility for the people of Hong Kong. In 1959, Reverend Stumpf, an advocate of international assistance to refugees through resettlement programs, and Father John Romaniello, sometimes referred to as "Father Noodle" because of the Catholic Welfare Services' well-known efforts in the area of food distribution, became involved in a heated exchange. Stumpf insisted that "nobody could make enough noodles to satisfy the demand" in Hong Kong and that humanitarians needed to think about securing resettlement opportunities abroad, particularly in Latin America where governments had expressed an openness to receiving Chinese refugees.[2] Romaniello, who was known for his jovial and "accepting attitude," disagreed, believing that direct relief in the colony was the most appropriate solution.[3]

In addition to several Western humanitarian workers in Hong Kong, Reverend Stumpf and Father Romaniello were two of the estimated 3,125 Western missionaries in the British colony in 1955.[4] Although many missionaries had attempted to remain in China after the Chinese Communist Party came to power, the government banned Western missions from entering its territory in 1951 and made it difficult for those who desired to stay to do so. The PRC government first ordered US citizens to leave, before targeting other Westerners. As a result of a series of show trials and public assemblies, by the spring of 1952, 90 percent of the missionaries had been expelled or had left in anticipation of expulsion orders. Another round of expulsions took place in 1955.[5] Rather than leave Asia entirely, many moved to Hong Kong, launching their relief services alongside Chinese mutual aid associations (*kaifong*), the Free China Relief Association (FCRA), and established Western missions in the colony such as the Roman Catholic Maryknoll Sisters who had begun their work in the area in 1911.[6]

The newly arriving missions, including representatives from the London Missionary Society, the World Council of Churches, the Christian Welfare Relief Council, the Church World Service, the Lutheran World Federation, and the Methodist Committee for Overseas Relief brought material resources as well as an abundance of human resources.[7] The missionaries' decision to stay in Hong Kong and provide a "holding operation . . . until work opened up in China again," contributed to the growth of Catholic, Lutheran, Methodist, and Protestant churches in the colony.[8] The Lutherans, like other denominations, had never considered Hong Kong "much of a field for missionary effort,"[9] and as a result, local Chinese often told Lutheran missionaries that before 1948, "we had never heard of the Lutheran Church."[10] By 1957 there were 144 Chinese Protestant Churches, 48 Chinese Protestant Preaching Places, a Gospel Tent, and a Roof-Top Preaching place listed in the Hong Kong Church Directory. At the time, the Anglican Diocese of Hong Kong included nine recognized parish churches and eight mission chapels. The Roman Catholic presence was also significant; the first church was built in 1841, and a little over a century later, the denomination counted twenty churches scattered throughout Hong Kong, Kowloon, and the New Territories.[11]

The churches' work on behalf of the colony's poorest residents was so critical, they became a "third force" in Hong Kong society.[12] They worked alongside a number of secular organizations interested in pursuing relief work in the colony, most notably ARCI, which was dedicated to "rescuing" Chinese intellectuals through resettlement programs to Taiwan and the United States. The government of Hong Kong relied on voluntary efforts to provide for much in terms of the health and welfare needs in the colony, but it provided little in the way of funds. Through communications abroad, Western humanitarians, of both secular and religious persuasion, raised funds to support their relief efforts by disseminating information about living conditions in Hong Kong. In the case of American organizations, their activities enabled the United States government to advance a Cold War refugee agenda in the colony. This was despite many differences in opinion about the most desirable forms and outcomes of relief based on worldviews that ranged from the evangelical to the ecumenical and the simply political.

Western humanitarians played a critical role in shaping international interest in the refugee question in Hong Kong. ARCI, the AFSC, and the Lutheran World Federation, among others, used careful representations of the situation in Hong Kong to garner support for their work in the colony. These organizations therefore shaped the international community's interest in life in Hong Kong and influenced how solutions for the crowded living conditions were imagined. The stream of informational materials created by religious as well as secular humanitarians created fertile grounds for discussions about the refugee population in Hong Kong at the United Nations, ultimately leading to the dispatch of the Hambro mission to investigate conditions in the colony in 1954 and an outpouring of support for Chinese refugees in Hong Kong during the United Nations' World Refugee Year (1959–1960). In looking at how missionaries and secular organizations presented social welfare needs for public consumption and how they elaborated notions of responsibility for refugees during World Refugee Year, one can see the broad currents of social, cultural, and political thought that animated humanitarian efforts on behalf of refugees during the early years of the Cold War. These trends were imbued with notions of freedom and liberty advanced by Western nations. Yet just below the rhetorical surface, one can also see the far more significant operation of racialized and territorialized notions of belonging that shaped how solutions to the crowded conditions in Hong Kong were construed. Humanitarian opinion was mixed on whether resettlement abroad, for instance, was a desirable solution.

The question of resettling refugees outside of the colony was perennially contentious because of the energy and resources required to organize resettlement programs, which inevitably involved only a small percentage of the targeted population. Moreover, there were a number of difficulties inherent in securing placements for people abroad. It took a great deal of advocacy work to convince white settler societies in particular of the value of resettling people from communist oppression in Asia. With the slight exception of the United States, barriers to entry generally remained in place after World Refugee Year (1959–1960), even though impressions of heartbreaking conditions in the British colony were sown around the globe. As a result, the agenda that emerged on refugee issues in Hong Kong was characterized by deep differences over who should bear responsibility for the health and welfare of refugees in Asia and the merits of short or long-term interventions. Debates amongst religious and secular humanitarians shaped how assistance to refugees was ultimately envisioned and delivered globally. ARCI, the AFSC, and the Lutheran World Federation reflect the wide range of work, as well as the robust debates, that took place in Hong Kong on refugee relief issues throughout the 1950s.

Aid Refugee Chinese Intellectuals Inc. was established in 1952 by Ernest Moy, who made no secret of his anticommunist sentiments. Moy was a Chinese American with Guomindang loyalties who wanted "a privately created and operated instrument for use in the war against Communist aggression."[13] On Eisenhower's election to office, Moy offered his services to the president in unequivocal terms,

> as an American citizen of Chinese ancestry, whose whole family rendered service to the country during World War II . . . I maintain relations with veterans of the war, and thus direct and indirect influence on a sizeable number of voters throughout the country. I will exert that influence to the fullest extent of my power . . . I am now ready to go to work for you. Please tell me whom I should contact.[14]

Convinced that intellectual refugees in Hong Kong could be "saved"— the religious parallels were not accidental—Moy recruited sympathetic supporters to make his idea of identifying and resettling "intellectual refugees" a reality. Moy considered an intellectual to be anyone who had studied at an American university. He believed that the alumni of US campuses (generations of Chinese students had been studying in the United States since the late 19th century) would be inclined towards America's Cold War pursuits and that they could, and should, be "saved" to ensure the future of a free China. This ideological commitment was crucial as most of ARCI's supporters, including Henry Luce, the publisher of *Life* magazine, were part of the vocal China Lobby in the United States and were committed to providing continued material and moral support to the Guomindang. Walter Judd, a Congressman from Minnesota and former medical missionary in China, eventually agreed to chair ARCI, which operated in Hong Kong from 1952 to 1959.

From 1950 to 1964, the American Friends Service Committee (AFSC) also worked in Hong Kong, though they did not begin to develop their substantive program in the colony until 1959. The AFSC was a Quaker relief organization founded in 1917, following the lead of Quakers who had been involved in war relief efforts in Britain from the early 1800s.[15] The AFSC began operations in China in 1941, a few years after the Japanese invasion, with an ambulance unit of 150 drivers and staff from England, Canada, the United States, and New Zealand. It continued its work over the course of the Chinese civil war, but in 1950, the AFSC learned that the communist regime was denying entry to newly arriving Western personnel. The AFSC's fledgling enterprise shriveled, and the

Friends decided to relocate to Hong Kong the following year when it became clear that Mao Zedong's animosity to the United States meant the
Friends' American status was getting in the way of "reconciliation and
the building up of understanding and goodwill."[16] Hong Kong was to be
a temporary home for the AFSC until its missionaries could go back to
the mainland.[17] In the spring of 1951, Mark Shaw, a graduate of the Yale
Divinity School who served in China for many years, reported from his
temporary home in CARE's office that "there's not enough work in Hong
Kong to justify having a Unit agent there, but there's too much work to
be able to get along without one."[18] In the end, the AFSC, like so many
others, not only stayed in Hong Kong but also became deeply invested in
improving social conditions in the colony.

The Lutheran World Federation, like the ecumenical World Council
of Churches (WCC), was an international organization that drew staff
and membership from congregations around the world. The Lutheran
World Federation was founded in Sweden in 1947 to coordinate the
activities of Lutheran churches worldwide. The federation was a late-
comer to refugee relief efforts in Europe, but it proceeded to play an
important role in resettling refugees and providing emergency food
supplies. It was responsible for the resettlement of 40 percent of all
Protestant refugees and displaced persons in Europe from 1948 to
1951, totaling 30,600 people.[19] German Lutheran missions that had
worked in the East River district area in Guangdong amongst the Hak-
ka people moved to Hong Kong after the establishment of the PRC,
inaugurating a "new era of Lutheran missionary activity."[20] In Hong
Kong, the Lutheran World Federation became involved in food distribution through eight centers and various community development
projects. The organization's major involvement with refugee resettlement work began in 1953 when the Lutheran World Federation purchased a four-story building at 33 Granville Road, intended "to serve
as a home for transient missionaries." Instead, when "the door was
opened in China for westerners to register for evacuation, a deluge descended." Many of the arriving migrants were White Russians, Tsarist
supporters who had fled to China following the Russian Revolution
in 1917. The Lutheran World Federation, working with the WCC, resettled thousands of White Russians, 14,000 of whom went to Australia. This cooperative program ran until July 1954, when the Lutheran

World Federation began "the task of assisting Chinese refugees" while the WCC continued to assist European refugees.[21]

The British colonial government in Hong Kong was rather ambivalent about the presence in so many Western humanitarians in the colony. Returning to govern a colony physically, economically, and psychologically damaged by the Japanese occupation, British officials were focused primarily on questions of infrastructure and economic recovery. They fully expected that the colony's Chinese residents would take care of themselves, as they had previously through the work of the *kaifong* and other clan and community endeavors such as the Tung Wah hospital.[22] However, the arrival and the permanent establishment of large numbers of returnees and new migrants fundamentally altered the nature of colonial governance in Hong Kong. The government addressed population pressures and concerns about potential political unrest by investing in unprecedented border controls and public housing projects. However, although the government spent money on housing resettlement projects, an estimated 30 to 35 percent of its annual budget by 1958, it remained largely aloof from the provision of direct relief such as food and medicine because of the sheer number of voluntary agencies engaged in such activities.[23] Estimates indicated that American agencies alone provided services to 25 percent of Hong Kong's populace, or 700,000 people.[24]

Relief efforts such as food distribution and medical care required considerable financial support from donors abroad. As a result, missionaries and humanitarians became adept at communicating need to audiences outside of Hong Kong. Through various fund-raising campaigns, humanitarians promoted their efforts on the ground, describing the provision of food and clothing and later, the organization of nurseries, mother's groups, and vocational training groups. They also suggested—in subtle and often not-so-subtle ways—the intangible virtue and benefits of donating to relief efforts in the colony. The receipt issued by ARCI for donations (Figure 1) is typical of the kinds of imagery and language used by Western organizations.[25]

The message at the heart of Western fund-raising and public-awareness campaigns was that the population in the colony was a refugee one. All of the campaigns invariably talked about "exiles", "refugees," "refugee movements," or "the needs of refugees." In actual practice, however, humanitarians administered to those in need with little consideration of what legal

Figure 1. The characters at the top left represent "freedom." The receipt reads, "This is to certify that (insert name) offers aid to members of the Chinese intelligentsia in exile by gladly contributing (insert amount) dollars." ARCI Donation Receipt, Marvin Liebman Papers, Box 88, Folder 1, Hoover Institution Archives.

or categorical status they might occupy. Western missionaries tended to evoke the term refugee in a rather casual manner to generate concern for the social welfare needs of their clients. By contrast, groups that were invested in the refugee situation in the colony for explicitly political reasons were far more pointed in their rhetoric, marrying the refugee situation in the colony directly with communist oppression on the Chinese mainland.

The ROC government, through the FCRA, undertook some of the earliest publicity campaigns about the refugee situation in Hong Kong. The FCRA deliberately crafted an image of the people in Hong Kong as refugees from an oppressive communist regime. In volumes of correspondence to the UNHCR and other United Nations' bodies, the FCRA emphasized this theme, declaring in one piece of correspondence:

> The refugee problem in the Far East, like those in some other areas, is chiefly an outgrowth of Communists' persecution. . . . The refugee problem would never have assumed so grave an aspect, nor would it have been a real problem, had the Chinese Communists not followed the pattern of the Communist International in purging and massacring.[26]

The FCRA's suggestion that the refugees in Hong Kong were victims of communist oppression meshed with the 1951 Convention's definition of a refugee as someone having a "fear of persecution." This pairing was used to simultaneously solicit international support at the United Nations for the refugee populace in Hong Kong and to demonstrate the Guomindang's capacity to advocate on behalf of the Chinese people.

At the United Nations, the FCRA and the ROC government played a key role in advancing the idea of a refugee population in Hong Kong. Yet the work of Western humanitarians, of both the secular and religious variety, proved far more significant in fostering perceptions and understandings about the refugee situation in Hong Kong amongst white settler societies. In soliciting funds to support their work in the British colony, ARCI, the AFSC, and the Lutheran World Federation each offered a particular vision of humanitarian need in Hong Kong and how it could best be addressed. Through their words and actions, they reflected the diversity of motives that inspired relief efforts in the British colony and the many variations in how need was understood, presented, and addressed. Moreover, their appeals to the general public shifted the sentimental terrain upon which advocacy and humanitarian work took place.

In ARCI's correspondence, much like communications produced by the FCRA, the idea of supporting refugees was intertwined with the battle against communism. ARCI's earliest solicitations were an impassioned plea to save refugee Chinese intellectuals from the evils of communism. In one typical missive, Walter Judd wrote,

It is in our power to give opportunity for a new life to many Chinese men and women who have made the greatest sacrifices to remain free. If we stand aside they will be destroyed or absorbed and enslaved. Nothing can be of greater importance to those of us who are concerned with the world-wide struggle to preserve freedom for all mankind.[27]

The American Friends Service Committee meanwhile talked about its "Refugee Program in Hong Kong," in terms of helping people with their "busy and overcrowded lives."[28]

Bill and Roberta Channel, who built the AFSC's program in the colony beginning in 1959, reported from Hong Kong that in the "crowded government housing projects. . . ."refugees with no previous relationships, speaking different languages and coming from different parts of China, are thrown closely together, with no sense of community developing." This resulted in "strangeness and underemployment," and as a result it was "toward these two problems that the AFSC program was directed."[29] The AFSC subsequently became involved with the six hundred residents of the Tsung Hau village who wanted a clean water supply and critical infrastructure such as a concrete path so that they could access agricultural lands. Although the AFSC referred to this work as their "Tsung Hau Refugee Village Project," they had only vague notions of the residents as refugees. The first generation of villagers had arrived in the 1920s, and the AFSC observed that those who had arrived after 1949 (almost one third of the village's population), "came from the same place in China as the original settlers and were members of the same clans."[30]

In order to determine how best to provide assistance, Helen Chen, one of the AFSC's local staff members, conducted interviews with each member of the village. Her purpose was not to determine refugee status but rather to obtain "a sort of 'profile' of the village," and "suggest problems and needs that something can be done about."[31] Similarly, the community centers established by the Lutheran World Federation were intended to serve the needs of the people of Hong Kong as a whole, "to develop, through the use of these services, a community sense or feeling of communal responsibility among the inhabitants."[32] While humanitarians crafted their appeals on the basis of particular refugee needs, their work was scoped much more broadly because, in practice, it was hard to distinguish between who was a refugee and who was not. Refugeehood was only ever one aspect of an individual's experience and quite often it was not even the defining one.

Despite, or perhaps because of, the fuzzy character of the refugee label, all of the humanitarian organizations in Hong Kong consistently used the generally accepted but unproven statistic of "1.5 million refugees in the colony" in their fund-raising campaigns and operational activities. Elaborating on this figure to describe Hong Kong as the most "crowded city anywhere in the world" had two important effects.[33] One, it thickened the association of refugees with humanitarian need. As a result of the focus on crowded, destitute conditions, refugees became increasingly conceptualized as people who needed to be assisted by more privileged individuals. The postwar linkage of refugee needs with economic poverty furthered the seemingly fixed status of refugees as destitute, desperate, and without recourse to assistance of their own. Second, the reference to 1.5 million refugees in Western solicitation campaigns solidified the limits of the possible, in terms of what kinds of solutions were envisioned and who was expected to bear responsibility for alleviating the needs of refugees. Solicitation campaigns highlighted material relief provided by individual citizens over any other kind of assistance.

What Western audiences did not realize was that the refugee subject presented in the promotional material bore little resemblance to the people who actually received aid. Missionaries and private organizations rarely distinguished amongst their clientele in terms of their local status, whether that of refugee, resident, or illegal migrant. The AFSC discussed the situation of "relative poverty" and noted the "special need" in the colony because "large numbers of people are under-nourished and there is a high mortality rate through sickness."[34] The actual status of the resident population mattered very little. The rhetoric of refugeehood therefore served one purpose, and the work on the ground served others.

At the same time, promotional materials needed to demonstrate concrete results to be effective. The need for tangible outcomes required humanitarians to provide evidence of their good work, and for ARCI, whose raison d'être was the "saving" of Chinese intellectuals to help build a Free China, the demands of its fund-raising strategies required that it prove the existence of a critical mass of intellectual refugees to potential donors. ARCI was therefore one of the first organizations to attempt an empirical assessment of the situation in the colony. The impact of its survey, which preceded a major United Nations mission by two years, was far greater than one might have expected given its relatively small scale and limited scope.

In the winter of 1952, Father Frederick A. McGuire, a missionary and ARCI Vice-Chairman, and James Ivy, a member of the Committee for a Free Asia, one of the US China lobby's many outlets, arrived in Hong Kong to conduct research on the resident population. McGuire was described by one observer "as someone who spoke with great knowledge, sobriety and concern" about the refugee situation in the colony.[35] However, McGuire and Ivy's month-long stay unnerved colonial officials who wanted to keep it secret that "an American organization using American personnel and

American funds was being permitted to carry on a program of assistance to a particular group of Chinese while the Red regime was prohibited from taking similar action in caring for their own people."[36]

Following their initial meetings with US representatives and colonial officials, who cautioned them against drawing any attention to their survey, Ivy and McGuire organized the distribution of a questionnaire to "get a fair sampling of the numbers of refugees, their conditions," as well as their general needs. ARCI's founder, Ernest Moy, crafted the questions in order to "obtain all the information" possible "about how many intellectual refugees there are in Hong Kong and what their conditions may be."[37] Of the 4,000 questionnaires distributed in the few short weeks that the team was on the ground, 1,207 were completed and returned. Based on this sampling, as well as conversations with "intellectual leaders," the ARCI team concluded that there were about 10,000 refugee intellectuals in the colony in need of assistance, contrary to the figure of 25,000 originally floated in ARCI correspondence's with supporters.[38] McGuire and Ivy's final report declared that the refugee intellectuals' sole hope lay in an "effort on the part of American philanthropy to save them for lives of future usefulness."[39] This rhetoric was deliberately constructed in order to obtain financial support from potential donors.

Such donors proved few and far between; there was considerable mistrust in philanthropic circles about the anticommunist fervor with which ARCI pursued its work. Edwin Arnold of the Ford Foundation solicited advice from Lewis Hoskins, executive director of the AFSC, about ARCI's proposed program in the colony. Hoskins was skeptical, observing that "irrespective of how hard Judd tries to make it non-political, the very fact that he is so intimately associated with its leadership means that ARCI will be regarded by many as an unofficial instrument of the Guomindang government."[40] Uneasiness about ARCI's work permeated the bureaucratic echelons of the Department of State as well, resulting in lukewarm and limited offers of support. B.A. Garside, ARCI's executive director, later complained, "all of (the bureaucrats) knew little and cared less about what ARCI was trying to do, or even what were the primary objectives of America's foreign aid program."[41] Perhaps for this reason, ARCI did not let the results of the McGuire and Ivy survey speak for themselves. Rather, the organization invested considerable resources in promoting the survey's findings amongst the highest levels of the American government. Their timing was auspicious. The survey, conducted in the midst of the Korean War, may have fed into the Eisenhower administration's unspoken apprehensions about the political situation in Asia. Shortly after the survey was undertaken, the American government provided for a small number of refugees from China in special refugee legislation.

The 1953 Refugee Relief Act allowed for 209,000 "non-quota" immigrant visas to be issued up to 31 December 1956 and included room for up to 3,000 Asian refugees in the Far East and 2,000 visas specifically for Chinese refugees.[42] The inclusion of refugees in Asia, largely at the behest of Walter Judd's efforts, was a token nod towards the large, and pressing, humanitarian situations in the region. Though unprecedented, it was still only a modest step towards opening American doors to migrants from Asia. Despite the passage of the Magnuson Act ten years prior, which had formally ended the Chinese exclusion era, and the McCarran-Walter Act the year before, the American government remained unsure about the merits of large-scale refugee admissions from China as a result of Cold War security concerns and the established practice of keeping Asian migrants beyond, rather than within, the nation.[43] Still, internal reports lauded the importance of the Refugee Relief Act and particularly the attention to refugees in Asia:

> Far East refugee aid signalizes to Free People everywhere the abiding character of American friendship for the people of the Far East and the traditional desire of the United States Government for free and independent nations. The Refugee Relief Act of 1953 can do very little quantitatively—only 7000 of the two to three million odd refugees in the Far East who fled Communism and were willing to go down to rags and starvation rather than fall again under its iron heel can benefit by the Act.[44] Nevertheless, the great body of "Free People" overseas readily recognize the sound American humanitarian purposes underlying the Act.[45]

In addition to the Refugee Relief Act, the Eisenhower administration expanded the United States Escapee Program (USEP), launched by President Truman in 1952 to encourage defections from the Soviet bloc, to Hong Kong in 1954 where it was known as the Far Eastern Refugee

Program (FERP).[46] This program helped qualified individuals fleeing communism resettle to the United States. It was, however, a program that configured "a typology of statelessness" that was particular to the Cold War in Europe. It operated distinctly in Hong Kong, focused less on "inspired defections" and more on relief and rehabilitation projects, including medical clinics run by the Maryknoll mission, relief to lepers in the colony, and a variety of food distribution projects.[47] The idea behind FERP funding was that it could provide support to seed efforts that would then be carried on by private US supporters. As Richard Brown, head of the Refugee Migration Unit in Hong Kong explained,

> it is the general policy of the United States government that the bulk of support for refugee assistance throughout the world should come from the free will private offerings of the American citizens rather than by government subsidy.[48]

It was American policy that assistance and resettlement projects would "be undertaken only for refugee groups or individuals where such assistance demonstrably contributes to the advancement of US political, psychological or intelligence objectives."[49]

FERP was fundamentally different from the Escapee Program that operated in Europe. Instead of a focus on resettling refugees to America, FERP program administrators prioritized integration projects in Hong Kong and the demonstration of US commitments to fighting the Cold War in Asia through financial assistance and resettlement to the ROC.[50] Resettlement to the United States was never a priority. The 5,701 who were resettled from Hong Kong under the Refugee Relief Act essentially represented the bare minimum that the administration felt it had to settle to deny charges of racism and unequal treatment.[51] The colonial government's sensitivities to overt displays of US activity in Hong Kong, meant that unlike in Europe, many of the US government's activities in the colony took place under the cover of voluntary agency activities. CARE received substantial FERP funds from the US government, and its relief efforts were promoted. The activities of the federal government were not.[52] As a result of this dynamic, voluntary agencies became responsible for resettlement activities to the United States. However, their modest resources, even with FERP funding, limited the capacity for resettlement activities. Of the 300,000–400,000 people in Hong Kong whom US authorities believed to be in "dire straits" by 1954, only a "small percentage"—namely "those who were in categories or groups identified as having unusual political or psychological significance"—were deemed eligible for resettlement abroad by the US government and partnering voluntary agencies.[53]

The AFSC was critical of boutique efforts such as the Refugee Relief Act and FERP, which it considered evidence of "political warfare" that did little to improve the condition of people in Hong Kong.[54] Frank Hunt, who later became Director of the AFSC's Overseas Refugees Programs, observed that it was only because the "large numbers of Chinese" leaving China appeared to symbolize "a condemnation of the Red Regime," that USEP had developed an interest in the migrants. He concluded that the people of Hong Kong had become "politically exploitable," which was "one of the ways a refugee is found eligible for USEP in Europe."[55]

As a result of such views, the AFSC did not participate in US government-led efforts in Hong Kong, but other groups did. With the Refugee Relief Act and the FERP, ARCI, the International Relief Committee, the Lutheran World Federation, Catholic Welfare Services, and the National Catholic Welfare Conference all began to manage caseloads for people admitted to the United States under the auspices of these programs. They provided advice to applicants on completing applications, obtaining the required medical exams, and preparing supporting documents; in many ways, they assumed the role that Chinese migration brokers had played in Hong Kong for decades, serving as helpful go-betweens armed with knowledge and a desire to help.[56]

The Refugee Relief Act and FERP came with important financial considerations, which were welcomed by humanitarians in the colony who depended on overseas support in undertaking their relief services. Under the terms of the act, the US government gave ARCI $250,000 for its proposed resettlement program. This government support was in addition to a secret fund of $50,000 provided to ARCI by the CIA in 1951. This government aid was important because ARCI and other Western humanitarians often had difficulty raising sufficient funds for the projects they envisioned. In ARCI's case, even the work of professional fund-raiser Harold Oram, who had worked on behalf of refugees from Nazi Germany and, later, the Eastern Bloc and exploited this experience in his fund-raising efforts, failed to garner the hoped-for donations. Private contributions came from the Committee for a Free Asia, Paul Hoffman of the Ford Foundation (who used his personal budget when the foundation's board refused ARCI's requests), Lilly Endowment Inc., and the Pew Foundation, but the American government was by far the most regular and most generous of ARCI's donors.[57] Similarly, the American government contributed funds and surplus agricultural commodities to the National Catholic Welfare Council, Lutheran World Federation, CARE, the FCRA, the Maryknoll Mission, the World Council of Churches, Catholic Welfare Services, and the Catholic Foreign Mission Society of America to stimulate food distribution and relief efforts in the colony in the belief that there were important political points to be amassed.

The significant sums invested by the American government in relief work, estimated at over 8 million dollars in resettlement and 30 million dollars in food products by 1962 (70 million and 262 million respectively in today's figures), shaped the kinds of solutions humanitarians advanced to address the population needs in Hong Kong.[58] Almost uniquely, the AFSC criticized the merits of both the resettlement and, to some extent, the food distribution programs undertaken in the colony as politically motivated and shortsighted. When AFSC began to prepare its own programs for the colony in 1958, it found the humanitarian arena to be rather crowded, prompting Friends' Dennis Moriarty to refer to a "denominational scramble in food distribution."[59]

In addition to a sense of there being too many organizations on the ground, some of the AFSC's reservations stemmed from the use of food for political and evangelical aims. CARE, for instance, labeled all of its boxes using a distinctive sticker (Figure 2), which referred to the enclosed as a "Gift from your American friend as a sign of care", and referred to the US food distribution program as a "Food Crusade" to ensure that recipients knew exactly to whom they should be grateful. The label showed a beaming American family and grateful Chinese recipients.[60] Food packages funded by Canadian donors contained a maple leaf label and referenced a "Friend in Canada."[61]

Some of the same groups initially involved in food distribution efforts later provided overseas resettlement services. While their involvement was initially motivated by their observations of the crowded conditions in the colony, resettlement cases put them at the heart of

Figure 2. Label used on CARE Packages for distribution in Hong Kong. CARE records. Manuscripts and Archives Division. The New York Public Library. Astor, Lenox, and Tilden Foundations.

political Cold War contests. The act of people moving across borders was perceived as a victory for one side, and a loss for the other. In the West, refugee resettlement was seen as evidence of a nation's commitment to the liberal democratic principles of freedom and justice. Yet, resettlement, particularly after it became a way of assisting "displaced persons" and "escapees" in Europe, also became a litmus test for racial equality. It was therefore a highly fraught exercise, rife with political and cultural implications. Humanitarian organizations, as active participants in the resettlement process, became implicated in the Cold War aspects of the resettlement contest, and also confronted questions about racial bias in their work.

ARCI believed in international resettlement as a solution because of the political advantages it created. Harold Oram described resettlement as a "campaign" that could "educate the American people to the realities of the situation in the Far East."[62] However, only a fraction of ARCI's total registrants were admitted to the United States from 1952 to 1959; the vast majority were resettled to Taiwan in keeping with the US government's inclination to settle refugees outside of the United States.[63] ARCI also looked to North Borneo, Portuguese Timor, Guam, Okinawa, Malaya, and South America for possible resettlement spaces, with little success.[64] Nevertheless, ARCI staff maintained that the resettlement of refugees was "proof to all Asia that men and women of whatever race, creed or color who stand with us in the world-wide battle between freedom and slavery can count on us."[65] The movement of people out of Hong Kong appeared, to supporters at least, to provide valuable political capital at a time when racism in the United States, and the treatment of African Americans specifically, was fodder for anti-American propaganda globally.[66] It was questionable, however, to what extent resettlement addressed the social welfare needs of the people in the colony and to what extent it served the political purposes of receiving nations. The AFSC, in particular, therefore remained ambivalent about the merits of international resettlement activities.

By the time the AFSC committed to operating a full program in Hong Kong in 1959, there was already a great deal of work being undertaken by Western humanitarians and even more by the thousands of *kaifong* in the colony. The AFSC therefore carved out a niche by focusing on rehabilitation, training, and community services. Working amongst the crowded tenement settlements, the AFSC organized a resettlement program to the Tsung Hau fishing village (with food provided by Christian Welfare Services), a cooperative day care (the first in Hong Kong), and a mother's program, through which women were provided with various kinds of training and that ultimately evolved into a family planning program in 1964.

Perhaps not surprisingly, Lewis Hoskins of the AFSC and Walter Judd of ARCI disagreed fundamentally about the nature of the problem in Hong Kong and, relatedly, on the most appropriate solutions. Hoskins believed that ARCI's blatant anticommunism risked exacerbating conditions on the mainland. He cautioned,

> The obsession of the Chinese government in Peking with fear of the possible return to power of the Generalissimo has made it difficult, if not impossible, for them to understand any non-partisan help to Chinese who have supported Chiang and still actively support the return of the Kuomintang . . . a sincere desire for helping Chinese friends in Hong Kong may have at times the effect of increasing the oppression and terror on the mainland because of the developing fears and insecurity. We are equally concerned about those who have chosen to remain behind and not become exiles.[67]

More than anything else, Hoskins questioned ARCI's explicit focus on political refugees and called Judd to task for privileging a single group of people. Judd was outraged and invoked his time as a medical missionary as evidence of the purity of his intentions:

> I will take second place to no man in my record of assistance, or effort to assist, all needy people of whatever political faith. I

ministered without favor to Chinese Nationalists and anti-Nationalists, Communists and anti-Communists, Japanese soldiers and civilians and those resisting Japan's armies.

Judd was bewildered by the AFSC's lack of support for ARCI's plans:

> The work of the AFSC in helping political refugees in Europe, in Palestine, etc. has been so outstanding that perhaps you will forgive my failure to understand what seems to me to be a different attitude with respect to political refugees in Hong Kong. Do you refuse to help an Arab in need just because you know that he is anti-Israel, and if his life is saved will certainly continue to do everything in his power to fight Israel in one way or another?[68]

Hoskins's resistance to ARCI's program may have been informed in part by vocal criticism from the British Friends, whose members maintained an interest in the situation in Hong Kong even though they did not have sufficient resources to provide relief programs in the colony themselves. Janet and Jack Shephard wrote to their American colleagues in 1958 and cautioned:

> If Quakers are to undertake an organic project which will take hold, we need the respect and confidence of the refugees themselves. Once the word Quaker becomes identified, even in a side issue, with the prevailing overtones of political suasion, that confidence will have been crippled from the start.

They acknowledged, with regard to the US government's Far East Refugee Program that "some denominations can and do resign themselves to the discriminatory aspects because the schemes do at least enable them to do *something*." They insisted, "For Friends such an attitude is impossible."[69] As a result of such views, which many Friends in the United States shared, the AFSC in Hong Kong never worked closely with the Refugee Migration Unit of the US Consulate, which was responsible for administering the Refugee Relief Act and FERP, despite repeated appeals to do so and the latter's proud promotion of the AFSC's work.[70]

As the Shephards observed, however, other denominations were interested in the small openings and financial support made available by the Refugee Relief Act and FERP. As much as the US government relied on private organizations to facilitate resettlement activities, Western humanitarians relied on these programs to solicit additional financial and operational support for their programs in Asia. They were willing participants in the US government's programs, so much so that ARCI, the Catholic Welfare Services, and the World Council of Churches ran into difficulty as a result of the very limited spaces available for Chinese refugees under the auspices of the Refugee Relief Act. Under the terms of the act, sponsoring organizations had to obtain "endorsing agency" status. Humanitarians competed to obtain this status, and then they competed again to secure the best candidates—meaning the ones most likely to be approved by the US government—for resettlement. ARCI obtained endorsing agency in 1954 with demonstrable relief. Up until then, its eligible cases were channeled through Catholic Welfare Services.[71] The problem with this, from ARCI's vantage point, was that Catholic Welfare Services gave priority to its own caseload. This practice frustrated ARCI staff because it slowed the progress on the files they were most invested in. Even with endorsing powers, however, ARCI could only do so much. Therefore, in 1956, ARCI was troubled to learn that the World Council of Churches office in New York, working with the Chinese Benevolent Association in the city, had sponsored one hundred Chinese cooks and their families. In Hong Kong, Bill Howard of ARCI was incensed, saying he could "not emphasize too strongly how serious this development is and what a heavy inroad it makes on the already very limited quota."[72]

Despite differences in priorities, personality conflicts (for instance, there was no love lost between the AFSC's Bill Channel and Dave Jack of CARE, whom Channel described as anti-Friends and resistant to any ideas that were not his own), and competition for scarce resources and clients, the religious and secular humanitarians in Hong Kong played an important, if quiet, advocacy role in both the colony and abroad.[73] Their status in the colony was somewhat precarious in that they relied on the government of Hong Kong's goodwill to pursue their work and therefore often reserved criticism of government initiatives, or lack thereof. The government of Hong Kong relied on voluntary agencies for the provision of health and welfare services, but officials were quick to deter initiatives they considered to be too generous, or those that were likely to improve conditions in the colony to such a degree that new migrants would be drawn in. Given its continued efforts to remain neutral in the contest between the communists and the Guomindang and the rivalries of the global Cold War more generally, the government of Hong Kong also disliked humanitarian appeals that drew attention explicitly to a refugee population in the colony.

Humanitarians also exerted unwelcome pressure on policymakers in white settler societies when they raised the question of racial equality on refugee issues.[74] Even international organizations were not immune. ARCI criticized the United Nations and the UNHCR for their "European-mindedness" and their "timidity" in dealing with the question of China.[75] From Bangkok, United Nations' Representative Aami Ali wrote the High Commissioner and reported on the harsh criticism he was hearing. Reports suggested that the UNHCR was "soft pedaling" the problem of Chinese refugees. Ali argued that it was hard to explain "to people in Asia why [the] UNCHR refuses to recognize the only Asian refugee problem which might fall within its scope."[76] Such observations were repeated at the United Nations where Dr. Yu Tsune-Chi, the ROC delegate, insisted that "refugees in Europe and refugees in Asia should be given equal attention."[77] Henry (Hank) Lieberman at the *New York Times* desk in Hong Kong, who had covered the Civil War in China, reported, "The impression of many Chinese refugees is, incidentally, that Western hearts bleed more for one Western refugee than for 10,000 Oriental refugees."[78] ARCI used this discrepancy to advance both its program and its fund-raising efforts. Judd explained to correspondents:

We are fighting for the minds of men in defense of freedom in the world, but those who stand on our side in East Asia are being alienated by our indifference. Is it any wonder that they speak of a double standard, that those with white skins have priority on our concerns.[79]

Arguments about racial equality on refugee issues linked the migrants in Hong Kong with preexisting, widely accepted notions of refugees from Europe and the Soviet Bloc as victims of communist oppression. Yet they were not one and the same. Many of the so-called refugees in Hong Kong were following the well-trodden routes that had historically bridged the two spaces, following friends and family to and from the colony and the mainland.[80] Advocates marginalized this reality only to have critics undermine claims to refugeehood and assistance on the very same basis.

Although the government of Hong Kong disavowed the term refugee to describe residents of the colony, the ROC government, its supporters, and a variety of Western humanitarians in the colony conceptualized the people from the mainland as refugees, specifically refugees from communist oppression in need of protection (in keeping with the spirit of the refugee definition in the 1951 Convention). As a result, in 1953 the ROC delegate introduced a motion during meetings of UNREF's Advisory Committee to have refugees in Hong Kong included within the scope of the High Commissioner for Refugees mandate.[81] After much discussion, the committee agreed that the question of eligibility could only be addressed if more concrete information was obtained about conditions in the colony.[82] In approaching the trustees at the Ford Foundation for financial support for a refugee survey, the High Commissioner for Refugees, Gerrit van Goedhart, explained he wanted to determine whether the people in Hong Kong fell under his mandate; more importantly, he wanted to look at substantive solutions.[83]

Funded with a $50,000 grant from the Ford Foundation, the resulting mission was tasked with ascertaining the size and composition of the refugee population, investigating all possible solutions and establishing "the necessary facts" required to make a determination about whether or not the refugees came within the scope of the High Commissioner's mandate. There was a great deal at stake. If the mission found that the migrants were eligible under the High Commissioner's office, then a new program would result; as one American authority indicated, it would probably bring about an extension of the High Commissioner's mandate beyond his second four-year term, set to expire in 1958.[84] However, it would also mean a United Nations presence in Hong Kong, which British authorities in both London and Hong Kong opposed, mostly on the grounds that it would be "politically embarrassing to have outside bodies administering camps or making relief payments in the colony."[85]

Governor Alexander Grantham, described as one of the "greatest governors" of Hong Kong and "progressive" in his approach to working with the local Chinese community, was "lukewarm" to the suggestion of a refugee survey as he was protective of British sovereignty in Hong

Kong.[86] Officials in London shared the Governor's reservations about the mission, but they confronted considerable pressure at the United Nations and therefore warned the Governor, who was trying to keep the mission's terms of reference from public view, against "carrying his 'caginess' too far."[87] Growing international attention to the situation in Hong Kong as a result of solicitations by humanitarians in the colony and ongoing discussions in various United Nations forums meant that British authorities had to be careful about how they presented their views on the refugee question. The Colonial Office was insistent that the mission proceed, and Governor Grantham only begrudgingly acquiesced. Nevertheless, he required that, in terms of financial assistance, no distinction be drawn between people defined as refugees and those considered residents of the colony. According to Grantham, preferential treatment for refugees would only sow discontent amongst the colony's residents and risk the precarious balance the colony had established amid various Cold War rivalries.[88]

From the outset, Dr. Edward Hambro—whom Governor Grantham described as a "rather conceited individual"—and his team took an expansive view of their mission's mandate.[89] They deemed the definition of a refugee according to the 1951 Convention too limiting and decided to reject the "juridical sense" of refugeehood, as established in the convention, in favor of providing "a broader and more comprehensive background."[90] The broad liberties Hambro and his team assumed in interpreting the mission's mandate were later reflected in the survey's recommendations, which dodged the question of whether or not the refugees fell under the High Commissioner's mandate. Instead, Hambro declared the refugees in Hong Kong to be of "international concern" regardless of their actual legal status. In his final report, *A Problem of People*, Hambro noted that although British officials considered the refugees "merely Chinese people living in a British colony," from the international point of view, "they were political refugees and as such, should be helped."[91]

The Hambro report elaborated three types of possible solutions: repatriation, emigration or resettlement in another country of asylum, or "firm establishment" in the colony.[92] On the question of emigration, the mission concluded, "the prospects of resettling Chinese refugees abroad are very limited, owing to the immigration policies practiced by most

Governments."[93] The only exception was the United States, where the 1953 Refugee Relief Act had created a small opening for sponsored refugee admissions. The Hambro report suggested that the High Commissioner intervene with other potential receiving countries to determine whether they would be willing to broaden existing categories of migration or introduce special measures akin to those in the United States. Hambro and his staff believed that the immigration policies of the white settler societies of Australia, New Zealand, and Canada in particular "could conceivably be modified."[94] This optimism was misplaced. It was precisely over concern that the UNHCR would press the Canadian government on refugee admissions that the latter refused to sign the 1951 Convention until 1969 and blocked the organization's requests to send a permanent representative to the country until 1975.[95]

The vast majority of Hambro's conclusions dealt with the question of refugee integration in Hong Kong, where he perceived major problems of "poverty, over-population and unemployment."[96] Instead of an enhanced role for the government of Hong Kong, the mission suggested expanding the practice of using voluntary agencies such as the International Social Service, the Lutheran World Federation, and the World Council of Churches to meet the needs of refugees. The report made some mention of ARCI's work, and Walter Judd was pleased with Hambro's assessment of ARCI's special training program "by which we are preparing some of these individuals for permanent professional activity in Hong Kong." He was particularly grateful that the mission recommended ARCI "be assisted in its work of promoting the resettlement of refugees to Formosa [Taiwan]."[97]

At the same time, Hambro and his team acknowledged that the voluntary agencies could not carry out expanded relief and rehabilitation schemes at their existing rate of financing. The inference seemed to be that the international community had a role to play in producing the estimated $35 million (HK dollars) required to care for the population in the colony on an annual basis.[98] On the related question of housing policy, Hambro proposed the creation of a refugee credit fund that could be used, in part, to provide grants and credits for accommodation. The fund was to be available to refugees only, contrary to the policies advocated by authorities in Hong Kong and London. In response, Governor Grantham insisted, as he had from the outset of the survey, that no distinction could be drawn between refugees and the rest of the populace in Hong Kong. The government of Hong Kong was determined to blur any distinctions between refugees and residents in order to keep international interest at bay and minimize its own responsibilities vis-à-vis the swollen population. The entire population was described as "decent, hardworking folk who only want to be left alone and they are self-reliant in so doing."[99] The government's strategy proved rather effective. By 1963, David Elder of the AFSC was explaining how he had "become so accustomed to regard[ing] Hong Kong as one whole entity, not separated into 'refugee' and 'resident' categories, that it requires some effort to think back to the time when I was more aware of 'refugees'."[100]

The government's insistence on the lack of distinctions between refugees and others, which intersected with what potential countries of resettlement wanted to hear, meant that discussions of the Hambro Report in UNREF's Advisory Committee achieved very little. The ROC delegate, Cheng Pao-Nan, lobbied forcefully to have the refugees included under the High Commissioner's mandate. However, there was very little appetite for this approach. Moreover, the Hambro report had stopped short of identifying mandated UNHCR responsibility as an appropriate solution. Reflecting the lack of enthusiasm for a major UNHCR presence in Hong Kong, and by association expanded responsibility for refugee situations outside of Europe, the resolution that eventually passed in UNREF's Advisory Committee was an empty one. It requested only that the High Commissioner "give sympathetic encouragement to Governments and organizations with a view to their assisting in alleviating the problems of Chinese refugees in Hong Kong and to report to the Committee, when he deemed it necessary, any progress made in the implementation of the Resolution."[101]

Although the Hambro Report failed to produce any substantial action at the United Nations, it garnered significant interest amongst humanitarians, who picked up the report's recommendations and referenced them in their campaigns for financial support for their program activities in Hong Kong.[102] In England, the Oxford Committee for Famine Relief (OXFAM) published advertisements in the *Manchester Guardian* and other newspapers, calling on the British government to address the situation in the colony.[103] CARE's Hong Kong office cited Hambro's report in its publicity materials, noting the "considerable time and effort" spent by the mission "in exploring ways and means for settling some of these people in Oceania and other Pacific regions." Still, the author of the promotional materials, Richard Shaefter, bemoaned the fact that the "proposed plans dealt only with a pitifully few thousand of the teeming refugee masses." As a result, he explained that CARE:

> is now engaged in a broad scale program to bring much-needed aid to political refugees throughout the free world. . . . What Berlin is for Central Europe that is Hong Kong for the Far East: Haven for tens of thousands who fled from Communist domination.[104]

Those on the ground were genuinely frustrated by the failure of the responsible authorities to act on any of the Hambro report's recommendations. Two years after the report was published, Dr. Elfan Rees of the World Council of Churches accused the British government of failing to address the situation in Hong Kong and demanded to know what action was being taken.[105] The answer, it seems, was very little.

In the years following the publication of the Hambro Report, the ROC delegate was often the only voice heard at the United Nations on the question of Chinese refugees and the High Commissioner's mandate. In the field, humanitarians continued their work in communicating need to audiences outside the colony. In circulars and letters home, missionaries and social workers stressed the "grim" conditions in which people lived and the need for critical social services.[106] In Hong Kong, the Civic Association and the United Nations Association of Hong Kong pursued Hambro's idea of a financial fund for the Chinese refugees in the colony.[107] In August 1957, organizations engaged with the refugee question in Hong Kong banded together to establish the "All Hong Kong Appeal to the United Nations for Relief to Chinese Refugees in Hong Kong," whose main purpose was to petition the United Nations for a $100 million (HK dollars) relief scheme for the refugees in the colony.[108]

Neither the Hong Kong nor the British governments liked the idea of a dedicated fund for refugees, although they were increasingly open to the idea of obtaining international funds to support the massive and costly public housing schemes in the colony as well as the relief efforts assumed by the churches.[109] Nevertheless, it remained official British policy not to provide the Hong Kong government with any money to address the refugee issue specifically. As such, discussions of a potential fund at the United Nations risked potential embarrassment.[110] The British delegation was irresolute about how it could lend support to the question of relief for Hong Kong without committing its own government to making targeted financial contributions. Meanwhile, the government of Hong Kong was concerned about its ability to retain discretionary control over the internal resettlement of the colony's squatter population and the delivery of social services if it accepted funds from the international community. Governor Grantham worried further about the possible political repercussions that deliberating on, and establishing, a refugee fund might have on the colony's delicate relationship with the People's Republic of China.[111] Still, Grantham conceded that it would be "most difficult to decline offers of assistance from any source," and therefore hoped that funds would come from private agencies and not national governments so that relief schemes would not be "complicated by conditions and special provisions."[112]

When the matter of the refugee fund was raised at the United Nations in the spring of 1957, delegates failed to reach a decision, and a US-sponsored resolution referred the matter to the General Assembly. In November 1957, the assembly recognized the refugee situation in Hong Kong as being of "international importance." Although the people in the colony still weren't included within the scope of the High Commissioner's mandate, the resolution enabled Auguste Lindt, appointed in 1956 after High Commissioner Goedhart's sudden passing, to use his "good offices" to issue financial appeals in aid of the migrants.[113] The "good offices" compromise was an important milestone in the growing international interest in the refugee situation in Hong Kong.[114] The ROC government, with American support, had exerted sufficient pressure, and Western humanitarians in the colony had produced enough publicity material to keep Chinese refugees in Hong Kong, if not at the center of the world's focus, then far enough from the outer periphery to ensure they were not forgotten completely. These determined efforts help explain why Hong Kong was such a prominent part of the United Nation's World Refugee Year (1959–1960).

In the spring of 1958, four young British lawyers published an article titled "Wanted: A World Refugee Year" in *Crossbow*, an influential London publication. Christopher Chataway, Colin Jones, Trevor Philpott, and Timothy Raison posited, "The refugee is the showing sore of the most bitter sickness of our time," and proposed a worldwide campaign to alleviate the suffering of refugees in Europe, Hong Kong, and the Middle East. Their call to action had an immediate impact. Officials in the High Commissioner's office were enamored with the idea, as they were mindful of the protracted refugee situation in Europe where there still almost 40,000 people in camps. They were also sensitive to their program's precarious financial situation: the annual pledging conference had only raised 50 percent of the funds required for the UNHCR's 1959 program.[115] World Refugee Year seemed like a wonderful way to increase awareness, raise funds, and close the remaining camps in Europe.

When the possibility of sponsoring a World Refugee Year was raised at the United Nations, governments tabled their support, along with their reservations. The Canadian delegate stated his government was in agreement with the proposed resolution, but it "did not want to take a national lead."[116] The Australian representative indicated that his government supported the initiative "subject to the understanding that the activities, which individual Governments may undertake, [are] a matter for determination by those Governments on an individual basis."[117] Many delegations echoed this concern. The British government made it clear that it would not be admitting refugees during World Refugee Year "except under normal immigration rules." It believed that "further contributions to the refugees problem must be financial, not by way of immigration."[118] No government wanted to be bound by a commitment to World Refugee Year to modify its immigration or refugee policies. The British government and white settler societies therefore insisted that refugee needs were best met by alleviating local conditions.[119] This approach was informed by perspectives that dictated that only certain migrants were desirable for permanent admission within national territories. This had serious implications for how the objectives of World Refugee Year were conceptualized and how they were ultimately pursued.

In preparation for World Refugee Year, there was considerable debate at the United Nations about which situations should be targeted and whether efforts should be limited to "mandated" UNHCR refugees, an approach that would have excluded the Chinese in Hong Kong. In a somewhat surprising move, British officials reversed their position regarding the international status of Chinese refugees, asserting "that Her Majesty's

Government have always considered this group of refugees to be eligible under the mandate of the High Commissioner" and expressing the hope that World Refugee Year "would provide an opportunity for further assistance" to Hong Kong.[120] This position was a radical departure from the government's strategy of keeping international interests at bay, as evidenced five years prior when the Hambro survey was commissioned.

The change in British policy resulted in large part from heightened tensions within the newly constituted UNHCR Executive Committee, which included a ROC delegate after the 1958 elections. Echoing concerns voiced previously by Governor Grantham, Foreign Service Officer Robin Black warned that the Guomindang delegate would "probably take the initiative in such a way to exploit the Cold War aspects of the refugee problem and spoil the chances of our doing something constructive."[121] Grantham had been antagonized by the way the Guomindang exploited the population situation in the colony, and insisted that resettlement or what the FCRA called "repatriation programmes" were unnecessary. All the Guomindang government had to do "to send more refugees to Formosa [Taiwan]," he said, "was make their immigration policy less restrictive."[122]

The presence of the ROC delegate seemed to portend problems for authorities in Hong Kong with the communist regime in Beijing as the issue of the refugees in the colony began to take on distinctly Cold War overtones. The British government therefore flipped on the question of the High Commissioner's mandate and made an initial commitment of £100,000 to World Refugee Year, the bulk of which was directed expressly to the situation in Hong Kong. The idea was to undermine the Guomindang's politicized claims. Although OXFAM and other organizations had pressed the British government to take more of an interest in the refugees' plight throughout the 1950s, it was the colony's vulnerable political position that proved the ultimate tipping point in securing British support for including Chinese refugees in the colony in the program for World Refugee Year. The British government's subsequent claim that the people in Hong Kong were "in every sense of the word, refugees," in the face of Soviet statements to the contrary, was evidence of how rhetoric about the population situation in Hong Kong disguised the political calculations that shaped so much of the decision-making on assistance to people in the colony.[123]

In the end, the UNHCR's Executive Committee decided that since the Chinese refugees in Hong Kong had been ruled of "international concern" in 1957, they should be included in the targets for World Refugee Year along with Arab refugees in Palestine, European refugees in China, and the main target, the people in the remaining camps in Europe.[124] Somewhat ironically, ARCI, which had been so enthusiastic in its efforts to assist refugees in Hong Kong in the early 1950s, was by World Refugee Year a name in correspondence only.[125] Faced with poor fund-raising prospects and a shifting legal framework with the expiry of the Refugee Relief Act and the introduction in 1957 of the Refugee-Escapee Act, ARCI transferred its residual operations in Hong Kong to the International Rescue Committee in 1959, missing out on the greatest publicity campaign ever mounted for refugee work in Hong Kong.[126]

A total of ninety-seven countries participated in World Refugee Year. National committees orchestrated a dizzying array of fund-raising activities. There were special events and presentations at the White House, refugee art exhibits and a promotional Austerity Week in Canada, candy sales and special ballet productions of *The Exile* in New Zealand, fund-raising screenings of *The Camp* in Australia, charity jazz concerts and amateur boxing tournaments in Hong Kong, and lavender sales and sponsored competitive boat races in England. The actor Yul Brynner, named Special Assistant to the UN High Commissioner for Refugees, lent his celebrity status to the cause, and musicians Edith Piaf and Bing Crosby contributed hit songs to the "All-Star Festival" album, which sold over a million copies in Europe alone in the first three months of sales. All of the participating countries set ambitious fund-raising objectives. The United Kingdom aimed for $5,600,000 (all figures in US dollars), Canada hoped to raise $3,300,000, Australia's goal was $1,120,000, and New Zealand's was $490,000. The Guomindang government aimed for $300,000 and proposed to dedicate 75 percent of the funds raised to support Chinese refugees in Hong Kong.[127]

World Refugee Year was a major undertaking, and it had a profound impact on the general public's engagement with refugee issues. Significantly, governments remained in the background in terms of advocating on behalf of refugees. If anything, they sought to dissuade humanitarian actors from going too far in their "elaborate" representations of "refugees and the begging-bowl."[128] Religious and secular humanitarians assumed the lead in presenting refugees and their needs to the public. Across the globe, the responsibility for generating support and interest in the refugee enterprise was left to the voluntary sector, with the result that it was private, and sometimes rather privileged, citizens who took the initiative in depicting refugees and characterizing their needs. Private fund-raising efforts simultaneously furthered the profile of Chinese refugees in Hong Kong, and contributed to the perception of unbridgeable distances between refugees in need and the citizens who raised funds and gathered material items for their relief.[129] The effect of these depictions was far-reaching both in terms of their visual and social impact, but also in terms of the ongoing debate over who should bear ultimate responsibility for providing assistance to refugees. Public and private engagement with refugee issues was mutually constituted and the balance shifted within particular national contexts. [130]

In South Africa, for instance, public and private apathy reinforced a general disinterest in refugee issues. By the 1950s, the government of South Africa was already beginning to diverge from those of other white settler societies in terms of the energy it invested in appearing to be humanitarian and in the effort it exerted in instrumentalizing refugee issues for larger political purposes. The apartheid government committed to World Refugee Year but it undertook little in the way of initiatives and voluntary efforts in the country lacked the enthusiasm evidenced elsewhere. South Africa's national committee for World Refugee Year included representatives from the Methodist Church, the South African National Committee for Child Welfare, and the South African Refugee Organization.[131] The committee decided that one of its top priorities was to demonstrate that refugees were good laborers to counter the "disgusting apathy" they perceived amongst policymakers and the general public. The committee's most ambitious plan was to build a refugee village in South Africa, modeled after Father George Pire's Nobel prize-winning work in Europe where he organized the construction of "refugee villages" after the Second World War. Organizers hoped to get land the size of a township where an architect could design residences. The idea was that refugees would then help in the construction of this village. Noting that they would need government permission to get the refugees to South Africa, and that this might be difficult, the committee nevertheless maintained:

True to our humanitarian ideas we must do all we can to get permission for the entry of an average cross-section of a village population. No average village ever consists only of able-bodied, first class artisans with 100% fit families within the specified immigration age groups. Existing legislation allows the entry of relatives and dependents of "sub-standard quality" and full advantage should be taken of that.[132]

Reflecting the insistence on physical racial separation that characterized life in apartheid South Africa, the committee felt that putting the refugees altogether in one place would permit them to "feel at home among their own kind and although the process of assimilation will be slower it will no doubt be easier."[133] This plan, like many of the committee's efforts to publicize World Refugee Year, did not amount to much. The government gave £5,000 to the Intergovernmental Committee on European Migration (ICEM) to assist with the cost of moving refugees, but little else was accomplished.[134] No refugee village was constructed.

President Eisenhower launched World Refugee Year with great fanfare, but the actual outcome—in terms of fund-raising objectives and public investment in the United States—was disappointing. Responsibility for promoting World Refugee Year fell to the United States Committee for Refugees, headed by Reverend Francis B. Sayre. The Reverend recruited Herbert Lehman, former head of UNRRA, to the committee as well as Edward Marks, who had worked in the camps in Europe and who became the committee's director. As the committee was responsible for leading fund-raising efforts, Marks called upon voluntary agencies in the United States to raise $20 million (US dollars) for World Refugee Year. Yet overall, the committee's aspirations were relatively modest. In fact, one of its main aims was to "to prevent the creation of the false impression that the present problems can all be solved in one year." Still, the committee also wanted to have a "lasting impact," and it consequently invested in educational campaigns and lobbied Congress to change the laws around the paroling of refugees.[135] As a result, Congress passed Public Law 86–648—the "Fair Share Law"—which allowed for "alien refugee-escapee[s]" to be paroled to the United States and which "committed the USA to accept up to one quarter of the total number of refugees admitted by all countries during World Refugee

Year."[136] At first glance, this seemed like an extraordinarily generous offer, and it was certainly one that suggested America's moral authority while encouraging other countries to do their "fair share." However, few countries chose resettlement as their preferred method of assisting refugees, and only 3,750 refugees were admitted to the United States in 1963.[137] As the law applied only to those eligible under Section 15(1)(c) of the 1953 Refugee Relief Act and to those who fell within the mandate of the United Nations High Commissioner for Refugees, Chinese refugees in Hong Kong were not eligible.

In the end, fund-raising efforts in the United States fell short of expectations. Though Abraham Lincoln's views on citizens' moral duties were held up by the US Committee for Refugees as a model of the American spirit for helping others ("I hold that while man exists, it is his duty to improve not only his own condition, but to assist in ameliorating mankind"), the year's financial and social results failed to match the expectations advanced by such lofty ideals.[138] As a result, American officials disguised the year's shortcomings by referencing the country's overall history, "not generally known," of engagement with refugee issues, including a history of admitting one million refugees to the United States as permanent residents and the expenditure of a billion tax dollars on refugees around the world.[139] From Geneva, Duncan Wood of the AFSC captured the sense of having fallen short of expectations in observing that even Iran, which has "quite a few more domestic problems than the United States," still "managed to contribute $40,000 to the refugees outside of Iran during World Refugee Year."[140]

In other white settler societies, public interest in refugees, including those in Hong Kong, outpaced government engagement with the issue. Compassionate appeals and fund-raising efforts led to attempts to resettle additional numbers of refugees, beyond the permissible limits defined by existing legislation, or endorsed by officials in power. For instance, Canadian groups sought to sponsor refugees from Europe and China and to organize orphan adoption schemes only to have their efforts consistently rebuffed by federal authorities. They did, however, manage to privately sponsor seventy European families, and their efforts laid the groundwork for future orphan adoption schemes.[141] Unlike other refugee groups, orphans were considered "safe" because they were, by definition, alone, and therefore did not pose a threat to the racial composition of white settler societies that relied on family sponsorship programs as part of their overall immigration admission frameworks.

Confronted by the question of whether to resettle refugees from Hong Kong, white settler society officials insisted on admissions based on notions of "assimilability," "absorptive capacity," and labor market needs.[142] They had little or no appetite for undertaking massive resettlement schemes, particularly for refugees from Asia. Australian officials referred to "psychological and environmental influences" in suggesting "certain categories of refugees in Europe" should be resettled to "a country which can provide, through its established and highly developed social services, appropriate institutional care and after-treatment."[143] Australia considered itself one of these countries and included the resettlement of people from Europe, including some with disabilities and health conditions, in its immigration priorities. The government of New Zealand also privileged the European refugee situation and only started contributing to the relief of refugee situations in Hong Kong and Korea once the situation in Europe had improved. Europe was certainly the focus of World Refugee Year because the UNHCR had committed to "clearing the camps," but humanitarian efforts also drew unprecedented attention, up to that point, to what was happening in Hong Kong.

In New Zealand, the Council of Organizations for Relief Services Overseas (CORSO) was the coordinating body for the country's World Refugee Year efforts.[144] Though it focused primarily on Europe, CORSO's World Refugee Year fund-raising efforts were so successful, it used some of the surplus funds to build cottages for indigent residents of Hong Kong under the auspices of the Chinese Methodist Church at Chai Wan. The Rotary Club in Wellington raised £300 for three cottages and school groups raised money for the construction of the huts. CORSO organizers believed "the practical nature of this help to Chinese refugees appealed to New Zealanders."[145] In Australia, all levels of society were engaged in efforts for World Refugee Year, including the Good Neighbor Councils, which were established in 1950 to smooth relations between arriving migrants and more established communities. Girl Guide groups as well as Rotary and Lions Clubs participated in the fund-raising and educational efforts. Local and regional voluntary agencies raised more than £880,000, with over £100,000 directed to Hong Kong to support hospitals in the colony and the construction of a housing settlement bearing the name "Australia Village."[146]

It was in England, however, that the story of life in Hong Kong figured most prominently in World Refugee Year campaigns. One of the most elaborate publicity stunts was constructed at Trafalgar Square. The installation consisted of forty huts, such as would be found in the squatter settlements in Hong Kong. Organized by the World Council of Churches and built by volunteer Rover Scouts, the huts featured "typical" refugee possessions that had been specially shipped from overseas. The designers also borrowed the replica of a Hong Kong street from the British Pinewood film studios to create an allegedly authentic atmosphere in the square. The space was organized so that the street led to the "open space where the shacks [could] be seen against a huge backcloth of the colony's hillsides."[147] The purpose of the exhibit was to demonstrate how refugees lived on a daily basis, with the ultimate objective of raising funds for a vocational training center. Combined with an exhibition of photographs on display in nearby St. Martin in the Fields (organized by the Inter-Church Aid and Refugee Service), the British public was left with an absolutely desperate picture of life in the colony. This same public subsequently gave over £200,000 to help people in Hong Kong.[148]

Displays such as the ones in Trafalgar Square and St. Martin in the Fields revealed the starkly different approaches that humanitarians took to relief issues in the colony, compared to those pursued by authorities in London and Hong Kong. For almost a decade, official government policy had sought to manage the refugee issue within Hong Kong's political and geographical borders. During World Refugee Year, humanitarians took center stage in disseminating information and images of the colony's people with seeming disregard for the careful dance of containment that officials in London and Hong Kong had executed in previous years. Around the world, images of refugees were instrumentalized for fund-raising purposes so that the refugee became a commodity that could be bought and sold.[149] Unable (or unwilling) to rely solely on rational arguments to appeal for donations and expenditures on behalf of refugees, volunteers used vivid descriptions and images that touched on cultural codes and conventions to tug at the heartstrings of would-be donors.[150] The creation of empathy was geared to the generation of funds.

In Australia, the state of Victoria's Committee for World Refugee Year decided that sheer emotion was the only "weapon" when it came to helping refugees in Hong Kong. Their appeal highlighted the plight of "children, sleeping in streets, ragged, cold and hungry through no fault of their own."[151] In Canada, the national committee used the image of a young refugee girl with dark eyes holding an empty bowl in their fund-raising efforts as there was "evidence from a number of countries" that indicated that this image had "a unique power of appeal."[152] The World Council of Churches hired Baden Hickman to cover the events and activities of World Refugee Year. As the WCC's journalist, Hickman's sole task was to disseminate information about refugee situations to the international public. In October 1959, Mr. Hickman went to Hong Kong and dispatched an account of the typical daily diet of a Chinese refugee. According to his report, refugees ate "nothing but two bowls of watery rice (congee) as they cannot afford to buy vegetables or beans." He explained that this "inadequate diet" led to malnutrition, which was "one of the causes of the epidemic-type of tuberculosis in over-crowded Hong Kong with its near 1,500,000 Chinese refugees."[153] Despite the unproven nature of the privation, and indeed the size of the refugee population, such representations conjured up notions about the deserving poor and their needs; by clearly delineating the role of donor and recipient, they also added an additional dimension to the existing landscape of difference.

Not surprisingly, officials in Hong Kong had mixed opinions about such efforts. Claude Burgess, the Colonial Secretary, thought that voluntary agencies were rather quick to "get their facts wrong and their publicity crooked," but the global interest generated by World Refugee Year caused the government of Hong Kong to see the population in the colony in a new light.[154] The government of Hong Kong welcomed the inflow of cash that World Refugee Year portended and developed a wish list of projects to be funded. The government's proposed projects amounted to a grand sum of $7,280,000 (US dollars). Many of the projects were left over from earlier discussions in 1957 about a possible refugee fund. Potential projects included a rehabilitation center ($5,250,000), primary schools in resettlement areas ($175,000), a technical secondary school ($375,000), library and teaching equipment, medical supplies, and expert assistance for the reclamation of land upon which refugee housing was to be constructed (estimated at a cost of $1.75–$4.2 million or $15.3–$36.7 million US in today's figures).[155] The chosen projects were designed to contribute to the overall health and welfare of the colony, and they were chosen strategically. When foreign governments suggested alternative projects that appeared to be politically sensitive, they were rebuffed. For instance, when the government of Norway proposed to fund the construction of a sanitarium in Rennie's Mill Camp, Governor Robin Black, who assumed office in 1958, objected. He indicated "proposals are welcome in so far as the money is to be spent otherwise than in Rennie's Mill."[156] Black wanted to avoid directing funds to projects that could serve the interests of the Guomindang in Taiwan or upset the communists on the mainland. Grants such as the $200,000 from the United States, which was handed directly to the government of Hong Kong, were most appreciated.[157]

The publicity and fund-raising campaigns undertaken by volunteers and humanitarians made World Refugee Year a financial success, amassing $620 million in today's figures.[158] However, other than the special refugee law in the United States and some incremental progress towards obtaining approval for adoptions and sponsorships in other white settler societies, very little changed structurally in terms of admission criteria. The overall philosophy that governed admissions amongst white settler societies limited the desire to open up migration streams to larger numbers of refugees, especially Chinese refugees. This reluctance forced humanitarians working on the ground in Hong Kong to become more vocal and explicit about how they perceived the responsibility of the international community. Resettlement, which had originally been advanced by ARCI with support from the United States government to move people from Hong Kong to Taiwan and elsewhere in Asia, became a frequently discussed solution, largely because of the moral imperative that animated humanitarians' worldviews, the political capital created by accusing societies of racism in the charged atmosphere of the Cold War and the many discussions generated by World Refugee Year activities.

The President of the Standing Conference of Voluntary Agencies Working for Refugees, Jean J. Chenard, proposed that resettlement was the only real solution for the situation in Hong Kong. He stated, "Everyone knows that Hong Kong is crowded up to and beyond saturation point. Everyone knows that the only real solution would be to resettle the Chinese refugees elsewhere." Chenard admonished the international community for not providing more in the way of resettlement opportunities, saying his organization "had hoped for better things from the Governments of the free world."[159] The World Council of Churches echoed Chenard's emphasis on the importance of resettlement. In a document titled *Observations on Emigration as a Solution to the Chinese Problem in Hong Kong*, the WCC declared:

> Even though the majority of Hong Kong refugees may never get to some other place, it is psychologically very important that a few are able to emigrate. The hope of resettlement abroad helps to reduce the despair and unrest at being hopelessly blocked in Hong Kong. While we stress that emigration cannot be the solution for the hundreds of thousands, we would like to press for a more generous attitude on the part of all countries so that the openings which exist can be made wider to admit, not a trickle, but a stream of refugees from this very-crowded city.[160]

The International Committee of the Red Cross believed that governments should use the momentum created by World Refugee Year to liberalize their immigration restrictions, both in terms of eligible categories of migrants and in the application of "artificial" age barriers that restricted mobility.[161] Governments rebuffed such suggestions. The British government maintained that there was "very little indication" that Chinese refugees wished to leave Hong Kong. Instead, it emphasized the importance of contributing monetarily to projects in the colony.[162] The leaders of white settler societies shared this sentiment.

Governments in the United States, Canada, Australia, New Zealand, and South Africa had committed to supporting World Refugee Year on the grounds that they would not be required to reform their respective immigration policies. Despite the outpouring of public support, the international campaign failed to convince governments or the broad public of the merits of large-scale refugee resettlement to their shores.[163] The images humanitarians used to raise money for World Refugee Year reinforced a sense of distance between citizens of white settler societies and refugees in Hong Kong, perpetuating the impression of refugees as alien others. There was therefore a disconnect between the ambitious objectives set out for World Refugee Year by the United Nations and what the intense fund-raising and promotional campaigns actually accomplished for people in Hong Kong. Fund-raising efforts for Hong Kong totaled over $5 million (or $44 million US in today's figures). However, the mobility potential for migrants in Hong Kong did not increase concurrent to the public profile of the Chinese refugee subject.

When it came time to prepare for the closing conference of World Refugee Year, the question of whether to use the leftover funds from the year's fund-raising activities to resettle Chinese refugees arose.[164] Australian officials indicated that they would only participate in discussions if they were not pressured to modify their immigration policies to accept Chinese refugees.[165] Similarly, Canadian officials informed the UNHCR that they "would not want to accept a quota of Chinese immigrants" though "naturally they would not want to admit this publicly."[166] For their part, staff in New Zealand's Department of External Affairs stated frankly, "any proposals for bringing Chinese to New Zealand would of course be out of the question."[167] The British Colonial Office returned to its earlier position, insisting that there was no room for an expanded UNHCR mandate in Hong Kong.[168] Having secured substantial funds for many development projects, the government of Hong Kong wanted to reassert its authority over the management of people in the colony. "Refugees" had served their instrumental purpose in Hong Kong and the colonial government wanted to build on the financial success of World Refugee Year, but it wanted to do so without outside interference. After World Refugee Year, the colonial government would once again seek to minimize external interest in the colony's subjects.

Attention to refugees in Hong Kong peaked at varying intensities over the better part of a decade, especially following the arrival of large numbers of Western missionaries in the colony in 1951. The ROC government and the FCRA, supported by the United States, introduced, and kept, the situation in Hong Kong on the agenda at UNREF meetings despite efforts by British colonial officials to handle the population situation in the colony by relying on *kaifongs*, Western missionaries and secular organizations for the provision of immediate health and welfare relief. The Guomindang's efforts as well as those of Western humanitarians in communicating needs in the colony to audiences abroad resulted in the United Nations organizing a survey to assess the refugee situation in Hong Kong. Following on the survey's results, the General Assembly later passed a resolution mandating the High Commissioner to use his "good offices" to appeal for funds on behalf of refugees in Hong Kong. In turn, this important resolution laid the groundwork for the Chinese refugees in the colony to be recognized as a key priority during the United Nations' World Refugee Year.

With World Refugee Year, the situation in Hong Kong came to the world's attention in an unparalleled manner. School groups, community organizations, and church congregations raised funds on behalf of the refugees in the colony and cultural and political elites did the same. Ironically, depictions of the refugees' daily lives and the publicity surrounding the situation in Hong Kong cemented the international public's perception of Chinese refugees as alien. For white settler societies, these images affirmed the idea of Chinese refugees as a problem, as reflected in the title of the Hambro mission's final report, *A Problem of People*.[169] Somewhat paradoxically, the activities of World Refugee Year cemented the prevailing sentiment that refugees in Hong Kong should be assisted through local integration efforts rather than cross-border resettlement programs. The outpouring of financial support suggested a willingness to assist refugees in Asia, but only from afar. No government, other than the ROC and two Latin American countries, offered to resettle Chinese refugees during World Refugee Year.[170] The United States, which passed the Fair Share Law as part of its World Refugee Year commitments, resettled only European refugees under the resulting quota. This preferred approach dovetailed with existing humanitarian efforts in the colony, which were focused almost exclusively on direct relief and vocational training. Reverend Karl Stumpf and Jean Chenard's appeals for resettlement opportunities abroad, voiced explicitly at the closing conference for World Refugee Year, had only tepid support from other humanitarians.

Even more critically, the appeals made by Reverend Stumpf and Jean Chenard for increased mobility fell on deaf ears in potential countries of resettlement. Perception was, if not everything, at least pivotal to facilitating the migration of Chinese people out of Hong Kong and into white settler societies on both sides of the Pacific. Exclusion-era narratives in white settler societies about the impossibility of integrating or assimilating Chinese migrants, which endured in the postwar period, were compounded by images of total destitution disseminated from Hong Kong during World Refugee Year. Following a year of intense publicity, fundraising and educational campaigns, the residents of white settler societies proved they were prepared to assist Chinese refugees in Hong Kong financially and materially but were still not quite ready to accept them as fellow citizens.

4

TROUBLED TIMES

Illegal Migration and the Refugee Subject

IN MAY 1966, a Chinese dry-cleaner in Toronto told immigration
authorities:

> I came to Canada as a Refugee. When I was examined in Hong
> Kong, I told the Canadian Immigration officials that I was single,
> when in fact, I was married and the father of two children. I told
> this lie to the Canadian Immigration officials because I thought
> it of no use to tell them the truth as my wife and children were on
> the mainland of China with very little chance of ever being able to
> get away.

Another man confessed,

> I escaped to Hong Kong from Communist China in May 1962. I
> approached the Canadian Immigration Office in Hong Kong and
> applied for admission to Canada as a refugee. At that time, I stated
> that my wife Wong Lui Yin was deceased and that I had no chil-
> dren. I concealed the true facts concerning my family because I was
> afraid that the Communists may do harmful things to my family
> in China if they found out that I came to Canada as a refugee. I

reduced my age as I knew that young people stand a better chance for employment in Hong Kong.[1]

The Canadian government elicited these two confessions, and that of almost twelve thousand others, with the promise of a "status adjustment."[2] Following their confessions, the gentlemen in question had their legal status, and that of their families, clarified and corrected. They were subsequently considered "normalized" by Canadian authorities. They thus became eligible for Canadian citizenship, with all the attendant benefits this entailed, including the possibility of sponsoring their wives and children from the Chinese mainland.[3]

The disclosures of fraudulent entry were obtained as part of the Canadian government's efforts to address, and resolve, the long-standing issue of illegal migration from China. It was an issue that had vexed officials in white settler societies almost from the moment they began to regulate and restrict Chinese admissions with legislation such as the 1881 Chinese Immigrants Act in New Zealand, the 1882 Chinese Exclusion Act in the United States, the 1885 Chinese Immigration Act in Canada, the 1901 Immigration Restriction Act in Australia, and the 1902 Transvaal Immigration Restriction Act in South Africa. In response to these restrictions, Chinese brokers developed paper son schemes that made possible the entry of migrants who would otherwise have been denied admission. "Paper sons," as suggested by a literal reading of the term, involved the creation of families on paper by repurposing the very documents demanded of the laws for admission. One commissioner from the Immigration and Naturalization Service (INS) described the practice as follows:

> For years, ever since the first Chinese had come over here, the male Chinese went back to the mainland from here, and appeared on his return trip with a man child. He'd come back the next year, stay a while with his so-called wife and he'd come back with another man child, and that went on. He'd come back with ten, eleven children, all male, over the years. We [knew], of course, it was a big fraud. He simply got a male child from a neighbor in his home town, or a nephew or a second nephew took his name, and brought him on back and he was an American citizen. He grew up to be an American citizen.

Although the Commissioner conceded that each of the sons "grew up to be an American citizen," he ultimately concluded, "going way back, the whole gang is illegal."[4]

Rather than reconcile the apparent contradictions in the notion of an illegal citizen, officials in white settler societies lived with this inconsistency. The seemingly impossible task of preventing illegal migration made it easier to simply live with the reality of residency achieved by illegal, or more precisely, fraudulent, means of entry. On occasion, when governments wanted to reinforce their authority on migration matters, they would bring discussions of illegal migration into the public realm, as in Australia and New Zealand in the immediate postwar period. Yet even though discussing illegal migration publicly was an effective political strategy for sowing fear and reinforcing the government's sovereign right to control and regulate admissions, this approach became more complicated as the growing humanitarian agenda around refugee protection gained currency. Ironically, governments resorted to the very instrument to which critics objected—the notion of migrants as illegal—to dismiss appeals to humanitarian action.

From the late 19th century, fake identity documents and elaborate coaching papers enabled Chinese migrants to adopt new personas and gain admission under false pretexts. Officials in white settler societies were well aware of the practice, but in the face of language barriers and brokers who benefited financially from the schemes (such as translators whose services could be purchased to facilitate entry), authorities found themselves at a loss as to how to effectively combat these practices.[5] In the United States, the massive 1906 fire in San Francisco, which destroyed reams of officials papers used to establish the identity of the Chinese in the United States, created an extraordinary opportunity for aspiring migrants. Over the course of the subsequent twenty-year period, an estimated 71,040 Chinese entered the United States as derivative sons.[6]

During the formal exclusion era (roughly from the 1880s to the 1940s in North America and three decades longer, to the 1970s, in Australia, New Zealand, and South Africa), officials recognized their efforts to exclude or limit the entry of migrants from China were being undermined by people purchasing forged documents, claiming false relationships, or deserting from passing vessels. In response, they ascribed illegality and deviance to Chinese migrants as if they were primordial traits as opposed to strategies developed to overcome the barriers created by restrictive immigration regimes.

Illegal migration was structurally embedded in regulatory regimes. As a result, as with the twinned practice of deporting undesirable migrants, it was a regular, rather than an exceptional, phenomenon. Efforts to enforce immigration laws in the United States and other white settler societies, which were harsher than any treatment meted out to European migrants, only furthered the impression that the very presence of Chinese migrants "was itself criminal."[7] The crime that marked the entry of Chinese migrants "ensured that they became even more deeply embedded in the existing networks of kinship and native place that made it possible for them to arrive."[8] Regular crackdowns on prostitution rings, the apparently "immense traffic" in opium, combined with rumors and allegations of fraudulent entry, fostered negative opinions about the suitability of admitting significant numbers of Chinese migrants as permanent residents.[9]

In the postwar period, immigration programs in white setter societies evolved beyond formal exclusion, but they remained structurally closed. Meanwhile, turbulent political conditions in Asia prompted people to seek out migration opportunities wherever possible. The unrest due to the Chinese Civil War, the Korean War, and French efforts to reoccupy Indochina, along with the prospect of future unrest as a result of decolonization efforts in the region, meant there were considerable numbers of people hoping to gain entry to the United States and other white settler societies. Yet race-based restrictions on permanent entry persisted. For instance, the 1952 Immigration and Naturalization Act in the United States allowed for a worldwide annual quota of only 105 Chinese annually. In South Africa, Chinese migration was banned almost entirely after 1953, and similarly restrictive measures operated in Canada, Australia, and New Zealand until the mid-1960s when signs of unprecedented openness to migration from Asia began to appear. Illegal migration in all its guises, from paper son schemes to violations of the terms of entry, continued.

At the same time, the issue of illegal migration assumed several new dimensions. The global Cold War fundamentally altered what was at stake in the debate over illegal migration. Violent conflicts created new population pressures, as did the fear and antipathy about living under communist regimes. The prosecution and punishment of migrants who entered countries under false pretexts, or violated the conditions of their entry, undermined the liberal democratic claims to equality, openness, and welcome advanced by white settler societies. Moreover, the question of how to best address illegal migration had particular implications for the emerging humanitarian agenda around refugees in Asia. Humanitarian appeals, particularly in the United States, were often framed in the context of Cold War value systems. Yet they were projected onto a canvas that was layered with the detritus of previous contests over legal admissions and exclusions. The legacy of the "legal racialization" of migrant subjects was more pernicious than the production of racialized categories of legal inclusion; it conditioned publics to attribute certain traits, namely criminality and amorality, to migrant groups caught up in the tangled mesh of multiple legal frameworks and transnational constructions of illegality.[10] These constructions were extremely convincing precisely because they were so broad and fluid in their manifestations. Public discussions of illegal migration, particularly from the People's Republic of China, therefore played a strategic role in the governance projects of white settler societies in the context of the Cold War. Public accusations of illegality were steeped in symbolic meaning about the nature of citizenship and belonging.[11] The significance of these charges varied according to the approach officials pursued in reconciling illegal migration with their evolving sense of race as a determinant of possible inclusion and the emerging postwar humanitarian agenda.

There was an immense gulf between the act of entering the country under false pretenses and the political leverage that governments sought in discussing the issue of illegal migration publicly. Public conversations about illegality existed above and beyond the legal systems that dictated "the legitimate means of movement."[12] Significantly, these discussions were spawned entirely by the state. No other entity could assign the label of illegality to an individual or group and ascribe essentialist motives to the people in question with such serious ramifications. Yet when governments discussed illegality in public, they did so from a position of insecurity. Their public pronouncements followed on the failure of initial control mechanisms such as border-point checks, passports, and visa requirements to produce the intended exclusion. Public discussions of illegality were a sign of a system under stress. For this reason, officials also discussed illegal migration publicly when they came under pressure to facilitate the migration of groups they considered undesirable. These discussions served instrumental ends, transforming illegal migration from an acknowledged though discouraged reality of cross-border movement to a public policy issue that served broad political objectives.

The use of illegality as a discursive strategy implied a situation of such gravity that governments were required to pursue extraordinary means to address the problem.[13] Significantly, the nature of the alleged threat that "illegal migrants" posed changed over time. In the late nineteenth and early twentieth centuries, illegality was ascribed in thickly racialized language. Chinese migrants were seen as "unscrupulous, devious and immoral," described in contemporary accounts as "heathens" at the mercy of a "shrewd coterie of fraudulent immigration boosters."[14] One news story described the woods near Port Townsend on the West Coast of the United States as being "full of Chinamen nearly all the time, who are skulking about evading customs."[15] Charges of illegal migration were imbued with suggestions of economic danger, in terms of labor market competition, as well as threatening racial impurities that risked the aspirations of whiteness amongst settler societies.

Over the course of the twentieth century, as it became increasingly difficult to justify exclusion on the basis of race, governments cast so-called illegal migrants primarily as potential threats to the nation's prosperity. Still, these allegations were consistently directed towards highly racialized subjects, often impoverished migrants from Asia.[16] Associations of illegality were aligned with those perceived to be at the margins of society and therefore undesirable.[17] By tracing the use of illegality as both a strategy of inclusion and exclusion after the Second World War, in a kind of "good migrant / bad migrant" dynamic, one can see how migrants deemed socially, politically, and economically undesirable continued to be marginalized and ultimately excluded at a time when progressively incorporated notions of universal human rights made discrimination on racial grounds not only difficult, but almost impossible, to justify.

In South Africa, for instance, discussions of illegality in the early twentieth century focused on the large Indian population, which had arrived and settled in the Cape territories in the early twentieth century. In response to the number of people arriving in the Cape, the government introduced the 1913 Aliens Act, which prohibited all new migration from

India. Those previously resident in the colony were required to register with the government. The result was the same kind of expansive bureaucracy that attended Chinese migrants in other white settler societies.[18] The Chinese in South Africa were eventually caught up in efforts to restrict Indian migration to the country, and their numbers were severely restricted as a result. Chinese migrants wishing to enter South Africa did so illegally, usually as stowaways on one of the many ships docking at the country's ports. Journalist Ufrieda Ho's grandfather, Ah Goung, arrived in South Africa in this manner. She recounts,

> Like most of the Chinese who entered the country, [Ah Goung's arrival] was by illegal means. The National Party was in power by 1948, probably coinciding with the year of my grandfather's arrival. There was a strictly enforced quota system for "free" Chinese, determining who was allowed to enter the country legally. The impossibly low quota numbers meant that many people chose to try their luck via the unofficial route . . . I have heard many stories of being smuggled into the country from my family members and other Chinese South Africans. They are stories of fear and terror of the unknown, dangerous journey; the helplessness of relying on strangers who are only mildly co-operative. Strangers such as the ship hands who took away the night buckets and brought food and water with the irregularity and disdain that came with knowing the stowaways were left with little choice but to take what they got during the miserable long sea voyage.[19]

As suggested by Ho's account, although Chinese migrants had entered the union illegally for years. However, the South African government's public crackdown on illegal Chinese migration only occurred in the 1960s. This repression coincided with the emergence of major fault lines in the apartheid project, characterized by the almost universal international condemnation of the Sharpeville Massacre in 1960. Chinese residents of Johannesburg recalled that after a failed assassination attempt on Prime Minister Hendrik Frensch Verwoerd in the same year, the South African government targeted the small Chinese communities in the country because of "false documentation" discovered in the assassin's possession.[20] The Verwoerd administration used public charges of illegal migration, along with the specter of communist infiltration from "Red China," to scapegoat the Chinese community and reassert the administration's legitimacy following the attack.[21]

In publicly responding to illegal entries or violations of the terms and conditions of entry, the South African government and other white settler societies ignored or suspended discussions of the restrictive structures that fostered the paper-son phenomenon and other forms of illegal entry in the first place.[22] Discussions of illegal migration, as an issue of public concern, were carefully constructed to disguise the persistent limitations on admission in the very white settler societies that were simultaneously advancing a platform of liberal superiority in the context of the global Cold War. In New Zealand, for instance, there were quiet discussions behind the scenes after five prominent Chinese were found to have entered the country illegally in 1954. Although they "were persons of considerable wealth and importance in China" and "it was suggested to us that it was not right that persons of such standing should be compelled to dodge the police as if criminals," the Department of Labor ultimately refused them entry. It was believed that "if the men concerned were of such importance and were well-known for their opposition to the Communist Regime in Peking then they should have no difficulty at all in obtaining permits to enter Formosa [Taiwan]."[23] Significantly, their illegal entry was not discussed publicly. The optics of turning away anticommunist elites did not allow for it.

Although restrictions on immigration were generally accepted as the prerogative of sovereign states, rhetorically they jeopardized claims to "freedom for all," particularly in Australia and the United States, where the virulence of anticommunist rhetoric dwarfed that employed by officials in other like-minded societies.[24] Yet Australia and the United States diverged profoundly in their responses to illegal migration from the People's Republic of China in the 1950s and 1960s. Cold War geopolitics therefore only partially explain why governments chose particular strategies to address the issue of illegal migration. The larger story rests with how people in white settler societies felt about the Chinese residents who had made their homes amongst them for decades and the prospect of additional migration from the PRC.

One measure of this sentiment was the public response to the practice of deporting migrants who entered countries illegally or violated the terms of their conditional entries. So entwined were regulation and deportation that when "large numbers of Chinese" were found to have entered Alaska illegally in 1903, the *San Francisco Chronicle Herald* assumed that once they were captured, the migrants' deportation would "undoubtedly follow."[25] In Australia, the historical association of illegality with Chinese migrants enabled immigration officials to proceed, virtually unchallenged until the 1960s, with the deportation of people who entered illegally or disobeyed the terms of their entry.[26] Deportations were crucial to protecting the principles enshrined in the 1901 Immigration Restriction Act, which created specific classes of eligible migrants and gave officers broad discretion to deny entry, particularly to non-Europeans. These powers, later affirmed in the 1905 Immigration Restriction Act, prevented Chinese residents in Australia from bringing in their family members and discouraged permanent Chinese settlement. Chinese were acceptable only as temporary, cheap labor.[27] Yet even with restrictive entry controls, such as dictation tests and elaborate documentary requirements, safeguarding the aspirations of the White Australia policy proved difficult.[28]

Officials pursued the White Australia policy with great determination because, in practice, Australia (like other white settler societies) was never monolithically white. Whiteness was only ever an aspiration. There were thousands of Chinese and other non-Europeans in the six colonies of Queensland, New South Wales, Victoria, Tasmania, South Australia, and Western Australia at the time of federation in 1901, not to mention the presence of 93,000 Indigenous people.[29] After federation, extensive coaching and document fraud meant that the Chinese population was always larger, and more permanent, than the government desired. The idea of a white Australia was therefore a fantasy, but it still proved to be a powerful animating desire. In times of heightened concern therefore, those most committed to the White Australia project resorted to colorful rhetoric about illegal migration to reinforce their authority in restricting the entry of undesirable migrants and pursuing deportations when initial controls failed.

During the Second World War, the Australian government afforded refuge to thousands of "non-Europeans" from Papua New Guinea, the Philippines, Malaya, Nauru, Singapore, and the Indonesian archipelago. The offer of refuge was a temporary one. In addition to the official evacuees, a number of uninvited refugees—sometimes called "temporaries" or "illegal immigrants" by officials—arrived in Australia during the war.[30] Although some historians suggest that the wartime offer of refuge marked the beginning of the end of the restrictive White Australia policy, the determination demonstrated by Australian authorities in countering people's attempts to remain in the country at war's end points to the enduring strength of the policy as a guiding nation-building principle.[31] Wartime resettlement could have been a progressive moment, but the government's inability to terminate the evacuation program sowed doubts about its ability to manage migration to Australia more generally. These concerns ultimately resulted in a postwar clampdown on Chinese migrants deemed illegal by virtue of the way they entered the country or the ways in which they conducted themselves in the nation's internal space.

At war's end, there were over 5,000 evacuees and refugees in the country. When the government announced they had to depart, many objected. While the majority did leave, about 800 wartime evacuees and refugees insisted they had established themselves in the country and should not be forced out.[32] Australian officials viewed these protests as a challenge to their authority and a threat to their cherished White Australia policy. In response to the demonstration of defiance, the Chifley government introduced an Aliens Deportation Act in 1948, with the specific goal of removing non-British residents from Australia. Despite criticism from Australia's Asian neighbors and from the evacuees' families, friends, and supporters, officials were determined to pursue deportations and affirm the message that Australia only had room for certain kinds of people.[33] However, efforts to deport wartime evacuees expeditiously were frustrated by the government of Hong Kong's decision to limit transit facilities due to the overcrowded conditions in the colony and by a series of court challenges that disputed the legitimacy of the Aliens Deportation Act. The case of Annie O'Keefe, an Indonesian woman who married an Australian national during the war, garnered international attention after she was ordered to leave. After receiving a deportation order, Annie asked to stay in Australia on humanitarian and compassionate grounds, given the age of her young children and the unsettled conditions in Indonesia as a result of efforts to end British colonial rule. The federal government refused her request. Arthur Calwell, the Immigration Minister, argued that if O'Keefe's arguments for humanitarian consideration became the basis for admission and entry, Australia would have to "let the starving millions of China in."[34] O'Keefe's case went all the way to the Australian High Court before the judges ruled that she could not be deported.

In response to the court's ruling, the Australian government introduced the 1949 Wartime Refugees Removals Act (WRRA), which gave it the power to counter the "impudent challenge" presented by those who refused to leave.[35] The WRRA gave the government a twelve-month window in which to deport non-residents and non-citizens who had sought refuge in Australia during the Second World War. The impetus for the legislation was the continued presence of the evacuees in the country, but the implications of the WRRA reached much further afield. The impact of the law proved to be particularly severe for the Chinese in Australia. With the WRRA, police assumed the power to investigate, seek out, and detain those who were in violation of their terms of entry. The WRRA gave authorities unprecedented access to Chinese businesses and private premises and heightened the suspicion with which policymakers, law enforcement, and the general public viewed Chinese communities in the country.[36]

The Chinese in Australia reacted by taking on the case of Kwan Ng and thirteen other deserter seamen who had arrived during the war. Their legal challenge went all the way to the High Court where their appeals were ultimately rejected. Only a change in government saved the remaining 853 wartime evacuees and refugees from deportation. The new Immigration Minister, Harold Holt, announced that the group could stay as a "wartime legacy."[37] Rather than a legacy, however, the treatment of the wartime refugees and evacuees was a precursor to the controls introduced to manage Chinese migration in the postwar period. As with earlier efforts to regulate and limit migration using complicated documentary requirements, new restrictions created new forms of illegal migration, which in turn led to public confrontations over who belonged, and more precisely, who deserved to be in Australia.

Fears about large numbers of Asian migrants looking for a place to settle, which underlay the early rationale for a White Australia policy, returned in the unsettled conditions of the immediate postwar period. Demographic projections indicated that Australia's birthrate was not at replacement level, and evidence suggested that migration from the United

Kingdom was on the decline.[38] Such statistics precipitated new calls and policies to guard against Asian migration. Minister Calwell declared in the House of Representatives that "we must fill this country or we will lose it." Calwell described the need for "the right people" who could be taught to lead lives of "civilized usefulness."[39] The Australian government aggressively recruited migrants and refugees from the United Kingdom and Europe. From 1945 to 1952, over 170,000 people were resettled from camps in Europe and another 90,000 were resettled between 1952 and 1970 as result of agreements with the International Refugee Organization and later the Intergovernmental Committee for European Migration.[40] The civil war in China and the rise of the Chinese Communist Party exacerbated the mood of the "anxious nation" and sensitivities around immigration.[41] Migrant bodies became "the fundamental site upon which territorial politics [were] constituted.[42] Chinese migrants, who had long been regarded with suspicion, were subject to further scrutiny. The Cold War in Asia perpetuated Australians' fears of being physically attacked by their Asian neighbors.[43] The fear of a physical invasion led to recriminations against those who appeared to physically undermine both the liberal democratic and the White Australia projects.

The problem was not only that Chinese migrants were seeking to enter Australia in increasing numbers; the unsettled conditions in Asia jeopardized the government's deportation program, which was at the heart of efforts to keep Australia white. In the early 1950s, the governments of the PRC, the ROC, and Hong Kong all began to restrict the number of deportees they were willing to accept and the conditions by which people could be returned. In 1951, as part of its general clampdown on inward and outward mobility, the PRC government decided to only accept the reentry of those migrants to whom it had issued permits. The identifying documentation for Chinese from the mainland who had moved to Australia before the establishment of the People's Republic of China was suddenly invalid.[44] Many stowaways carried no documentation at all, making it especially difficult to convince PRC officials to accept their return. Similarly restrictive reentry policies in Hong Kong and the ROC meant that Australia's system of entry based on temporary exemptions guaranteed by the ability to deport was suddenly rather precarious.

After 1951, therefore, Chinese migrants from the People's Republic of China were denied entry to Australia. Officials needed to be sure that when "the time came for Chinese to leave Australia, they would have somewhere to go and we would not be obliged to let them stay here indefinitely."[45] When immigration officials could no longer secure deportations to the People's Republic of China, they stopped allowing even temporary admissions. In 1956, this organizing principle also led the government to tighten the rules around admissions from Hong Kong. Australia's regulations permitted only permanent residents of the British colony to enter for twelve-month terms. When Australian officials discovered that the colonial government—facing major population pressures—was providing residence permits to people seeking to move abroad, regardless of whether or not they were permanent residents of the colony, they tightened their definition of "permanent domicile."[46] Despite these tactics, migrants from the Chinese mainland continued to access Australia, often via Hong Kong, as stowaways or through one of the classes eligible for temporary entry from the colony such as restaurant workers, merchants, or students. All of these classes were subject to strict reporting and registration requirements under the terms of the 1947 Aliens Registration Act.

Critics described the act as a "fascist measure" and the "first step in the creation of a police state."[47] The Aliens Registration Act required all aliens, European and Asian alike, to register with authorities and to request approval before proceeding with any alteration to their names or change in employment. The act provided for workplace inspections and the surveillance of politically active individuals in the community. Significantly, the impact of the act was far more severe for Chinese migrants than for other groups. Europeans could apply to be naturalized after five years while Chinese persons remained ineligible for permanent residence. Investigations of Chinese businesses and workplaces were also more numerous and more invasive. If Chinese workers attempted to improve their situations by switching jobs without official permission, they quickly slipped into the realm of illegality. In a 1996 interview, Arthur Locke Chang, a founding member of the Chinese Seamen's Union, recalled that because of the lack of mobility created by the WRRA's restrictions, Chinese migrants were "virtually slaves" and vulnerable to exploitation at the hands of corrupt employers.[48] Moreover, as in other white settler societies, the very act of dedicating resources or offering reward money to explicitly manage the entry and existence of Chinese migrants suggested there was a problem with the Chinese character.[49]

The layers of rules and regulations that governed legal entry and residence gave corrupt individuals on all sides, including immigration officials, an opportunity to exploit the system. In 1954, information emerged suggesting that a certain Officer Cayley was accepting payoffs to facilitate the entry of Chinese workers. The Department of Immigration investigated and found that Cayley had clearly lied in his reports on the operation of market gardens in Sydney.[50] Instead of finding fault with one of their own however, the department blamed the corruption on the Chinese proclivity for offering "not only money, but goods and entertainment," in the hope of a "quid pro quo."[51] Critics viewed migrant strategies to navigate the complex immigration regime as evidence of immoral and un-Australian behavior. The Under-Secretary of Immigration, H. McGinness, alleged that Chinese, "even men of standing," think "nothing of making false statements to officialdom."[52] The system of registrations and inspections, intended to control and regulate the entry and behavior of Chinese migrants in Australia, worked in practice to ostracize all classes of Chinese Australians all the while proving rather ineffective in actually controlling temporary entries.

Many migrants who arrived illegally, or violated their conditions of entry, were ultimately never punished. Deportations to the People's Republic of China were difficult to effect, and loopholes gave migrants who figured out how to maneuver their way around various categories of admission the opportunity to extend their time in Australia.[53] For instance, Jap Kuan Wong first entered the country as a student in 1938. When his permit expired, he successfully evaded immigration officials and established a small business in Sydney. His illegal status was discovered in 1954, sixteen years later, and it is not clear from the archival record whether or not he was deported.[54] His story is significant, however, for it offers a reminder of the difference between exclusionary legislation in theory and in practice. Although the government made a show of its crusade against so-called "illegal migrants," many people entered and stayed, living beyond the reach of the government's intermittent efforts to uncover and punish evidence of illegal entry and residence. These "able bodied men and women" became contributing members of society, paying union dues and aiding in patriotic ventures.[55] In doing so, they blurred and complicated the frontiers of legitimacy. When migrants who entered illegally or violated the terms of their stay were pursued in police raids and other enforcement efforts, sympathetic supporters questioned the moral correctness of these campaigns as well as the government's rhetoric about the questionable character of the targeted migrants.

The Chinese in Australia blocked government efforts to deport members of their communities by hiding suspects from officials and taking their cases to the media. In 1952, local residents established the Chinese Workers Association when Sydney's Chinese community was hit by a wave of deportation orders. Students found with corns on their hands were accused of working in market gardens and shopkeepers who changed jobs for restaurant positions were harassed by police officers and ordered to leave by immigration officials.[56] The Chinese Youth League, Chinese Seamen's Union, and the New South Wales Chinese Society, led by the ubiquitous William Liu, the English-speaking Secretary of the Chinese Consulate in Melbourne who dedicated his life to improving Chinese-Australian relations, came to the defense of the migrants. The Chinese Youth League charged the Immigration Department with "punishing the victims of the system instead of tracing the cause of all this trouble."[57] Advocates urged the government to cease the practice of deportations and used the print media to alert people about the deportation of their friends and neighbors.[58] William Liu also lobbied supporters such as Bishop Burgmann (an outspoken Anglican who opposed Prime Minister Menzies' efforts to ban the Australian Communist Party in 1951) about the plight of individual migrants.

In 1957, Liu publicized the case of Ng Chuck You who worked at the Eastern Restaurant in Sydney. According to Liu, "whilst on a few days visit to Brisbane to seek another position from a friend, he was arrested and deported . . . without being given a chance again to see his aged Father." Liu called the deportation "a most unfortunate mistake," speculating that You had probably been returned to the Chinese mainland. Liu imagined, "this man being over there carrying that bitter experience with him for the rest of his life."[59] Such lobbying humanized the deportation issue and complicated the question of how to prevent and control illegal migration. Newspaper stories provided the reading public with the names, life stories and, on occasion, the photographs of previously anonymous deportees. Still, while the stories may have resonated amongst some concerned publics in Australia, they had little effect in curbing the government's enthusiasm for deporting Chinese migrants found to be in violation of their conditions of entry or without the proper documentation. From 1953 to 1962, 255 Chinese migrants were deported to the People's Republic of China, despite the difficult administrative challenges and costs associated with the practice.[60]

Even as Australian officials pursued the deportations of people from the People's Republic of China who entered the country under false pretenses or violated their conditional terms of entry throughout the 1950s, they recognized that their enforcement measures had little effect on curbing the number of people entering or staying in the country illegally. At various intervals, staff in the Department of Immigration contemplated whether their strategy of allowing temporary admissions under the threat of deportation was the most appropriate course of action. Advocates, including William Liu, pressed the government to grant Chinese migrants permanent residence. Yet the seemingly infallible rhetorical power of illegal migration, married with the threat of deportations, proved persistently alluring. The government concluded that since it could not prevent stowaways from gaining entry at one of Australia's many ports and since people continued to reappropriate legal categories of entry to gain admission, deportations, along with public discussions of illegality, were potent weapons. Immigration officials believed that Chinese migrants would "behave better" if it were "known that we had the power to deport."[61]

The government's approach to enforcing the terms of entry enabled it to coerce what it deemed to be appropriate behavior and to reaffirm a White Australia "built on the twin pillars of Anglo-Celtic origins and cultural heritage."[62] In the context of the Cold War, this heritage was imbued with anticommunist rhetoric that painted life on the Chinese mainland in stark, foreboding terms.[63] Still, despite its disdain for the communist regime in Beijing, the Menzies' government was quite cavalier about deporting individuals to the People's Republic of China throughout the 1950s and 1960s. When the Consul General of Taiwan approached the Australian government in 1954 with a request that no Chinese nationals be deported to the Chinese mainland, as they were "liable to be executed," the Australian government refused to cooperate. It expected that such a commitment would lead to an increase in desertions "and further defiance under exemption of our immigration requirements."[64] Officials wanted to retain possible deportation to the People's Republic of China as an enforcement tool, one that discouraged ineligible migrants from attempting to make their way into the country beyond the categories of legally permissible entries.

Aside from the determined protests by Chinese leaders and their supporters, there was little public opposition to deportations to the People's Republic of China in the immediate postwar period. Like many Americans, the Australian public was afraid of potential communist infiltration. Unlike their US counterparts, however, officials in the Menzies government refused to think about immigration, and refugee issues in particular, as part of its Cold War strategy. Nevertheless, by the late 1950s, members of the Australian public were becoming increasingly aware, and increasingly uncomfortable, with the practice of sending people back to "Red China." As much as Australians feared possible infiltrators amongst migrants from communist countries, they were nevertheless concerned about the fate of individuals returned to these same places. In the United States, where by the mid-1950s the People's Republic of China was the country's "number one enemy" and where President Eisenhower perceived the *huáqiáo* "as a fifth column for China," there was still a desire amongst officials to resettle Chinese refugees under the terms of the 1953 Refugee Relief Act and the Far East Refugee Program run by the Department of State.[65] There was no comparable impulse amongst Australian officials. Instead, it was members of the Australian public who, having absorbed anticommunist rhetoric depicting the brutality of the Beijing regime during the devastating famine years of the Great Leap Forward (1958–61), ultimately proved most sympathetic to the plight of those they understood to be escaping from the People's Republic of China.[66]

In 1959, residents of Sydney were scandalized by the so-called "*Taiyuan* incident" in which two Chinese migrants seeking entry to Australia suffocated while hiding from immigration officials.[67] The smugglers unceremoniously dumped their bodies into the Sydney Harbor. They were found floating in the water a few days later. This incident created an immediate call for the government to prevent harm from coming to people fleeing communist oppression. This pressure, along with the case of Wong Yew, which came to light shortly after the *Taiyuan* incident, sparked a modification in Australia's deportation policy. Yew was a ship deserter who had been in the country for eleven years. When he was apprehended, officials argued that since he had entered the country illegally, he should be deported. They deemed that Yew "himself had little in his personal favor," given that he flitted from job to job. They further insisted that "a policy of allowing Asian illegal entrants to stay posed difficulties of principle and administration generally."[68] Yet Tasman Heyes, the Secretary for Immigration, who had enthusiastically defended deportations to the People's Republic of China in early 1950s, was one official who had come to believe that deportations to the Chinese mainland were damaging Australia's reputation domestically as well as internationally and that deportations were, in fact, hampering the government's ability to manage its immigration program effectively.[69]

Heyes recognized the innate difficulties involved in deporting migrants to the Chinese mainland, specifically the need to confirm the subjects' identities, secure documentation, and obtain permission to return the migrants. He therefore recommended that Yew be permitted to stay and that those Asian deserters who had been in Australia for five years or more and who could only be sent back to communist countries be permitted to remain as long as they were of good character and there were no security objections.[70] His recommendations were accepted. This was an important concession to the Chinese population in Australia, many of whom officials believed had either entered the country using fraudulent means or had violated their terms of entry. Yet despite these modifications, deportation remained an important enforcement tool and nation-building instrument. When this state practice was criticized, the government reintroduced the issue of illegal migration, and most importantly the supposedly illegal character of the people in question, as a way of legitimizing deportations. The sensational case of Willie Wong brought all of the problems inherent in a discretionary immigration program based on temporary admissions, limited concessions, and enforced deportations to the fore.

Willie Wong was apprehended in Matraville on 9 February 1962. When he was caught, he had no identification papers, no possessions except for his work clothes, and little money. He claimed to have been in Australia for seven years (sufficient time to be protected from deportation under the 1959 policy decision championed by Heyes) and produced income tax returns to prove his case. Officials in the Department of Immigration viewed this action as an "old ruse," given that the returns were all in the same handwriting and had only recently been completed.[71]

The court agreed and ordered Wong deported, an instruction that was summarily executed. Wong's lawyer went to the press, with impressive results. Although newspaper editors did not contest the court's actual decision, commentary after commentary cast doubt on the wisdom of the government's actions in sending Wong back to the People's Republic of China.[72] Critics, including respected parliamentarians Kent Hughes and Bill Wentworth, used Wong's case to question the morality of the government's actions.[73] An editorial in the *Sunday Telegraph* raged:

> Does Mr. Downer (Minister of Immigration) seriously believe there is ANY freedom in China? Does he seriously believe Wong arrived back over the border with no Red welcoming committee to greet him? The Immigration Department must be told that humanity is more important than the strict letter of the law.[74]

The government retorted that stowaways such as Willie Wong were not refugees and had no grounds for contesting deportation. Stowaways were "more in the nature of 'economic refugees' who, in seeking a better life, leave China and its privations."[75] To move for economic reasons was portrayed as a crime against the collective, an affront to all law-abiding and hardworking Australians. Several newspaper editorials lent support to the government's approach. The editors of the *Hobart Mercury*, published in Tasmania, declared:

> Wong was smuggled into this country . . . if it were known that an illegal migrant could get round the law by establishing "squatter's right," it would be an open invitation to smuggling activities on a far larger scale. From every point of view the act of deportation was justified . . . like all other illegal migrants who enter Australia, Wong was an economic refugee.[76]

Nevertheless, the debate over Willie Wong led to a brief reprieve in the government's practice of deporting people to the Chinese mainland. Following on Wong's case, five stowaways successfully remained in Australia after they expressed fears about being returned to the People's Republic of China. Their claims received significant media attention.[77] Twenty-six-year-old Fun Cheong Wong told lawyers that he was afraid of being sent back to "Red China" from which he had fled after famine conditions limited him to two bowls of rice a day. Confronted with renewed opposition, immigration officials buckled, despairing of the new potency that the rhetoric of Chinese migrants as "refugees from Communist tyranny" had on the Australian public.[78] It was, however, a short-lived concession.

In the longer term, the outcry over Wong's deportation and subsequent removals to the Chinese mainland via Hong Kong only caused the Australian government to become more determined in its efforts to use deportation and depictions of illegality as enforcement strategies to discourage claims for admission based on humanitarian and compassionate grounds. Critically, officials consistently emphasized migrants' unscrupulous economic motives in public discussions of their actions. With this strategy, the government created a space in which it could continue to defend deportations, especially when migrants, such as the five stowaways in Sydney, seized upon public sensibilities about sending people back to communist China to make their case. In May 1962, weeks after Willie Wong was deported to the People's Republic of China, Cabinet affirmed "as a matter of principle, that if people refuse to go to Formosa [Taiwan], they should be sent to the Mainland." Thus, the enforcement and deportation program against migrants from the People's Republic of China continued and, in fact, became more sophisticated. Two years after Willie Wong was deported, the Australian government recruited additional staff to organize a formal investigation section in Hong Kong to deal with what their British correspondents called the "wily Oriental" so that they could more efficiently secure the identity of the migrants and ensure their deportations.[79]

Concurrent with and connected to developments in Australia, authorities in the United States and Canada were confronting the reality of illegal migration from the People's Republic of China and elsewhere in their own countries and, fatefully, their apparent inability to effectively curb its operation. Though the solutions pursued by officials in the United States and Canada were similar, there were significant differences in impulse and tone. The Cold War flavored the American government's decision to pursue a highly discretionary Chinese Confession Program.[80] The program resulted from the increasingly untenable situation at the American Consulate in Hong Kong, fears about the possible infiltration of communist agents, and apprehension about how race relations in the United States were viewed amongst allies and enemies alike.

After the establishment of the People's Republic of China, the United States terminated its diplomatic presence on the Chinese mainland. As a result, staff in the American Consulate in Hong Kong became responsible for making decisions about admissions to the United States. By 1954, the consulate had a caseload of 117,000 applications and a backlog of four to twelve years.[81] The situation deteriorated with the appointment of Everett Drumright. Drumright was both a fierce anticommunist and a quiet racist. In a 1955 report, Drumright described a "smile campaign, conducted by the Communists towards the *huáqiáo* and their families in southern China" as "part of a Communist strategy to gain influence in the United States."[82] Rather than expedite family sponsorship cases, Drumright insisted on full investigations and high standards of proof to guard against possible infiltration. The backlog grew under Drumright's watch and only exacerbated the demand for fraudulent documents, fostering further illegal immigration. Drumright's methods troubled British colonial officials in Hong Kong as well as American authorities in Washington. Colonial officials attributed the presence of large numbers of migrants in Hong Kong in part to Western consulates in the colony, all of whom required hopeful migrants to present themselves at their offices for inspection. Given the strict exit controls in the PRC, many of these migrants made their way to Hong Kong illegally.[83] The backlog at the US consulate compounded population pressures in the colony. In the United States, meanwhile, Congressional representatives were receiving regular appeals from Chinese Americans seeking to sponsor their relatives.[84] The American government ultimately determined that it needed to halt the paper son phenomenon if it was to successfully manage Chinese migration to the United States.

In February 1956, the Justice Department convened a series of grand juries to investigate the issue of immigration fraud and compel people to disclose what they knew about the practice. Chinese Americans, terrified at the prospects of being hauled before a grand jury, refused to cooperate and criticized the blanket crackdown. The Chinese Consolidated Benevolent Association charged that the mass campaign was a gift to communist agents producing anti-American propaganda.[85] When the threat of being subpoenaed failed to obtain the desired results, the INS introduced a confessions program to solicit information about fraudulent entries in return for the promised possibility of legal citizenship. A total of 13,895 people participated in the program, resulting in the exposure of 22,083 persons and the closure of 11,924 so-called slots.[86] In a 1967 interview, General Joseph May Swing, a decorated war veteran who served as INS Commissioner from 1954 to 1961, expressed his personal satisfaction with the program, given his own views on the Chinese "character":

> I never saw a really bad Chinese in my life. All the Chinese I've seen, including a lot of the soldiers under me, were hell of a fine men. I don't see them in the newspapers all the time committing armed robbery, rape and this and that.

He objected to criticisms of the Chinese Confession Program declaring, "we adjusted them. We haven't deported a one of them that came in. And yet lawyers have gotten ahold of them, to try to say we're persecuting them."[87]

In actual fact, a small number of people were deported.[88] More importantly, the very threat of deportation meant that the confession program was a fraught experience for the Chinese in the United States, just as living in quotidian Australia could be disquieting for communities under suspicion. The confession program created feelings of "mutual paranoia" given that "it was the first time that many Chinese immigrants had been afforded such a clear opportunity for legal status."[89] There was the fear of reprisals but there were also serious debates about testifying, and extended repercussions for those who did. Fathers testified against sons, neighbors exposed neighbors and whole families had long, divisive debates about whether or not to participate in the program.[90] Although participants made public loyalty statements following their confessions, these were induced by the promise of citizenship and failed to entirely convince the American public and authorities alike of the authors' sincerity. Rather, "the cultural arrogance of the authorities, combined with the politics of the times, dictated that paper immigration be cast as a mass criminal conspiracy."[91] The contradictory makeup of the program, that of inclusion through coerced government processes, contributed to the confession program's disturbing legacy. Though the program created grounds for family reunification and the "renegotiation of membership in the nation," it failed to entirely legitimate Chinese Americans as fully desirable members of society, as the allegations "reproduced racialized perceptions that Chinese immigrants were unalterably foreign, illegal and dangerous."[92]

A similarly troubling process was reenacted in Canada after the Royal Canadian Mounted Police (RCMP) uncovered evidence of large-scale immigration fraud. In 1959, the RCMP Commissioner in Hong Kong explained,

> We have evidence of the operation of a ring which obtains Canadian passports from the Department of External Affairs by fraudulent means. These passports are sent to Hong Kong to enable Chinese there to enter Canada illegally by passing themselves off as returning Canadian citizens. Recently a Chinese admitted paying 9,000$ for two of these passports which were used to bring two Chinese into Canada unlawfully.[93]

Fake documents facilitated migration to Canada as did paper son schemes which, as in the United States, made it possible for Chinese Canadians to sponsor family members who were ineligible for entry after 1885 or were unable to afford the punitive head tax that increased incrementally from $50 in 1885 to $500 by 1904. In the early 1950s, there were over one hundred *gam saan jong* (Gold Mountain firms) in Hong Kong, half of which "made it their principal business to facilitate immigration to the Americas."[94] Canadian officials viewed the ongoing operation of paper son schemes in the postwar period as a deeply destabilizing act of fraud. The federal government's continued immigration restrictions depended on limiting family sponsorships for Chinese Canadians to specific, and more limited, categories of relatives than other Canadians. Officials believed that if these categories were compromised, an undesirable level of Chinese migration would result.

Upon confirmation of fraud in Hong Kong, the RCMP, aided by plainclothes officers from the Royal Hong Kong Police Force, raided Chinese homes and businesses across Canada. Their targets included the Chinese Benevolent Association in Vancouver, which the RCMP alleged was overseeing the paper son scheme. Many Chinese felt unjustly discriminated against, much like the Chinese in Australia when police and immigration officials subjected them to intense workplace investigations or the

Chinese in the United States who were confronted by grand jury processes and a coercive confession program. The very act of being monitored and investigated seemed to cast doubt on the character of the Chinese in these various communities. Yet this was not an inevitable outcome. Authorities wielded considerable influence over the messaging around illegal migration and their efforts to resolve it.

Although there was some internal speculation about whether the Canadian public would tolerate a mass deportation program as a result of the discovery of organized fraud, the federal government ultimately decided against this strategy.[95] As the RCMP's investigation unfolded, the Canadian government, repeatedly lobbied by concerned Chinese community leaders and their supporters, determined that the best course of action would be to recognize and treat the migrants as victims rather than perpetrators of fraud.[96] The costs of enforcement were politically and economically high enough and the phenomenon of illegal entry sufficiently widespread to convince Canadian authorities that prosecution and deportation were not viable solutions to the problem of illegal entry. Instead of punishing paper families, the Canadian government introduced a Status Adjustment Program in 1960 whereby all those who had moved to the country illegally could confess and then apply to be naturalized, receiving all the rights of other naturalized Canadians, including family sponsorship. The only exceptions were those found guilty of organizing illegal immigration schemes; they were subject to criminal proceedings and deported.[97] The program was clearly modeled on the Chinese Confession Program in the United States and, indeed, INS Commissioner Joseph May Swing described Canadian officials visiting Washington "to go over with my people how we were doing this" and then adopting the "the same thing up there in Canada."[98]

The Status Adjustment Program represented a marked departure from earlier efforts to curb illegal migration in Canada which, as in other white settler societies, had consisted largely of enforced deportations. As a result, the Canadian government invested significant resources in ensuring the success of the program. The federal government took out advertisements in newspapers across Canada and convinced the government of Hong Kong to halt its own prosecutions in order to encourage migrants who had entered Canada under false pretenses, or lied about their status or that of their families, to confess. Governor Black cooperated, indicating that he had "no wish to jeopardize the Canadian amnesty pro-gramme" and would therefore "overlook offences which are uncovered as a result of the programme unless there is some serious aspect to a case over and above the deception of the Canadian authorities."[99]

The careful distinction officials made in differentiating between the organizers of smuggling rings and those who used their services was part of the government's larger strategy to reaffirm the real and sym-bolic value of Canadian citizenship. Confessants in Canada received a form letter from Citizenship and Immigration Minister Jean March-and. It read in part:

> I wish to thank you for volunteering the information which has enabled us to adjust your status in Canada. I am certain that, hav-ing taken this important step, you have paved the way for a much happier life in this country of your choice.[100]

This strategy appears to have reverberated with the Canadian public, which was largely supportive of the program.[101]

Normalization marked a fundamental departure in the way the Amer-ican and Canadian governments managed migration from China. By "normalizing" the status of Chinese who had entered under false pre-tenses or violated their conditions of entry, governments knowingly fa-cilitated the possibility of family sponsorship and increased Chinese mi-gration.[102] In both the United States and Canada, the respective Chinese Confession and Status Adjustment Programs were terminated immedi-ately following the introduction of universal family sponsorship rules in the 1965 US Immigration and Nationality Act, which established admis-sions on the basis of skills and family preference, and the negotiation of a family reunification agreement between Canada and the People's Re-public of China in 1973. The timing of the programs' termination shows that they were designed to resolve the long-standing problem of illegal entries and paper families specifically. They were never intended to de-liberately increase Chinese migration. Continued status adjustment and confession programs, combined with new rules and measures for family sponsorship, would have done just that.

The Chinese Confession and Status Adjustment Programs had obvi-ous benefits for those who entered the United States and Canada under false pretenses, and especially for the "sons" who often did so unknowingly. In a 2009 interview, Sid Chow Tan, a community activist in Vancouver, chuckled about being shepherded through the adjustment process as a young boy. His humor seemed to disguise more troubling emotions, however, as he then talked openly about his fear of being deported until he was "normalized" in 1964.[103] Douglas Lam moved to Australia in part because of his fears about becoming a paper son in Canada. He worried about possible "snitches" in the Chinese community in Vancouver and the complications of trying to pretend that his grandfather was his father. He worried further about being deported.[104] As Douglas Lam and Sid Tan's stories illustrate, entering the country illegally made migrants vulnerable to prosecution and deportation. Yet the state-proffered solution to their liminal status made them susceptible to the subjective operation of power: they were accused and interrogated and their possible futures in the United States and Canada ultimately depended on the discretion of immigration officials. Still, the large-scale participation in the Chinese Confession and Status Adjustment Programs suggests that many preferred the state's solution over a continued existence outside the boundaries of national citizenship. It is unclear, however, how many hundreds or thousands of other migrants never came forward to have their legal statuses adjusted or, more accurately, readjusted by the state.

The nature of the programs introduced in the United States and Canada worked to affirm the authority of the federal governments through the process of forgiving the initial act of fraudulent entry or the violation of conditions of entry. The Chinese Confession and the Status Adjustment Programs were meant to signify the governments' authority to determine, as well as enforce, the legal terms of entry and residence. The programs' internal contradictions were crucial for preparing "a tacit but increasing inscription of individuals' lives within the state order."[105] Through the Chinese Confession and Status Adjustment Programs, Chinese migrants were included on the governments' terms, but the very process of inclusion served as a cautionary note about the cost of doing so. Exclusionary and restrictive structures were not put on trial, only the statements and admissions of the Chinese who moved through these frameworks.

In Australia, the government made illegal migration a public issue to dissuade the entry of Chinese migrants and appeals for compassion based on humanitarian grounds. In the United States and Canada, governments reconciled illegal entries with their desire to regain control of their immigration programs and, in the case of the United States, to avoid the appearance of unfairly punishing migrants from Asia given the racially charged optics of the global Cold War. In both instances, whether the issue of illegal migration was used for instrumental aims or whether it was disregarded in favor of a normalizing discourse, the concept of illegality and of people living outside the margins of society reaffirmed the government as the ultimate arbitrator of the legitimate and illegitimate means of entry.

Although the impulses for the Chinese Confession and Status Adjustment Programs in the United States and Canada were slightly different, correspondence between officials in the two countries reveals that they learned from each other and that ultimately, their programs had the same objectives.[106] American and Canadian officials understood that the presence of migrants from China who had entered illegally was a permanent reality and one that needed to be resolved so that officials could pursue other related, if distinct, political objectives such as the crafting of citizenship norms. By contrast, in Australia, the government worked to expel wartime refugees and evacuees, perfecting the use of deportation tactics and notions of illegality as enforcement tools to physically and conceptually cast out those whom authorities deemed objectionable and undesirable. In the immediate postwar period, charges of illegality were bound up with concerns about the racial makeup of the nation as authorities attempted to safeguard the principles of the White Australia policy. By the early 1960s, migrants who gained entry under false pretenses were described as "economic migrants." Race still mattered, as evidenced by the Australian government's concentrated efforts vis-à-vis Chinese migrants, but the evolving human rights and humanitarian agendas of the postwar period meant that targeted exclusion on racial grounds was harder and harder to justify.

Illegality, as an issue of public concern, was a flexible discursive strategy that governments across the spectrum of white settler societies used to target a variety of unwanted migrants. The manner in which Australia's immigration program was structured and enforced after the Second World War, particularly the government's heavy reliance on limited temporary entry permits, impressed the idea of Chinese migrants as reprobates amongst law-abiding Australians. Although the government actively selected and resettled thousands of displaced people from Europe, it insisted on the deportation of non-European wartime evacuees and restrictions on Chinese migration more broadly. Efforts to resist deportation seemed to confirm suspicions about the dubious Chinese character. The resulting association of illegality with Chinese people in Australia was so powerful, it became "established as an identity of its own."[107]

The effects of the federal government's approach to structural illegal migration in Australia led to the crisis over the deportation of Willie Wong in 1962. Officials met the public outcry over Wong's deportation to communist China with stubborn resistance. In the face of humanitarian appeals and outrage, authorities insisted on Wong's illegality and the need to pursue deportations in order to ensure that unwanted migrants did not abuse Australia's immigration system. The government defended its deportation of Wong on two grounds: first, that Willie Wong was in no real danger on the Chinese mainland; and second, by implying that he deserved his fate because he was illegal and motivated by economic gain. The term *economic migrant* represented a fusion of both illegal entry or residence and the state's position that people had to move through officially sanctioned categories of migration to be considered eligible for entry. The second part of the government's defense was especially powerful because the anticommunist rhetoric of the previous years and reports of the widespread devastation following the Great Leap Forward had established "Red China" as a place of danger and oppression in the minds of many Australians. The movement of thousands of migrants from the mainland into Hong Kong in the spring of 1962 reinforced this impression. Decades of public discussions about Chinese migrants as illegal amongst white settler societies shaped the context in which news of the crisis was communicated and received. Yet unlike the invisible qualities of the socially constructed "illegal migrant," whose crimes were evident on paper, the refugee qualities of the people moving into Hong Kong seemed unequivocally clear to many observers as a result of the visual choreography that depicted the migrants' movements. Governments and humanitarians alike exploited the unprecedented media attention and instrumentalized the situation in Hong Kong for their own political ends. These tactics had a profound impact on the manner in which expectations of an authentic refugee experience came to influence responses to humanitarian crises in Asia in subsequent decades.

5

COLD WAR VISUALS

Capturing the Politics of Resettlement

ON 8 JUNE, 1962, *Life* magazine ran a three-page spread titled, "Hong Kong: Refugees Rejected," using images taken by American freelance photographer Larry Burrows.

Sixty thousand migrants sought refuge in Hong Kong in the spring of 1962 following devastating famines in the People's Republic of China and amidst rumors of future, potentially greater, ruinous grain shortages. The essay showcased images of some of the migrants who made their way into the colony as well as those (Figure 3) who were forcefully turned back at the border by order of the colonial government.

Caught up in the debate over the government of Hong Kong's response, Western journalists filed news stories that featured gripping images of individual refugees, and wide-frame images of long lines of people grouped near the border. With the unprecedented media coverage, photography proved to be a powerful medium for creating a "visual encounter" with refugee suffering.[1] Viewers brought their personal perspectives to bear on how they viewed the images and were, in turn, variously affected by the encounter. Photographic essays and daily news coverage consistently implied a terrible state of desperation that prompted the flight of thousands. The images of impoverished, haggard women and men and serious, bewildered children aroused sympathy in some, and fear in others. As such, the visual medium proved to be an evocative one.

Migrants leaving difficult conditions in Asia started their journeys at a deficit in terms of public backing or appreciation for their circumstances amongst white settler societies. In some instances, providing a visual representation portended unprecedented benefits in terms of moral or material support. Robert Capa's famous photographs of lines of refugees fleeing in advance of the Japanese invasion of China in 1937, for instance, compelled significant public sympathy for allied China. The searing image of Kim Phuc, the so-called "Girl in the Photo"—captured as she ran naked down a village road in Vietnam following an American napalm attack—was critical in sensitizing viewing publics to the conflict in Indochina.[2]

The images of the 1962 refugees that circulated globally reflected a similar subjectivity. The photographs' subjects were carefully selected, so too were the composition of the visuals and the narrative sub-texts. As with the Capa and Phuc images, individual subjects were "consigned to visuality" resulting in "a blanketing and generalizing depoliticized depiction of refugees as helpless victims."[3] As such, it became difficult for "people in the refugee category" and specifically the migrants attempting to make their way into Hong Kong "to be approached as historical actors rather than simply as mute victims."[4]

Yet it was precisely because news images of the refugees in Hong Kong in 1962 erased the agency of the migrants that some Western audiences became convinced of the benefits of assisting a few, selected refugees. This was particularly true in the case of young children and families. The seeming lack of agency evidenced by the depiction of lonely children and broken, ruined families, made the migrants seem safer, an important quality given the ongoing Chinese Confession and Status Adjustment Programs in the United States and Canada and discussions of illegal migration in other white settler societies. The carefully crafted visual narrative, from flight to reception, created unprecedented empathy for the Chinese in Hong Kong, even as it perpetuated difference. This ambiguous response resulted from the unequal power dynamics between the subjects of the images and the citizens of white settler societies. These relationships defined the horizon of possible solutions—including resettlement across national borders—that humanitarians and governments subsequently envisioned.

Figure 3. Migrants at the Hong Kong border. Photograph by Larry Burrows, *Life* Magazine, 8 June 1962. LIFE © Time Inc. Courtesy Lenny Burrows Collection.

The pursuit of resettlement as a solution resulted from the visual record's particular capacity to reproduce and reinforce "dominant social relations" in "the act of imagining those who do not have access to the means of representation themselves."[5] The very act of photographing migrants on the border between mainland China and the British colony of Hong Kong and then displaying their images in photographic essays, on nightly newscasts and the front pages of newspapers implied the vulnerability of the migrants and the need for more privileged individuals, namely the citizens of white settler societies, to assist in some way. The visual nature of the migrants' movements in 1962, twinned with the carefully constructed narrative about "the hungry masses fleeing Red China" as advanced by US Senator Kenneth Keating, meant that the idea of saving individuals for better lives and restoring broken families in the West resonated more powerfully than ever before.[6] The hard work that religious and secular humanitarians had been doing on the ground in Hong Kong in previous years, and the publicity generated by World Refugee Year, informed the landscape in which news of the refugees was received and possible solutions were imagined. So too did ongoing suggestions of illegality.

Before analyzing the visual encounters sparked by images of the migrants' movements, it bears noting that the overall impact of these encounters, while significant, was nevertheless limited. The visual encounter was short-lived. Senator Philip Hart—later a cosponsor of the Immigration and Nationality Act of 1965, which put an end to the 1924 national origins quota system in the United States—observed,

> Interest in refugees . . . follows a pretty predictable path—virtually no interest until something hits the front page, and then, if there is enough emotional overtone to it, everybody is anxious to help. Once refugees disappear from the front page there are very few left around to help.

In South Africa, for instance, newspapers carried wire stories about intensified migration to the British colony, but there was none of what Hart called the "emotional overtone" to the coverage, and the apartheid government ignored the events in Hong Kong completely. The only Chinese migrants authorities contemplated during the spring of 1962 were the migrants found to have entered the Union illegally.[7] Australian authorities, dealing with the crisis over the deportation of Willie Wong to the People's Republic of China, downplayed the significance of the migrants' movements and voiced support for the strategy of forced expulsions adopted by the government of Hong Kong. By contrast, the Canadian government made the unprecedented offer to formally resettle 100 Chinese refugee families, puncturing a history of discrimination with a proactive effort to welcome Chinese migrants. The government of New Zealand also made a novel commitment, organizing the adoption of fifty Chinese orphans from Hong Kong, though this initiative was less generous than the New Zealand public was led to believe. In the United States, where the emotional rhetoric was perhaps most pronounced, Attorney General Robert Kennedy authorized the parole of 5,000 refugees from Hong Kong on 23 May 1962, resulting in the largest single number of refugees to be resettled from Asia to the United States up to that point.[8] The particular character of these overtures, especially their simultaneously progressive and cautious nature, stemmed in significant measure from the media coverage in Hong Kong and the insistence by many journalists and observers, though by no means all, that the migrants were victims of communist oppression. While there had been media coverage of the refugee situation in Hong Kong prior to 1962, the intensity of the visual coverage surrounding the migrants' movement was unprecedented. Combined with a narrative about communist oppression, the visual record shifted the grounds upon which politicians and publics alike imagined providing assistance.

News of large numbers of people leaving the Chinese mainland for Hong Kong first reached Western audiences on the nightly news and in the form of newspaper accounts that described a "flood of illegal migrants,"[9] a "lemming-like invasion of people,"[10] or as the *Cape Argus* in South Africa announced, a "Red Refugee Flow."[11] There was a great deal of speculation about what was causing the movement, including rumors of famine and forced collectivization. Witnesses disagreed on how malnourished the migrants actually were. Dave Elder of the American Friends Service Committee reported that at the time of the influx about one million, two-pound food packages were being sent from Hong Kong to the PRC on a monthly basis. He noted that "the senders have generally been people from the lower economic brackets, and hence ones who would not send unless they really felt there was a dire need."[12] Claude Curtis, President of Gospel Missions Inc., conducted interviews with fifty migrants and reported the following:

> Starvation is prevalent in Red China. It is common practice in west China to sell new-born babies for human consumption. The grain that is being imported into China from foreign countries is being stockpiled in west China in preparation for the needs of the Communist leaders when they find it necessary to establish a second line of defense there.[13]

Anglican missionary James Atkinson, who worked with the World Council of Churches and the Hong Kong Christian Welfare and Relief Council, wrote,

> A lot of rubbish is talked by the government [of Hong Kong] . . . about the refugees showing "no signs of malnutrition" but anyone at Sheung Shui now could see the truth for themselves . . . the hunger in Po On county that drove them to swarm over must be truly appalling.[14]

Atkinson's account was contradicted by representatives from the International Committee of the Red Cross who observed "the relatively good physical condition of a large number of these refugees" and wondered "whether one should look for other motives behind this sudden displacement of the population."[15] The inconsistencies in the accounts of deliberate starvation as opposed to general economic distress caused by a "system breaking down" pointed to the unknowns surrounding life in the People's Republic of China during the inward-looking years of the Great Leap Forward and its aftermath.[16] Many journalists speculated that authorities in Beijing were deliberately trying to embarrass Western nations, knowing that they would be unlikely to provide significant assistance.[17] Others emphasized the rumored food shortages and Hong Kong's history as a "haven" from communist oppression to explain the sudden influx.[18] British authorities in London and Hong Kong attributed the movement to loosened border controls and to the "connivance of local officials in anticipation of serious famine conditions."[19] The lack of reliable factual information about what was going on in China enlarged the space in which interested parties could depict the 1962 migrants. In *Exodus from China*, published shortly after migrants began to appear at the border in significant numbers, the journalist and rabid anticommunist Harry Redl depicted the migrants as desperate refugees from communism:

> Those who entered Hong Kong brought with them an authentic and desolate picture of these conditions: a grey, barren landscape of hardship and scarcity, of failing food and dwindling hope, of hungry uprooted thousands, either conscripted to farm work or wandering in search of greener fields and happier lives.[20]

The broad freedom to explain the movement led to a range of interpretations about the people involved, from illegals who should be deported to innocent victims in need of compassion.

In determining how to respond to the arrival of significant numbers of people, colonial officials were preoccupied with the potential problems a major influx would create. They kept in mind former Governor Alexander Grantham's earlier warning that the risk of violent "outbreaks" was "ever present" and required "vigilance."[21] Risk was assessed in terms of sheer population numbers and, after the destructive riots in Kowloon in 1956, increasingly in terms of the possibility that communist agitators were amongst those arriving in the colony. After the October riots, the colonial government became more aggressive in removing people, including new arrivals, under the guise of ensuring the colony's internal security. Deportation orders were executed rapidly and colonial officials expanded their practice of "informally expelling" people from the border area. People caught just inside of the frontier area were immediately returned to the mainland without any formalities or paperwork. These deportations were effected in secret, often taking place at night. Thousands of people were returned to the Chinese mainland using this illicit method, one that ran counter to the spirit of *non-refoulement* enshrined in the 1951 Convention Relating to the Status of Refugees. The genius of this system, according to the colonial secretary, Claude Burgess, was that there was no possibility of publicity as people were "returned so quickly after their illegal entry" they didn't have time "to find their feet and start protesting."[22]

Officials in London disapproved of the deportations even though the British government had ratified the 1951 Convention with the reservation that Hong Kong was to be exempted from the scope of its application. The Foreign Office nevertheless found the colonial government's strategy "questionable" in terms of international law and the moral weight of the 1951 Convention.[23] Still, under sustained criticism from the international community, the interests of authorities in Hong Kong and London tended to converge. This is exactly what happened in the spring of 1962. Officials in London shared Governor Robin Black's concerns about the diplomatic implications of the migrants' movements to the border. They further recognized the potentially destabilizing effect of a sudden increase in the population of the colony. They also appreciated that the government of Hong Kong had few options, other than to send the migrants back, if it wanted to manage population pressures in the colony, which had continued largely unabated since the 1950s.

After some initial hesitation about how to respond to people's movements to the border, the government of Hong Kong adopted a policy of indiscriminate returns. The wire fence that had demarcated the border since 1950 was reinforced, and contingents of the British army, including many Gurkha brigades, along with the Hong Kong Royal Police, were dispatched to patrol the border and prevent incursions. When migrants tried to enter, they were physically pushed back through the fence. Those that made it further into the colony were captured, detained, and returned to the mainland to what missionary James Atkinson described as a "certain death."[24] Bishop Swanstrom, executive director of relief services for the National Catholic Welfare Conference, reported seeing "truckload after truckload of refugees being returned to the border to be sent back into China," describing it as "a very sad and distressing experience." In his opinion, the migrants were well and truly being sent back to China to "starve with their families."[25] Sensitive to the optics of this practice, the government of Hong Kong barred journalists from the frontier and imposed a publication ban. Yet in a precursor to the intense media coverage of the Vietnam War, photojournalists defied the Hong Kong government's pronouncements. Images of the migrants circulated as a result.

The visual depictions of the migrants encouraged action and commentary from those who were politically invested in the situation in

Hong Kong and questions of refugee protection more generally. For instance, the ROC government offered food and refuge while the UNHCR cautioned against returning "bona fide" refugees to the mainland. Such responses required British authorities to convince the international community that the migrants were not, in fact, refugees.[26] Without refugees, outside intervention from the Guomindang government and the UNHCR was unnecessary. Yet as the world absorbed images of people streaming across the border with gaunt faces and bony hands reaching out for food and medical aid, such a pretense became difficult to maintain. The government of Hong Kong therefore resorted to discussions of illegality in an attempt to counter the visual evidence of a large, and apparently destitute, refugee population. The ensuing focus on illegal migration to Hong Kong, akin to the discussions taking place concurrently in Australia, was intended to erase the apparent refugeehood of the migrants and create conditions in which authorities could justify mass expulsions.

Building on the strategy adopted in the early 1950s, that of refusing to refer to any arrivals in the colony as refugees, the government of Hong Kong moved its private discussions of people as "illegal" into the public arena.[27] Colonial officials pointed to the permit and quota systems in place to argue that not only were the migrants amassing at the border not refugees, they were "illegal" and had to be dealt with accordingly. In the Legislative Council of Hong Kong, Colonial Secretary Claude Burgess—whom missionary James Atkinson described as a "small and pompous man" declared:

> When we decided some seven years ago . . . to integrate every immigrant into our community, we were in effect making a decision that put the word "refugee" out of our dictionary. Refugees live in camps; they do not normally earn their keep; by definition they believe that "home" is somewhere other than where they are now; their well-being depends on someone else's charity; perhaps because they do not expect rice or bread on someone else's charity to come to them from the conscience of humanity, but it comes nevertheless; and it brings with [it] the humiliation of the zoo. . . . This we would not have. The new people became our people. . . . We have accepted our heavy burden to be intolerably increased, and we

must be allowed to pursue our policy of containment in the immigration sphere.[28]

The 1962 migrants, Burgess insisted, were illegal and therefore the government's policy of "containing" illegal migration had to be maintained.[29] The government's casting of the migrants as illegal was a deliberate attempt to undermine claims to refugeehood advanced by migrants and the humanitarians campaigning on their behalf. At UNHCR meetings in Geneva, the British delegate argued that these "would-be immigrants are not all political refugees in the normal sense of the word" as they had a number of reasons, including the presence of close relatives in Hong Kong, for leaving the mainland. For some observers, such as Bishop Swanstrom, this effort to avoid responsibility based on the ambiguous categorical status of the migrants was outrageous. "Call them economic refugees," he said, "but they are escaping from an economic system under which they cannot live."[30] According to the bishop, they deserved to be assisted regardless of the categories under which they moved or the labels ascribed to them.

This expansive view of need and assistance was common amongst various humanitarians working in Hong Kong who thought of refugee assistance in terms of the broader public good. Indeed, part of missionary James Atkinson's outrage over the government's practice of returning people across the border, which he characterized as "wholly selfish," and the decision to reinforce the barbed-wire fence that he equated to the Berlin Wall, stemmed from his belief that such stopgap measures didn't benefit the public good. Atkinson viewed these measures as "unnecessary compared with the real necessity" of curbing population growth in the colony. He contended that the "real problem" lay with "the 2,200 babies born every week as against the 400 old people who die."[31]

Equally important, given the ongoing efforts by CARE, Catholic Relief Services, the International Rescue Committee, and the Lutheran World Federation to provide for the nutritional needs of the colony's population, Atkinson noted that with two million Hong Kong dollars, the cost of building the fence, "you could buy a lot of rice."[32] Feeding programs were valuable, as was the development of infrastructure programming and education, but they lacked the sensational impact of dramatic rescue efforts afforded by physically assisting refugees from communism during the Cold War. ARCI had wrapped up operations in Hong Kong in 1959, but other organizations, inspired by ARCI's work, advanced the refugee cause as proof positive of the evils of life in communist China. Chief among these organizations was Chinese Refugee Relief.

The head of Chinese Refugee Relief was Anna Chennault, the widow of decorated American General Claire Chennault whom Walter Judd described as a "courageous fighter for the Chinese people."[33] The general had been commander of the famous Flying Tigers, a celebrated group of air squadrons that operated in Asia during the Second World War. Chinese Refugee Relief focused on the rhetoric of assistance so as to create conditions in which American leaders and the general public would be receptive to the resettlement of refugees to the United States. Chennault promoted the organization's work by explaining that its first aim was "to raise money to feed, clothe, and re-settle the Chinese refugees." Chinese Refugee Relief also considered "it equally important to dramatize to the world that the American people are as sympathetic to Oriental refugees as they have been to European and Cuban refugees."[34]

Over the six weeks of significant migration to Hong Kong, Chennault focused her energies on raising funds and support for refugees, all the while advancing a pointed, anticommunist platform.[35] Chinese Refugee Relief married the refugee issue with America's crusade against communism—much to the dismay of the deliberately apolitical AFSC, whose leaders mocked Chennault's tendency to talk about "freedom" if nothing else came to mind.[36] In contrast to Chinese Refugee Relief, organizations based in Hong Kong focused primarily on the practical implications of the migrants' movements. For instance, the Human Rights Council of Hong Kong expressed concern "at the continuously large number of refugee-immigrants, men, women and children alike, seeking to enter . . . at great personal peril." [37] The Council recommended that those "countries with vast open spaces and unexploited resources, such as Canada and Australia, amend their immigration laws to absorb at least a few thousand refugee-immigrants from Hong Kong every year."[38]

Governments were generally not keen on resettlement as a solution. The British government was opposed to resettlement in part because it feared that it would be called upon to admit Chinese migrants to the United Kingdom.[39] The American government supported only token admissions in an effort to demonstrate its commitment to fighting the

Cold War in Asia. Resettlement programs led by ARCI or administered through FERP had been kept deliberately small, and yet the size of the programs, and their relatively insignificant impact, was used to reinforce normative understandings that resettlement was not a viable solution. Richard Brown of the United States Refugee and Migration Unit in Hong Kong insisted,

> resettlement is not the answer. It has helped. But unfortunately the numbers who have moved from Hong Kong elsewhere are pitifully small compared with the numbers that the Hong Kong Government has been forced to integrate and to try to assimilate into the economy of the crown colony.[40]

With resettlement, the question of assimilation loomed large. The AFSC, reflecting its emphasis on long-term development-oriented relief, believed that resettlement did not address the fundamental causes animating population movements and that, furthermore, only Chinese-speaking countries could absorb "any great numbers" of "illiterate Cantonese peasants."[41]

Neither British nor American authorities expected other governments to initiate resettlement measures, although US officials were certainly pleased by Guomindang efforts in this regard.[42] It would have been hypocritical to call on other countries to resettle refugees when they themselves were unwilling to do so. Still, previous humanitarian efforts such as the mass campaigns during World Refugee Year, which had sensitized audiences to the refugee issue in Hong Kong, created an atmosphere in which circulating photographs of the migrants could convey powerful impressions about the scale of the movement.[43] Moreover, the photographs seemed to reveal deep depths of personal anguish. As a result, visual encounters altered the way in which solutions to the migrants' movements, including resettlement, were imagined.

Larry Burrows, an American photojournalist known for his "searing" war photography in Vietnam, created some of the most dramatic representations of the refugees.[44] *Life* magazine used many of Burrows' images in its photographic essays of the springtime migrants. *Life* was cofounded by Henry Luce, a child of Protestant missionaries in China and an active member of the China Lobby. It was not hard to discern an anticommunist agenda in the essays that "America's weekly picture book" produced during the six weeks of visible activity at Hong Kong's territorial borders.[45] As with all of the magazine's essays, the photographs were the heart of the story and the accompanying textual narratives created the interpretive frameworks in which the photographs were to be understood. In the narrative that accompanied the magazine's major pictorial spread on 8 June 1962, *Life*'s editors insisted on the possibility of understanding the migrants' refugeehood simply by looking at the photographs, explaining, "it was in their faces for all the world to read—the hunger for enough food and a little joy. Both were just out of reach."[46] The narrative was crucial because of long-standing impressions of an "inscrutable" Oriental character.[47] Readers needed to be told what they were seeing.

To ensure that readers, and viewers, understood the photographic essay, the editors at *Life* provided the following context:

> Over the border into British territory flooded thousands after thousands of refugees from Red China. They struggled in crowds by day down hot, bare mountainsides, and by night lost their families and friends in the confusion of the dark. They cowered bewildered in the underbrush, listening to Chinese from Hong Kong hopefully calling out the names of relatives who might be in hiding.[48]

In highlighting flight, desperation, and human suffering, the text and images implicitly condemned life in communist China. At the same time, the combined narratives conveyed the message that there was a special role for white settler societies to play in resolving the crisis in terms of healing broken families. Included in *Life*'s photographic essay was a full-page image of a small boy (Figure 4) with the caption:

> Alone and Scared: A little boy weeps after getting separated from his father the night before while crossing the Hong Kong border. Now, trying to hide with a group of strangers in some bushes, he refuses to eat, drink or speak to anybody, believing that if he does he will never see his family again.

The hand and lower leg of an anonymous individual were discernable in the upper left portion of the image. This disembodied presence seemed

Figure 4. Young boy featured prominently in *Life* photographic essay. Photograph by Larry Burrows, *Life*, 8 June 1962. LIFE © Time Inc. Courtesy Lenny Burrows Collection.

to confirm the caption's claim that the boy was with strangers. Nevertheless, the image was open to multiple readings given the veiled nature of the juxtaposition.[49]

Visual encounters with the migrants in Hong Kong were shaped by what was present, as well as what was absent, from the photographs. Missing fathers were particularly conspicuous in the context of societal preoccupations with the health and welfare of nuclear families that characterized Western societies in the aftermath of major social upheavals such as the Great Depression, the First and Second World Wars, and the onset of the Cold War.[50] Absent fathers spoke to families in distress, as did images of mothers and children separated from one another. In the spring of 1962, several newspaper outlets published an image of a woman on her knees with her empty hands spread open by her sides. In accompanying narratives, readers and viewers were told that the woman had been torn away from her children and had little hope of ever seeing them again. The absent children, and the missing husband, meant that the disrupted bonds of "normal" family life were palpably evident.[51] This broken scene resonated with families in the West, where the tensions of the Cold War contributed to widespread anxiety around the strength of the nuclear family unit.[52]

In another arresting family image, published in the *New York Times* under the heading "Hong Kong Builds Refugee Barrier: Barbed Wire is Going Up as Influx of Chinese Grows," a woman was shown on her knees, head hunched, attempting to spoon-feed her small daughter.[53] The child's eyes were closed, as though in prayer or gratitude. While the image conveyed a close bond between mother and child, the presumed father was noticeably absent. This reinforced the suggestion that not only were people displaced from their homes, but that the family unit was also under duress. Such images informed the solutions that leaders in white settler societies pursued in response to the crisis. Their approach was profoundly influenced not only by the migrants' movements but also by the general public's sense of being able salvage the broken lives of people in flight. The religious impulse to "save people" was ubiquitous despite the apparent secularization of life in the West in the postwar period.

On 23 May 1962, in the face of continued media coverage about the "exodus" into Hong Kong, US Attorney General Robert Kennedy announced the parole of 5,000 people from the British colony, to be selected from an existing pool of prescreened migrants. Migrants were responsible for covering their own travel costs.[54] The act of paroling saw the arrival of 14,757 Chinese migrants in the United States between 1962 and 1966. Originating from the French word *parole* ("to speak"), paroling is most often associated with the release of prisoners who have given their word.[55] In the case of the migrants who were paroled to the United States, their entry was conditional on meeting high standards of selection. The idea was that they would then become good American citizens.

The first family to arrive in America under the 1962 parole program for Hong Kong consisted of See Suey Eng, aged forty-five, along with his wife and three children. Eng's father, Frank Jing Eng, had migrated to the United States in 1916. The younger Eng had been in Hong Kong since 1953 after the communists in the Toishan district confiscated his land. According to the *New York Times* profile story, the family's fourth child, a son, had not qualified to enter the United States because he had tuberculosis. However, the author reported, the family's "joy was complete" upon their arrival in Chicago because they learned that their son had been cleared for admission. They could proceed with their plans to work in their father's restaurant and send their children to American schools as a whole family. Journalist Donald Janson did not critique or dwell on the fact that US government restrictions had delayed Eng's application in the first place and then led to the family's separation. The focus of the article was on the family's joy at being in the United States and their delight at being together.[56]

Eng's celebrated status was further enhanced by his appearance before the US Senate Subcommittee on Refugees on 8 June, 1962. With Anna Chennault of Chinese Refugee Relief as his translator, Eng told the hearing on the refugee problem in Hong Kong and Macao,

> He is very happy and very grateful that he comes to America, a free country, and he feels like a different person. It was wonderful to leave the misery as a refugee and come into this country as a free citizen.[57]

Senator Hart, cochair of the Subcommittee, told him he was "most welcome" before explaining by way of illustration,

> I think that the more people in this country see the Engs and families like them, the greater the opportunity will develop for understanding and appreciating the need to improve the immigration

attitude in this country . . . we had better make sure that our response to the hopes and the aspirations of the rest of the world is consistent with what we preach and for what we stand . . . I am sure your presence here serves to remind the conscience of America about this point, and we are the richer for having you.[58]

Then, in a moment of heightened drama at the conclusion of Eng's testimony, Chennault announced,

Mr. Eng has just presented me with a check of $20 to the Chinese refugee relief. He has just told me, even he himself, a refugee, and they do not have much money. But he feels that he is now in this country, he is more fortunate than the rest, and he wants to do whatever he can. And he has presented a check of $20 in helping Chinese Refugee Committee.[59]

The rebirth of the refugee subject was complete.

Another person who appeared at the hearings, which were convened to determine what form of "effective relief and assistance" the United States could provide, was Deanna Chu, introduced by the International Rescue Committee as evidence of their good work in Hong Kong.[60] At the hearings, Senator Hart exclaimed repeatedly at her physical attractiveness. He declared, "I wish the record included photographs. I am sure that the reception of Chinese in this country would be stepped up appreciably if they could just see you."[61] Deanna was captured for the American public in *Life* magazine on 15 June 1962. The photographic essay showed a happy family. Deanna's father was seated in the middle of a couch. Deanna and one of her sisters sat on either side of him. Mrs. Chu was posed behind the couch along with another one of the daughters. All the women wore simple *cheongsams*. What appeared to be the stars and stripes of a large American flag were visible in the uppermost corner of the image. Although no one was looking directly at the camera, the Chus seemed to be bursting with joy. The associated caption read, "Refuge for a lucky few from Hong Kong."[62] Readers were informed of how Deanna was able to join her family in America as a result of the parole program. Deanna's success story embodied the tropes about fortune and gratitude, which audiences have since come to expect from newly arriving refugees.[63] Deanna told *Life* readers, "I cannot . . . express my feelings at being here."[64] The contrast between the narratives, from the despair and hopelessness in the initial *Life* essays to the joy and euphoria of the final one, captures how the media's visual representations of refugees in pre- and post-resettlement situations sustained international attention and shaped diverse responses to the situation in Hong Kong.

Photographs were used to depict need and to applaud Western responses to the crisis. Yet although they seemed to offer a window onto the experience of displacement and resettlement, they concealed a number of aspects that should have troubled the celebratory tone of the narratives. Deanna Chu's application was one of many that were approved as a result of population pressures in Hong Kong in the spring of 1962, but she had been waiting for years to gain entry into the United States which, with the exception of limited special refugee legislation, maintained a strict annual quota of 105 Chinese admissions until 1965. The special refugee quota did nothing for the new arrivals to Hong Kong other than free up space in the processing backlog. The refugees who left Hong Kong for the United States in 1962 had been there for years. Even the parole program itself was a means by which the American authorities could avoid taking on the contentious issue of broader immigration reforms.[65] Visual accounts of the resettlement process disguised these practical realities. Ultimately, they also created humanitarian interest in the refugee situation beyond what governments were prepared to do.

On 22 May 1962, the Canadian *Globe and Mail*'s top headline read "Hong Kong Police Take Panic Steps." Journalist Frederick Nossal reported that the colony's morning papers showed "ugly pictures of a young British police detective-inspector in plainclothes drawing his pistol against a defenseless crowd at Shengshui Township."[66] Nossal reported,

> During the weekend a Hong Kong resident found his impoverished and hungry wife who had escaped from China with their child, after searching for her for three days in the hills. Colonial authorities allowed the man to keep his son but sent the weeping, shouting wife back into China.[67]

It was a heartbreaking tale. Discerning political opportunity, Prime Minister John Diefenbaker, who was in the thick of a federal election campaign, announced a day later and without any prior consultation with officials in Ottawa that Canada would set an example to the world by resettling one hundred refugee families. His announcement coincided with the American notice of a parole program for 5,000 people. A lawyer, born and raised in rural Canada, Diefenbaker had a strong sense of social justice and was a fervent anticommunist.[68] The initiative that resulted from his campaign promise has since been commemorated as "the first time that Canada served as a haven for non-European refugees."[69] It was an effort that focused on families, revealing the importance the federal government attributed to the nuclear family unit as a way of ensuring the future health of Canadian society.

The Chinese Refugee Program, as Diefenbaker's overture became known, was a significant milestone in the history of Chinese migration to Canada, for it denoted the first time that the government actively facilitated the entry of Chinese migrants. Only fifteen years prior, most migration from China was still prohibited under the terms of the Chinese Immigration Act, repealed in 1947. With the repeal came the promise of greater migration opportunities but these were not forthcoming. Even the refugee resettlement program marked only modest progress in the dismantling of whiteness as a structuring element of Canadian society. While church leaders in Canada applauded Diefenbaker's initiative and subsequently lobbied for an even more expansive effort, public servants in the Department of Citizenship and Immigration administered the refugee program with reluctance given the possibility of fraud and abuse, confirmed by the revelations garnered as a result of the ongoing Status Adjustment Program.[70] Officials therefore designed a resettlement program that was deliberately off-limits to Chinese Canadians and their families in China. They wanted to prevent people from using the refugee program to sponsor relatives who had previously been deemed inadmissible.[71] This news was poorly received amongst the Chinese in Canada who had been campaigning for faster, more expedient, and broader family sponsorship opportunities.

Beginning in 1950, Foon Sien Wong, President of Vancouver's Chinese Benevolent Association, made annual pilgrimages to Ottawa to petition the government on immigration reform and family reunification issues in particular. In 1958, Wong's annual petition to Ottawa focused explicitly on the plight of refugees in Hong Kong. Citing the 1953 Refuge

Relief Act in the United States, Wong proposed that 500 Chinese refugees in Hong Kong be admitted to Canada over the next five years and that they all be relatives of Chinese Canadians. He described the refugees as follows:

> There are many outstanding professional men living under conditions which are most deplorable. These include doctors, dentists, engineers, technicians, artists, writers, newspapermen and men whose talents and genius would contribute in a large measure to the future progress of Canada. It would seem tragic that these minds should be condemned to a life of poverty and suffering when they could be used so extensively to enrich the new world. Some of these men are relatives of Chinese Canadians.[72]

Officials in Ottawa contemplated Wong's request at length, since the issue of refugees from China had come up at key intervals in previous years.[73] In doing so, some immigration officials thought Canada could derive great benefits from such an initiative, particularly if a family member became responsible for the migrant's care.[74] However, Laval Fortier, deputy minister of the Department of Citizenship and Immigration, did not regard the proposal as "practical" under the Canadian system and was adamantly opposed to blurring the categorical distinctions between refugees and family class migrants.[75] Other departmental officials concurred, suggesting that if a refugee movement was "authorized and based on [the] relationship to a Canadian sponsor, it would simply open up another area for misrepresentation." They pointed to difficulties in identifying bona fide refugees and mused, "the most desirable refugees now in Hong Kong will not necessarily be relatives of Canadian residents."[76] Wong charged that the government's decision destined "families of Chinese Canadians who are refugees in Hong Kong . . . to return to China where an alien political philosophy and possibly severe punishment or death awaits them."[77] Yet raising the possibility of persecution or danger at the hands of the communist regime in Beijing had little effect on the Canadian government's determination to tightly control family-class migration from China. In 1962, Chinese Canadians still could not sponsor their brothers, sisters, sons, and daughters over the age of twenty-one. This contrasted with much more permissive family sponsorship rules for other, notably white, Canadians. Not surprisingly, therefore, the government's refugee program met with a mixed response amongst Chinese communities across the country. Chinese Canadians resented the fact that people with no ties to Canada were gaining admission before their own family members. Mrs. Jean Lum, President of the Chinese Women's Association in Toronto, said there were "hard feelings among Chinese about these refugees. . . . It's a crime refugees who have been waiting in Hong Kong so long are still there, while these recent refugees are admitted."[78]

To recruit applicants for the Chinese Refugee Program, the Canadian government advertised in local Hong Kong newspapers. Wui Shun Lau, who was resettled to Canada under the terms of the program, told journalist Val Werier, "At first we were scared. . . . We thought it was a trap. Then the word got around that it was legitimate and thousands applied." He added, "We knew nothing of Canada . . . except that it was extremely cold. We also heard from people that if you were willing to work you would never starve."[79] The reference to working was significant because the Canadian program was highly selective. It targeted family units that were altogether in Hong Kong, where the head of the family had skills that officials expected would facilitate integration in Canada. Desired skills included experience as a market gardener, chef, tailor, or restaurant worker. Individuals could not apply. The program was only open to people who moved to Hong Kong after 1 May 1962. Ultimately, 3,500 applications involving 8,000 people were received. However, few applicants met the stated selection criteria, and officials feared a public relations fiasco if they could not fill the promised quota. The problem was that the people the government wanted to resettle, namely skilled workers with families, were not the people who had fled the Chinese mainland in the spring of 1962. The bulk of the migrants who had arrived in the six-week period were single, laboring men.[80] They were not the families depicted in visual accounts of the movement. As a result, the Canadian government amended the cutoff date for eligibility to 1 January 1962. Individuals also became eligible to apply. The government provided free transportation from Hong Kong and then relied on local community groups and supporters to find shelter and employment for the refugees. Despite their criticisms of the program, Chinese community groups were often the first to receive the refugees upon their arrival in Canada.

In the end, the Canadian government resettled 109 individuals and families, totaling 259 people. It is questionable how many of those selected conformed to Diefenbaker's original conception of a refugee from the Chinese mainland. Consider the case of Ton-Son Chu who worked as a translator for the American military in China during the Second World War. After the war, he returned to his small business, but life in the People's Republic of China was difficult. Soon, Ton-Son began to organize for his family's departure. Due to exit controls introduced by the communist regime, it was difficult for the family to leave the mainland. He sent his wife, Show Hwa, to Hong Kong first. "Knowing my father," recalls his son Jim Chu, "he would have devised a plan and he probably knew she could always come back if the rest of the family couldn't follow her." According to Jim, Ton-Son "applied several times to leave China. He appealed on humanitarian grounds saying the children needed their mother . . . he was finally given permission to leave after he made a special lathe for the local communist authorities." Once in Hong Kong, Ton-Son applied to the American government. He was confident that he would be admitted to the United States as a result of his wartime service. His application, however, was refused. As Jim tells it, his father then looked to Canada and chanced upon the Chinese Refugee Program. He was accepted and the Chu family arrived in Calgary in December 1962.

Ton-Son Chu left Shanghai as a result of anxieties about his future in communist China, but he had also been planning for a better life for his family, what some might call economic migration. Yet this ambiguous status did not deter immigration officials from selecting the Chu family for the resettlement program. The Canadian government was not interested in selecting refugees for the program on the basis of who had suffered most in the People's Republic of China. At no time during the selection process were applicants asked about their fear of persecution at the hands of communist officials. Rather, all of the applicants were required to provide information about their name, birth, height, weight, ethnic origin, family and dependents, and present address, as well as respond to questions such as "Can you pay your own passage to Canada? Why do you wish to migrate? Why did you select Canada?"[81] They were also required to list any languages they could speak as well as any training, practical experience, or employment they had gained. There was no box to check about the kind of persecution they might have endured.

The focus was on selecting individuals who seemed likely to integrate with ease and generate positive feedback for the resettlement program.

Given that the government-sanctioned resettlement of refugees from Asia was unprecedented, the Canadian government used local and national media to generate positive impressions of individual migrants and the refugee program generally. Press conferences and interviews were organized immediately upon entry, often in the arrivals hall of the airport, and immigration officers reported with pleasure when local media gave prominence to the public receptions that greeted refugees upon arrival. Press clippings were carefully preserved at immigration headquarters in Ottawa. Often, images and stories featured smiling families and saccharine comments about young children trying spoons for the first time or observations about the refugees' exemplary behavior. Upon their arrival in Calgary, Ton-Son Chu's wide-eyed children were photographed "enjoying" Christmas candies for the first time. Jim later recalled his dislike of the licorice-flavored All Sorts they were offered.[82] Another reporter regaled readers with the story of the Lau family and explained how on "the day they left the immigration hall, Moy Kam Moy, Lau's wife, asked for an interpreter. She wanted to know where she could wash the sheets and linens the family had used."[83]

Images of children, families, and hopeful young couples were typical. Invariably, all of the individuals were attired in Western dress and shown smiling for the camera. Government officials reported, "We have been agreeably surprised with the quality of the refugees selected. They have been in the main neatly dressed, appear well-fed and most are skilled or semi-skilled."[84] Journalists emphasized the high quality of the refugees and the bright prospects for their integration into Canadian society. News accounts were meant to leave readers with feel-good sentiments, both about the people being resettled as well as Canadians' generosity. Most of the news reports made a point of referencing the extensive support provided by local churches and Chinese community organizations and provided readers with thick details about the nature of the government's assistance, including the $5 that all the refugees received upon arrival. Such accounts normalized both the arriving refugees and the Chinese Canadians who provided support, since they were understood to be acting as one would expect of good Canadian citizens. An *Edmonton Journal* news piece recounted the following anecdote to its readers:

Five-year old Kuen Szeto, whose family arrived in Edmonton from Hong Kong Monday, is bewildered. Momentarily left alone during welcome ceremonies at the CPR station, a rag doll and a little bouquet failed to bring reassurance in her strange surroundings. Her tears soon were brushed away in the warmth of the welcome staged by Edmonton Chinese.[85]

Significantly, the names of individual migrants were rarely mentioned in press coverage of the situation in Hong Kong. Only when a refugee had been safely received in a country of resettlement was their name provided to journalists, feeding impressions of broken lives made whole.[86] Moreover, the voices of the 1962 migrants were only heard in the English-language press after they were resettled and could speak of their gratitude and good fortune at being selected. Even then, there was a discernible tendency amongst the media to use carefully chosen narratives as representative of the experience of the whole.[87] One of the few published profile pieces was of Mr. Kam Hung Fung who arrived in Winnipeg in August 1962 with his wife and two children.

The front-page article featured a photograph of the family (Figure 5), with the mother foregrounded along with her two small children. The mother's face exudes strength and determination, and one has the sense that she is firmly focused on her family's future. Her husband appears just behind her right shoulder and he too seems intent only on what lies ahead. The children gaze away from the camera and appear somewhat dazed. The caption described them as "fugitives" from "Red China." Mrs. Fung described their journey to Canada:

> We managed to escape from interior China to the city of Canton in 1957. . . . We waited for the opportune time and then after paying border guards 1,000 HK dollars, myself and the children went to "visit" in Hong Kong and did not bother to return. Last June my husband made his bid for freedom, walking over treacherous roads and mountains from Canton to Hong Kong past armed border guards, for four days without food.

The article revealed, "The Fungs have to start building their home from the beginning" because, as Mr. Fung explained, "the Communists took

Figure 5. Fung Family Arriving in Winnipeg, Manitoba, Canada, *Winnipeg Free Press*, 11 August 1962.

everything away." The author closed with the following observation: "the Fung family was brought to Canada by the Canadian immigration department in order to give them a new chance in life and the children a future." The article suggested that the government had chosen well because Mr. Fung had "five years of primary education and has been a qualified electrician for five years."[88] The focus on whole families, as in the coverage of the Fungs' arrival in Winnipeg, countered the depiction of lost individuals and broken families that characterized the initial movement of people into Hong Kong. It was also crucial to the government's efforts to ease the reception of the refugees in the face of the ongoing Status Adjustment Program and accusations that some of the refugees being resettled had bought their way into the country.[89] Kim Abbott, a former visa officer to Hong Kong who argued consistently against facilitating Chinese migration alleged, "some of these persons paid as much as $1,500 for 'refugee papers.'" He accused one of the refugees of being "the son of a wealthy Hong Kong merchant."[90] In response, departmental officials reported that the RCMP and Hong Kong Royal Police had investigated and were "satisfied that the persons concerned appear to be genuine refugees." They concluded that the allegations were intended to "discredit the refugee movement through attack on the individual refugees."[91]

The carefully managed arrivals and public communications proved effective. As a result of the positive publicity, the Canadian government's initiative to resettle refugees excited church groups who believed in the humanitarian value of the government's overture and hoped that the Chinese Refugee Program would be the beginning of a much larger resettlement effort. The idea of saving people was an appealing one. During World Refugee Year (1959–1960), an assorted collection of church and social groups had arranged for the private sponsorship of seventy refugees from Europe.[92] On the same day that Prime Minister Diefenbaker announced the government's program for Chinese refugees, the Canadian Council of Churches issued a call for the government to take in 10,000 refugees, calling it Canada's "fair share" of the refugee burden in Hong Kong. The Canadian government dismissed this appeal, but the council's public lobbying inspired other groups that had supported missions in China prior to the expulsion of Western missionaries from the mainland in 1951.

In October 1963, the Anglican Church of Canada asked the federal government for permission to sponsor fifty orphaned children from Hong Kong. Church leaders had in mind young, single men between the ages of 18–21 who had been deserted or were "foundlings in their earlier years" and who had no family in Hong Kong. They knew "British authorities in Hong Kong [did] not see in emigration schemes a means of solving their over-population problem," but church representatives said they were "seriously concerned over the welfare of Chinese in Hong Kong and would like to be of concrete help to even a number of youths."[93] The desire to produce tangible, concrete results was manifest in the engagement of all the Canadian churches involved in the provision of aid and social services in Hong Kong. It was difficult to ask for financial or moral support from Canadians for missions overseas without being able to show returns on investments.[94] Over the course of the postwar period, as population pressures in Hong Kong persisted, the appeal of resettling people to Canada, to share in the nation's prosperity, grew.

The Anglican Church promised the government that congregations would provide each refugee "with complete care and maintenance, educate him and help him to become successfully established and integrated into the community." The Acting Director of Immigration, Don Reid, a highly respected and influential civil servant, deemed the Anglican Church's proposal worthy of support but he expressed reservations as he saw the situation in Hong Kong as more of a population problem than a refugee one. He argued, "Canada cannot hope to solve the over-population problems of the world by immigration."[95] Discussions about how to respond to the Anglican Church's request for sponsorship dragged on for months. Immigration officials worried that if they rejected the church's proposal, the Minister for Citizenship and Immigration would be tarred as a racist; whereas if they accepted it, they would be opening the door to even more petitions.[96]

While officials stalled on responding to the Anglican Church's resettlement proposal, the United Church approached the government with another idea. Characterized by government officials as "ultra-liberal," the United Church's leadership proposed a pilot project to sponsor 100 families totaling 300 to 400 people.[97] In contrast to the government's 1962 program, which distinguished expressly between Chinese family migration and Chinese refugees, the United Church intended its pilot project to be a family reunification one. Eleven United Church congregations across Canada sought to sponsor the refugee relatives of members of their assemblies. Reverend Ernest E. Long, who later became a vocal advocate on behalf of American draft dodgers and their right to claim refuge in Canada, agreed that only by sponsoring family members could congregations help so many refugees.[98] He explained that as a matter of "face" the Chinese in Canada "could not ask non-relative refugees to accept crowded living conditions nor the ordinary family fare whereas they would not hesitate to explain the necessity for this treatment to relatives."[99] With such comments, Long demonstrated the important bridging role that humanitarians assumed in translating Chinese refugee needs, experiences, and behavior to wider audiences, a role that Western humanitarians in Hong Kong had undertaken for years.

Despite these efforts at translating need, senior officials in the Department of Citizenship and Immigration insisted that Long's proposal "be viewed with extreme caution."[100] They believed that the families the United Church wanted to use in its pilot project had "relatives who have been found, or are, inadmissible under the Regulations."[101] The specter of illegal migration continued to haunt Ottawa's policy decisions on Chinese admissions. As a result, the department refused the United Church's request. Furthermore, when the first four individuals the Anglican Church proposed to sponsor turned out to have "fairly substantial families" in Hong Kong and the PRC, formal support for any refugee resettlement program also evaporated. Officials assumed the refugees would then want to sponsor their relatives to Canada, leading to more Chinese migration than the government deemed desirable.[102] Expanding refugee resettlement opportunities that would result in the sponsorship of more Chinese relatives was not an option the government wanted to endorse. Officials consequently told church groups they should focus on the adoption of orphans, rather than the sponsorship of refugees. The Canadian government preferred orphan adoptions to refugee resettlement schemes because orphans, by definition, were alone, and their resettlement would not create any impetus for significant family reunification initiatives.[103] The government of New Zealand pursued this same strategy as it too confronted pressure from church groups to address the refugee situation in Hong Kong.

Unlike in Canada, the first Chinese refugees officially admitted to New Zealand arrived decades before events in Hong Kong in 1962. In February 1939, the New Zealand government, under the leadership of Prime Minister Michael Savage, decided to allow the entry of Chinese wives and children affected by the Japanese invasion of Manchuria and the spreading conflict in China. They were the first Chinese in New Zealand to "approximate refugee status."[104] However, because the government had no intention of encouraging substantial or permanent migration from Asia, the entry of the women and children was intended as "a special, one-off, temporary permit concession."[105] The refugees were granted admission for two years. They were responsible for their own fares, and the adult women had to pay a £200 bond each, agreeing to return to China at the end of the conflict along with their children and any new children born to them in New Zealand during their time in the country. Despite these many controls, the offer of refuge lasted only a few short months. The government stopped issuing entry permits in the beginning of 1940 after complaints that the refugee women and children were working in shops while Chinese assistants started their own businesses, exploiting opportunities created by the departure of white New Zealanders who enlisted to fight.[106] In the short period the program was in operation, 249 women and 244 children moved to New Zealand from China. When the war ended, the government initiated plans for their return. However, the effective lobbying by churches and Chinese community organizations, which coincided with the establishment of the communist regime in Beijing, led to a reprieve from their forced returns and to additional, if incremental, concessions on the admission of Chinese families to New Zealand.[107]

These reforms included an end to quotas in 1952 and the right for permanent residents as well as New Zealand-born Chinese to sponsor their wives. Additionally, beginning in 1954, humanitarians encouraged the government of New Zealand to alleviate the refugee situation in Hong Kong by opening up resettlement opportunities for people from the PRC. The bulk of this pressure came from the National Council of Churches in New Zealand (NCC), fronted by Reverend Alan Brash, a leader in the worldwide Ecumenical movement and a man who embraced an activist, redistributive vision of social justice.[108] While Chinese community groups in New Zealand focused their lobbying on family re-unification issues, Brash advanced a refugee resettlement agenda. Brash was supported by Protestant and Catholic missionaries who had been active in China both before and after the Japanese invasion and who were equally passionate about their work in Hong Kong.[109] Missionary reports about poverty and suffering in the British colony encouraged church congregations in New Zealand to think about the various ways in which they could assist what they understood to be a refugee population. By the late 1950s, church congregations were actively promoting the idea of refugee resettlement to New Zealand with the idea that they could support the children and families, ensuring their successful integration into New Zealand society.

In 1957, the NCC formally proposed the resettlement of Chinese ref-ugee families from Hong Kong.[110] Inspired by American initiatives such as those undertaken by ARCI, Reverend Brash argued that even a "token response" of two or three families would help alleviate the situation in Hong Kong.[111] Brash's proposal split government opinion. Authorities did not want to encourage the active resettlement of Chinese refugees, but at the same time the NCC's appeals based on notions of Christian charity and obligations were difficult to reject. Calls for humanitarian action resonated with the government's notion of New Zealand as a wel-coming, progressive society, evidenced in practice by the government's leadership in resettling handicapped refugees and their families from Eu-rope during World Refugee Year.[112] Still, the government in Wellington also remained loyal to the general principle of a White New Zealand.[113]

Unlike in Australia, where a series of laws ensured the general exclusion of Asian migrants, discrimination in New Zealand was far more subjective. A poll tax operated from 1901 to 1944 but exclusion operated more broadly through the discretion enjoyed by immigration officials in granting admissions. In the postwar period, it persisted most obviously in the discretion on granting admissions based on humanitarian and compassionate grounds. Officials were reluctant to exercise this discretion in favor of migrants from Asia, and did so only on rare occasions. For instance, in August 1961, the Minister of Labor, Thomas Shand gave Mr. and Mrs. Norman Perry rare permission to adopt a child from China because of Mr. Perry's "special interest" as a result of his active involvement in the Ecumenical movement and Mrs. Perry's earlier work as a missionary in China. Shand declared,

> I consider that this case is quite outstanding and need not be regarded as a precedent. Mr. Perry has been an outstanding worker in the field of race relations; his work for the Maori people and for the integration of Maori and European in this country is well known. . . . Mrs. Perry was for some years a missionary in China. When the Communist Government began imprisoning Europeans in the area where she was working, she was hidden by local Chinese friends at great risk to themselves and smuggled out of the country. It is the special position of Mrs. Perry which I feel distinguishes this case from all others which have come to my notice.[114]

News of the Perry's adoption initiative appeared in the newspapers and encouraged other applicants who, in due course, were dissuaded from their hopeful efforts. The perception of Chinese nationals as unassimilable aliens remained, and latent suspicions about Chinese communities in New Zealand were compounded by evidence in the 1950s of illegal migration in addition to information that the communist regime in Beijing was seeking to foster better relations with *huáqiáo* communities. As a result of the considerable concern about the loyalty of Chinese residents, workers and laborers were only permitted entry on a temporary basis, and family sponsorships were limited until 1963 when some concessions were made for entry on compassionate grounds.[115] Despite these structural barriers and an equally cautious outlook on the part of the government, the NCC ultimately proved persuasive in its campaign for a discretionary refugee resettlement program. The government operated the program with reluctance, resettling only three families in four years, but the small opening encouraged missionaries in Hong Kong and church congregations in New Zealand to hope that further concessions might be forthcoming.

In Hong Kong, the Reverend Robert Sprackett of the Presbyterian Case-Work Centre in Kowloon carried the torch lit by Reverend Brash. After visiting a home with ninety abandoned children in August 1960, Sprackett wrote to Norman Kirk, the Member of Parliament for Lyttleton, to inquire whether the government would follow the lead of countries such as the United States and Canada and permit the entry of fifteen to twenty-five Chinese orphans for adoption.[116] Sprackett described the children as "fine looking," asserting that they could be "integrated into New Zealand family and social life" and "become useful New Zealanders."[117]

Officials in New Zealand were sympathetic to intercountry adoption efforts, having previously resettled European children after the Second World War and Anglo-Indian orphans from institutions in India.[118] World Refugee Year in New Zealand, much like in Canada, excited further interest in adoption as a way of improving not only the children's personal prospects but also that of humanity generally.[119] According to one New Zealand church member, families were "motivated by a desire to give one of these unfortunate children the care and comforts which their own family enjoy."[120] The New Zealand government committed to giving the matter further consideration, but from all evidence, officials simply let Reverend Sprackett's initiative quietly wither. Reports from Hong Kong indicated, "There were very active organizations attending to their welfare and the orphans were generally very well cared for," and so there was no sense of urgency, despite the reverend's efforts.[121] When Reverend Sprackett returned to Christchurch the following year, he renewed his appeal to the government, this time providing a detailed proposal outlining the rationale for an adoption program for twenty-five children from Hong Kong. He told officials that 30 babies a month were being abandoned in the colony and claimed that there were over 2,000 Chinese babies and children in Hong Kong's "baby homes" and orphanages. Reverend Sprackett argued:

It would be a humanitarian act to meet the need(s) of some of them. We are a Christian country with a growing Asian relationship. . . . It would be a token of friendship and goodwill not only to Hong Kong, a member of our Commonwealth, but also to Asia. Such acts of goodwill are part of the answer to communism.[122]

Again, immigration officials debated the merits of Revered Sprackett's proposal. Perhaps because of the reverend's direct linkage between adoptions and the fight against communism in Asia, this time they approved a plan for twenty orphans. Although the government had intended to proceed with the program quietly, the events in Hong Kong in the spring of 1962 altered the manner in which the orphan adoption program was presented to the New Zealand public.

Absorbing news of the migrants on the Hong Kong border, Reverend Alan Brash insisted, "New Zealand ought to make some practical effort to help. If we were to accept even 50 families it would be a token response at least and would be appreciated."[123] Persistent lobbying by the churches propelled the government to act, even though general public opinion was rather apathetic about the idea of resettling refugees as a solution to events in Hong Kong. The traditional inclination to give funds rather than welcome new citizens persisted. A letter in *The Dominion* on 10 May 1962 proposed that assistance be provided in Hong Kong through the Red Cross Society. The author, a "Thankful New Zealander," stated, "I am willing to subscribe £5 . . . I haven't a lot but what I have is a fortune compared to what these unfortunate victims of Communist tyranny have."[124] The *New Zealand Herald* declared, "the United States, Canada and other countries have been moved to consider offering homes to refugees. This is a humanitarian gesture, but it is utterly impractical as a solution to a massive exodus from China."[125] Despite such opinions, the government of New Zealand still felt pressed to respond proactively to the crisis in some way.

On 12 June 1962, Prime Minister Holyoake announced that the government of New Zealand would resettle twenty orphans, "most of whom would be of refugee origin."[126] The announcement implied that the orphan adoption program was a direct response to the 1962 spring influx. In fact, the government had been working on the program for months in response to Reverend Sprackett's appeals.[127] Officials in

External Affairs explained to their Australian counterparts that the decision to admit the orphans was taken two months prior as a "gesture to the many church organizations and private individuals" that were pressing the government to resettle Chinese orphans. The decision to publicize the program in the spring of 1962 "was taken because of press interest in the plight of refugees in Hong Kong and numerous representations to the Prime Minister that the Government should admit some Chinese refugees."[128] The government of New Zealand was fully aware that the orphan adoption scheme did nothing to address the fate of migrants who had moved into Hong Kong in the spring of 1962. The Minister of Labor, Thomas Shand, acknowledged, "the attempted large scale immigration into Hong Kong from China has not led to any increase in the number of children abandoned or placed in the care of institutions there."[129] The government pursued the public promotion of the adoption initiative regardless.

The optics of the adoption program enabled the government to deflect calls for additional humanitarian relief—especially from Chinese communities in New Zealand—by taking an initiative already in place and using it for political advantage.[130] When the government faced renewed calls to resettle refugees from Hong Kong following the initial "spring exodus," it responded by expanding the orphan adoption scheme from twenty to fifty children even though it knew this was an inappropriate gesture, given local conditions in the colony.[131] It had been difficult for the government to find the first twenty orphans. J. P. Costello, New Zealand's trade commissioner in Hong Kong had informed officials in Wellington that there were not enough orphans for the expanded program even though staff at the International Social Service (ISS)—an organization established in 1924 dedicated to assisting families and minors with cross-border migration issues—repeatedly referenced significant numbers of orphans in the colony in their communications.[132] It was with the help of the ISS that the orphan adoption quota was eventually filled.[133]

Forty-nine of the fifty children resettled to New Zealand were girls. Their ages ranged from two to eight. Many of the 275 families who expressed an interest in adopting children were from the Chinese community. Government officials, however, were reluctant about placing the orphans with Chinese families, since they believed this would affect the children's ability to assimilate into New Zealand society.[134] One official, casting aspersions on Chinese parenting skills, feared that the children might simply "become laborers in market gardens or shop assistants in fruit shops with the result that they would be denied the opportunity that the greater majority of our children are given."[135] Ultimately, only five children were placed with Chinese families. Instead, the orphans were adopted and sponsored along religious lines, with Protestant congregations obtaining the bulk of the sponsorships—a total of forty.[136] Applicants who demonstrated a strong sensibility about the challenge of raising a Chinese family in a European home were preferred. According to official assessments, Mr. and Mrs. Malpas of Remuera had "a genuine concern for race relations and see this adoption as a possible contribution to breaking down barriers."[137] They were desirable parents. By contrast, Mr. and Mrs. Donegan's application was refused because they had

> little conception as to the problems which may beset them in bringing up a Chinese child, and [were] only motivated by a desire to give one of these unfortunate children the care and comforts which their own family enjoy.[138]

The commentaries on individual applications show that the New Zealand government handled the adoption issue with extreme caution. In this, they were sabotaged somewhat by the excited media attention that greeted the arrival of the orphan adoptees.

As in Canada and the United States, journalists were often on hand at the airport when the children arrived. In New Zealand, however, officials were dismayed by the press attention and tried to keep news of the arrivals secret so as to protect the privacy of the children and their adoptive parents. Only a few news stories ultimately circulated as a result. One surviving clipping, preserved by Archives New Zealand, featured the headline "Doorway to Happiness."[139] The article contained minimal text but featured ten portraits of the youngest infant orphans. Presented in two rows of five images, the dark-haired and dark-eyed children conveyed a range of emotions from delight and surprise to sadness and despondency. The vacant backgrounds of the images implied the presumed emptiness that filled the children's lives before their arrival in New Zealand.

The visual record that accompanied the movement of people to Hong Kong in the spring of 1962, and in some cases abroad, concealed the fact that migrants moving to the British colony in the spring of 1962 and those resettled to the United States, Canada, and New Zealand were hardly one and the same. The charade succeeded because the subtext to the refugee resettlement efforts in the United States and Canada and the orphan adoption program in New Zealand was that of broken families being mended, united, and reborn as a result of the generosity of white settler societies. Even though the orphans' images did not mesh with the images of migrants in Hong Kong, they worked in the context of the larger narrative about benevolent societies saving people from communist China.

The events in Hong Kong in the spring of 1962 marked a critical juncture in the experience of Chinese migrants seeking refuge in Hong Kong and abroad. The visuality of the migrants' movements was constructed to suggest large-scale human need. This construction undermined alternative readings of the movement, especially the notion of the migrants as illegal—a categorization produced by officials in Hong Kong, echoing the strategy pursued in Australia in the same period. Even though efforts to normalize the status of Chinese migrants in the United States and Canada were ongoing in 1962, the powerful visual element of migration meant that for people empathized in an unprecedented manner with the refugee subjects depicted in photographs and news stories. The refugee story in Hong Kong became far more immediate and intimate for people around the globe than in previous years. This individualized humanity resonated with shifting sensitivities around refugee issues, which had been nourished during the intense media and fund-raising campaigns of World Refugee Year two years prior and affirmed by people charged with illegal and fraudulent entries who defended their infractions by referencing the oppression in communist China.

In the policy contortions that evolved from the initial, visceral response to visual and narrative accounts of refugees moving into Hong Kong, a few, carefully selected migrants were offered resettlement opportunities in the United States, Canada, and New Zealand. These offers were an explicit attempt to advance America's Cold War efforts globally, to gain political advantage domestically in Canada, and in New Zealand, to limit the scope of obligation by recycling a preexisting program for public consumption. In each case, the response reflected immigration officials' efforts to reconcile calls for humanitarian action, whether from the US Attorney General, the Canadian prime minister or New Zealand church groups, with their persistent reservations about migration from China. Rather than establishing a precedent for continued assistance, the response to the 1962 crisis was a minor interruption in the general practice among white settler societies to ignore migration out of the PRC as well as relief issues in Hong Kong. The colonial government's insistence on migrants from China as illegal suited the moods of authorities in white settler societies who wanted to manage—read limit—their responsibilities vis-à-vis Chinese migrants. Canadian officials ultimately recommended against expanding the original Chinese Refugee Program, using the migrants' illegal entry to the colony as justification.[140] They also followed the British lead in terms of how the migrants were conceptualized and portrayed. René Tremblay, who became Minister of Citizenship and Immigration in 1964, reported that the British maintained, and he agreed, that the migrants from the mainland were "not political refugees at all, but (were) simply seeking a better economic life." The proof, he said was the fact that "once they (were) accepted as Hong Kong residents they flock back to China to visit by the hundreds of thousands, apparently without fear of persecution."[141] Officials disinclined to assist refugees through resettlement programs pointed to the lack of tangible evidence about the migrants' refugee status (avoiding the question of how this should be demonstrated) and their failure to conform to the expected norms of refugee behavior. Despite the potential benefits of refugee resettlement in terms of positioning white settler societies as generous and humanitarian, the gulf between the visual representation of refugees, humanitarian rhetoric, and how people moved was simply too great to justify resettlement as a sustainable approach to the "problem of people" in Hong Kong.

The visuality of the migrants' movement into Hong Kong in the spring of 1962 was unique in the history of population flows out of the People's Republic of China. It was never again reproduced, not even in the spring of 1989 when Chinese authorities clashed with pro-democracy activists at Tiananmen Square.[142] Millions of people witnessed the violence on television, most famously the image of Wang Weilin standing alone in front of a row of tanks. What they did not see were the many activists who escaped to Hong Kong after the PRC closed its borders to prevent departures. Activists left in secret, away from the media spotlight and were, on occasion, aided under "Operation Yellowbird" by criminal triads in Hong Kong experienced at facilitating illegal entries into the colony.[143] After 1962, without the spectacle of large numbers of people moving across the border, associations of refugeehood with migrants from the People's Republic of China diminished. Instead, perceptions of Chinese migrants were bound up with the formalization of various immigration categories. Migrants moved through official, and increasingly delineated, categories of migration and navigated discrete humanitarian opportunities for resettlement. When they fell out of line, atavistic impressions of illegality, morally bankrupt personal characters, and unassimilable aliens salvaged the authority and legitimacy of officially sanctioned categories and programs.

6

NAVIGATING CHANGE

Migrants and Regulated Movement

IN 1955, Shang-Ling Fu registered with Aid Refugee Chinese Intellectuals Inc. (ARCI). His profession was listed as "University Professor and College President in China; as a refugee, lecturer in Hong Kong." Fu had obtained a PhD from the University of London in 1928. He was a married father of three and sought employment in lecturing, research, editing and translation, social work, "Christian Services"—with specific mention of "moral rearmament" and United Nations' services with UNESCO, ILO, and the IMF. ARCI staff observed, "This applicant is presently employed as a Professor by Hong Kong University, but he strongly desires to immigrate to the US. He is considered outstanding in the field of Sociology. Makes an unusually good impression."[1]

In the same year, Paul B. Bien registered with ARCI. His profession was listed as "science teaching, specialist in Chemistry." He had received a PhD from Brown University in Chicago in 1932, and on his application, he listed his sponsors as Senator Theodore Green of the US Senate, the provost of Brown University, and professors from Yale, Indiana University, and the University of Rochester. He explained that he preferred "to teach undergraduate Chemistry or some physics and mathematics" but he "also had experience with alcohol distillation and making of glassware." He affirmed that he was a "Christian belonging to the

Baptist denomination" and that he had "no objection to other convictions." ARCI staff noted, the "applicant recently retired as President of the American University Club here in Hong Kong, a prominent association of graduates of American universities and colleges. He is influential and highly regarded in the education field and among Chinese. His English is very good, appearance neat, dignified and self-possessed. We are favorably impressed and hope that we can assist."[2]

In the 1950s, migrants such as Shang-Ling Fu and Paul B. Bien navigated discrete resettlement programs orchestrated by the likes of ARCI. Later, migrants seeking refuge learned to read the intricate web of humanitarian programs and regulations that developed alongside the formalization of migration categories. It was a complicated dance. Changing immigration laws and governments' use of increasingly sophisticated categories of migration for selection and admission portended greater equality of treatment. The immigration reforms initiated in the 1960s and 1970s included the 1965 Immigration and Nationality Act in the United States, Canada's universal skilled worker and family migration programs in 1967, the formal end of the White Australia Policy in 1973, and an immigration policy review in New Zealand in 1974. Each initiative was celebrated for its progressive openness, yet the genealogy of these reforms belied their true character. Universally, they grew out of earlier efforts to restrict and control admissions, especially with regard to migrants and refugees from Asia. The restrictive nature of immigration in white settler societies endured because, at their core, admissions remained selective. A significant change, however, was that governments began to explicitly incorporate humanitarian principles into legislation that governed the movement of people. As a result, humanitarianism became regulated and institutionalized. Migrants shifted from navigating discrete resettlement opportunities to deciphering a web of laws, humanitarian regulations, and special programs.

This state humanitarianism differed dramatically from the expansive humanitarianism that advocates had championed in the postwar years. In the case of New Zealand, authorities sought to preserve executive discretion over admissions using a variety of refugee definitions to select some Chinese migrants instead of others. In this, their efforts dovetailed with developments in Hong Kong, where the colonial government began to formally categorize residents in order to deliberately minimize its humanitarian obligations. In Canada, humanitarian principles were included in the country's overall immigration program using the narrow definition of a refugee set out in the 1951 Convention Relating to the Status of Refugees and the 1967 amending protocol, reflecting an increased engagement on the part of white settler societies more broadly with institutionalized refugee protection. Canada signed the 1951 Convention and the amending protocol in 1969.[3] In doing so, it followed the lead of the United States, which signed the protocol on 1 November 1968.[4] Although Australia signed the convention in 1954, it did not sign the protocol until 1973, introducing formal refugee determination processes four years later in response to the Indochinese refugee crisis of the late 1970s.[5] New Zealand signed the convention in 1960, as part of its World Refugee Year efforts. It signed the amending protocol in 1973, but only introduced formal refugee determination processes in 1987. South Africa did not sign the convention or protocol until 1996.[6]

For the most part, governments continued to define refugees on an ad hoc basis until the 1970s. Canada defined a refugee in law for the first time in 1976, Australia and New Zealand did so four years later. South Africa defined a refugee in domestic law in 1995, in one of the first acts of the new government in the post-apartheid era. The refugee definition established by the 1951 Convention was the basis for refugee definitions that appeared in domestic legislation. The convention was therefore critical in securing a legal commitment to refugee protection. Yet it was the actual movement of people that forced governments to reconcile the convention's limited legal definition of a refugee with political pressure to provide for generous humanitarian admissions and their ongoing interest in securing the best migrants for settlement, even if the latter were not necessarily the most in need of protection or assistance. New Zealand, Hong Kong, and Canada provide examples of how governments reconciled the increasingly potent appeals to humanitarianism with their ongoing desire to regulate the movement of people in this period.

Legal and administrative changes in the 1960s and 1970s meant that migrants faced inordinate pressure to conform to idealized notions of a refugee in order to meet the eligibility criteria for officially sanctioned migration and resettlement opportunities. In this respect, these later reforms mirrored early efforts by the United States to define refugees in domestic legislation for the purposes of securing people, and political points, in the global Cold War. Refugees admitted under the terms of the 1953 Refugee Relief Act were held to high standards of refugeehood, as were the refugees admitted under the Far East Refugee Program. All carried stories of communist persecution, but as the examples of Shang Ling Fu and Paul B. Bien illustrate, they were also highly skilled individuals selected to ensure their successful settlement.

In this regard, other white settler societies mirrored the American strategy, selecting migrants to advanced political objectives while also securing desirable migrants. Yet while the Cold War was important to the governments of Australia, Canada, New Zealand, and South Africa, their more fundamental preoccupation was with ensuring social stability and economic prosperity. For this reason, refugee policies in these countries were consistently crafted on an ad hoc basis, designed with particular refugee situations in mind to maximize the possibility for state discretion. This ambiguous strategy, at once accidental and deliberate, enabled authorities to exert some control over where, when, and how refugees would be assisted. This control was nevertheless limited. Organizations such as the National Council of Churches in New Zealand (NCC) and the Canadian Council of Churches (CCC) could, and did, lobby governments for humanitarian assistance from their position as the providers of frontline care and support. The humanitarians' conservative but determined efforts on behalf of refugees, along with sizable population flows born of political and environmental factors around the globe, eroded officials' capacity to make decisions about admission, or exclusion, without considering the political fallout. Confronted with ongoing challenges to their power, authorities evolved their loose discretion over admissions into formal, and seemingly scientific, categories of admission. These efforts continued until the 1970s, when admission on humanitarian grounds became codified in law in many white settler societies.

To discourage migrants from China, the government of New Zealand operated a poll tax from 1901 until 1944. More critically, under the terms of the 1920 Immigration Restriction Amendment Act, the minister of customs in New Zealand had almost absolute discretion on admissions until 1964 through a permit system, which was expressly designed to limit the number of Chinese migrants in the country.[7] British citizens were exempt from the system. In introducing the legislation, Prime Minister Massey stated,

This Bill is the result of a deep-seated sentiment on the part of the huge majority of the people of this country that the Dominion shall be what is called a White New Zealand.[8]

The permit system endured for decades due to reservations about the desirability of increasing the Chinese population in New Zealand, estimated at 5,723 people—approximately 6 percent of the total population in the early postwar period.[9] In his capacity as minister of labor, Thomas Shand was responsible for discretionary admissions from 1960 until his sudden death from lung cancer in 1969. He consistently turned down family sponsorship applications from Chinese New Zealanders out of fear that "too much" migration would result.[10] Shand observed:

> The [Chinese] community would increase their numbers very quickly if we allowed them to but it is necessary to operate our immigration policy in such a way that we do not build up our racial minorities so quickly that we jeopardize our future race relationships in this country.[11]

When one childless Chinese couple applied to sponsor their niece and nephew from Hong Kong to raise as their own, Shand refused their request on the basis that most Chinese families in New Zealand had "many relatives resident in China and Hong Kong."[12] From Minister Shand's perspective, to make an exception for one couple would only invite similar, and far too numerous, petitions.

This was not a position that the government in Wellington wished to voice explicitly. Instead of discussing the admission of Chinese relatives in terms of an ongoing process of negotiating the presence of a permanent Chinese community, the government made general comments about the state of race relations in the country, suggesting that too much migration would threaten a fragile state of affairs. By the 1960s, the New Zealand government was invested in integration as a way of avoiding racial tensions of the sort witnessed in South Africa and the United States.[13] Emphasizing the importance of managed integration, the government regularly invoked its work with the Maori, the Indigenous people of Polynesia, who made up 23.9 percent of the country's total population according to the 1966 census.[14] The government treated Chinese migration as a threat to its efforts to smoothly integrate the Maori into the wider fabric of New Zealand society.[15] In correspondence with Reverend Alan Brash of the NCC, Minister Shand explained,

> We have an average of 1600 to 2000 rural Maoris, unskilled and inadequately educated for city life, to absorb each year into our industrial structure. Added to this we have a responsibility to take increasing numbers of our own island peoples and the people of Samoa. Every Chinese refugee of the type available from Hong Kong aggravates this problem with which we are scarcely coping adequately as I am sure you will agree.[16]

Reverend Brash, who was an outspoken advocate for refugees in Asia, did not agree, and the NCC pressed repeatedly for a refugee sponsorship program from Hong Kong to New Zealand. Instead of people sponsoring their relatives through some kind of family reunification program, the NCC proposed that church congregations sponsor needy and deserving families from Hong Kong. Refugee resettlement was seen as a way to situate New Zealand amongst other nations that considered themselves enlightened and humanitarian. Although the NCC's proposal to resettle refugee families was extremely modest in scope, its suggestion still presented a challenge to the government in Wellington, which like those of other white settler societies, sought to advance a liberal humanitarian image in the context of the global Cold War, while at the same time limiting migration from Asia.

In 1961, following persistent NCC pressure, the New Zealand government reluctantly agreed to admit three refugee families from Hong Kong. The government approved the program essentially because it preferred to initiate a refugee movement under the auspices of the churches rather than open the doors to family reunification, as requested by local Chinese communities.[17] Believing that a church-run refugee resettlement initiative would be better controlled and less open to abuse, the government agreed to a trial sponsorship program on the condition that the NCC find sponsors and employers for the group.[18] There was no mass publicity for this undertaking and government information about the program was distributed only to church congregations.

With the assistance of the World Council of Churches (WCC), the NCC identified and submitted for official consideration the dossiers of twelve families in Hong Kong, whose primary breadwinners (all male) had "valuable occupations" and a "good command" of the English language. Candidates deemed to have too many relatives were rejected outright. Still, selecting from the many applicants in Hong Kong proved difficult because few candidates met the language and employability criteria in addition to expectations about the substance of their refugee experiences. The previous decades had conditioned officials in New Zealand to think of refugees as economically destitute, but the refugees in Hong Kong rarely met the expected standards of poverty envisioned by immigration staff. H. C. J. Thompson, assistant to the secretary of labor, observed, "Technically these people might be refugees because they are no longer on the main-land but their circumstances are much better than any of the European refugees we generally accept."[19] Next to the names of potential candidates, immigration officials scrawled notes such as "Not a pressing case but more needy than others" or "the only pressing case."[20] The government selected three professionally qualified individuals and their families. One of the chosen, Lai Kwong-Chun, 54, was not considered an urgent case at all, but he was a business manager and could speak and write English, and so he and his family were approved despite doubts about their humanitarian needs.[21]

It took four years for the three families to arrive in New Zealand.[22] During this time, the NCC struggled to find appropriate employers and sponsors. People were reluctant to provide assistance without having met the prospective employee-refugee in person. Even once the families were successfully resettled, the amount of work and the degree of trepidation with which the government of New Zealand approached questions of refugee resettlement discouraged all the officials involved from expanding the program beyond the original three test cases. Moreover, the trial period coincided with the discovery of new immigration fraud involving the sale of passports in Hong Kong for as much as £1,200 (£28,000 in today's figures). This made the government nervous about the moral character of the people being resettled as well as the authenticity of their qualifications.[23] Officials were loath to pursue further resettlement programs from Hong Kong as a result.

Despite this reluctance, the events in Hong Kong in the spring of 1962 and the orphan adoption scheme that resulted inspired the NCC to press the government for additional refugee resettlement programs. In 1963, six families were approved for resettlement from Hong Kong. From then on, the NCC's sponsorship efforts became progressively formalized. In 1964, it established an office in Christchurch and hired a resettlement officer from the WCC.[24] Through its connections in Hong Kong and its work in New Zealand, the NCC became increasingly part of the machinery of transnational resettlement efforts. The WCC and the UNHCR would refer cases to the NCC, which would then submit them to the New Zealand government. Once approval was given, the NCC matched sponsors with refugees.[25]

In 1966, the government granted NCC sponsorships for another six families.[26] Minister Shand liked the fact that the NCC coordinated the work of individual congregations, which accepted responsibility for the refugees' accommodation, welfare, and in some cases, employment.[27] The government was also pleased with the quality of the individuals recommended by the NCC:

> The acceptance of six refugee families from Hong Kong has proved to be quite successful, because in practically all cases the breadwinners have possessed the occupational skills that we need here. For instance, one man was a qualified medical practitioner and is now completing a qualifying period at Otago University so that he can obtain New Zealand registration. Two other Chinese are working as accountants.[28]

Officials in the Department of Labor concluded, "the entry of six families like this over a period of eighteen months to two years at a time is not likely to create any problem."[29] The government was so delighted with the skilled individuals being resettled that when the NCC recommended another twelve families for resettlement in 1969, Minister Shand unilaterally approved the program. Shand did not consult with his cabinet colleagues as he had in previous years; the merit of the program had become self-evident. His only condition was that the resettlement effort be limited to six families. Shand felt it "would be less difficult to resettle the smaller number and they would attract less attention."[30] To reconcile the contradiction between refusing applications for family sponsorship from Chinese New Zealanders while approving ongoing refugee resettlement initiatives from Hong Kong under the auspices of the NCC, the government insisted that the individuals being sponsored had to be clearly, and unquestionably, refugees in need of assistance. Here one can see the productive work of applied categorizations even though refugees had yet to be defined in New Zealand law. By creating the parameters for who was to be considered a "genuine refugee," the New Zealand government worked to curtail criticism from Chinese New Zealanders who were being denied the chance to sponsor their loved ones. This careful construction required serious discussions amongst officials in New Zealand about how they should be defining refugees and evaluating the merits of the cases promoted by the WCC.

One official explained to a colleague, "We have always understood a Refugee [sic] to be a person who has been forced to leave his homeland in order to escape from oppression etc."[31] Yet the sheer number of people who left the Chinese mainland after 1949 prompted the government to put limits on this expansive definition in order to curtail the perceived scope of its humanitarian obligations. The government considered the WCC "naïve" in suggesting "that the many thousands who have left mainland China since 1949 should be eligible . . . with no other qualification than that they are refugees."[32] Instead, authorities proposed that refugeehood be defined in relation to others who had left in similar circumstances. This meant identifying "persons who are suffering genuine hardship compared with their contemporaries in the country of residence."[33] Admission on humanitarian grounds was therefore considered impossible for those who had successfully established themselves in a second country, especially if they seemed to be doing as well as (or better than) their fellow residents.[34] Still, the government of New Zealand wanted to ensure the admission of people capable of assimilating; this assumed a degree of skills and education that did not necessarily reflect the desired refugee-type. Nevertheless, officials cautioned the WCC "that the success or otherwise of continuing our refugee quota must be restricted to *genuine refugees* [emphasis added]" and that "New Zealand should not be a dumping group for people who have been registered with the World Council of Churches as alleged refugees."[35] It was a difficult to pretext to uphold.

The New Zealand government's criteria for admissions consisted of the following:

a)   The applicants should be genuine refugees who are having difficulty in establishing themselves in Hong Kong;

b) The head of the family should not be more than 45 years and should have not more than four children;

c) He should be able to engage in a worthwhile occupation in New Zealand; preferably as a tradesman, technician or as an experienced factory operative;

d) All members of the family must be of good health and character.[36]

In going through the recommended cases in 1969, officials were dismayed to discover that very few cases fell within the department's stated parameters, this despite the movement of large numbers of people to Hong Kong following the extreme violence of the Cultural Revolution in the People's Republic of China, which had begun three years prior. It seemed that most of the recommended families had "established themselves quite well" and had "a standard of living equal to the local residents" of Hong Kong.[37] In 1971, the NCC proposed a fourth quota and submitted thirty cases for consideration based, in theory, on the refugee selection criteria established by the department. The commissioner in Hong Kong, C. S. Crawford, checked the list for possible candidates. He found none, but because of what he later described as the WCC's "sob story," he felt compelled to select six families.[38] When the list was forwarded to the Department of Labor in Wellington, officials rejected all of the suggested applicants. They too found nothing refugee-like about the proposed families. Officials were adamant that the people chosen for resettlement to New Zealand had to meet the government's standard for genuine refugees. This was the only way to justify the admission of NCC-sponsored families over perennial requests by Chinese New Zealanders to sponsor their relatives.

When news of the rejection was communicated in Hong Kong, WCC staff were distressed. Some of the families involved had already begun to make preparations to move to New Zealand. Mr. Chiang Kaom Ng, a married father of one, had resigned his position in anticipation of an imminent departure. Officials in Wellington suspected that Reverend O'Grady, the NCC's resettlement officer, had been too enthusiastic in his communications with the families. Torn between the government and the interests of the NCC and the WCC, the commissioner in Hong Kong suggested there were valid grounds for considering Mr. and Mrs. Ng as refugees:

He was born in Macao in 1938, went to China in 1947 and escaped from China in 1950 when he returned to Macao and completed his studies there in 1957 prior to coming to Hong Kong. Mrs. Ng was born in China in 1938. Her father fled from China about 1955 leaving behind a wife and three children. Mrs. Ng managed to escape from China in 1961 when she came to Hong Kong. Her mother and two sisters still live in China and her father died in Hong Kong in 1969.[39]

In this case, Crawford proposed that merely leaving the Chinese mainland was sufficient evidence of refugeehood. It was the kind of broad argument advanced by the WCC that authorities in Wellington had come to suspect and reject as they sought to define refugeehood in a way that narrowed the scope of their obligations and guaranteed, in theory, the successful settlement of prospective migrants. Reverend O'Grady petitioned further on behalf of two other refused cases. He described Kin Yip Peter Chan as "an orphan who has endured considerable hardship under the Communists in China. His salary is not sufficient to support himself without help from a cousin. He has a sponsoring church, and guaranteed employment in his own field of motor mechanic." The second case involved Mr. and Mrs. Bernard Hui. Reverend O'Grady explained that Mr. Hui had "long been unable to find steady employment in Hong Kong, and although both he and Mrs. Hui work their combined earnings are insufficient to keep the family. In addition the baby has to be boarded out so Mrs. Hui can work."[40] It was difficult to see what was so exceptional about these cases that they required resettlement to New Zealand. Officials in Wellington concluded the applicants were "suitable as migrants" but could not ascertain on what grounds "they had been presented as refugee cases."[41]

The NCC's resettlement program created an opening for people seeking to move if they could meet the government's expectations of a "genuine refugee" and prove that they were capable of adapting to life in New Zealand. The NCC and the WCC made the case for the families desiring to move, but in 1971 the WCC misjudged where the dividing line between desirable migrant and deserving refugee was located. After 1971 there were no further resettlement schemes for Chinese refugees in Hong Kong. This may have been because the pretext for a refugee resettlement program to New Zealand was no longer viable.[42] It may also have been the result of the newly elected government of Norman Kirk's immigration policy statement, published in 1974, which itself was the result of a major policy review.

Reflecting the growing tendency to categorize migrants as a way of managing movement, the 1974 statement privileged migrants' potential economic and cultural contributions as skilled workers over the traditional family ties requirement. Exceptions were made for humanitarian admissions, which were often linked to questions of family reunification.[43] Moreover, the policy indicated, "efforts should be directed towards the early removal of discrimination on ethnic grounds between citizens of any one country" and emphasized that in considering applications from Chinese migrants and other "ethnic origins already represented here as minority groups, emphasis should progressively be placed on the cultural and economic contribution they can make in terms of selection criteria, rather than on their relationship with families resident in New Zealand."[44] For the first time, immigration policy required British and Irish migrants to obtain permits before leaving their homelands, subjecting them to the same requirements as all other migrants and, in theory, rendering New Zealand's immigration regulations race-neutral.

The 1974 policy statement was part of a global wave of reforms that began in the mid-1960s, which established a whole new slate of categories of admission. Yet the immigration reforms in New Zealand were paradoxical in nature. They incorporated humanitarian admissions as a principle and therefore facilitated the movement of some, but they also established criteria for admissions based on decades of efforts to curb the scope of humanitarian largesse and secure the most skilled migrants for settlement. As in other white settler societies, New Zealand's migration categories served three key purposes: to select, regulate, and exclude. This paralleled developments in Hong Kong, as the colonial government responded to unwanted migration from China during the turmoil of the Cultural Revolution.

Years after the establishment of the People's Republic of China, British colonial officials in Hong Kong continued to wrestle with the issue of sizable migration from the Chinese mainland. After 1966, these pressures were exacerbated by the launch of the massive, and extremely violent, Cultural Revolution. Fearing that the communist project was being corrupted by bourgeois elements, Mao Zedong planned to rebuild the Chinese Communist Party by cleansing it of ideological impurities. What was intended to be a controlled revitalization, however, became an unexpectedly chaotic and violent upheaval.[45] Top leaders from the Chinese Communist Party were purged, along with senior military officials and university educators. Hundreds of thousands of people were relocated as seventeen million urban youth were sent to the countryside to labor on collective farms as part of the massive *xiafang* (sent down) campaigns.[46] Cadres of paramilitary youth groups, known as Red Guards, were organized across the country. Thousands of people were physically and psychologically persecuted for allegedly failing to uphold the class struggle.[47] The "most gruesome aspects" of the Cultural Revolution involved the "torture and killing of innocent people and the suicides that were the final options of many who had suffered intolerable physical and mental abuse."[48] Estimates suggest that in the elementary schools of Beijing's six urban districts, 994 people were beaten between 1 June and 25 June 1966.[49] After Mao announced that "to rebel is justified," conditions worsened. In two months alone, 1,772 people were murdered in Beijing. In September, another 704 people committed suicide and 534 people were killed in Shanghai.[50] Although the violence lessened after 1969, only with Mao's death in 1976 and the arrests of the Gang of Four (Jiang Qing, Zhang Chunqiao, Yao Wenyuan, and Wang Hongwen) did the decade of upheaval finally conclude. At the Eleventh Party Congress in 1977, the Chinese Communist Party declared the Cultural Revolution officially over.

Many of the people who moved to Hong Kong legally or illegally after 1966 were "sent-down youth" who did not want to work in the Chinese countryside.[51] During the "mass stage" of the Cultural Revolution, from 1966 to 1969, over a thousand people a month sought refuge and better opportunities in the colony.[52] Along with its traditional role as a site of refuge, Hong Kong continued to be a listening post for events on the Chinese mainland as the territory remained largely off-limits to Western observers. Interviews conducted with arriving migrants hinted at the turmoil in the PRC. One individual described being getting sent down to a rubber plantation in Hainan. "No matter how I resisted," he said, "I couldn't escape my fate. I tried to hide out in Canton, but they caught me. Then I disappeared a second time and they put pressure on my family to make me go."[53] In the evolving dynamics of the Cold War, many Westerners either couldn't, or didn't want to, believe the migrants' stories. As one observer noted:

> Refugees complained about elitism, lack of responsiveness to mass needs, inept policies, over politicization, unnecessary political purges, harsh life in forced labor camps, and so on. These complaints were often dismissed as sour grapes and made us question the credibility of such accounts.[54]

The eruption of violence in Hong Kong suddenly affirmed what many observers had been inclined to dismiss. For weeks in the spring of 1967, Hong Kong's youth demonstrated and rioted in the streets.[55] Agitators broadcast propaganda from loudspeakers on communist-owned buildings. Large character posters and slogans championing Maoist thinking appeared everywhere. Bombs and decoys were planted in urban areas. By the end of the year, 51 people had been killed in the violence and another 800 injured. A total of 5,000 people had been arrested. The WCC worried about the excesses of the Cultural Revolution, as well as the fate of the church in China, which it feared had been dealt a "fatal shock."[56]

The violence and unrest created great uncertainty amongst Hong Kong's residents, who looked to colonial authorities to restore peace and security. The government responded by restricting the display of propaganda materials, limiting inflammatory speeches, imposing curfews, providing additional police presence on the streets, and militarizing the border as a precaution against both individual agitators moving into the colony and the possibility of a potentially destabilizing influx akin to the movement that occurred in the spring of 1962.[57] A new fence was constructed along the Shun Chun River immediately north of San Tin to Sha Tau Ko. Military and police forces were posted permanently to the frontier to defend the border against illegal entries.[58] In hindsight, one British official observed, "as far as we know, there were no refugees or attempts at illegal immigration," but, he concluded, "the danger was there and the Hong Kong government planned against this contingency."[59]

The militarized border proved relatively effective in preventing entries, at least for those who attempted to transgress the territorial frontier. Stories of people swimming across Mirs Bay or arriving by boat were still common. This led to a renewed interest in managing migration in all its forms. In 1971, the government of Hong Kong introduced an Immigration Ordinance, defining for the first time who was to be considered a resident of the colony.[60] This included Hong Kong Belongers (all British subjects born in Hong Kong) and Chinese Residents who were defined as persons "wholly or partly" of Chinese race who had lived in Hong Kong continuously for at least seven years. The system prevented anyone falling outside of these categories from legally establishing himself or herself in Hong Kong, dovetailing with efforts in white settler societies to manage the admission and settlement of migrants through the use of various migration categories.[61] Not surprisingly, given the colonial government's history of trying to limit population flows, authorities did not provide a category for refugee admissions. Instead, colonial officials blurred formal and informal distinctions when arriving migrants threatened the fragile conceptual structures upon which categories of admission and residency were constructed.

In 1972, the government in Beijing issued a series of instructions to district authorities to the effect that they should assist, rather than deter, people who desired to emigrate. There was a tangible increase in entries to Hong Kong as a result.[62] Many of the people moving into Hong Kong in the early 1970s were *huáqiáo* from Indonesia, Malaysia, Cambodia, and Vietnam who had returned to China a decade prior, heeding appeals from authorities in Beijing to help rebuild the motherland. They were disillusioned by the Cultural Revolution and the *xiafang* campaigns and wanted to leave. By the early 1970s, the communist regime was happy to help them do so; authorities furnished exit documents to aspiring migrants who then became part of the official flow of people from the mainland.[63] According to one man who successfully obtained a visa, "there was a long waiting list, but from gossip and a few concrete examples it appeared that almost everyone who applied eventually received an exit visa, although in some cases it took over a year."[64]

The number of people moving illegally also grew in these years. Their departures stemmed from the same unhappy conditions on the mainland that were encouraging people to pursue legal methods of admission. One survey, reported in the *Hong Kong Standard*, suggested that many of the illegal migrants were "discontented young people" from the towns and cities who had been forced to go to the communes to work as well as "village youngsters" near the border who moved to Hong Kong "to look for a job, or with the intention of sending money home to their families who were suffering from the effects of two bad harvests."[65] The colonial government feared a relentless stream of migrants from the mainland of the sort the colony had witnessed after 1949. To prevent this from happening, in November 1974, after negotiations with Chinese officials, authorities in Hong Kong announced that all migrants who entered the territory illegally, and who were later apprehended, would be repatriated. This policy built on the new, prescribed categories of belonging introduced in the 1971 Immigration Ordinance. Previously, those who had made their way to urban areas had been protected from deportation. The new policy put an end to this practice; it echoed the temporary measures introduced in 1962 and applied to people found within the colony's urban centers as well as its frontier areas.[66]

In creating new legal categories of residency and belonging, the government of Hong Kong altered the manner in which those who violated their conditions of entry were treated.[67] The careful categorization of people in the 1971 Immigration Ordinance meant that in 1974 there were many more ways for someone to be considered illegal and returned to the mainland than had been case historically. Importantly, the government of Hong Kong's approach affected how other countries understood the nature of migration out of the PRC. For instance, the Canadian government heeded British caution on proposing large-scale resettlement schemes out of Hong Kong in the early 1970s.[68] Raph Girard, former Director of Refugee Policy, conceded that the Canadian government could have done more to assist refugees in Hong Kong but explained that they were dissuaded by British officials who did not want to create a "tidal wave" of movement into the colony, an outcome they deemed likely if resettlement became a known option amongst migrants from mainland China.[69] The policies and practices of other countries and territories factored into how the Canadian government understood the character of cross-border migrant populations as well as its own capacity to manage these movements.

The signing of the 1951 Convention and the associated protocol had only a limited impact on how governments organized their overall responsibilities vis-à-vis refugee populations. Indeed, as the case of New Zealand illustrates, even the movement of people to Hong Kong during the Cultural Revolution was peripheral to the impulse behind its humanitarian program for refugees in the British colony. The biggest imperative for refugee resettlement schemes was the challenge of incorporating humanitarian principles into immigration legislation while retaining control over admissions. In Canada, this process was born of efforts to reconcile discrete humanitarian programs with a growing impulse to institutionalize humanitarian initiatives so as to better manage the country's immigration programs.

In 1973, the Canadian government negotiated a family reunification agreement with PRC authorities. The agreement was struck three years before the introduction of a new Immigration Act that formalized the humanitarian aspects of Canada's immigration program and five years before the communist regime lifted exit controls on its nationals, permitting open movement to and from China. This agreement therefore foreshadowed more profound structural changes as it addressed the specific case of family class migrants, using notions of humanitarianism to reunite families. Moreover, the family reunification agreement created an unprecedented opportunity for Chinese migrants to leave the PRC for Canada, as a result of the government in Beijing's surprising initiative in pursuing the accord.

As in other white settler societies, the normative inclination in Canada was to manage rather than actively facilitate migration from China. Despite regular petitions from Chinese Canadians hoping to sponsor their relatives, Canadian officials sidelined the question of migration to Canada given the "known sensitivities" of PRC officials to the subject in the lead-up to formal diplomatic relations between the two countries in 1970.[70] In 1972, a surprise overture by the PRC government on the family reunification issue forced the Canadian government to address the issue of actively managing significant Chinese migration for the first time in decades.[71] Under the terms of the agreement, negotiated as part of a larger package on consular affairs, a member of Canada's Hong Kong Commission was accredited to Beijing to conduct interviews and process applications. The agreement committed the governments of both countries to give "sympathetic consideration . . . to the issuance of entry or exit visas to citizens of one country applying to go to the other country in order to join members of their families."[72] Officials in both Canada and the PRC were to assist with the provisions of necessary documents, and visas were to be issued by authorities in Beijing and Ottawa.

The family reunification agreement was sealed during Prime Minister Pierre Trudeau's first visit to the People's Republic of China as head of state in 1973.[73] Excitement and interest in the visit abounded amongst the Canadian public. The *Globe and Mail*, a national newspaper, carried front-page stories about every aspect of the trip from the gift of four beavers to the Peking Zoo to the warm reception that greeted the prime minister to details of his meetings with Chairman Mao.[74] The family reunification agreement was one of the few concrete results from the visit and it therefore assumed important political dimensions. Don Cameron, the visa officer in Hong Kong responsible for administering the agreement, recalls that even after the formal signatures, the prime minister retained a strong interest in the agreement's success. The prime minister's office was attentive to many of the program's smallest details, including the press coverage that greeted Ching Ma, the first person to arrive in Canada under the terms of the program.[75]

The fact that Prime Minister Trudeau was personally invested in the family reunification agreement with the People's Republic of China set the tone in which visa officers considered applications. Much in the way that the State Department in the United States was able to forge progress, albeit limited, on the refugee file in Asia in the face of continued opposition from their colleagues (the traditional "gatekeepers" in the Immigration and Naturalization Service), foreign policy considerations advanced the family reunification agreement beyond what senior Canadian immigration officials had envisioned.[76]

Immigration regulations dating from 1967 provided for the sponsorship of two classes of relatives. The first was for spouses and children. The admission criteria for this category were rather liberal given the importance the federal government attributed to family reunification as a means of ensuring social stability. The second category was for nominated relatives such as brothers, sisters, aunts, and uncles. The admission criteria were somewhat more rigorous for this category, given that the family connections were more distant. Nevertheless, the same premise applied— namely that having a relative in the country was a means of ensuring that the new migrant would be supported and would be able to find work and integrate without becoming dependent on social welfare services.

Standard selection criteria for sponsored and nominated relatives should have applied to all cases. Yet, as evidenced in Hong Kong in 1962, selection criteria were not the only consideration in selecting applicants. Political factors also played a key part. After 1973, one of the goals of the selection process for family class migrants was to ensure that the agreement with the PRC, which the Department of External Affairs was promoting as a "great achievement," was, indeed, a success. Don Cameron was charged with the responsibility of visiting the PRC to conduct interviews with prospective migrants. As Cameron recalls, he "didn't ask" senior officials in the Department of Manpower and Immigration and they "didn't tell him what category to use." There was an unspoken understanding that Cameron would not be turning people away.[77] Cameron and his successors applied the selection criteria generously in order to assure that the family reunification program would be a diplomatic success. Officials in Ottawa appeared none the wiser, reporting that the "quality of the movement was very high indeed."[78] In recounting what has become known as the "chicken farmer" story, Gerry Campbell, former assistant deputy minister in the Department of Manpower and Immigration, recounted how Chinese applicants from Guangdong were routinely assessed as poultry farmers by Canadian visa officers. According to Campbell, "All these applicants were in the nominated category, usually with siblings in Canada who had sponsored them, and with limited education and no English or French. Few would have qualified if assessed in lower demand occupations."[79] Suggesting to people that they had experience in the poultry business helped ease their applications, especially as word traveled amongst prospective applicants.

Despite the Canadian government's apparent commitment to the program, new regulations scheduled to come into effect in 1975 threatened to curb the numbers of nominated relatives admitted into the country. Staff in Hong Kong communicated their concerns, and Allan Gotlieb, deputy minister of the Department of Manpower and Immigration, worried immediately about the impact of these regulations on the "goodwill" that was being generated by the family reunification program.[80] Gotlieb and other senior bureaucrats in the department were sensitive to Prime Minister Trudeau's investment in the family reunification agreement, but faced a practical dilemma. Due to the diplomatic aspects of the agreement, they had "inherited a special Family Reunification program without acquiring, or developing ourselves, a policy by which to implement this program."[81] Immigration officials essentially had to formulate a policy on family reunification after the fact. One proposed response was to administer the program as a refugee one. However, in a briefing to Cabinet, officials in the Department of Manpower and Immigration insisted that family reunification immigrants

> should not be thought of as refugees no matter how their situation is viewed by family members in Canada. These persons normally wish to come to Canada for a combination of economic and family reasons. To have them thought of as refugees will not only confuse the public about our actual refugee program, but it will make it much more difficult (if not impossible) to administer a special family reunification program.[82]

Calling migrants "refugees" or refugees "migrants" jeopardized the pretense that people naturally belonged to different migration categories or that the categories themselves were organic rather than carefully constructed, as evidenced by the development of refugee selection criteria in New Zealand and ongoing efforts to define, and assist, refugees in Canada.

As in New Zealand, ad hoc humanitarian initiatives such as the family reunification program evolved into the basis for legislative reforms in Canada in 1970s. In 1974, the government of Canada launched a major policy evaluation of the country's immigration programs, the same year that New Zealand undertook its own major review. Following on extensive public consultations about the substance of Canada's immigration and refugee policies, the Canadian government introduced an Immigration Act in 1976 that provided for a new migration category: Designated Classes.[83] Reflecting public interest in having a "humanitarian" immigration program, this category provided for humanitarian admissions for cases that did not mesh with the 1951 Convention's emphasis on individual persecution.[84]

The 1976 Immigration Act, the first since 1952 when the government of Mackenzie King crafted legislation to explicitly preserve official discretion on immigration admissions, marked an important step in how the federal government gradually modified its approach to managing global migration flows, including the movement of refugees. According to Mike Molloy, then director of refugee policy in the Department of Manpower and Immigration, the legislative drafters did not have any particular groups in mind when they created the Designated Class criteria. What they were most aware of was the need to modernize Canada's approach to refugee issues in the face of population movements from all over the globe. According to Molloy, the Canadian government "wanted to be able to cut definitions to meet specific situations." He says, politicians "knew they were going to need alternatives to the Convention Refugee category, given what was happening in the world."[85] In other words, they wanted to establish criteria that would guide humanitarian assistance broadly, beyond the limited scope for protection offered in the 1951 Convention. Raph Girard, who was instrumental in designing the system, affirms that the Designated Classes were a mechanism "to deliver what [the government] knew it already wanted to deal with."[86] Refugee movements out of Chile and Uganda in the early 1970s had sensitized officials in an immediate way to the global, and multifaceted, nature of migration in a world where people were increasingly attuned to events abroad. For instance, in 1973, Canadian church groups lobbied passionately for the admission of 7,000 refugees from Chile and Latin America based on their active engagement with the liberation theology movement.[87]

A year later, following on their involvement with the resettlement of Chilean refugees, the Anglican and United Churches presented a joint brief to Parliament as part of the discussions around reforming Canada's immigration regime. They proposed "new legislation [that would] make it easier for those seeking asylum to be admitted to Canada." Specifically, they wanted a special asylum category to address occasions of "special crisis in the lives of nations and of individuals which plead for [a] special movement." The churches recommended an expansive understanding of what constituted a political refugee. They argued that the term "political" should be understood in the "widest sense" to include those who are suffering due to "war or changes in government, those who find themselves in an environment where legislation . . . Removes "or" curtails their freedom of movement and speech, thus preventing their living up to the dictates of their conscience as well as those who are the victims of a revolutionary or military coup." Significantly, the brief made no mention of refugees as defined by the 1951 Convention. The narrow legal definition did not mesh with the churches' expansive vision.[88]

In contrast to the largesse imagined by the Anglican Church and others, the federal Liberal government preferred discrete, selective solutions. Along with the Designated Classes, new regulations introduced a Self-Exiled Persons category for individuals fleeing communist-controlled countries in Europe. Unlike the token numbers provided for in the United States' 1953 Refugee Relief Act, migrants from the People's Republic of China were not included in the Self-Exiled class category. They continued to be largely absent from the Canadian government's conceptual field.[89] Even though the federal government increasingly considered refugee issues in global terms and had paid some attention to refugees from the People's Republic of China in the 1960s, it still continued to associate the idea of oppressive communist regimes primarily with the Soviet Union and the Eastern Bloc. Still, because the 1976 Immigration Act established new categories of migration, migrants had novel opportunities through which to move.

Most notably, the 1976 Immigration Act elevated refugee determination processes to a new level in Canada by creating the Refugee Status Advisory Committee (RSAC)—the first dedicated refugee determination body in Canada.[90] RSAC was mandated to ensure that "no person claiming refugee status [was] deported in contravention of the provisions of the UN Convention." The minister of Employment and Immigration appointed officials from their department, the Department of External Affairs, and from the general public to consider claims. The UNHCR representative in Canada was permitted to attend as an observer with a modest advisory role. Refugee claimants, their lawyers, churches, NGOs, and the general public were not allowed to assist at the committee's deliberations.

Two general summaries of cases that were appealed to the Immigration Appeal Board hint at what appellants before RSAC went through as they stated their cases for why they should not be returned to the People's Republic of China.[91] On 25 April 1979, the board heard the case of Jut Wong Cheung, who arrived in Canada as a member of a ship's crew and then deserted. The board refused Cheung's claims because the members doubted the legitimacy of his asserted persecution. The board declared: "the appellant's desire to stay in Canada as a refugee is prompted not by persecution but by the fact that he does not agree with the political ideologies of the Red Chinese regime and does not approve of the existing social economic base of their society."[92] The fact that it took him four years to make a refugee claim after his arrival in Canada cast suspicion on the veracity of his allegations of persecution.

RSAC heard Hua Kien Hui's claim on 8 March 1988. Hui claimed Convention refugee status "for reasons of his family background and political opinion." Hui was a landowner and was therefore forced to undergo political reeducation involving forced manual labor and mandatory indoctrination classes. He claimed that he was frequently arrested and insisted, at the time of his appearance before the board, that the police were still looking for him. He told the board that if he was returned to China, "he expected to be treated as a traitor for having left the Communist system and to be jailed for a long period of time." The board ruled against Hui on the grounds that "political re-education through manual labor combined with indoctrination classes is carried on in many countries and for many large social groups." The board concluded that Hui's treatment was neither "so onerous [nor] unpleasant as to amount to a basis for well-founded fear of persecution." As for the frequent arrests, the board did not "regard such questioning as unusual in a heavily regimented Communist society" and determined that it did not constitute a well-founded fear of persecution. Ultimately, the board declared that there was "little doubt that Hui was likely to be subject to some disciplinary action as a result of leaving China without proper authority," but the board was not overly concerned about this possibility.[93]

The decisions in the Cheung and Hui cases were quite telling, especially considering the grounds upon which the board rejected their claims. Neither case met the strict definition of a convention refugee because Cheung and Hui had each left conditions of generalized violence. Although the 1967 Protocol had removed the geographic and temporal limitations of the convention, the definition of a refugee as someone with a well-founded fear of persecution remained. It was a limited definition, born of the immediate postwar situation in Europe, and meant that for people in conditions of generalized violence, the search for refuge, ironically, had to be undertaken beyond the convention's narrow legal framework. Occasionally, discrete programs that incorporated, and also supplemented, the legally established categories of migration enabled migrants to do this.

To benefit from discretionary humanitarianism, migrants had to figure out how to exploit their personal stories and backgrounds in order to profit from changing rules and categories that had little to do with their individual life experiences and histories and everything to do with selecting and admitting potential citizens to develop nations along particular lines. In the 1970s, selection had less to do with whiteness, although race continued to play a major role in suggesting desirability, and much more to do with obtaining skilled workers, fostering social stability, and responding to humanitarian advocacy that, more than ever, was bound up with global human rights and social justice campaigns.[94] Migrant populations found themselves occupying unstable terrain, especially those who sought protection as refugees. Governments felt compelled to present their immigration laws as just and humanitarian while also seeking skilled migrants who could be readily assimilated into the workforce. The rhetoric of being humanitarian nations embodied language that Canadians and New Zealanders came to believe in. It was also language that ultimately lead to reforms meant to incorporate humanitarianism into formal selection and admission structures, unlike in Hong Kong where such an identity was never celebrated as part of the colonial project.

Over the course of the postwar period, diverse opportunities emerged for migrants to move by official means to white settler societies. Some appeared as a result of humanitarian interventions, such as those initiated by ARCI and the NCC, which created discrete opportunities for those who left the Chinese mainland for Hong Kong. Others materialized as governments nuanced and refined official categories of migration. While the regulation of migration categories and limited resettlement efforts were meant to restrict and regulate movement, migrants moved according to whatever means were available to them. Chiang Kaom Ng, with the help of the NCC, was able to take advantage of the refugee sponsorship program to move to New Zealand. Jut Wong Cheung and Hua Kien Hui were not so fortunate. They failed to convince RSAC and the Immigration Appeal Board of Canada of their claims to refugeehood.

Humanitarian reforms and the refugee determination processes introduced in the 1970s became an additional layer in the complex web of laws, rules, and regulations that governed the movement of people in the twentieth century. They layered and moderated, but did not erase, the discrimination at the heart of immigration programs amongst white settler societies, which remained invested in securing the most desirable migrants. At the same time, in response to shifting public sentiments born of concerted lobbying, governments created room for humanitarian admissions, disguising the fact that these were often based on the potential economic benefits that migrants—admitted on humanitarian and compassionate grounds—might bring. The refugees selected for resettlement to New Zealand were consistently chosen on the basis of their employability, rather than the depth of their "genuine refugee" experiences.

The exception was the family reunification agreement in Canada, which—because of political considerations—facilitated the admission of non-skilled relatives whose suitability for the Canadian job market was questionable. Critically, this humanitarian program was limited to the relatives of Chinese Canadians. Authorities insisted that refugee issues had to be handled distinctly in order to ensure that overall admission numbers could be carefully managed. Humanitarian admissions were a loose, and easily enlarged, class of migrants that governments felt compelled to regulate closely so as to guard against "too much" migration. Refugee determination processes such as those of RSAC in Canada, which had the potential to create a significant opening in otherwise restrictive migration regimes as they were beyond the purview of government discretion, employed the narrow convention definition of a refugee in their decision-making processes. This approach limited the number of people who could benefit from their mandated operations.

For migrants, the growing formalization of admission categories in New Zealand, Hong Kong, and Canada, as well as the introduction of independent refugee determination processes, changed the circumstances in which they contemplated cross-border movement. Migrants moved from navigating discrete resettlement opportunities to defined categories of movement. While the structures underpinning immigration programs in white settler societies remained selective, new generations of immigration officers facilitated the admission of migrants who, a few decades prior, would have been considered perpetually, and incorrigibly, alien. Many of these officers would be sent to Hong Kong and Southeast Asia in response to the flight of hundreds of thousands of refugees from Vietnam, Cambodia, and Laos in the 1970s.

7

HUMANITARIANISM IN MYTH AND PRACTICE

From Hong Kong to Indochina

IN 1975, the United States lost the fight in Vietnam. The American War had raged for two decades, starting shortly after the French defeat in 1954. An estimated 195,000–430,000 civilians in South Vietnam and another 50,000–65,000 in North Vietnam perished during the conflict. A total of 58,220 Americans were killed, and these losses, along with the profoundly divisive nature of the war, severely damaged the national American psyche.[1] Since then, the meaning of the loss in Vietnam has been refashioned again and again, shifting from an "incomprehensible loss" to a "good war," representative of America's principled global interventions.[2] At the core of this evolution has been the story of the 130,000 refugees resettled to the United States in 1975 and the nearly one million others resettled as the political situation in Vietnam, Cambodia, and Laos—collectively known as Indochina—deteriorated in the late 1970s. As a result of the turmoil, over three million people risked their lives by boarding sea vessels of dubious quality to seek security and more promising futures elsewhere.[3]

Along with the United States, Canada, Australia, and New Zealand all assisted Indochinese refugees in some way, marking the first time that white settler societies responded en masse to refugees in Asia. South Africa did not, having failed to develop "a discourse of refugee rights or institutionalized protections."[4] As in the United States, other white settler societies used the refugee movement to instrumentalize the myth of generous compassion. They did so for slightly different ends, though all sought to erase the history of racial discrimination that had historically privileged migrants from the United Kingdom and Europe over migrants from Asia by advancing a humanitarian identity. In Canada, the resettlement of 60,000 refugees from Vietnam, Cambodia, and Laos was, and continues to be, regularly used as evidence of the country's "humanitarian character."[5] New Zealand resettled 11,000 refugees and this gesture resulted in what observers describe as a "boon to the nation." Critics used the example of the Indochinese refugees to criticize New Zealand's reluctant response to Syrian refugees in 2015.[6] Similarly, in Australia, the resettlement and reception of 100,000 Indochinese refugees has since served critics of the federal government's restrictive asylum policies and its use of prison-like detention centers to segregate arriving migrants from the general populace.[7] Government documents, however, insist that the resettlement of Indochinese refugees established, and continues to reflect, the country's "proud record of resettling refugees and people in humanitarian need from around the world."[8]

Indeed, the actions of white settler societies have been mythologized to such an extent that all other aspects of events in Indochina, including the critical role played by territories of first asylum (places where migrants landed before moving elsewhere), notably Hong Kong, and the resourcefulness of the migrants themselves, have been eclipsed. While contemporaries recognized refugees from Indochina as victims of communist oppression, history has remembered the resettlement of refugees in this period first and foremost as a "gift of freedom" and evidence of white settler societies' "heartwarming" generosity.[9] There is a real problem with this mythology, and it lies with the myth of beneficence itself, which suggests that the generosity of white settler societies was somehow to be expected and typical of earlier, and later, interventions. It was not. For almost thirty years, humanitarians presented refugees from the Chinese mainland to the governments of white settler societies as persons deserving of assistance, and even resettlement. Although members of the public provided financial and material assistance, humanitarians were generally rebuffed in their efforts. Still, these contests laid the fragile foundations for the way the United States, Australia, New Zealand,

and Canada responded to the people who fled their homes in Indochina in the 1970s.

The established, if delicate, underpinnings of international humanitarian assistance shaped the way white settler societies responded to the evolving situation in Indochina, especially since Hong Kong played a pivotal role as a site of first asylum. Amongst such territories, which included Thailand, Malaysia, and Indonesia, Hong Kong was most closely allied with the Western liberal democratic project. Moreover, white settler societies had worked with the colonial government in Hong Kong for years on issues around refugee protection and assistance. There was, therefore, an expectation amongst observers that authorities in Hong Kong would adopt responses in keeping with their own evolving vision of enlightened humanitarianism, even if the colonial government had proven obstinate in the face of previous humanitarian situations.[10] The Hong Kong government certainly did so initially, as did numerous humanitarian organizations in the colony. However, when resettlement activities appeared to encourage the continued movement of people out of Vietnam, the colonial government shifted course. White settler societies followed suit. In order to curb migration out of Indochina, countries relied on previous strategies to limit responsibility for refugees from Asia through the production of discussions about how only "genuine refugees" should be assisted. Efforts to restrict mobility based on categorical definitions of who was a "genuine refugee" ultimately curbed the scope of the humanitarian intervention in Southeast Asia in the 1970s. The exception was the United States, which because of its wartime experiences in Vietnam remained committed throughout the 1980s to the propaganda value of resettling people fleeing communist oppression regardless of their degree of genuine refugeehood.

The French and American wars in Vietnam displaced millions of people within North and South Vietnam. After French forces were defeated in 1954, 900,000 civilians fled the communist zone for the south.[11] Thousands more followed in subsequent years as war ravaged the country. By 1971, there were an estimated six million refugees in South Vietnam.[12] The fall of Saigon in 1975 marked a new, and distinct, phase in the movement of migrants as people sought refuge outside of the country.[13] In May 1975, weeks after the fall of Saigon, the US Congress passed the Indochina Migration and Refugee Assistance Act, which authorized the admission of 130,000 Vietnamese refugees to the United States. Distinct migration categories and quotas were established to designate eligibility. These included 4,000 orphans under "Operation Babylift" (other countries participated in this endeavor, but their involvement was relatively minor. New Zealand, for instance, resettled only three orphans).[14] The relatives of American citizens or permanent resident aliens, as well as high-risk Vietnamese, including government employees, collaborators, people who knew about US intelligence operations, prominent political and intellectual figures, communist defectors, and the employees of American firms were assisted under "Operation New Life."[15] These resettlement programs were born of a sense of obligation and a desire to rescue people rendered vulnerable because of the war. Policymakers in Washington commonly held that evacuation efforts would discredit the new communist regime.[16] As with "Operation Babylift," US officials sought broad support for the evacuation program and urged other countries, including Canada, France, and Australia, to participate.[17] Each of these countries did so, in a limited capacity. France became involved in the relief efforts as a result of its own imperial history in Indochina.[18] Australia and Canada both responded to US pressures based on their involvement with the American war in Vietnam.[19] However, it was events in Indochina that ultimately enlarged the scope of their engagement.

Beginning in the fall of 1978 through to the spring of 1979, the number of migrants departing over land and sea from Vietnam increased sharply. The invasion of Cambodia by Vietnamese forces and the pursuit of repressive programs by Laos authorities contributed to the growing numbers of people in flight. Still, most of the increased movement was provoked by the Vietnamese authorities' decision to persecute certain groups considered undesirable or threatening to the new regime. This included the ethnic Hao Chinese, who were relatively affluent. As authorities charged migrants an exit tax before allowing them to depart, the Vietnamese state derived pecuniary benefit from its targeted oppression. Some estimates suggest that Vietnamese authorities garnered $115 million US dollars in 1978 alone with this strategy.[20] Moreover, organized syndicates profited from the traffic in refugees by arranging large vessels to transport migrants, including the Hao Chinese and others desperate to leave.[21] According to contemporary accounts:

Refugees are exploited at every turn once they declare their intention to leave. . . . They generally sell all their personal property or forfeit it to the state. The price of passage does not include a safe conduct pass to the point of embarkation, so bribes must be paid at each check-point along the way.

The cost of passage ranged from $1,800 to $3,000, and the voyages were treacherous.[22] By mid-1979, over 700,000 people had left Indochina. Of these, 235,000 had fled north into China, 277,000 had fled by boat, and 21,000 had gone overland to Thailand.[23] An estimated 40 to 70 percent of the boats never landed.[24]

The Australian government was acutely aware of the pressures that caused people to leave. As one briefing document from May 1978 surmised:

Conditions in Indo-China are severe. Expropriation and confiscation of goods and means of livelihood have been followed up by redirection to labor and re-education zones. Food is short. People will take enormous risks to escape.

The conclusion was that Cabinet faced "some difficult decisions."[25] Reports of increased departures at the behest of the Vietnamese government triggered a mix of outrage at the actions of communist authorities and anxiety because officials believed that the departing migrants were going to try and make their way to Australian territory. This apprehension stemmed from two years of boat arrivals in Australia.

The first boat had arrived in Darwin, on the northern coast, in 1976.[26] By 1978, thirty-six vessels had landed, bringing a total of 1,254 people. This created considerable alarm amongst officials who were accustomed to a sense of remove from the world's refugee situations. This same mentality shaped how the government of New Zealand initially viewed migration out of Southeast Asia. Previously, "it never had to face the problem of refugees arriving empty-handed on its shores."[27] As a result, the initial strategy in both Australia and New Zealand was to deter migrants from gaining access to their shores by making admissions more difficult. In 1977, the government in Canberra established the Determination of Refugee Status Committee, with the express purpose of distinguishing refugees who met the Convention definition of persecution from those who might be more readily classified as economic migrants.

In the spring of 1978, reports appeared in Australia of an estimated twenty-five vessels with 800 people "in or near Indonesian waters."[28] Cabinet members noted with considerable apprehension, "the refugees are significantly altering the ethnic composition of our total intake (21% in 1978 from Asia) with significant long-term consequences for Australian society."[29] When the government received news in the fall of 1978 that a large boat, the *Hai Hong*, carrying almost 2,000 passengers, had left Vietnam and was presumably headed for Darwin, politicians vehemently opposed its arrival. They did so by emphasizing their humanitarian commitments to assisting refugees in an organized fashion while at the same time casting doubt on the *Hai Hong* migrants' claims to refugeehood.

Michael MacKellar, the minister for the Department of Immigration and Ethnic Affairs, explained to the Australian public:

> We now have the first clear indications that unscrupulous people are attempting to profiteer in the present Indo-Chinese refugee situation . . ."bona fides" of the group are doubtful . . . Australia has played a major part in accepting many thousands of genuine refugees but I give strong warning that we shall not accept cases involving subterfuge.[30]

This statement reflected a continued effort to identify "genuine refugees" and it was rhetoric that the government would use repeatedly over the following months and years. Arrivals in Darwin were described as having "escaped the net" or "jumped the queue."[31] In addition to publicly denigrating migrants that sought to make their way directly to Australia, the government developed legal measures to circumvent arrivals, most notably the Immigration (Unauthorized Arrivals) Act of 1980, which "discouraged the operators of vessels from conveying to Australia large numbers of persons who do not possess proper documentation for travel to Australia."[32]

Perhaps because of the Australian government's rhetoric and its pursuit of legal powers to deal with the arrival of unwanted migrants in international waters, the *Hai Hong* changed course. Instead of heading to

Australia, the captain of the ship sought to reach Malaysian territory, following the trajectory of other boats that left Vietnam after 1975. However, the government of Malaysia refused to allow the migrants to disembark by echoing Australian claims that the people aboard were not real refugees but rather had "paid handsomely" to be on the "profit ship."[33] Officials argued that people who could afford to pay to leave were not "genuine refugees" and should therefore be returned.[34]

By not permitting the *Hai Hong* to land, the government of Malaysia was attempting to curb the business that was developing around the transportation of migrants out of Vietnam. Yet the Malaysian government's response appeared harsh and uncaring to observers, and the case of the *Hai Hong* became an international media sensation. There were daily news stories and images about the boat's precarious situation as well as accounts of tragic deaths and perilous escapes at sea involving other migrant vessels. The cumulative media coverage sparked considerable public concern and, as a result, France, the United States, and Canada committed to the resettlement of the *Hai Hong*'s passengers, breaking the deteriorating impasse. The decision also made these countries more attentive to the plight of migrants arriving in territories of first asylum, including Hong Kong.

In contrast to the manner in which arriving migrants were received by the governments of Malaysia and other countries in Southeast Asia between 1978 and 1979, the British colony of Hong Kong appeared to observers and migrants alike, as a beacon of civility.[35] Hong Kong was the only territory of first asylum that did not threaten "push-backs" or advocate some kind of expansive exclusionary strategy (though it deported a number of boat people individually) in the face of growing departures from Vietnam. After 1975, it was identified as a liberal territory by countries of resettlement and migrants alike. Over 200,000 people arrived in Hong Kong from Indochina between 1975 and 1993.[36]

The government of Hong Kong's immediate response to the increased, and very visible, arrival of Indochinese migrants in the mid-1970s was formulated almost entirely based on its decades of experience in attempting to limit and regulate the size of population flows from the Chinese mainland and its ongoing efforts in this regard. Even with a major cholera outbreak in the colony in 1979, an average of 495 people were caught trying to enter Hong Kong from the mainland on a daily basis. There were frequent reports of bloated corpses found in the harbor as "freedom swimmers" sought to leave the People's Republic of China illegally, only to lose their lives at sea.[37] Nevertheless, the government of Hong Kong continued its policy of returning migrants who entered the colony without proper authorization upon detection and, in fact, enforced this practice even more severely after 1980. Reinforcements were brought into the colony so that additional British soldiers could patrol the colony's territorial borders and waters.[38] In a twelve-month period, 77,000 "illegal migrants" were discovered and returned.[39] Yet an estimated three quarters of the migrants who entered the colony without permits were never apprehended.[40] It was against this backdrop of growing legal and illegal migration from the People's Republic of China that migrants began to arrive from Indochina in growing numbers, much to the dismay of the colonial government.

The first sizable group, composed of 119 ethnic Chinese from Vietnam, arrived in June 1974. They were arrested and returned to Vietnam, sparking considerable, and somewhat surprising, public opposition in Hong Kong.[41] Their deportation was in keeping with the government's approach to illegal migration from the People's Republic of China, but it did not sit well with those concerned about the ongoing conflict in Vietnam. The colonial government's approach shifted with the fall of Saigon. The end of the war and the growing urgency of the humanitarian situation caused authorities to adopt a more liberal attitude vis-à-vis migrants from Indochina. Residents of Hong Kong awoke to the reality of greater numbers of refugees and different kinds of political contingencies when a Norwegian ship arrived in harbor on 4 May 1975 carrying 3,740 refugees. Instead of repatriating the people aboard the *Clara Maersk*, the government housed them in temporary camps.[42] As the situation in Vietnam worsened, the number of people making their way to Hong Kong and other places increased. In 1977, approximately 1,000 people arrived in Hong Kong from Indochina. This number jumped to over 9,000 people in 1978. Although most arrived via small boats, the *Huey Fong*, which arrived in December 1978, carried 3,318 passengers.[43] In 1979, 68,749 migrants arrived from Indochina.[44]

Even as the number of arrivals grew, the colonial government pursued a relatively liberal policy. Rather than screening the new arrivals for evidence of genuine refugeehood, the government assumed that all of the boat people were refugees and provided them with temporary accommodation until they could be resettled abroad. The government operated on the assumption that other countries should, and would, offer more permanent solutions.[45] By 1979, there were thirteen camps in Hong Kong, administered by various government departments and supported by the Hong Kong Civil Aid Society. Voluntary agencies, including the Red Cross, the International Rescue Committee, Caritas, and the YMCA, supported operations on the ground. The UNHCR was present, though too thinly staffed to offer substantial assistance.[46] In comparison, Caritas (a Catholic Relief organization) proved so efficient, it soon began operating the Kai Tak East Transit Centre on behalf of the government.[47] Until 1982, most of the camps were open. This meant that refugees could work in Hong Kong and send their children to local schools. This generous policy stood in stark contrast to the government's approach to migration from the People's Republic of China, where people found without proper documentation were summarily, and regularly, returned to the mainland.

Hong Kong's contradictory strategies with regard to arrivals from Vietnam and those from the mainland stemmed in part from American pressure on Hong Kong and other countries in Southeast Asia to provide temporary asylum for Indochinese refugees until a more permanent solution could be found. They also resulted from the fact that Hong Kong had no formal refugee policy, and so its response to arriving migrants was ad hoc, constructed in the immediacy of the moment but informed by decades of population controls at the border. As there was no legal category for refugees, colonial officials sought to reconcile the expectations of the international community, and the Western camp in particular, with their own interests in managing arrivals from Indochina.[48] This "mixture of pragmatism and moral restraint" led the Hong Kong government to focus on temporary asylum with the expectation that other countries would resettle the refugees permanently.[49] This did not occur.

Significantly, given its status as the last British colony, the government of Hong Kong received very little support from the imperial government in London. Between 1975 and 1993, Britain resettled only 13,000 Indochinese refugees from Hong Kong. In the same period, the government of Hong Kong spent an estimated $635 million (US dollars) on the care and maintenance of the refugees.[50] Prime Minister Margaret Thatcher viewed the boat people as a political problem, not a humanitarian one. Her immediate reaction to the growing numbers of refugees in 1979 was to seek a way to avoid responsibility. Persistent campaigning from the shipping lobby, which was reluctant to rescue people at sea if they were not able to deposit them in a country of first asylum, made the British government eager to find a solution to the crisis. Yet it proved deeply reluctant to assume any kind of responsibility for resettlement, much to the dismay of officials in the United States and Australia, who strategized about how they could convince Britain to resettle more refugees.[51] Instead of addressing such concerns, Prime Minister Thatcher dispatched staff to investigate the possibility of withdrawing from the 1951 Convention Relating to the Status of Refugees.[52] When such a withdrawal proved unworkable, Thatcher emphasized the need to "internationalize the situation." Such calls were critical in convening the first Geneva Conference on Indochinese refugees in 1979 and ensuring that Western obligations were limited ones.[53]

Sixty-five countries participated in the conference, which was held in July 1979. The atmosphere was hostile as countries of first asylum and those involved in resettlement efforts engaged in heated debates in the lead-up to the conference about the degree to which Vietnamese authorities should be held publicly responsible for the crisis. Australia was adamant that authorities in the Socialist Republic of Vietnam needed to be held accountable. Officials in Canberra believed that the Vietnamese government needed to curtail departures, otherwise, "as a large, under-populated 'white' country Australia would be especially vulnerable to international criticism if [it] failed to respond in a humane manner to the arrival of boat refugees from Asia on Australian territory."[54] Privately, officials referenced the potential for a "hostile public reaction", stimulated by traditional fears of the "yellow peril." In doing so, they made it clear that they were only prepared to do so much, arguing that the responsibility for the situation lay with the government of Vietnam.[55] American and British officials were sympathetic to this approach, believing that public criticism would embarrass the communist government and elevate the moral authority of the Western camp. The UNHCR, however, maintained that public condemnation would discourage Vietnamese authorities from even attending the conference in Geneva.

In the end, public criticism was muted, and participants simply noted that the Vietnamese government had a "responsibility" in managing
the crisis. Most importantly, in terms of substance, the conference established a system whereby Hong Kong and receiving countries in Southeast Asia would provide temporary asylum to people fleeing Indochina
with the understanding that resettlement countries would then facilitate
the relocation of people to their shores. The Orderly Departure Program,
which the UNHCR had negotiated with Vietnamese authorities in May
1979, was supported as a mechanism for easing the crisis despite reservations about the extent to which officials in Vietnam could be trusted
to cooperate with these arrangements. The Orderly Departure Program
was essentially a family reunification arrangement whereby people who
were sponsored by relatives abroad were given official permission to leave
by Vietnamese authorities. With official sanction, people did not have to
resort to dangerous escape routes.[56] In Geneva, countries of first asylum
agreed not to return boats to sea or deny admission to vulnerable migrants. Resettlement countries committed to accepting refugees in Indochina as well as from countries of first asylum.

As a result of the 1979 Geneva Conference, the lines of responsibility
were drawn between countries of first asylum and potential countries of
resettlement. White settler societies, with the exception of South Africa,
were marked as resettlement countries. The humanitarian largesse of the
United States resulted from pressing ideological and psychological reasons for investing in the resettlement of the refugees. Other white settler
societies committed to the resettlement process for reasons that were
much more aligned with nation-building settlement issues than geopo-
litical concerns. The scale of the crisis, the ensuing public pressure, their
signatures on the 1951 Convention, as well as their confidence in their
ability to carefully manage and control the resettlement program, contributed to their engagement.[57] The fear in Australia that refugee boats
might continue to arrive on its shores propelled the government to act.
So, too, did the need to respond to ongoing lobbying by promoters of
immigration reform.

In 1979, Kenneth Rivett, an outspoken advocate for immigration
reform in Australia and cofounder of the Immigration Reform Group
(which published the highly influential *Control or Color Bar?* in 1962 in
an effort to convince the government to formally terminate the White

Australia Policy) learned of the high percentage of boats that left Vietnam and never made it to shore. He observed,

> the whole situation reflects not just our greater involvement in Asia but also the demand, from outside and within Australia, that we assume responsibilities which an earlier generation would not have acknowledged.[58]

Rivett emphasized Australia's "special responsibilities" to the United States, its wartime ally, and suggested that Australia was in a superior position to assist refugees from Indochina, compared to other white settler societies. He explained, since Australians were "more accustomed than many 'white' nations to 'yellow' (actually light brown) skins and to Chinese-type features," they should do more.[59] Yet instead of an enlightened, color-blind response, the Australian government remained wary of the impact of significant Asian migration. Its response to the refugee flows out of Southeast Asia was first and foremost about ensuring that it could manage entries and that it could select people for admission based on an individual migrant's capacity for integration. In practice, this was a much more subjective exercise than the government might have hoped, as evidenced by the case of Van Thi-The Huynh and her family.

Worried about their future and those of their children, Van Thi-The Huynh and her husband (who worked for the Electric Authority in Saigon before 1975), paid a substantial sum to obtain a passage on a departing boat. To gain access to the boat, they also had to pretend to be members of the targeted ethnic Hao Chinese minority:

> at that time the government want to put the Chinese people away from Vietnam, so they have the scheme for the Chinese people to pay, and they close their eye for them to escape. And that . . . my husband knew that and he asked my cousin for him to, to pay for the . . . my family to join that . . . organize to escape from Vietnam. . . . Yes. We all had to pretend to be Chinese so we can join the Chinese family to escape. The government, I think they knew that, but they just didn't care and as long as they get more money, and if we escape they can . . . took our house and our . . . all of the things we left for them they very happy to do that.

They landed in Pilau Bidong, Malaysia, and were eventually resettled to Canberra in 1979. Van Thi-The Huynh and her family were able to buy their way out of Vietnam, but given that they had more resources available to them than others, they could easily have been accused of being economic migrants or "rice refugees." What worked in their favor was the threat of communist indoctrination:

> they train the children just think about the Communist Party, and the family to the child is nothing. And they sometimes try to train . . . the child become spy on [his] own family. And with the thing happen with the . . . every young man at that time and my husband were very worried if my son have to grow up in that situation. And not only for him difficult at his work, he have to work for somebody know nothing, and he thought if his son have to go in the same way if he doing in that time, and even if my son how clever my son is, he still can't get into university or doing any better for, for himself at all. So, that time my husband start to think about to escape from, . . . Vietnam, and that time it's a lot of people organize.[60]

The production of evidence that spoke to an authentic refugee experience was critical to gaining acceptance in Australia just as the use of categories to distinguish between authentic and inauthentic refugees was critical to the government of Australia's efforts to manage arrivals on its shores and shape the size and scope of its resettlement program.

The capacity for integration was often a key determinant in an applicant's bid for admission. The case of "PA," for instance, shows that she had few of the qualifications, including education, employability, and family connections that the government preferred. She was described by the assessing officer "as a single woman, Cantonese speaker" with no "relatives in Australia." The officer noted, "She seeks early resettlement. Has cousin in USA but cannot sponsor her. PA has 6 years education only but seems reasonably intelligent. She has some skills as a dressmaker and was a factory worker after [19]73. Well presented and seems reasonably intelligent. Pleasant woman who seems capable of settlement." The officer's conclusion was that she was "acceptable."[61] Migrants still had to prove their worthiness, as humanitarianism was only part of the

Australian government's selection strategy and it remained a very subjective component of the selection and admission process.[62]

The same was true of the government of New Zealand's approach, which relied on resettlement as a way of managing its humanitarian obligations. The idea behind the resettlement of selected individuals was that the government could retain control over who was admitted, and downplay any responsibility for refugees that arrived uninvited. In 1978, the government of New Zealand resettled 535 people using special airlifts from Vietnam. The migrants were assisted by the Inter-Church Commission on Immigration, commonly recognized as the "traditional agent for refugee resettlement," though they had not previously engaged significantly with the settlement of refugees from Asia.[63] Continued pressure, both domestically from church groups and internationally from allied nations, led the government to airlift another 600 people in 1979.

New Zealand shared the concerns of other white settler societies about migrant assimilation, and as a result, its resettlement process was highly selective. At first the government sought refugees with "professional or technical qualifications recognized in New Zealand" who were "readily employable in a job equal to or near equal to their present qualifications and experience and with English language skills."[64] However, as the situation evolved and the refugees became both more numerous and more desperate, the government "was forced to give up many immigration-type ideals of what a new settler should be, and adopt more realistic expectations of a new settler appropriate to refugee status."[65] At the international meetings in Geneva in July 1979, the government of New Zealand committed to resettling an additional 3,235 migrants.[66]

The Canadian government's commitments in Geneva were shaped by similar concerns about integration, though the country continued to benefit from its geographic remove from the crisis, enjoying the luxury of determining if and when to become involved. The government's sense of responsibility became amplified as the severity of the crisis deepened and images of the boat people, including those aboard the *Hai Hong*, exacted ever more empathy from the Canadian public. Over the course of 1978 and into 1979, immigration officials and elected politicians not only came to believe that something needed to be done, but that they had the capacity to make a difference. Sections of Irving Abella and Harold Troper's book, *None Is Too Many: Canada and the Jews of Europe 1933–1948*, circulated amongst immigration officials at the height of the crisis. The authors detailed in dramatic terms the failure of the Canadian state to come to the aid of Jewish refugees fleeing Nazi persecution. Minister Ron Atkey made the work required reading, and Jack Manion, the Deputy Minister, informed officials that nothing akin to the voyage of the *St. Louis* was to occur on his watch.[67]

In the lead-up to the Geneva Conference, the Canadian government created an Indochinese Designated Class, based on the provisions of the 1976 Immigration Act, to facilitate the resettlement of people who did not meet the strict definition of a Convention refugee. This initiative resulted from public pressure in the aftermath of the *Hai Hong* stalemate and concern about the ugly overtones detected in countries of first asylum.[68] On 31 January 1979, the Liberal government of Pierre Trudeau approved a plan to resettle 5,000 refugees to be selected according to Designated Class regulations. Pressure persisted from critics who charged that the government should be doing more. As in New Zealand, it was public pressure that encouraged elected officials to become more involved in the humanitarian efforts in Indochina.[69] Following the election of a Conservative government, Flora McDonald, freshly installed as secretary of state for external affairs, decided that being able to talk about a commitment "ten times" the original figure advanced by her party's political opponents was sufficiently dramatic.[70] As a result, just prior to the start of the Geneva Conference, the Conservative government announced that it would resettle 50,000 people in a private-government partnership called the Indochinese Refugee Program.[71] Under the 1976 Immigration Act, groups of five or more could organize themselves to privately sponsor refugees. Due to government sponsorships already in place, an outstanding quota of 21,000 slots was dedicated to private sponsorships.

The announcement of the quota, which was contingent on a matching program whereby the state would sponsor one refugee for every individual sponsored privately, was met with a mix of optimism and suspicion. Much of the negative sentiment came from the leadership of the Anglican and United Churches in Canada. They had been at the forefront of campaigns to assist refugees in Hong Kong in the 1950s and 1960s, but by the late 1970s, they mistrusted the government's intentions and suspected that their congregations were being asked to assume excessive responsibilities for the care and assistance of refugees.[72] This mistrust had built up over the preceding decade as the contest between public and private responsibility for the protection of refugees became more intense. Protestant churches were particularly disappointed with the Liberal government's response to the violent right-wing coup in Chile in 1973. They had lobbied intensely for the Canadian state to take action on behalf of refugees fleeing the Pinochet regime and were dismayed when swift action never came. While over 6,000 refugees were eventually admitted to Canada, the whole episode soured the relationship between the Protestant churches and the federal government. According to one official who surveyed the landscape following the introduction of the Indochinese Refugee Program:

> Certain elements of the Canadian Council of Churches, reflecting the views of certain national officials of the Anglican and United Churches, including those who continue to criticize the government for not doing more, have to date been decidedly lukewarm ... [this] reflects the strongly held view, on the part of a few influential officials at headquarters, that refugees from rightist regimes, e.g. Chile, are somehow more deserving than those from leftist regimes like Vietnam.[73]

Relations were so poor that by the time of the Indochinese refugee crisis, officials were differentiating between "good churches" that wanted to help and those they considered obstructionist.[74]

Senior officials in the Department of Manpower and Immigration, including Cal Best—the formidable assistant deputy minister—resented the combination of public pressure "to do something" about the boat people in Indochina and the lack of progress on sponsorship issues because of Protestant opposition.[75] There was a sense amongst officials that certain churches were willing to criticize the government but were not prepared to actively participate in the resettlement of refugees from Southeast Asia. Frustrated, Best instructed Gord Barnett—a senior bureaucrat and skilled negotiator—to test the churches and essentially pawn off as much responsibility as he could in order to "let them flounder."[76] The instruction coincided with an overture by the Mennonite Central Committee (MCC) to work with the government on the sponsorship issue. The MCC had been active in Vietnam since 1954 and had long been invested in the plight of the Vietnamese people.[77]

Gord Barnett began meeting with Bill Janzen of the MCC's Ottawa office in early 1979 and discovered a man, and a church, with a sincere and profound desire to help. Barnett returned to Assistant Deputy Minister Best and argued that burdening sponsoring organizations with too much responsibility would be wrong, given the sincerity with which the MCC was negotiating. Best relented, and the MCC became the first organization to sign a master agreement with the federal government on 5 March 1979. Under the terms of the agreement, the national organization guaranteed the sponsorship of smaller independent congregations. The master agreement alleviated the considerable paperwork and processing inefficiencies that would have resulted from individual congregations and sponsorship groups submitting separate applications to sponsor refugees to Canada.[78]

The Canadian government eventually signed over fifty master agreements to facilitate the sponsorship of Indochinese refugees. The majority of these were with religious organizations. The Christian Reformed Church, under the leadership of Reverend Arie van Eek, followed the MCC's lead, and Barnett recalls that the whole atmosphere around the undertaking was "joyous and positive."[79] The two churches had powerful memories of persecution and were attuned to what was unfolding in Indochina. Mennonites had fled the Soviet Union in the 1920s, and as Bill Janzen notes, "they had quite a feeling for the Communist threat."[80] The Christian Reformed Church had been active in attempting to save Jews during the Second World War. The Jewish Immigrant Aid Services of Canada also became involved in the resettlement of Indochinese refugees, for similar reasons. Other denominations required more persuasion, and Barnett used his personal connections with the Roman Catholic bishop in Pembroke, Ontario to encourage the participation of the Canadian Council of Catholic Bishops.

The participation of the "big churches" was important to the government, as it legitimized resettlement efforts. There were some misgivings that early sponsorships were being pursued by organizations with a more fundamentalist bent. This sentiment was compounded by the eager and active participation of World Vision, an Evangelical Christian humanitarian, in the camps in Southeast Asia. American Dr. Bob Pierce had established World Vision in 1953 to help children orphaned by the Korean War. There was concern that World Vision was pushing an aggressive religious agenda in the camps, and the Canadian government sought to moderate its influence on the resettlement process.[81] The Anglican and United Churches eventually signed master agreements, although the level of participation amongst their congregations was never as great as it was amongst the Mennonites and the Christian Reformed Church.

The largesse of the public-private resettlement program was the product of decades of work towards making Canada's immigration program more humanitarian. By the 1970s, the Canadian government had incorporated certain humanitarian principles and structures into its immigration program even if they were never as large or expansive as certain advocates might have desired. In managing the Indochinese Refugee Program, the Canadian government retained a sense of responsibility for the larger immigration and settlement programs in Canada. This sense of responsibility entailed selecting the candidates most in need of assistance who could successfully establish themselves.[82] Often, having relatives in Canada was the key determinant in the selection process, since officials believed that the presence of relatives helped with the acculturation process.[83] Officials believed that, otherwise, many would face "loneliness and isolation" if they were resettled without any family members.[84] Policymakers preferred to select people with relatives in Canada or to resettle entire family units.[85]

News about these preferences soon circulated amongst the camps in Hong Kong and Southeast Asia, and there were clearly some cases of fraudulent representations put forward by people hoping to be resettled as a family unit. Nevertheless, visa officers in the field were committed to the resettlement program, believing that they had the support of the government and the Canadian public.[86] When one man appeared with two wives, the responsible officer explained that he "should figure out which one was his wife and which one was his dead brother's wife before returning to complete the interview process."[87] Such discretion led to embarrassing discoveries later by church groups who sponsored families only to discover that some of them were comprised of several wives.[88] The Canadian government eventually adopted the use of family trees in Hong Kong, similar to those developed during the 1960–1974 Status Adjustment Program for Chinese migrants.[89] Family trees enabled officials to establish "true" relations amongst those in the camps.

Even as authorities pursued a largely humanitarian endeavor, their desire to manage and regulate the program remained. Significantly, the emphasis on regulating the program and the preference for families and refugees capable of integration meant that the most difficult cases were not necessarily addressed. Mennonite workers in Thailand told their colleagues in Ottawa that the lowland Laos were least in need of resettlement as they were middle-class, educated, and capable of making their own way out of the camps. Yet the MCC's final statistics revealed that 60 percent of those resettled were lowland Lao.[90] As a result of the so-called "seeding" of refugees, camps ended up being filled with people without relations or qualifications, leading to "delinquent" behavior that only exacerbated the strain of being in camps without any sense of a future.[91] One observer noted that the sense of "desperation grows and grows, as they see that refugees who have arrived in the camp after them are allowed to depart for a third country while they must remain."[92] Selection biases affected more than just the people chosen for resettlement; they had an immediate impact on all residents of the camps and on the capacity and willingness of territories of first asylum to provide assistance.

By October 1979, it appeared that the Canadian quota for 21,000 private sponsorships would soon be reached. The federal government faced a dilemma: there was obviously a great deal of interest among Canadians in being actively involved in the relief efforts, but an ongoing resettlement program would be costly and risked perpetuating movement out of Indochina.[93] According to the relevant Memorandum to Cabinet:

> Some groups are already sponsoring their second or even third family. While the refugee outflow continues at a much reduced level, sponsorship interest may well increase should the situation in Indochina produce a new surge of refugees requiring overseas resettlement.[94]

The danger, if sponsorship levels continued, was that the program would simply encourage more people to leave. To slow the process, Cabinet decided to allow the number of refugees sponsored privately to exceed the allotted figure of 21,000, while reducing the number of government-supported refugees proportionately to keep the intake figure for 1979–1980 at

50,000.[95] When the change in policy was announced at an infamous breakfast meeting on 6 December 1979, church groups and NGOs were, not surprisingly, dismayed.[96] Mike Molloy recalls that attendees received the announcement like a "slap in the face."[97] To cynics in the crowd, the government's reversal on the matching agreement confirmed allegations that the government had been intent on "off-loading" responsibilities all along.[98] Yet the reality was that the government was seeking to manage an outpouring of support for a crisis that it believed was abating. The government of Australia shared this assessment. One official alleged: the country's "humanitarian response is now being exploited in some ways which amount to back-door migration."[99] Sponsors in Canada did not share this impression, nor did officials in Hong Kong.

As the Canadian and Australian examples suggest, by the 1980s support for resettlement was dwindling amongst responsible authorities in white settler societies. As a result, Hong Kong faced a growing imbalance in resettlement figures.[100] Resettlement efforts had slowed, but people continued to arrive, making camp stays longer and longer and straining the public's tolerance of open-ended support to the refugees. Reports of Kai Tak North, which opened in 1979 under the auspices of the Red Cross with funding from the UNHCR, indicated "prevailing housing conditions make it extremely difficult to maintain a reasonable standard of sanitation and health." This situation was exacerbated by the fact that people often waited in the camp for two years or more leading to "tendencies of frustration and desperation."[101] As one resident explained, "the worst of living here" is "you never know a thing. You just hope to be told to go—but you never have any idea when that is going to happen."[102]

Adopting a policy of "humane deterrence," the government of Hong Kong established closed camps in July 1982. People were no longer permitted to work outside of the camps, and individuals who were found guilty of some kind of infraction could be sent to a closed camp as punishment. Comparisons to prisons were obvious and apt. Staff from OXFAM Hong Kong toured the camps and reported:

the overwhelming impression of all closed camps is that they are prisons. They are surrounded by tall fences and there are uniformed officers everywhere. Even moving within the camps involves an endless unlocking and locking of gates.[103]

The closed camps were intended to deter new migrants from seeking refuge in Hong Kong and to encourage "longstayers" to return to Vietnam. The closed camps were geographically remote, and humanitarians worried especially about the "effects of confinement on the individuals involved," particularly if they were detained for long periods of time.[104] The staff of various voluntary agencies and church representatives considered the closed camps inhumane and lacking in dignity. Representatives from OXFAM Hong Kong remarked:

the overriding impression of camp life is of people standing around doing nothing. Walk into a hut at any time of the day and you see people sitting on their beds doing nothing. There is a total lack of purpose to life.[105]

Staff found such scenes "very odd" in "purposeful Hong Kong."[106] Humanitarians attached considerable importance on productivity as a desirable end, and they believed that the closed camps were the equivalent of squandering lives. Voluntary agencies suggested local settlement as a preferred solution to the closed camps; however, the government of Hong Kong rejected this idea. Authorities believed such a policy would only encourage the movement of more people to the colony, an effect they were seeking to counter.

The closed camps proved to be a significant financial burden for the government of Hong Kong, which covered the cost of constructing new buildings, security perimeters, and hiring additional security staff. The camps were located on outlying islands, far away from Hong Kong's urban centers. With this novel strategy, the government "compartmentalized" the refugee problem.[107] The closed camp policy essentially scapegoated the refugees: "they were classified, labeled, and stigmatized; they became a category of their own, totally disposable and dispensable."[108] Still, the government appeared to be taking action, and its initiative met with approbation from the local populace. White settler societies were unhappy with the policy, however, since it seemed to contradict their own humanitarian efforts on behalf of Indochinese refugees and undermined American efforts in particular to demonize communist regimes in Asia.[109] Nevertheless, officials could say little without committing themselves to larger and more expansive resettlement programs. Given that population flows from Indochina lasted for almost two decades, they were disinclined to do so.

When another increase in population numbers in the colony was observed in the late 1980s, the government of Hong Kong's policies became even more restrictive. In the summer of 1987 alone, 7,000 people crossed over the border from the Chinese mainland. Many were ethnic Chinese from Vietnam who had moved into China during the border war in 1979 and had been living in Guanxi and Guangdong.[110] The same forces that had encouraged generations of South Chinese migrants to leave the mainland were compelling a new generation of migrants to seek political and economic refuge in Hong Kong. Chinese officials did little to dissuade people from Vietnam from leaving the mainland, and authorities in Hong Kong were frustrated by the lack of control on the Chinese side of the border. Residents of Hong Kong, who wrote letters to their relatives informing them that there were opportunities in the colony, aggravated the situation. Correspondents suggested that people could be resettled overseas to the United States and other countries. Migration from the mainland increased as a result.[111] The number of arrivals from Indochina also grew as the Orderly Departure Program in Vietnam slowed down and people sought other avenues of escape. Hong Kong authorities recorded a new influx of 5,000 people in the early months of 1988.[112] As a result, in June of the same year, the government introduced a screening process for newly arriving migrants. "Genuine refugees" were permitted to stay in the camps to be resettled. However, after 16 June, 1988, those found not to be refugees were to be repatriated. It was a unilateral decision and one that had profound implications for countries of resettlement seeking to preserve the humanitarian character of their efforts.

With its repatriation initiative, Hong Kong went from the most liberal site of first asylum to the most restrictive. It took the lead in adopting the long-debated and much-criticized refugee screening procedure and in promoting regional discussions about voluntary as well as forced repatriation.[113] Part of this impulse came from pressure from authorities in Beijing, who demanded that Hong Kong address the situation before 1997, when the colony was scheduled to revert to Chinese control.[114] More immediately, however, the change in Hong Kong's policies coincided with a shift in how the arriving migrants were perceived. There were growing suspicions that the people leaving Indochina were no longer "genuine refugees" but were instead economic migrants searching for opportunity. While such arguments had only minimal impact at the height of the crisis in 1979, the perception of fraud thickened as the urgency of the crisis abated. By the late 1980s, the conventional dichotomy of genuine / fraudulent refugee was being fully employed to remove any sense of obligation towards the migrant population. The colonial government claimed that only 10 percent of the migrants were "real refugees."[115] The logical corollary of this claim was that 90 percent of the arrivals were not and were therefore did not deserve accommodation in Hong Kong. Many white settler societies shared this impression. American officials, more ideologically and emotionally invested than their counterparts, remained committed to helping anyone who left Indochina, regardless of their formal refugee status. US authorities objected to forced repatriations to communist countries and maintained that the "principle of first asylum must continue to be the cornerstone of our, and others', approach to continuing refugee flows."[116]

British officials in Hong Kong and London disagreed, believing that different mechanisms, including screenings and repatriation, were required to stem the continued movement of people out of Indochina. They were supported in this stance by the Australian government, which also believed that the urgency of the crisis had abated.[117] Officials in Canberra were doubtful about the degree to which later arrivals were truly in need of protection. Canadian officials also supported the screening process, albeit reluctantly.[118] The Canadian government had its own doubts about the optics of the screening and repatriation option, but it also had deep reservations about the desirability of continuing the resettlement program in perpetuity. Canadian officials shared the impression that refugees out of Indochina were no longer "genuine." Furthermore, there was growing discomfort about the resettlement program being used as a family reunification program. The Canadian government had relied on the resettlement of family units and relatives to ensure the successful establishment of new arrivals. By the late 1980s, however, it believed the Indochinese Refugee Program was becoming "unsustainable."[119] Freshly arrived refugees in Canada were petitioning their sponsorship groups to assist relatives who were still in the camps. Officials believed this practice undermined the original intent of the Indochinese Refugee Program. The Family Class and Assisted Relatives categories, outlined in the Immigration Act, existed for the purpose of family reunification. The Designated Classes were for people in need of humanitarian assistance.[120] By 1989, the diminishing refugee character of the migrant population and pressure from newly arrived Indochinese refugees, which was turning the resettlement program into a family reunification program, convinced the Canadian state that screening and repatriation were necessary to prevent the refugee flow from continuing in perpetuity.

The Comprehensive Plan of Action (CPA), which was developed at the second Geneva conference in 1989, represented an attempt at compromising between conceptions of genuine and fraudulent refugees. It established the mechanisms for a region-wide refugee determination process based on the 1951 Convention definition of a refugee. People found to be non-refugees were to be repatriated. At the same time, the CPA sought to encourage the use of the Orderly Departure Program in Vietnam and to improve conditions in Indochina so as to discourage future migration. As a result of insistence by officials in the United States, screenings only began in 1990 (except in Hong Kong, where the mechanisms were already in place). The Canadian government committed to the CPA in the hopes that involuntary repatriations could be avoided and that more emphasis would be given to the ongoing Orderly Departure Program. The solution to the suffering caused by dangerous escapes seemed to lie with managing the way people were leaving Vietnam. Encouraging people to stay in Indochina likewise meant that resettlement countries would not face as many demands for assistance.[121]

As a result of the CPA, Canada amended its Designated Class regulations. People from Vietnam and Laos were no longer eligible for sponsorship under this category. Only Cambodians remained as a scheduled class given the ongoing political turmoil in the country.[122] This had an immediate impact on the sponsorship program. People screened before the cutoff date were still eligible to be sponsored. However, sponsorship groups were told they should not try to help people who had not yet been screened. Officials in the field also requested that sponsors be told about the challenges they faced in accessing populations in an effort to diminish sponsorship pressures more generally. The embassy in Bangkok explained:

Access to persons in refugee camps is controlled by the host government. Under the CPA an individual who is determined not to be a refugee in the screening process, or who has not yet been screened, is not eligible for third country resettlement. Even when such an individual has close family links with persons in Canada our visa officers have no access.[123]

With the CPA, screening and voluntary repatriation, along with local settlement, became the priority solutions. Resettlement and forced repatriation were secondary options. In light of this approach, the MCC ceased its efforts to resettle refugees from Southeast Asia in March 1990. In a press release, the MCC observed that given the changing patterns of migration, it saw the ongoing resettlement of Vietnamese abroad as unwittingly enabling the "the U.S. government to continue its war against Vietnam . . . by luring people out of the country." The MCC believed that most of the people leaving Indochina were now economic migrants and declared that it would cease its resettlement efforts out of concern for people who were "dying in their attempts to flee in small boats" and others who survived but then faced "years of awful conditions in camps."[124] The MCC in Canada had facilitated the resettlement of 5,000 people since 1979, and their efforts were highly regarded by the country's officials who described them as "one of the most serious and effective groups in the resettlement of refugees in Canada."[125] The MCC's announcement was therefore a powerful statement about the manner in which the organization had come to see its responsibilities and obligations towards the Indochinese refugees. By the time the CPA was negotiated in Geneva, the MCC no longer believed that it was improving the plight of the refugees. Rather, it felt complicit in a program that was no longer effectively humanitarian in practice. As Bill Janzen of the MCC recalls, "humanitarian efforts to do good are often more complicated than they appear."[126] It is an important and telling reflection, at once applicable to the ordinary citizens, humanitarians, and government officials in countries of first asylum and those in resettlement countries who responded to the millions of people who left Vietnam, Cambodia, and Laos after 1975.

The size of the movement that emerged in Indochina after the American War and the intensity with which the media documented the plight of the "boat people" meant there was unprecedented global awareness of refugees in Asia. The outpouring of support was at once a departure from previous practices and an evolution in long-standing approaches to the issue of refugees in Asia. On no other occasion did white settler societies respond so convincingly to the plight of refugees in the region. The crisis was unique in terms of the size and scale of the response. The British colony of Hong Kong, as well as the countries of Indonesia, Malaysia, and Thailand, enjoyed unprecedented success in engaging white settler societies on the continued movement of people out of Indochina. Yet some historical antecedents endured, most obviously in the persistent effort to distinguish between "genuine refugees" and seemingly less deserving migrants. Historical connections were also pivotal.

Hong Kong was a critical node between countries of resettlement, such as the United States, Canada, Australia, and New Zealand, and countries of first asylum in Southeast Asia. Authorities in Hong Kong were able to pursue questionable practices such as closed camps, screening, and the repatriation of migrants because to international observers, their practices were inherently liberal and were simply an extraordinary response to extraordinary circumstances. The colony therefore played a crucial role in shaping the global response to refugees from Indochina. As a result of the government of Hong Kong's initiative, a region-wide screening and repatriation mechanism was in place after 1989, monitored by the UNHCR. Rather than sheltering white settler societies from the movement of refugees, the government of Hong Kong's actions forced potential countries of resettlement to confront protection issues more directly.

The dynamics of the Indochinese movement, most notably the number of people involved and the attendant media coverage, meant that white settler societies were confronted with the issue of refugees from Asia in a manner analogous only to the events in Hong Kong in 1962. The apparent largesse of their response belies the extent to which white settler societies remained highly selective in their approach. Australia and New Zealand's geographic proximity to the epicenter of the crisis informed their desire to manage the resettlement program rather than have boats of migrants arrive uninvited. As in Canada, the governments of both countries selected refugees based on family ties and the capacity for individual migrants to successfully establish themselves.[127] As the people out of Indochina increasingly assumed the characteristics of economic migrants or family class migrants, Canadian, Australian, and New Zealand officials worried about operating a resettlement program in perpetuity. By 1989, they were willing to concede on the issue of involuntary repatriation. American officials were not. The United States was unique in terms of the depth of responsibility it felt for the crisis. Determined negotiations were required to convince American authorities to accept repatriation for non-refugees as a possible solution.

The approval of a screening mechanism at the second Geneva Conference served to limit the scope of responsibility to "real refugees." Those whom states believed were taking advantage of an opening in an otherwise restrictive global immigration regime were excluded from resettlement programs. The new screening and repatriation mechanisms, adopted in all the territories of first asylum, effectively limited the number of people eligible for resettlement. It was a policy reminiscent of earlier strategies that directed migrants to clearly defined categories of migration. Those that fell outside of these categories became illegal and unwanted. Even in the case of the celebrated Indochinese resettlement efforts, migration categories worked to restrict rather than facilitate migration. There was refuge for many, but for many others it remained elusive.

EPILOGUE

JIM CHU is best known as the first Chinese Canadian to be appointed chief of police in a major Canadian city. A 36-year veteran of the Vancouver Police Department, Jim became chief of police in 2007 and retired from the post in 2015. During his time as chief, he was a prominent figure in the city's social and political landscape: addressing concerns about violence in the Downtown Eastside neighborhood, taking responsibility for the police department's failure to fully investigate the abduction and murder of Indigenous women, managing security around the 2010 Winter Olympics, and then handling riots that tore through city's downtown during the spring hockey playoff season a year later.

I first contacted Jim in the spring of 2012 after he spoke at Pier 21, the Canadian Museum of Immigration. I was looking for people to interview for my research, and from what I gathered, Jim's family had come to Canada in the early 1960s. I suspected the Chus might be one of the families resettled to Canada in 1962. Jim promptly responded to my e-mail, but indicated that while his family had moved from Shanghai to Hong Kong and then to Canada, he was not a refugee. Generously, he offered to describe his family's story, which is featured in Chapter 5. What followed was quite remarkable.

During the Second World War, Jim's father, Ton-Son Chu, worked as a translator for the American military in China. After the war, he returned to his small business, but life under the communist regime was difficult. Soon, Ton-Son began to organize for his family's departure. Due to exit controls introduced by the Chinese Communist authorities, it was difficult for the family to leave the mainland. After numerous applications, he was finally given permission to depart for Hong Kong. Ton-Son then applied for admission to the United States, but his application was refused. As Jim tells it, his father then looked to Canada and was accepted. Jim and his family arrived in Calgary in December 1962.

Neither Jim nor his sister Joanne, who is presently a school principal in Vancouver, ever had any sense that they were refugees. But by piecing the bits of the archival puzzle together, I realized that, in fact, their family was part of the first group of Chinese refugees ever resettled to Canada. Using his parents' names, we were able to identify the Chu's immigration case file at Library and Archives Canada. It is one of only twenty-five surviving case files from the group of over one hundred families and individuals who came to Canada in 1962.

When we first discovered his family's history, I asked Jim if I could tell his family's story publicly. Their arrival in Canada, it seemed to me, was terribly important for shedding light on the workings of the refugee resettlement process and for dispelling some of the myths surrounding the idea of a "genuine refugee." Jim refused my request. He was worried about the public reaction if it was known that he was a refugee. Jim was proud but cautious about his status as the first Chinese Canadian chief of police for a major urban center in Canada. His detractors referred to him as the "Chief of the Chinese," and he didn't want to be further stigmatized. Once Jim obtained copies of his family's immigration case file, however, his outlook changed completely. As a result of the Canadian government's careful monitoring of all the refugee families, Jim and his sister Joanne were able to glean information from the file that had previously been unavailable to them. Jim explained:

The files contained newspaper stories and field reports that allowed me and my older sister Joanne to connect to events we vaguely recalled from our early childhood. It also confirmed some things that my parents did not talk about much. Such as why (my father's) typewriter repair shop in Calgary didn't succeed and why we moved to Peterborough. One immigration officer memo called it a "freeze out" by his former employer. This official's speech at the ribbon cutting of my father's business was a heart-warming read.[1]

It was after reading the file that Jim, in accord with his sister Joanne, agreed to talk about his family's history publicly. He felt his family's story could be an "inspiration" to refugees in Vancouver who might be struggling with their new lives in Canada. Joanne agreed.[2]

I was astonished at the complicated ways in which the notion of being a refugee family resonated with Jim and Joanne, particularly with Jim. Here was an obviously accomplished community leader who was wary of being associated with the term refugee because of potential political blowback. How was it that the refugee label carried such stigma?

It seems fitting to close this book on how Chinese migrants were alternatively assisted, marginalized, excluded, and welcomed as refugees by white settler societies during the Cold War with a reflection on the stigma associated with refugees more generally. A number of scholars have explored how refugees have historically been seen as threatening outsiders and how governments have exploited their marginalized status to reify the bonds between citizens and states. But the stigma that refugees confronted, and continue to encounter, runs deeper than their political relationships with citizens and states.[3]

Historian Peter Gatrell suggests that refugees, more than other migrants, "confront the weight of history" in their movements.[4] They follow in the footsteps of previous generations of displaced persons, for instance, who met with anxious concern about their capacity to integrate, rehabilitate, prosper, and even thrive.[5] This has negatively affected the inclination of many migrants to be thought of as refugees. Raph Girard, formerly of Canada's Department of Manpower and Immigration, recalls that in 1970s Geneva, he couldn't convince Jewish migrants from Russia to participate in the Canadian government's Self-Exile program for people who did not quite meet the Convention definition of a refugee. They thought the term refugee was perjorative and, as a result, "they wouldn't play the game."[6]

During the Cold War, migrants from Asia had to overcome the obstacles imposed by white settler society mentalities that treated them as outsiders and threats. There was such a strong onus on territorial and political belonging, cross-border migration was treated as an extraordinary rather than regular state of affairs. Observers did not think of the world as one of perpetual human motion, where the bonds of loyalty and citizenship were constantly being negotiated and renegotiated. As a result, refugees were treated as a problem.

In documenting the refugee situation in Hong Kong in 1954, Edward Hambro described "a problem of people." This term became a constant refrain in discussions about what to do with, and for, people in Hong Kong. The "problem" of the boat people also established the parameters in which assistance was provided to migrants leaving Indochina in the late 1970s. The perpetual notion of refugees as a problem highlights the discrimination that continues to structure contemporary discussions about population displacement and humanitarian assistance.

Refugees and migrants not only confronted extraordinary measures to regulate and control their movements, they also had to prove that they were not a problem. They did so by testifying to their gratitude at being assisted, their love of their new countries, and by a commitment to civic participation that was unmatched by the native-born.[7] The records of ARCI, for instance, are replete with testimonials from individuals the organization resettled to the United States. Recipients speak of "coming out of the darkness" and how they were "most grateful for the help given."[8] Despite these efforts, Jim Chu's reservations about being described as a refugee demonstrate how the term continues to be negatively construed.

Today's refugees—most recently the millions of people leaving Syria—are stigmatized even as they are held to high expectations about who is a refugee and what constitutes a legitimate refugee experience. As with earlier generations, in order to be assisted or protected, they must convince decision-makers that they are "genuine refugees." They must demonstrate gratitude, conform to social norms, and ultimately be—not only good citizens—but exemplary citizens. For some, these societal pressures dovetail with their own personal ambitions. But for others, the burden of such expectations can be suffocating and oppressive, especially for those whose communities have been historically marginalized.

Humanitarians who advocated on behalf of refugees in Asia started from a greater deficit than those who worked on behalf of refugees and displaced people in Europe. The refugees they presented for consideration to white settler societies needed to be extraordinary so that charges of alienness and doubts about the capacity for assimilation and integration could be rebuffed. In the very act of raising awareness and support for refugees in Asia, humanitarians widened the gulf between benefactor and recipient, between the "saved" and the "saviors." It is a gulf that remains unbridged and one that may, in fact, be widening as people in motion must now meet exaggerated standards of need and deprivation to be assisted.

In April 2013, when I interviewed Tony Enns, who worked energetically with the Mennonite Central Committee on sponsoring refugees from Indochina in the late 1970s, he paused during our conversation and said, "I want to tell you that I am depressed."[9] He had been watching the news about the humanitarian crisis in Syria. At the time, four million people had already left their homes as a result of the devastating civil war. As world leaders debated how to deal with the regime of Bashar al-Assad and its use of chemical weapons on its own people, the UNHCR and other humanitarians worked to draw attention to the people who were moving in large numbers to Lebanon, Jordan, Iraq, Turkey, Egypt, and Europe. Like the countries of first asylum that received the boat people out of Indochina in the late 1970s, Syria's neighbors were doing the lion's share on behalf of refugees while traditional countries of resettlement, cloaked in new conceptions of whiteness, looked on. In the post-9/11 world, the fear and discrimination that once attended refugees from Asia enveloped migrants from the Middle East.

The humanitarian agenda that evolved from the experience of distinct groups of refugees after the Second World War is more fragile than ever. Unrealistic notions about refugeehood and the insistence on a genuine refugee experience have confused expectations about the character of government relief, the nature of cross-border movement in the modern world, and the extent to which the identity of contemporary white settler societies can truly be called humanitarian. People have consumed the idea of being humanitarian nations with abandon, and it has fueled contemporary relief efforts, but it remains a distorted mythologizing of the past. Rather than saying, "We should assist people because we are humanitarian nations," it would be more accurate if the publics and governments of white settler societies declared, "We have never been as humanitarian as we could be, let us work on that now."

Part of that work involves seeing beyond labels. The term *refugee*, and even that of *migrant*, disguise the humanity of people in motion, precisely because for most of the twentieth century, governments used migration categories to restrict movement and disguise the multi-faceted lives of individuals in motion even as their admission policies became seemingly more liberal and progressive. Even when people were actively recruited and selected for admission, there was underlying anxiety about their capacity to integrate and lead rich, productive lives. The mythology of being a "nation of immigrants," which has animated national identity claims in the United States, Canada, Australia, and New Zealand, disguises how much has been asked of arriving migrants. Moreover, this mythology also disguises the histories of slavery, Indigenous displacement, and settler colonialism that are essential, and ugly, dimensions of aspirational humanitarian national identities.[10]

Over the course of writing of this book, I regularly despaired of humanity's capacity for compassion, kindness, and generosity. Too often, I was discouraged by the treatment of people as a "problem" and by the cynical and self-serving way in which the humanitarian agenda of the late twentieth century was instrumentalized for political purposes that had little to do with the migrants in question. Yet I retain hope for a more compassionate world. This hope springs from the encounters I witnessed between people and history, as in the case of Jim and Joanne Chu, and the surprising empathy between groups that scholars have previously positioned in conflictual, exploitative relationships.

In 2005, Bonita Lawrence and Enakshi Dua penned a piece titled "Decolonizing antiracism."[11] In it, they charged that migrants and refugees perpetuate settler colonialism through their failure to acknowledge the history of forced Indigenous displacement and by their presence on unceded lands. Though I was sympathetic to their arguments, I believed Lawrence and Dua failed to fully account for how the very notion of a settler was based on privileged notions of race and class. I was intrigued therefore when I attended a workshop that included a session dedicated to connecting the experiences of Indigenous peoples and newcomers. It deliberately brought together the two groups that Lawrence and Dua had painted as diametrically opposed.

In a meeting room, a circle of thirty chairs was arranged. We were a rather earnest group and we all sat rather nervously, I thought, unaccustomed to this kind of set-up. One of the Elders who was hosting the workshop, perhaps detecting some of our uneasiness, opened by saying, "a sharing circle is a concept. It doesn't literally mean you have to be in a circle." This brought some chuckles and a collective release. What followed was more intense: a discussion of Indigenous displacement, residential schools, the loss of language, the disruption of traditional ways of life, the strain on relations with family and friends, and through it all, an attempt to be recognized as human beings, to be treated with dignity. The workshop participants, many of whom were first-generation refugees—some young, and some more elderly—were clearly moved.

There was then an open discussion about flight, home, and loss of language, and most powerfully, an identification with the history of Indigenous displacement and the oppression of Indigenous identities and ways of life. One gentleman began by saying, "Thank you for sharing your stories." He then proceeded to recount how as a member of the Kurdish minority in Turkey, his family had lost their property and he had been forced to attend government schools where he had been prevented from speaking his own language. He didn't say, "my experience is your experience," but in his sharing he recognized and validated what so many citizens of white settler societies have denied about the history of settler colonialism.

Some of the more youthful members of the workshop talked about how they didn't know about Indigenous peoples before being resettled to Canada. Information about Indigenous histories and their contemporary experiences was not included in the government materials distributed to refugee camps in Africa and elsewhere. It seemed to me that this too validated what the Elders had been saying in terms of communicating knowledge, history and life experiences. In the sharing of stories, the Elders and the workshop participants moved beyond typifications and met as human beings, discarding labels and identities that so often obscure rather than reveal the humanity at the heart of any experience, regardless of how it is categorized. It is this kind of openness and generosity that makes possible a world where refuge won't be so elusive and people will not be punished, stigmatized, or unduly celebrated for overcoming barriers to mobility.

NOTES

BIBLIOGRAPHY

ACKNOWLEDGMENTS

INDEX

NOTES

INTRODUCTION

1. *Refugee Problem in Hong Kong.* United States. Congress. House of Representatives. Report of a Special Subcommittee of the Committee on the Judiciary. Washington: U.S.G.P.O., 1962.
2. See discussion in Special Movement of Chinese Refugees from Hong Kong – Operational Control, RG 76, File 555-54-526-3, Part 1, Vol. 861, Library and Archives Canada (LAC).
3. Ronald O. Hall, *Hong Kong: What of the Church?* (London: Edinburgh House Press, 1952), 9. On Hong Kong's position as the last of the British Empire's colonies, see Robert Edward Mitchell, *Velvet Colonialism's Legacy to Hong Kong, 1967 and 1997* (Hong Kong: Hong Kong Institute of Asia-Pacific Studies, 1998); John Darwin, "Hong Kong in British Decolonisation," in *Hong Kong's Transitions 1842–1997,* ed. Judith Brown and Rosemary Foot (New York, NY: St. Martin's Press, 1997).
4. *Oxford English Dictionary*, 3rd ed.. For an overview of the evolving legal definitions for refugees, see Susan Kneebone, ed., *Refugees, Asylum Seekers, and the Rule of Law: Comparative Perspectives* (Cambridge: Cambridge University Press, 2009).
5. See Paul Tabori, *The Anatomy of Exile: A Semantic and Historical Study* (London: George G. Harrap, 1972).
6. Gunther Beyer, "The Political Refugee: 35 Years Later," *International Migration Review* 15, no. 1/2 (Spring–Summer 1981): 26–34.

7. The actual number of people who moved to Taiwan after the war is in dispute. For a discussion of the inflated estimates, see Joshua Fan, *China's Homeless Generation: Voices from the Veterans of the Chinese Civil War, 1940s–1990s* (London: Routledge, 2012). See also Meng-Hsuan Yang, "The Great Exodus: Chinese Mainlanders in Taiwan" (Paper Prepared for the Canadian Asian Studies Association Conference, Waterloo, 13–16 November 2008).

8. Wen-Chin Chang, "From War Refugees to Immigrants: The Case of the KMT Yunnanese Chinese in Northern Thailand," *International Migration Review* 35, no. 4 (Winter 2001): 1088.

9. Richard Hughes, "Hong Kong: An Urban Study," *The Geographical Journal* 117, no. 1 (1951): 1–23.

10. Ronald Skeldon, "Migration from China," *Journal of International Affairs* 49, no. 2 (1996): 43–65.

11. See contributions including Kit-ching Lau Chan, "Hong Kong in Sino-British Diplomacy, 1926–45," in *Precarious Balance: Hong Kong between China and Britain, 1842–1992,* ed. Ming K. Chan (London: M. E. Sharpe, 1994), 71–90. See also Chi-Kwan Mark, *Hong Kong and the Cold War: Anglo-American Relations 1949–1957* (Oxford, UK: Oxford University Press, 2004).

12. See Ming K. Chan, ed., *Precarious Balance: Hong Kong between China and Britain, 1842–1992,* with collaboration from John Young (Armonk, NY: M. E. Sharpe, 1994).

13. On the historic work by religious groups with migrant populations, see Roberto Perin, "Churches and Immigrant Integration in Toronto, 1947–65," in *The Churches and Social Order in Nineteenth- and Twentieth-Century Canada,* ed. Michael Gauvreau and Olivier Hubert (Montreal: McGill-Queen's University Press, 2006), 274–291; National Catholic Welfare Conference Administrative Board in the Name of the Bishops of the United States, *People on the Move: A Compendium of Church Documents on the Pastoral Concern for Migrants and Refugees* (Bishops' Committee on Priestly Formation: Bishops' Committee on Migration, National Conference of Catholic Bishops, 1988); Kathleen Ptolemy, "Ministering to the Uprooted," in *Hope in the Desert: The Churches' United Response to Human Need, 1944–1984,* ed. Kenneth Slack (Geneva: World Council of Churches, 1986), 107–118; Australian Council of Churches, *Strangers in Our Midst: Guidelines and Suggestions for Helping Refugees* (Migration and Ethnic Affairs: A Review of the Work of the Australian Council of Churches. Sydney: Australian Council of Churches, 1979).

14. On missionary and NGO advocacy work generally, see Ruth Brouwer, "When Missions Became Development: Ironies of 'NGO-ization' in Mainstream Canadian Churches in the 1960s," *Canadian Historical Review*

91, no. 4 (2010): 661–693. doi: 10.1353/can.2010.0027; Andrew S. Thompson, *In Defence of Principles: NGOs and Human Rights in Canada* (Vancouver: UBC Press, 2010); Rachel M. McCleary, *Global Compassion: Private Voluntary Organizations and U.S. Foreign Policy since 1939* (Oxford, UK: Oxford University Press, 2009); Andrew S. Thompson and Stephanie Bangarth, "Transnational Christian Charity: The Canadian Council of Churches, the World Council of Churches, and the Hungarian Refugee Crisis, 1956–1957," *American Review of Canadian Studies* 38, no. 3 (2008): 295–316; Alvyn Austin, *China's Millions: The China Inland Mission and Late Qing Society, 1832–1905* (Grand Rapids, MI: William B. Eerdmans, 2007); Nicholas Reid, "Struggle for Souls: Catholicism and Communism in Twentieth Century New Zealand," *Australian Historical Studies* 128 (2006): 72–88; Rosemary Gagan, *A Sensitive Independence: Canadian Methodist Missionaries in Canada and the Orient, 1881–1925* (Montreal: McGill-Queen's University Press, 1992); Bonnie Greene, ed., *Canadian Churches and Foreign Policy* (Toronto: Lorimer, 1990); Alvyn Austin and Jamie S. Scott, *Canadian Missionaries, Indigenous Peoples: Representing Religion at Home and Abroad* (Toronto: University of Toronto Press, 2005); Robert Wright, *A World Mission: Canadian Protestantism and the Quest for a New International Order, 1918–1939* (Montreal: McGill-Queen's University Press, 1991); Alvyn Austin, *Saving China: Canadian Missionaries in the Middle Kingdom, 1888–1959* (Toronto: University of Toronto Press, 1986); Peter Ward, "The Oriental Immigrant and Canada's Protestant Clergy," *BC Studies* 22 (Summer 1974): 40–55.

15. For instance, many workers use temporary migration opportunities to establish more permanent residence. Stephen Castles, "Guestworkers in Europe: A Resurrection?" *International Migration Review* 40, no. 4 (December 2006): 741–766.

16. On the refugeeing process, see Nezvat Soguk, *States and Strangers: Refugees and Displacement of Statecraft* (Minneapolis: University of Minnesota Press, 1999).

17. See, for instance, Myron Weiner, "Bad Neighbors, Bad Neighborhoods: An Inquiry into the Causes of Refugee Flows," *International Security* 21, no. 1 (1996): 5–42; Aristide Zolberg, Astri Suhrke, and Sergio Aguayo, "International Factors in the Formation of Refugee Movements," *International Migration Review* 20, no. 2 (1986): 151–169; E. F. Kunz, "The Refugee in Flight: Kinetic Models and Forms of Displacement," *International Migration Review* 7, no. 2 (Summer 1973): 125–146.

18. Roger Zetter, "Labelling Refugees: Forming and Transforming a Bureaucratic Identity," *Journal of Refugee Studies* 4, no. 1 (1991): 39–62 and "More Labels, Fewer Refugees: Remaking the Refugee Label in an Era of Globalization," *Journal of Refugee Studies* 20, no. 2 (2007). See also Oliver Bakewell, "Research beyond the Categories: The Importance of Policy

Irrelevant Research into Forced Migration," *Journal of Refugee Studies* 21, no. 4 (2008): 432–453. The language around migration has also shifted as scholars have advocated a move away from *immigrant* and *emigrant* to *migrant*, as a way of capturing the continuous movement of people and re-thinking the national narratives that characterized studies of migration for most of the twentieth century. Nina Glick Schiller, Linda Basch, and Cristina Szanton Blanc, "From Immigrant to Transmigrant: Theorizing Transnational Migration," *Anthropological Quarterly* 68, no. 1 (January 1995): 48–63.

19. In the fall of 2015, the news network Al Jazeera announced that it would no longer use the term *migrant* to describe people making the danger-ous journey from Syria, Lebanon, and Jordan across the Mediterranean to Europe, http://www.aljazeera.com/blogs/editors-blog/2015/08/al-jazeera-mediterranean-migrants-150820082226309.html. The network argued that the term provided ammunition to those who were casting doubts on the humanitarian needs of the migrants. Al Jazeera's decision sparked considerable debate. See http://www.lapresse.ca/debats/chro-niques/agnes-gruda/201509/02/01-4897263-parlons-de-refugies.php; http://www.bbc.com/news/magazine-34061097; and http://www.unhcr.org/55df0e556.html.

20. Andrew Shacknove, "Who Is a Refugee?" *Ethics* 85, no. 2 (1985): 275. On borders and the filtering of migrants, see Alison Bashford, "At the Bor-der: Contagion, Immigration, Nation," *Australian Historical Studies* 33, no. 120 (2002): 344–358.

212. Daniel Cohen argues that the question of displaced persons was deeply influential in hardening the lines of the global Cold War. See *In War's Wake: Europe's Displaced Persons in the Postwar Order* (Oxford, UK: Oxford University Press, 2011). On the contested history of refugee resettle-ment, see Christopher Lee, "Humanitarian Assistance as Containment: New Codes for a New Order" (Working Paper No. 72, Oxford, UK, Ref-ugee Studies Centre, 2010), http://www.rsc.ox.ac.uk/publications/work-ing-papers-folder_contents/RSCworkingpaper72.pdf; Shauna Labman, "Invisibles: An Examination of Refugee Resettlement" (MLaw Thesis, University of British Columbia, 2007); Stephanie Nawyn, "Making a Place to Call Home: Refugee Resettlement Organizations, Religion, and the State" (PhD Diss., University of Southern California, 2006); T. Al-exander Aleinikoff "State-Centred Refugee Law: From Resettlement to Containment," in *Mistrusting Refugees,* ed. E. Valentine Daniel and John Chr. Knudsen (Berkeley: University of California Press, 1995), 257–278; Anthony Richmond, *Global Apartheid: Refugees, Racism, and the New World Order* (Toronto: Oxford University Press, 1994).

22. Cohen, *In War's Wake*, 5.

23. On the relationship between migration and the labor market, see Nandita Sharma, *Home Economics: Nationalism and the Making of 'Migrant Workers' in Canada* (Toronto: University of Toronto Press, 2006); Ravi Pendakur, *Immigrants and the Labour Force: Policy, Regulation, and Impact* (Montreal: McGill-Queen's University Press, 2001). On refugees and labor markets, see Gerald Dirks, *Canada's Refugee Policy: Indifference or Opportunism?* (Montreal: McGill-Queen's University Press, 1977).

24. Louise Holborn, *The International Refugee Organization, A Specialized Agency of the United Nations: Its History and Work, 1946–1952* (New York, NY: Oxford University Press, 1956), 366. For a discussion of the IRO's operations, see Dennis Gallagher, "The Evolution of the International Refugee System," *International Migration Review* 23, no. 3 (Autumn 1989): 579–598.

25. Cohen, *In War's Wake*, 11.

26. Historian Susan Carruthers notes that alongside the public celebration of defectors and refugees, there were concerns about the desirability of refugee subjects as potential citizens, largely in terms of their capacity to conform to American ideals of the model citizen. See *Cold War Captives: Imprisonment, Escape, and Brainwashing* (Berkeley: University of California Press, 2009).

27. B. S. Chimni has been a leading critic of the Eurocentric focus of the 1951 Convention as well as the field of refugee studies. See "From Resettlement to Involuntary Repatriation: Towards a Critical History of Durable Solutions to Refugee Problems," *Refugee Survey Quarterly* 23, no. 3 (2004): 55–73; "Globalisation, Humanitarianism, and the Erosion of Refugee Protection," *Journal of Refugee Studies* 13, no. 3 (2000): 243–263; "The Geopolitics of Refugee Studies: A View from the South," *Journal of Refugee Studies* 11, no. 4 (1998): 350–375.

28. Peter Gatrell, *The Making of the Modern Refugee* (Cambridge: Cambridge University Press, 2013), 138. See also Stephen MacKinnon, *Wuhan, 1938: War, Refugees, and the Making of Modern China* (Berkeley: University of California Press, 2008).

29. See Zheng Yangwen, Hong Liu, and Michael Szonyi, eds, *The Cold War in Asia: The Battle for Hearts and Minds* (Leiden: Brill, 2010); Tuong Wu and Wasana Wongsurawat, eds., *Dynamics of the Cold War in Asia: Ideology, Identity and Culture* (New York: Palgrave Macmillan, 2009); Akira Iriye, *The Cold War in Asia: A Historical Introduction* (Englewood Cliffs, NJ: Prentice-Hall, 1974).

30. On perceptions of the People's Republic of China, see Christina Klein, *Cold War Orientalism: Asia in the Middlebrow Imagination, 1945–1961* (Berkeley: University of California Press, 2003).

31. The Ming Dynasty (1368–1644) encouraged a continental focus so much of the early migration was internal. Sunil S. Amrith, *Crossing the Bay of Bengal: The Furies of Nature and the Fortunes of Migrants* (Cambridge, MA: Harvard University Press, 2013), 18.

32. Robin Cohen, ed., *Cambridge Survey of World Migration* (Cambridge: Cambridge University Press, 1995), 47.

33. Ibid., 45. Other estimates place the number of migrants from 1876 to 1907 as high as 6.75 million. Dirk Hoerder, *Cultures in Contact: World Migrations in the Second Millienium.* (Durham, NC: Duke University Press 2002), 366.

34. Ibid., 377. For a full discussion, see Adam McKeown, *Chinese Migrant Networks and Cultural Change: Peru, Chicago, Hawaii, 1900–1936* (Chicago: University of Chicago Press, 2001).

35. On the history of sojourning, see Wang Gungwu, *Don't Leave Home: Migration and the Chinese* (Singapore: Eastern Universities Press, 2001); Wang Gungwu, *The Chinese Overseas: From Earthbound China to the Quest for Autonomy* (Cambridge, MA: Harvard University Press, 2000).

36. Nayan Shah, *Contagious Divides: Epidemics and Race in San Francisco's Chinatown* (Berkeley: University of California Press, 2001); Kay Anderson, *Vancouver's Chinatown: Racial Discourse in Canada, 1875–1980* (Montreal: McGill-Queen's University Press, 1995).

37. Charles A. Price, *The Great White Walls Are Built: Restrictive Immigration to North America and Australasia 1836–1888* (Canberra: Australian Institute of International Affairs in association with Australian National University Press, 1974); Patrick Ettinger, *Imaginary Lines: Border Enforcement and the Origins of Undocumented Immigration, 1882–1930* (Austin: University of Texas Press, 2009); Adam McKeown, *Melancholy Order: Asian Migration and the Globalization of Borders* (New York: Columbia University Press, 2008); Michael Kearney, "The Classifying and Value-Filtering Missions of Borders," *Anthropological Theory* 4, no. 2 (2004): 131–156.

38. Hannah Arendt, "Race-Thinking before Racism," *Review of Politics* 6 (1944): 36. Arendt later refined this piece, which became Chapter 6 in *The Origins of Totalitarianism* (New York: Harcourt Brace & World, 1966).

39. Ibid. Scholars have built on the concept of race-thinking to move beyond racism alone as a means of qualifying the deserving and undeserving. Sherene Razack, for instance, points to the dangers implicit in discussions of "Canadian values" for their effectiveness in excluding those who do not seem to share these values. See *Casting Out: The Eviction of Muslims from Western Law & Politics* (Toronto: Toronto University Press, 2008). Relatedly, Paul Gilroy moves from Arendt's focus on the state in arguing that race-thinking is a social phenomenon and one that results in distinctive social structures. See *Against Race: Imagining Political Culture*

Beyond the Color Line (Cambridge, MA: Belknap Press of Harvard University Press, 2000), 12.

40. This wording is inspired by Peter Gatrell, who uses the phrase "the contours of refugee history" to describe his methodological approach to researching the subjective history of refugees. See *Free World? The Campaign to Save the World's Refugees, 1959–63* (Cambridge: Cambridge University Press, 2011), 3.

41. "Hong Kong: Refugees Rejected," *Life*, 8 June 1962, 40. See also Dudley L. Poston Jr. and Mei-Yu Yu, "The Distribution of the Overseas Chinese in the Contemporary World," *International Migration Review* 24, no. 3 (1990): 480–508.

42. Daiva Satsiulis and Nira Yuval-Davis, eds., *Unsettling Settler Societies: Articulations of Gender, Race, Ethnicity, and Class* (London: SAGE, 1995).

43. Settler colonialism is defined as the movement of migrants to a colony with the express purpose of securing control over the colony and expanding the empire. Settler colonialism, as a field of inquiry, is relatively new, born of the desire to mitigate the earlier historiography that neutralized the devastating effects of colonialism by erasing the presence of previously settled indigenous populations and the violence of the settler-indigenous encounter. Annie E. Coombes, ed., *Rethinking Settler Colonialism: History and Memory in Australia, Canada, Aoetearoa New Zealand, and South Africa* (Manchester: Manchester University Press, 2006), 2; Adele Perry, *On the Edge of Empire: Gender, Race, and the Making of British Columbia, 1849–1871* (Toronto: University of Toronto Press, 1994), 196.

44. See Marilyn Lake and Henry Reynolds, *Drawing the Global Colour Line: White Men's Countries and the International Challenge of Racial Equality* (New York: Cambridge University Press, 2007).

45. See Noel Ignatiev, *How the Irish became White* (London: Routledge, 1996). There is an extensive literature on race, settler colonialism, and the British imperial project. See Lorenzo Veracini, *Settler Colonialism: A Theoretical Overview* (New York: Palgrave Macmillan, 2010); James Belich, *Replenishing the Earth: The Settler Revolution and the Rise of the Angloworld* (Oxford, UK: Oxford University Press, 2009) and *Paradise Reforged: A History of the New Zealanders from 1880s to the Year 2000* (Honolulu: University of Hawai'i Press, 2001); Catherine Hall and Keith McLelland, eds., *Race, Nation, and Empire: Making Histories, 1750 to the Present* (Manchester: Manchester University Press, 2007); Radhika Mohanram, *Imperial White: Race, Diaspora, and the British Empire* (Minneapolis: University of Minnesota Press, 2007); Alan Lester, "Imperial Circuits and Networks: Geographies of the British Empire," *History Compass* 4, no. 1 (2006): 124–141; Tony Ballantyne, "Writing Out Asia: Race, Colonialism and Chinese Migration in New Zealand History," in *East by South: China in the Australasian Imagination*, ed.

Charles Ferrall, Paul Millar, and Keren Smith (Wellington, NZ: Victoria University Press, 2005), 87–109; Ann Laura Stoler, *Carnal Knowledge and Imperial Power: Race and the Intimate in Colonial Rule* (Berkeley: University of California Press, 2002); Tony Ballantyne, *Orientalism and Race: Aryanism in the British Empire* (Cambridge: Cambridge Imperial and Post-Colonial Studies Series, Palgrave, 2001); David Pearson, *The Politics of Ethnicity in Settler Societies: States of Unease* (New York: Palgrave, 2001), Patrick Wolfe, *Settler Colonialism and the Transformation of Anthropology* (London: Cassell, 1999); David Pearson and Patrick Ongley, "Post-1945 International Migration: New Zealand, Australia and Canada Compared," *International Migration Review* 29, no. 3 (1995): 765–793; R. A. Huttenbach, "The British Empire as a 'White Man's Country': Racial Attitudes and Immigration Legislation in the Colonies of White Settlement," *Journal of British Studies* 13, no. 1 (November 1973): 108–137.

46. Bonita Lawrence and Enakshi Dua, "Decolonizing Antiracism," *Social Justice* 32, no. 4 (2005): 120–143.

47. Caroline Elkins and Susan Pedersen, *Settler Colonialism in the Twentieth Century* (New York, NY: Routledge, 2002), 4. See also, John Fitzgerald, *Big White Lie: Chinese Australians in White Australia* (Sydney: UNSW Press, 2007); David Goutor, "Constructing the 'Great Menace': Canadian Labour's Opposition to Asian Immigration, 1880–1915," *The Canadian Historical Review* 88, no. 4 (December 2007): 549–576. Karen L. Harris, "Scattered and Silent Sources: Researching the Chinese in South Africa," in *Chinese Overseas: Migration, Research, and Documentation*, ed. Tan Chee-Beng, Colin Storey, and Julia Zimmerman (Hong Kong: The Chinese University Press of Hong Kong, 2003), 139–165; Patricia Roy, *Oriental Question: Consolidating a White Man's Province, 1914–1941* (Vancouver: University of British Columbia Press, 2003); Peter Ward, *White Canada Forever: Popular Attitudes and Public Policy Toward Orientals in British Columbia* (Montreal: McGill-Queen's University Press, 2002); Price, *The Great White Walls Are Built.*

48. Manying Ip refers to Chinese migrants as "essential outsiders" in *Unfolding History, Evolving Identity: The Chinese in New Zealand* (Auckland: Auckland University Press, 2003), xi. On Australia's ambivalent embrace of multiculturalism, see Andrew Jakubowicz, "Chinese Walls: Australian Multiculturalism and the Necessity for Human Rights," *Journal of Intercultural Studies* 2, no. 6 (December 2011): 691–706.

49. Historian Adam McKeown breaks this down into notions of civilized and uncivilized peoples. See *Melancholy Order: Asian Migration and the Globalization of Borders* (New York: Columbia University Press, 2008); John Fitzgerald, *Big White Lie: Chinese Australians in White Australia* (Sydney: UNSW Press, 2007).

50. Patrick Wolfe, *Settler Colonialism and the Transformation of Anthropology* (London: Cassell, 1999), 163.

51. "Memoranda to Cabinet on Immigration Policy," RG 76, SF-C-1-1, Part 3, Vol. 948, LAC.

52. Governor of Hong Kong to the Secretary of State for the Colonies, 17 May 1950, CO 537/6068, NAUK.

53. Claims to freedom included appeals to the freedom of movement, especially as mobility became more restricted in the Soviet Bloc and in the People's Republic of China. Alan Dowty, *Closed Borders: The Contemporary Assault on Freedom of Movement* (New Haven, CT: Yale University Press, 1987).

54. Mary L. Dudziak, *Cold War Civil Rights: Race and the Image of American Democracy* (Princeton, NJ: Princeton University Press, 2011).

55. B. A. Garside to Howard, 18 March 1955, File: Letters to Hong Kong, 1955, Box 20, Aid Refugee Chinese Intellectuals, Hoover Institution, Stanford University. On US settler colonialism as imperialism, see Alyosha Goldstein, "Where the Nation Takes Place: Proprietary Regimes, Antistatism, and U.S. Settler Colonialism," in *Settler Colonialism, The South Atlantic Quarterly*, ed. Alyosha Goldstein and Alex Lubin (Durham, NC: Duke University Press, 2008), 833–861.

56. Mimi Thi Nguyen, *Gift of Freedom: War, Debt, and Other Refugee Passages* (Durham, NC: Duke University Press, 2012); Yen Le Espiritu, *Body Counts: The Vietnam War and Militarized Refugees* (Berkeley: University of California Press, 2014).

57. The central role of humanitarians in reshaping the outlook of white settler societies after the Second World War becomes evident in reading the archival records of humanitarian organizations in conjunction with those of state authorities responsible for determining refugee policies. The research for this book created a unique archive based on the holdings of state archives as well as the repositories of NGOs, churches, and humanitarian workers. Interviews were also conducted with migrants, refugees, policymakers, humanitarians, and politicians. The historian's archive that resulted became the basis for reading the archival record in new ways, looking for points of intersection between diverse organizations and different levels of authority. There were many. In working with these collections as a holistic whole, numerous points of connections amongst the transnational operations of humanitarian activists were revealed. So too were the myriad ways in which humanitarians challenged, pressed, and transgressed government efforts to limit responsibilities for refugees. Perhaps most critically, the holistic archive also revealed the frequency with which white settler societies looked to one another as they sought to manage the growing

humanitarian impulse on behalf of refugees in Asia. On strategies for reading the archives, see Ann Laura Stoler, *Along the Archival Grain: Epistemic Anxieties and Colonial Common Sense* (Princeton: Princeton University Press, 2009).

58. Nevzat Soguk, *States and Strangers: Refugees and Displacement of Statecraft* (Minneapolis: University of Minnesota Press, 1999), 15.

59. See Tony Ballantyne, *Webs of Empire: Locating New Zealand's Colonial Past* (Vancouver: UBC Press, 2014); Lake and Reynolds, *Drawing the Global Colour Line: White Men's Countries and the International Challenge of Racial Equality*; Price, *The Great White Walls Are Built*.

60. Catherine Dauvergne, *Humanitarianism, Identity, and Nation: Migration Laws in Canada and Australia* (Vancouver: UBC Press, 2005), 4. See also Matthew Gibney, *The Ethics and Politics of Asylum: Liberal Democracy and the Response to Refugees* (Cambridge: Cambridge University Press, 2004).

61. See, for instance, discussion of Canadian prime minister, John Diefenbaker, and his handling of the question of South Africa's membership in the British Commonwealth. In Robert Bothwell, *Alliance and Illusion: Canada and the World, 1945–1984* (Vancouver: UBC Press, 2007), 143; "John Diefenbaker: Staring Down South Africa," CBC-Radio Canada, CBC Player, 16 March 1961, http://www.cbc.ca/player/play/1771019570.

62. See correspondence between Royal Canadian Mounted Police and South African officials. BTS 59/6 Vol. 9 Immigration Policy, 1952–54, National Archives of South Africa (NASA) (Pretoria).

63. Sally Peberdy, *Selecting Immigrants: National Identity and South Africa's Immigration Policies, 1910–2005* (Johannesburg: Wits University Press, 2009), 171. See also Audie Klotz, *Migration and National Identity in South Africa, 1860–2010* (Cambridge: Cambridge University Press, 2013).

64. Just as the idea of universal human rights was instrumentalized for the purposes of advancing the Western cause in the global Cold War, so too was the notion of being a humanitarian nation. See discussion in Samuel Moyn, *The Last Utopia: Human Rights in History* (Boston: Harvard University Press, 2010), 10. On the pursuit of legitimacy, see K. Cronin, "A Culture of Control: An Overview of Immigration Policy-Making," in *The Politics of Australian Immigration,* ed. James Jupp and M. Kabala (Canberra: Australian Government Publishing Service, 1993), 83–104; Alan B. Simmons and Keiran Keohane, "Shifts in Canadian Immigration Policy: State Strategies and the Quest for Legitimacy," *Canadian Review of Anthropology and Sociology* 29, no. 4 (1990): 421–452.

65. Libby Garland, *After They Closed the Gates: Jewish Illegal Immigration to the United States, 1921–1965* (Chicago: University of Chicago Press, 2014), 177.

66. For details on the American response, see Carl Bon Tempo, *Americans at the Gate: The United States and Refugees during the Cold War* (Princeton, NJ: Princeton University Press, 2008), 109.

67. "President Lyndon B. Johnson's Remarks at the Signing of the Immigration Bill, Liberty Island, New York, October 3, 1965," LBJ Presidential Library, http://www.lbjlib.utexas.edu/johnson/archives.hom/speeches.hom/651003.asp.

68. Gil Loescher with Jon Scanlan, *Calculated Kindness: Refugees and America's Half-Open Door, 1945 to the Present* (New York: Simon and Schuster, 1998).

69. "Four out of five migrants are NOT from Syria: EU figures expose the 'lie' that the majority of refugees are fleeing war zone," *Daily Mail*, 18 September 2015, http://www.dailymail.co.uk/news/article-3240010/Number-refugees-arriving-Europe-soars-85-year-just-one-five-war-torn-Syria.html.

70. "Crossings of Mediterranean Sea Exceed 300,000, Including 200,000 to Greece," UNHCR, 28 August 2015, http://www.unhcr.org/55e06a5b6.html.

1. WRITTEN OUT

1. Robert Cribb and Li Narangoa, "Orphans of Empire: Divided Peoples, Dilemmas of Identity, and Old Imperial Borders in East and Southeast Asia," *Comparative Studies in Society and History* 46, no. 1 (January 2004): 164–187.

2. Historian Daniel Cohen, for instance, in his effort to argue for the significance of displaced persons and refugees in shaping the postwar order, focuses entirely on the situation in Europe with no attention to the dynamics of the Cold War in Asia and how the region's population movements shaped the postwar order: *In War's Wake: Europe's Displaced Persons in the Postwar Order* (New York, NY: Oxford University Press, 2012). Gil Loescher traces the formation of the UNHCR to Europe and then treats the rest of the world as secondary aspect in his analysis of the UNHCR's efforts to grow beyond its initial mandate, *The UNHCR and World Politics: A Perilous Path* (Oxford, UK: Oxford University Press, 2001). Much of the focus in the refugee literature on Europe and refugees has to do with the manner in which the Cold War has also been understood as a predominantly European affair, or the product of multiple theatres where Europe was foremost. See Kim Salomon, *Refugees in the Cold War: Toward a New International Refugee Regime in the Early Postwar Era* (Lund: Lund University Press, 1991).

3. Cohen, *In War's Wake*, 52. Cohen observes that it was only in the 1930s "with the spread of economic depression and the refugee exodus form

Nazi Germany" that people began to call for labor migrants to be excluded from international asylum programs.

4. Building on earlier legislation introduced in the United States in 1882 and its own Chinese capitation tax laws, Canada introduced the Chinese Immigration Act in 1923, which effectively banned almost all migration from China. In 1924, the United States passed the Immigration Act, which imposed 2 percent quota limitations based on national origins and excluded migrants from Asia entirely.

5. Refugees from fascist Italy and Spanish Republicans sought refuge independently, many of them making their way to France. Claudena Skran, *Refugees in Inter-War Europe: The Emergence of a Regime* (London: Clarendon Press, 1995), 55, 57.

6. Legal scholar James Hathaway describes the Nansen passports as the most successful aspect of the League's work on behalf of refugees. See "The Evolution of Refugee Status in International Law: 1920-1950," *International and Comparative Law Quarterly* 33, no. 2 (1984): 352.

7. Fifty-four countries accepted the Nansen passport for Russian refugees but only thirty-eight did so for Armenian refugees, for whom the terms of the passport were extended in 1924. See Keith David Watenpaugh, "The League of Nations' Rescue of Armenian Genocide Survivors and the Making of Modern Humanitarianism, 1920-1927," *The American Historical Review* 115, no. 5 (2010): 1315-1339; Isabel Kaprielian-Churchill, "'Misfits': Canada and the Nansen Passport," *International Migration Review* 28, no. 2 (Summer 1994): 281-306. The years of genocidal violence, including a terrible attack on Smyrna in 1922, in which an estimated 500,000 to 1,000,000 people were killed, caused the flight of thousands of Armenian refugees, many of whom were housed in camps in the Caucasus, Greece, the Balkan countries, and the Middle East by the mid-1920s. Skran, *Refugees in Inter-War Europe,* 55, 57.

8. Due to German opposition, Nansen passports were never provided to refugees leaving Nazi Germany, who numbered over 400,000 by the end of the 1930s. Instead, the League of Nations created a general convention to provide refugees with the same treatment, in terms of economic and social rights, as the citizens of countries of asylum: Skran, 48, 128. In 1933, it also created the High Commission for Refugees from Germany. The organization was privately funded, and the first High Commissioner, the American James G. MacDonald, was tasked with negotiating the admission of German refugees, who were mainly Jewish, with individual countries. It was an uphill battle, and MacDonald eventually resigned in frustration. Later efforts to address the German refugee situation, including the Evian Conference, which is generally considered a failure because participating nations failed to commit

to admitting Jewish refugees, and the 1938 Convention on Refugees Coming from Germany, achieved little in terms of protection. Skran, 230–240.

9. Ernest Lapointe, Minister of Justice, quoted in Irving Abella and Harold Troper, *None Is Too Many: Canada and the Jews of Europe, 1933–1948* (Toronto: University of Toronto Press, 1983, reprinted in 2013), 64. On the treatment of Jewish refugees elsewhere, see Bob Moore and Frank Caestecker, eds., *Refugees from Nazi Germany and the Liberal European States* (New York: Berghahn Books, 2010); Deborah Dwork, *Flight from the Reich: Refugee Jews, 1933–1946* (New York: W. W. Norton, 2009).

10. Hathaway, "The Evolution of Refugee Status in International Law: 1920–1950", 350.

11. Cohen, *In War's Wake*, 6. The American Jewish Committee was a key participant in the drafting of the UN Charter, and the Consultative Council of Jewish Organizations, the Coordinating Board of Jewish Organizations, and the World Jewish Congress participated in the development of the 1951 Convention.

12. Samuel Moyn rejects the idea that the Holocaust led to the advancement of universal human rights as a kind of utopic vision for how humankind might progress and prosper. *The Last Utopia: Human Rights in History* (Boston: Harvard University Press, 2010), 7. See also Daniel Cohen's argument that it was the question of displaced persons that was instrumental in solidifying the emerging fault lines of the global Cold War. *In War's Wake*, 8, 15.

13. UN Relief and Rehabilitation Administration, "Agreement for UNRRA," 9 November 1943, http://www.ibiblio.org/pha/policy/1943/431109a.html.

14. Peter Gatrell, *The Making of the Modern Refugee* (Cambridge: Cambridge University Press, 2013), 90.

15. Ibid., 107.

16. Cohen, *In War's Wake*, 67.

17. For a discussion of the IRO as an institutional organization that balanced humanitarian interests with political ones, see John Stoessinger, *The Refugee and the World Community* (Minneapolis: University of Minnesota Press, 1957).

18. Gatrell, *The Making of the Modern Refugee*, 86.

19. Ibid., 108.

20. Meredith Oyen, "The Right of Return: Chinese Displaced Persons and the International Refugee Organization, 1947–56," *Modern Asian Studies* 49, no. 2 (2015): 546–571. For a broader diplomatic history on the subject of Chinese refugees, see Meredith Oyen, *The Diplomacy of Migration: Transnational Lives and the Making of U.S.-Chinese relations in the Cold War* (Ithaca, NY: Cornell University Press, 2015).

21. Louise Holborn, *The International Refugee Organization, A Specialized Agency of the United Nations: Its History and Work, 1946–1952* (New York, NY: Oxford University Press, 1956), 366. For a discussion of the IRO's operations and impact, see Eric Richards, *Destination Australia: Migration to Australia since 1901* (Melbourne: UNSW Press, 2008); James Jupp, *Exile or Refuge? The Settlement of Refugee, Humanitarian, and Displaced Immigrants* (Canberra: Australian Government Publishing Service, 1994); Dennis Gallagher, "The Evolution of the International Refugee System," *International Migration Review* 23, no. 3 (Autumn 1989): 579–598.

22. Eugene M. Kulischer, "Displaced Persons in the Modern World," *Annals of the American Academy of Political and Social Science* 262 (March 1949): 174.

23. Gatrell, *The Making of the Modern Refugee,* 91. On the IRO's impact, see, for example, Jock Collins, *Migrant Hands in a Distant Land: Australia's Post-War Immigration* (Leichhardt, NSW: Pluto Press Australia, 1988).

24. Historian Daniel Cohen observes that the IRO's constitution "expanded the notion of displaced persons and brought it closer to the concept of political refugees." It did so by including in its list of valid objections to being repatriated "persecution, or fear based on reasonable grounds of persecution because of race, religion, nationality or political opinion." The notion of persecution, Cohen observes, had not appeared in previous legal instruments created to assist refugees, which consistently used the notion of statelessness as the basis for assistance. Its introduction in the IRO Constitution was the result of heightened Cold War tensions and was the product of unique historical circumstances: *In War's Wake,* 33. As legal scholar James Hathaway has observed, the basic notion "underlying the IRO definition was that an individual who might be described as a victim of recognized state intolerance or as a genuinely motivated political dissident was a refugee until he either did not require or was determined to be unworthy of international protection and assistance." See "The Evolution of Refugee Status in International Law", 376.

25. "The IRO," Memorandum dated 8 April 1950, RG25, File 5475-T-40 (International Refugee Organization General File: Committee on Refugees and Displaced Persons Established by the U.N.), Part 12.2, Vol. 6407, LAC.

26. Paul Weis, "The International Protection of Refugees," *The American Journal of International Law* 48, no. 2 (April 1954): 194. For details on the drafting of the convention, see Terje Einarsen, "Drafting History of the 1951 Convention and the 1967 Protocol," in *The 1951 Convention Relating to the Status of Refugees and Its 1967 Protocol,* ed. Andreas Zimmerman (Oxford, UK: Oxford University Press, 2011), 37–74.

27. See Michael Marrus, *The Unwanted: European Refugees from the First World War Through the Cold War* (Philadelphia: Temple University Press, 2002).

Marrus mentions refugees in Africa as the successors to early postwar efforts in Europe. The need to decenter regional stories that are presented as universal histories is one that global and transnational historians have insisted upon in recent years. See Akira Iriye, *Global and Transnational History: The Past, Present, and Future* (London: Palgrave, 2012), 31. On the history of how the refugee regime evolved in Asia, see Sam Blay, "Regional Developments: Asia," in *The 1951 Convention Relating to the Status of Refugees and its 1967 Protocol*, ed. Andreas Zimmerman (Oxford, UK: Oxford University Press, 2011), 145–184.

28. Sunil Amrith, *Migration and Diaspora in Modern Asia* (Cambridge: Cambridge University Press, 2011), 89.

29. Anjali Gera Roy and Nandi Bhatia, eds., *Partitioned Lives: Narratives of Home, Displacement, and Resettlement* (New Delhi: Dorling Kindersley (India), 2008), 62.

30. Vazira Fazila-Yacoobali Zamindar, *The Long Partition and the Making of Modern South Asia* (New York: Columbia University Press, 2010), 6.

31. Statement by Robert Rochefort, French delegate, Conference of Plenipotentiaries on the Status of Refugees and Stateless Persons: Summary Record of the Twenty-Fourth Meeting, 27 November 1951, http://www.unhcr.org. Scholars have pointed to the fact that India was considered a "peripheral location" in the "postwar international order" as further reason for the lack of international engagement. See *The Long Partition and the Making of Modern South Asia*, 6.

32. Gatrell, *The Making of the Modern Refugee*, 182.

33. Sahr Conway-Lanz suggests that the United States needed to fight a more humanitarian war in a climate where the horrors of the Second World War were still fresh in the minds of policymakers and publics alike and where instruments such as the Universal Declaration of Human Rights elevated the notion of human dignity and the protection of rights to new heights. See "Beyond No Gun Ri: Refugees and the United States Military in the Korean War," *Diplomatic History* 29, no. 1 (January 2005): 49–81.

34. Ibid., 50.

35. See Steven Lee, "The United States, the United Nations, and the Second Occupation of Korea, 1950–1951," *The Asia-Pacific Journal* 7 (2009): 1–9.

36. Conference of Plenipotentiaries on the Status of Refugees and Stateless Persons: Summary Record of the Twenty-Second Meeting, 27 November 1951, http://www.unhcr.org.

37. Sunil S. Amrith, *Crossing the Bay of Bengal: The Furies of Nature and the Fortunes of Migrants* (Harvard: Harvard University Press, 2013), 3. On contemporary migration and refugee networks as a global phenomenon, see Khalid Koser and Charles Pinkerton, *The Social Networks of Asylum Seekers and the Dissemination of Information about Countries of Asylum* (London:

Home Office, 2002), http://library.npia.police.uk/docs/hordsolr/social-network.pdf; Khalid Koser, "Social Networks and the Asylum Cycle: The Case of Iranians in the Netherlands," *International Migration Review* 31, no. 3 (1997): 591–611.

38. Amrith, *Crossing the Bay*, 1.

39. Ibid., 18.

40. This experience determined the kinds of concerns and issues that delegate Cha presented to the conference. Cha was invested in the question of equal treatment for aliens and nationals, knowing that during the war, the Chinese government had distinguished between refugee populations and its own citizens. "During the Second World War," he said, "certain difficulties had arisen from the fact that the staple food of the Chinese population was rice, while refugees preferred bread as their basic food; moreover, refugees, particularly Russians and Jews, consumed far more sugar than the Chinese. The Chinese Government had given satisfaction to the refugees as far as had been possible; but, by doing so, it had not treated them on the same footing as nationals." See Ad Hoc Committee on Statelessness and Related Problems, First Session: Summary Record of the Fifteenth Meeting Held at Lake Success, New York, on Friday, 27 January 1950, at 10.30 a.m, www.unhcr.org.

41. Don Page, "The Representation of China in the United Nations: Canadian Perspectives and Initiatives, 1949–1971," in *Reluctant Adversaries: Canada and the People's Republic of China, 1949–1970,* ed. Paul Evans and B. Michael Frolic. (Toronto: University of Toronto Press, 1991), 73–84.

42. For a discussion, see Gil Loescher, *The UNHCR and World Politics: A Perilous Path* (Oxford, UK: Oxford University Press, 2001), 45.

43. "Leslie Chance to USSEA, 21 January 1950," Stateless Persons & Refugees, Microfilm reel C-10675, File C76724, Part 2, Vol. 672, LAC.

44. Conference of Plenipotentiaries on the Status of Refugees and Stateless Persons: Summary Record of the Nineteenth Meeting, 26 November 1951, www.unhcr.org.

45. Ad Hoc Committee on Statelessness and Related Problems, First Session: Summary Record of the Fifth Meeting Held at Lake Success, New York, on Wednesday, 18 January 1950, at 2.15 p.m., www.unhcr.org.

46. Ad Hoc Committee on Statelessness and Related Problems, First Session: Summary Record of the Sixth Meeting Held at Lake Success, New York, on Thursday, 19 January 1950, at 11 a.m., www.unhcr.org.

47. "The Refugee Convention, 1951 – The Travaux Preparatoires Analyzed with a Commentary by Dr. Paul Weis," UNHCR, www.unhcr.org/4ca34be29.html.

48. Conference of Plenipotentiaries on the Status of Refugees and Stateless Persons: Summary Record of the Nineteenth Meeting, 26 November 1951, www.unhcr.org.

49. Amongst the countries invited to participate in the conference were Albania, Austria, Bulgaria, Cambodia, Ceylon, the Federal Republic of Germany, Finland, the Hashemite Kingdom of Jordan, Hungary, Ireland, Italy, Japan, Laos, Liechtenstein, Monaco, Nepal, Portugal, the Republic of Korea, Romania, Switzerland, and Vietnam.

50. Irial Glynn, "The Genesis and Development of Article 1 of the 1951 Refugee Convention," *Journal of Refugee Studies* 25, no. 1 (December 2011): 137.

51. Discussion by Mr. Hoare at Conference of Plenipotentiaries on the Status of Refugees and Stateless Persons: Summary Record of the Thirty-Third Meeting, 30 November 1951, www.unhcr.org.

52. Conference of Plenipotentiaries on the Status of Refugees and Stateless Persons: Summary Record of the Nineteenth Meeting, 26 November 1951, www.unhcr.org.

53. Ibid. Rochefort also believed that those arguing for a broad definition were unprepared to assume responsibility for the effects of such an approach.

54. *House of Commons Debates*, 1 May 1947 (Ottawa: Queen's Printers, 1947), 2644–2546.

55. Conference of Plenipotentiaries on the Status of Refugees and Stateless Persons: Summary Record of the Nineteenth Meeting, 26 November 1951, www.unhcr.org.

56. Ibid.

57. Ibid.

58. Ibid.

59. Ibid.

60. The PRC could not send a representative as the country was not accepted as a member of the United Nations until 1971. The following countries sent delegates to the conference of plenipotentiaries: Australia, Austria, Belgium, Brazil, Canada, Colombia, Denmark, Egypt, France, Federal Republic of Germany, Greece, the Holy See, Iraq, Israel, Italy, Luxembourg, Monaco, Netherlands, Norway, Sweden, Switzerland (the Swiss delegation also represented Liechtenstein), Turkey, the United Kingdom, the United States, Venezuela, and Yugoslavia.

61. Conference of Plenipotentiaries on the Status of Refugees and Stateless Persons: Summary Record of the Fourteenth Meeting, 22 November 1951, www.unhcr.org. The government of New Zealand debated participating in the conference, but didn't feel immediately affected by the convention's discussions. Officials in Wellington were reassured about not participating after confirming that Australian officials were like-minded in their

thinking on the scope of the convention and the refugee definition and would be able to adequately represent their views at the meetings.

62. Australian Mission to UN to Secretary, DEA, 5 December 1950, A1838 855/11/11, Part 2, NAA (Canberra). Cited in David Palmer, "The Quest for 'Wriggle Room': Australia and the Refugees Convention, 1951–73," *Australian Journal of International Affairs* 63, no. 2 (2009): 292.

63. Conference of Plenipotentiaries on the Status of Refugees and Stateless Persons: Summary Record of the Nineteenth Meeting, 26 November 1951, www.unhcr.org.

64. Hakan G. Sicakkan, "The Modern State, the Citizen, and the Perilous Refugee," *Journal of Human Rights* 3, no. 4 (December 2004): 447.

2. BORDER CROSSINGS

1. Douglas Lam, interview with author, 11 July 2010, Sydney, Australia.

2. Roxanne Doty emphasizes how much of the work of governments is aspirational, attending to what states desire in their efforts to govern and regulate the body politic. See *Anti-Immigrantism in Western Democracies: Statecraft and the Politics of Exclusion* (New York: Routledge, 2004).

3. The population of Hong Kong and the New Territories was estimated at 3,129,648 by 1961. Fan Shu Shing, *The Population of Hong Kong* (United Nations: The Committee for International Coordination of National Research in Demography, 1974), 2.

4. Press Release by Richard A. Shafter, "Hong Kong—Refugees," Box 330, CARE records. Manuscripts and Archives Division. The New York Public Library. Astor, Lenox, and Tilden Foundations.

5. Governor of Hong Kong to Secretary of State for Colonial Affairs, 5 May 1949, CO 537/4802, National Archives of the United Kingdom (NAUK).

6. See Siu-Lun Wong, *Emigrant Entrepreneurs: Shanghai Industrialists in Hong Kong* (New York, NY: Oxford University Press, 1988).

7. John Carroll, *Edge of Empires: Chinese Elites and British Colonials in Hong Kong* (Cambridge, MA: Harvard University Press, 2005), 48; Governor of Hong Kong to Secretary of State for the Colonies, 30 May 1938, CO 129/570/2, NAUK.

8. Britain acquired Hong Kong, Kowloon, and the New Territories in a series of treaties with China from 1842 to 1898. Steven Tsang, *A Modern History of Hong Kong* (London, UK: I. B. Tauris, 2004), 145; Ming K. Chan, "The Legacy of the British Administration of Hong Kong: A View from Hong Kong," *The China Quarterly* 151 (September 1997): 567: \Elizabeth Sinn, ed., *Hong Kong, British Crown Colony, Revisited* (Centre of Asian Studies: University of Hong Kong, 2001), 8.

9. Harold Ingrams, *Hong Kong* (London: Her Majesty's Stationery Office, 1952), 64.

10. Nicholas Thomas argues that the migrants increased permanency meant that the government began to think of them as "potential citizens" rather than sojourners. See discussion in *Democracy Denied: Identity, Civil Society, and Illiberal Democracy in Hong Kong* (London, UK: Ashgate, 1999).

11. Daily Information Bulletin: Rotarian K. M. Barnett Details Government Plans for Squatter Resettlement, 30 January 1952, CO 1023/164, NAUK.

12. Cindy Yik-yi Chu, ed., *Diaries of the Maryknoll Sisters in Hong Kong* (London, UK: Palgrave Macmillan, 2007), 178.

13. "Housing Hong Kong's 600,000 Homeless" by Sir Alexander Grantham in *Geographic Magazine,* April 1958. Republished in "Hong Kong—As Others See It," CO 1030/782, NAUK.

14. Extract, *Hong Kong Annual Reports 1950–1951*, Medical and Health Services Department, CO 1023/164, NAUK.

15. Folder— "Hong Kong: Refugees," CARE records. Manuscripts and Archives Division. The New York Public Library. Astor, Lenox and Tilden Foundations.

16. Ingrams, *Hong Kong,* 72.

17. Chu, *Diaries of the Maryknoll Sisters in Hong Kong,* 147.

18. The only exemptions were members of the military who had identity cards, members of the Hong Kong Police force, bona fide travelers in transit (in possession of a passport), and children under the age of twelve.

19. Allen Chun, "Colonial 'Govern-mentality' in Transition: Hong Kong as Object and Subject," *Cultural Studies* 14, no. 3/4 (2000): 437.

20. Governor of Hong Kong to the Secretary State for the Colonies, 6 November 1954, CO 1030 / 382, File 418/403/02, NAUK.

21. Governor of Hong Kong to Secretary of State for the Colonies, 17 May 1949, FO 371/83515, NAUK. British officials in Beijing, particularly the Chargé d'Affaires, Mr. Hutchinson, had great affinity for the idea of traditional ties and lobbied against the controls contemplated by Hong Kong.

22. See correspondence in FC 10112/45 regarding the Expulsion of Undesirables Ordinance, FO 371/83262, NAUK.

23. Report by Security Liaison Officer, March 1950, FO 371/83267, NAUK.

24. Sunil S. Amrith, *Migration and Diaspora in Modern Asia* (Cambridge: Cambridge University Press, 2011), 1.

25. For a full discussion, see John Torpey, *Invention of the Passport: Surveillance, Citizenship, and the State* (Cambridge: Cambridge University Press, 2000).

26. Peter Nyers, *Rethinking Refugees: Beyond States of Emergency* (New York: Routledge, 2006), 7.

27. Note by the Immigration Officer on Border Controls, CO 1030 / 383, NAUK.

28. Commonwealth Relations Office to Governor of Hong Kong re. Restrictions on the Entry of Chinese into Hong Kong, 7 April 1955, DO 35 / 10411, NAUK.

29. As scholars of the new imperial history have demonstrated, the so-called periphery exerted considerable influence from the metropole and regularly developed independently from the "center." Diplomatic historians have made similar suggestions about seemingly unequal alliances such as that of the United States and Taiwan. See Nancy Bernkopf Tucker, *Taiwan, Hong Kong, and the United States, 1945–1992* (New York: Twayne Publishers, Maxwell Macmillan International, 1994).

30. See correspondence in CO 537 / 3718 Chinese Communist Activities in Hong Kong, 1949, NAUK.

31. Beijing Embassy to Foreign Office, 10 May 1950, FO 371/83515, NAUK.

32. Alan Smart and Josephine Smart argue that 1950 was a significant turning point because up until then "borders were less significant for Hong Kong than for most other political territories." See "Time-Space Punctuation: Hong Kong's Border Regime and Limits on Mobility," *Pacific Affairs* 81, no. 2 (2008): 181, http://www.pacificaffairs.ubc.ca/files/2011/09/smart.pdf.

33. James Scott, *Seeing Like a State: How Certain Schemes to Improve the Human Condition Have Failed* (Binghamton, NY: Vail-Ballou Press, 1998), 77.

34. Note by the Immigration Officer on Border Controls, CO 1030/383, NAUK.

35. Maggie Ip, interview with author, 27 October 2009, Vancouver, British Columbia.

36. "Years of Constant Caution," in *Out of China: A Collection of Interviews with Refugees from China,* ed. Francis Harper (Hong Kong: Dragonfly Books, 1964).

37. Beijing Embassy to Foreign Office, 6 January 1951, FO 371/ 92371, NAUK.

38. Memorandum to Executive Council, CO 1023/164, NAUK.

39. Royal Hong Kong Police, *Annual Review / Commissioner of Police, Hong Kong* (Hong Kong: Government Printer, 1951–1952), 46.

40. Governor of Hong Kong to the Secretary of State for the Colonies, 17 May 1950. Handwriting in margin by J. D. Anderson, CO 537/6068, NAUK.

41. Ibid.

42. Wong Yiu Chung, "The Policies of the Hong Kong Government toward the Chinese Refugee Problem, 1945–1962" (PhD Diss., Hong Kong

Baptist University, 2008), 166; Beatrice Leung and Shun-hing Chan, *Changing Church and State Relations in Hong Kong, 1950–2000* (Hong Kong: Hong Kong University Press, 2003), 27.

43. Sir Robin Black Transcript, interview with Steve Tsang. Mss. Ind. Ocn.s.348, Rhodes House Library, Oxford University, 64.

44. Sir David Trench Transcript, interview with Steve Tsang, 23 April 1987, Mss. Ind.Ocn.s.337, Rhodes House Library, Oxford University, 16.

45. Maggie Black, *A Cause for Our Times: OXFAM, The First Fifty Years* (Oxford, UK: Oxfam Professional, 1992), 49.

46. Keith Hopkins, *Hong Kong: The Industrial Colony: A Political, Social, and Economic Survey* (Oxford, UK: Oxford University Press, 1971), 283.

47. Diary Entry, 19 April 1959, Diary of Captain James B. Atkinson, MSS. Eng. misc. c. 510/2, New Bodleian Library, Oxford University.

48. Black, *A Cause for Our Times,* 50.

49. Reuters, 4 April 1956, Binder: Newspaper Clippings, Box 330, CARE records. Manuscripts and Archives Division. The New York Public Library. Astor, Lenox, and Tilden Foundations.

50. Press Release, "1956 Food Crusade to Send 300,000 Packages to Hong Kong," File Hong Kong 1954–1957, CARE records. Manuscripts and Archives Division. The New York Public Library. Astor, Lenox, and Tilden Foundations.

51. Folder – "Hong Kong: Refugees," Box 330, CARE records. Manuscripts and Archives Division. The New York Public Library. Astor, Lenox, and Tilden Foundations.

52. Correspondence from Ogden Meeker to CARE New York, 11 August 1956, "August 1956," Box 562, CARE records. Manuscripts and Archives Division. The New York Public Library. Astor, Lenox, and Tilden Foundations.

53. Ibid.

54. Bill Hanson to Duncan Wood, 17 February 56, Box: Foreign Service, 1956, AFSC Archives.

55. Studies of Hong Kong in the 1950s rely heavily on data from 1931 to establish a demographic picture of the colony. This data is undoubtedly inaccurate given the significant population movements between China and Hong Kong during the Second World War. A 1931 government report revealed that 56 percent of Chinese had been in the colony for ten years or under and 35 percent of the Chinese had been there for less than five years. At the time of the report, 33 percent of the colony's residents were born in Hong Kong, compared to 46 percent in Canton. See R. H. Hughes, "Hong Kong: An Urban Study," *The Geographical Journal* 117, no. 1 (March 1951): 14.

56. Extract, *Hong Kong Annual Reports*, Urban Council and Sanitary Department (1950–1951), CO 1023/164, NAUK.

57. Ibid.

58. The Hong Kong police blamed the ex-soldiers for problems in the colony. "The Civil War across our borders let loose upon the Colony numbers of unscrupulous men supplied with arms and well skilled in their use." Foreword, Royal Hong Kong Police, *Annual Review / Commissioner of Police, Hong Kong* (Hong Kong: Government Printer, 1949–1950).

59. File Note to Mr. Paskin, 14 October 1949, CO 537 / 5024, NAUK. Legal counsel in London maintained that the government of Hong Kong could not send able-bodied soldiers to Taiwan, regardless of their political persuasion, because they had come from villages and cities across China and should be sent back there. Foreign Office to Governor of Hong Kong, 21 March 1950, CO 537/ 6314, NAUK.

60. Governor of Hong Kong to Secretary of State for the Colonies, 24 February 1950, CO 537/ 6314, NAUK.

61. Deportation from Hong Kong of Fourteen Members of the "Chinese Anti-Communist National Salvation Youth Corps," 1953, FC 2041/2, FO 371/10532, NAUK.

62. Extract, *Hong Kong Annual Reports*, Urban Council and Sanitary Department (1950–1951), CO 1023/164, NAUK.

63. Kenneth On Wai Lan, "Rennie's Mill: The Origin and Evolution of a Special Enclave in Hong Kong" (PhD Diss., University of Hong Kong, 2006), 12.

64. Description by David Jack, head of CARE Hong Kong. As a result, it was only in 1960 when Hong Kong's Social Welfare Department organized a distribution scheme for families not helped by religious organizations that CARE began to work in Rennie's Mill Camp. Correspondence by David Jack, 1 June 1960, Box 590, Hong Kong Correspondence 1960, CARE records. Manuscripts and Archives Division. The New York Public Library. Astor, Lenox, and Tilden Foundations.

65. David Trench to the Secretary of State for the Colonies, 23 October 1957, CO1030/ 778. Cited in Wong Yiu Chung, "The Policies of the Hong Kong Government towards the Chinese Refugee Problem, 1945–1962" (PhD Diss., Hong Kong Baptist University, 2008). The FCRA "became" a private voluntary organization after 1950 in order to continue operating in countries that no longer recognized the Republic of China.

66. This debate culminated with a General Assembly resolution in 1971 that expelled representatives for the Republic of China and declared the People's Republic of China to be the sole and legitimate representative of China to the United Nations.

67. Chi-Kwan Mark, "The 'Problem of People': British Colonials, Cold War Powers, and the Chinese Refugees in Hong Kong, 1949–62," *Modern Asian Studies* 41, no. 6 (2007): 1154, http://digirep.rhul.ac.uk/items/919d118d-10ad-5583-20c7-20db29f3fe31/1/.

68. Joshua Fan, *China's Homeless Generation: Voices from the Veterans of the Chinese Civil War, 1940s–1990s* (New York: Routledge, 2011).

69. Edward Hambro, *The Problem of Chinese Refugees in Hong Kong: Report Submitted to the United Nations High Commissioner for Refugees* (Leyden: A. W. Sijthoff, 1955), 53; Governor of Hong Kong to the Secretary of State for the Colonies, 6 June 1961, CO 1030/1321, NAUK.

70. Sir David Trench Transcript, interview with Steve Tsang, 23 April 1987, Mss. Ind.Ocn.s.337, Rhodes House Library, Oxford University, 25.

71. Sir Robin Black Transcript, interview with Steve Tsang, Mss. Ind. Ocn.s.348, Rhodes House Library, Oxford University, 26.

72. Reuters Report, 31 January 1953, CO 1023/117, NAUK.

73. According to historian Glen Peterson, ARCI was "was intended to be the equivalent in Asia of the National Committee for a Free Europe, a joint CIA and State Department creation for promoting the 'rollback of communism' in Europe." See "To Be or Not to Be a Refugee: The International Politics of the Hong Kong Refugee Crisis, 1949–1955," *The Journal of Imperial and Commonwealth History* 36, no. 2 (2008): 177. Governor of Hong Kong to Secretary of State for the Colonies, 31 January 1953, CO 1023/117, NAUK.

74. $20 Hong Kong dollars was given to each of the 12,880 refugees who registered for relief. The rest was held in reserve to provide food for the camp. CO 1023/117, NAUK.

75. Royal Hong Kong Police, *Annual Review / Commissioner of Police, Hong Kong* (Hong Kong: Government Printer, 1949–1950 and 1950–1951).

76. *Refugee Questions in Various Countries, 1946–1954,* 425.02.09.025 Commission of Inter-Church Aid, Refugee, and World Service (CICARWS), World Council of Churches Archives, Geneva.

77. Selwyn-Lloyd, the Foreign Secretary, observed that between June 1954 and June 1955, 2,741 refugees were settled abroad. Of these, 2,703 went to Formosa. "Memorandum for the Executive Council: The Squatter Problem," CO 1023/164, NAUK.

78. Sir Robin Black Transcript, interview with Steven Tsang, 6 February 1989, Mss. Ind.Ocn.s.348, Rhodes House Library, Oxford University.

79. See discussions of restrictive refugee policies in Prakash A. Shah, *Refugees, Race, and the Legal Concept of Asylum in Britain* (London, UK: Cavendish, 2000).

80. Ogden Meeker, April 1956, "File Hong Kong 1956–63," Box 840, Overseas Operations Discursive Reports, CARE records. Manuscripts and Archives Division. The New York Public Library. Astor, Lenox, and Tilden Foundations.

81. Rotarian K. M. Barnett Details Government Plans for Squatter Resettlement, 30 January 1952, Daily Information Bulletin, CO 1023/164, NAUK.

82. Daily Information Bulletin, 7 February 1954, CO 1030/390, NAUK. For details, see Alan Smart, *The Shek Kip Mei Myth: Squatters, Fires, and Colonial Rulers in Hong Kong* (Hong Kong: Hong Kong University, 2006). On public housing generally, see David Drakakis-Smith, *High Society: Housing Provision in Metropolitan Hong Kong, 1954 to 1979: A Jubilee Critique* (Hong Kong: Centre of Asian Studies, University of Hong Kong, 1979).

83. Sir Robin Black Transcript, interview with Steven Tsang, 6 February 1989, Mss. Ind.Ocn.s.348, Rhodes House Library, Oxford University, 74.

84. Ibid.

85. Peterson, "To Be or Not to Be," 182. For an overview of the refugee situation in Hong Kong, see Eugene Perry Link, *Refugees in Hong Kong* (n.p: s.n., 1976?).

86. Peterson, "To Be or Not to Be," 182.

87. Ogden Meeker, August 1956, "File Hong Kong 1956-63," Box 840, Overseas Operations Discursive Reports, CARE records. Manuscripts and Archives Division. The New York Public Library. Astor, Lenox, and Tilden Foundations.

88. Governor of Hong Kong to the Secretary of State for the Colonies, 26 January 1954, CO 1030/390, NAUK.

89. Ibid.

90. Lorenz Luthi, *Sino-Soviet Split: Cold War in the Communist World* (Princeton, NJ: Princeton University Press, 2008), 78. Mao was dismayed by the Soviet response to the Hungarian Revolution, in part because of the implications for his own ambitions.

91. Intelligence Report, 28 February 1956, CO 1030/250, NAUK.

92. Governor's Public Announcement on Immigration Control, 31 August 1956, CO 1030/384, NAUK.

93. Ashton (Foreign Office) to Comfort (Colonial Office), 16 June 1956, FO 371/121165, NAUK. The resettlement figures were measured and explained differently. Governor Grantham estimated the rate at 40,000. See "Refugees in Hong Kong," CO 1030/384, NAUK. By the late 1950s, the squatter population was estimated at 530,000. Despite years of resettlement, Governor Grantham expected it would still take a full six years to resettle everyone given the economic state of the colony and the resources available. Governor of Hong Kong to the Secretary of State for the Colonies, 23 April 1957, CO 1030/777, NAUK.

94. Note from Willan to de la Mare, 3 October 1962, CO 1030/1114, NAUK.

95. Ogden Meeker, July 1956, "File Hong Kong 1956-63," Box 840, Overseas Operations Discursive Reports, CARE records. Manuscripts and Archives Division. The New York Public Library. Astor, Lenox, and Tilden Foundations.

96. Fortnightly Intelligence Report, 23 October 1956, CO 1030/250, NAUK.

97. There were frequent appeals in the local Hong Kong press for the return of students and intellectuals to China. Intelligence Report, 25 September 1956, CO 1030/250, NAUK.

98. Governor of Hong Kong to the Secretary of State for the Colonies, 17 May 1950. Handwriting in margin by J. D. Anderson, CO 537/6068, NAUK.

99. The colonial government's desire to shelter itself from any kind of outside disturbance was further reflected in the great reluctance with which authorities permitted the transit of White Russians from China in the early 1950s. The International Refugee Organization was forced to campaign aggressively to facilitate passage for migrants destined to Australia and other parts abroad. Correspondence from UNHCR to Foreign Office, 16 April 1953, CO 1023/117, NAUK.

3. CAMPAIGNING FOR REFUGEES, CARING FOR PEOPLE

1. Walter Judd to Dr. Victoria Beckett, 4 January 1960, 167.3, File Correspondence – General, 1960–1980, Box 167, ARCI, Hoover Institution Archives, Stanford University.

2. Meeting with Refugee Migration Unit and World Refugee Year, 4 May 1960, File: Letters from Hong Kong, Box 25, ARCI, Hoover Institution Archives, Stanford University.

3. Bill Channel to Charles Read, 16 October 1959, File: Foreign Service, 1959, AFSC Archives.

4. Père Paul Duchesne, "Activités Catholiques à Hong Kong," *Mission Bulletin* 7, no. 4 (April 1955): 298.

5. Beatrice Leung, *Sino-Vatican Relations: Problems in Conflicting Authority, 1976–1986* (Cambridge: Cambridge University Press, 1992), 91. For discussions of persecution in China in the early 1950s, see "No Persecution?" *Mission Bulletin* 7, no. 9 (November 1955): 767–771.

6. At its height, the United Church of Canada had fifteen missionaries working in Hong Kong. The Anglican Church had anywhere from four to six. Most missionaries worked with the Church of Christ in China, which was based in Hong Kong after 1951. See Tom Newnham, *New Zealand Women in China* (Auckland: Graphic Publications, 1995).

7. *Hong Kong Council of Social Services – 40th Anniversary: A Commemorative Issue* (Hong Kong: Hong Kong Council of Social Services, 1988), 30.

8. Evangelical Lutheran Church of Hong Kong, *The Church Doth Stand: A Report of the Work of the Evangelical Lutheran Church of Hong Kong* [Kowloon?: The Church, 1958?], 17.

9. *The Church Doth Stand*, 17.

10. Ruth Sovik, *Mission in Formosa and Hong Kong: Studies in the Beginning and Development of the Indigenous Lutheran Church in Formosa and Hong Kong* (Minneapolis, MN: Augsburg Publishing House, 1957), 36.

11. *The Church Doth Stand*, 13.

12. Cindy Yik-yi Chu, ed., *Diaries of the Maryknoll Sisters in Hong Kong* (London, UK: Palgrave Macmillan, 2007), 363. See also Eliza W. Y. Lee, "Nonprofit Development in Hong Kong: The Case of a Statist–Corporatist Regime," *Voluntas: International Journal of Voluntary and Nonprofit Organizations* 16, no. 1 (2005): 51–68. On the work of voluntary organizations, see Hong Kong Council of Social Services, *Working Together: A Survey of the Work of Voluntary and Government Social Service Organizations in Hong Kong* (Hong Kong: Hong Kong Council of Social Services, 1958).

13. Ernest Moy to Walter Judd and Christopher Emmet, 7 March 1952, ARCI, File 167.4 ARCI – Correspondence – Internal, 1951-52, Box 167, ARCI, Hoover Institution Archives, Stanford University.

14. Ernest Moy to President Eisenhower, 14 August 1952, File 167.5 ARCI – Internal Correspondence, May – Aug 1952, Box 167, ARCI, Hoover Institution Archives, Stanford University.

15. Rebecca Gill, *Calculating Compassion: Humanity and Relief in War, Britain 1870–1914* (Cambridge, UK: Cambridge University Press, 2013), 2.

16. Hong Kong to London, January 1951, File: 1950 Correspondence, AFSC Archives.

17. Ibid.

18. Mark Shaw, 18 April 1951, File: Philadelphia to Hong Kong, 1950-52, AFSC Archives.

19. Guide to Lutheran World Federation Archives, Geneva. The guide counters Jacques Vernant's relatively low impression of the work of the Lutheran World Federation, *The Refugee in the Post-War World* (New Haven, CT: Yale University Press, 1953), 591.

20. Ronald O. Hall, *Hong Kong: What of the Church?* (London, UK: Edinburgh House Press, 1952), 17.

21. *The Church Doth Stand*, 38.

22. Elizabeth Sinn argues the Tung Wah Hospital operated as a distinctly Chinese enterprise, which simultaneously served as a bridge between the socially distinct European and Chinese spheres in Hong Kong. *Power and Charity: A Chinese Merchant Elite in Colonial Hong Kong* (Hong Kong: Hong Kong University Press, 2003).

23. Extract from UN A/AC79/124, "Chinese Refugees in Hong Kong," CO 1030, NAUK.

24. United States. Congress. Senate. *Refugee Problem in Hong Kong and Macao: Hearings Before the United States Senate Committee on the Judiciary, Subcommittee to Investigate Problems Connected with Refugees and Escapees*, 87th Cong. 2nd Sess. 18 (1962).

25. See Akira Iriye, *Global Community: The Role of International Organizations in the Making of the Contemporary World* (Berkeley: University of California Press, 2002) on the general trend to provide direct relief and then to provide vocational training. Michael Barnett traces the history of activist humanitarianism to the immediate postwar period. See *Empire of Humanity: A History of Humanitarianism* (Ithaca, NY: Cornell University Press, 2011). However, most analysts identify the post-1989 period as the era of activist humanitarian work and see the Cold War as more of a freeze. See Bonnie Greene, ed., *Canadian Churches and Foreign Policy* (Toronto: Lorimer, 1990), 6; Geert van Dok, Christian Varga, and Romain Schroeder, "Humanitarian Challenges: The Political Dilemmas of Emergency Aid," (Caritas Switzerland: Position Paper 11, Caritas Luxembourg: LES CAHIERS CARITAS No 3, Lucerne/Luxembourg, November 2005), 20.

26. Fang Chui to Thomas Jamieson, 28 July 1952, 15/2/HK/1 Chinese Refugees in Hong Kong, Fonds UNHCR 11 Records of the Central Registry, Series 1, Classified Subject Files, 1951–1970 15/2/HK, Box 262, Part 2, UNHCR Archives.

27. Walter Judd to Whitney Shepardson, 17 September 1952, III.A.1. A-B, Box 6, File 5, ARCI, Carnegie Corporation of New York, Columbia University Archives.

28. 1959 AFSC Newsletter, File: Country – Hong Kong, Refugee Program, General, Box: Foreign Service, 1959, AFSC Archives.

29. "Refugee Program – Hong Kong" Box: International Service Division, 1961, AFSC Archives.

30. See correspondence from Bill Channel, 15 April 1962, Hong Kong Projects, File 61886, Box: International Service Division, 1961, AFSC Archives.

31. Ibid.

32. *Hong Kong Working Committee for WRY: Quarterly Progress Report*, no. 1, March 1960, Lutheran World Federation.

33. Country – Hong Kong, Refugee Program, General, Box: Foreign Service, 1959, AFSC Archives.

34. Denis Moriarty to Frank Hunt, 5 September 1958, Box: Foreign Service, 1958 Letters: London to P, Foreign Service Section, AFSC Archives.

35. Walter Judd to Whitney Shepardson, 5 June 1962, III.A.1. A-B, Box 6, File 5 ARCI, Carnegie Corporation of New York, Columbia University Archives.

36. "Preliminary Report," PA 52-90, Reel 645, Ford Foundation Archives.

37. Moy to Emmet, 19 February 1952, File 167.4 ARCI – Correspondence – Internal, 1951–52, Box 167, ARCI, Hoover Institution Archives, Stanford University.

38. Ibid.

39. "Preliminary Report," PA 52-90, Reel 645, Ford Foundation Archives.

40. Arnold to Gladieux, 9 May 1952, PA 52-90 Reel 645, Ford Archives Foundation.

41. Garside to Judd, 8 August 1957, File 169.1 ARCI Correspondence / Internal 1957, Box 169, ARCI, Hoover Institution Archives, Stanford University Archives.

42. "Asian Refugees in the Far East" were defined as "refugees, including Chinese persons, who: a) At the time of application for a visa are residing within the district of an American consular office in the Far East, and 2) are attributable by as much as one-half of their ancestry to a people or peoples indigenous in the Far East." "Chinese refugees" were defined as "refugees who: a) are of Chinese ethnic origin, and 2) whose passports for travel to the United States are endorsed by the Chinese Nationalist Government or its authorized representatives."

43. For an overview see Meredith Oyen, *The Diplomacy of Migration: Transnational Lives and the Making of U.S.-Chinese relations in the Cold War* (Ithaca, NY: Cornell University Press, 2015).

44. The figure of 7000 individuals referred to in this report included admission for 2000 people who had taken refuge in US consular offices in East Asia but were not indigenous to the region; 3000 people who had taken refuge in U.S. consular offices in East Asia and were indigenous to the region; and 2000 Chinese refugees. The act also enabled thousands of Chinese residents in the United States before 7 August 1953 to have their status adjusted to become eligible for permanent residence and citizenship. See Madeline Y. Hsu, *The Good Immigrants: How the Yellow Peril became the Model Minority* (Princeton, NJ: Princeton University Press, 2015), 127.

45. "The Refugee Relief Act of 1953: What It Is – How It Works for the Far East," Background on Refugee Program in Hong Kong, Turkey and Jordan, 1953–1956, A1 5495, Record Group 59: General Records of the Department of State, 1763–2002, National Archives and Records Administration (NARA).

46. On Truman's Cold War politics, see Elizabeth Edwards Spalding, *The First Cold Warrior: Harry Truman, Containment, and the Remaking of Liberal Internationalism* (Lexington: University Press of Kentucky, 2006); Melvyn P. Leffler, *A Preponderance of Power: National Security, The Truman Administration, and the Cold War* (Stanford, CA: Stanford University Press, 1992).

47. Susan L. Carruthers, "Between Camps: Eastern Bloc 'Escapees' and Cold War Borderlands," *American Quarterly* 57, no. 3 (2005): 913. For a fuller discussion of the program as it operated in Eastern Europe and the Soviet Union, including its important publicity components, see Susan Carruthers, "Chapter Two: Bloc-Busters," in *Cold War Captives: Imprisonment, Escape, and Brainwashing* (Berkeley: University of California Press, 2009).

48. Richard Brown to Rep. Magnuson, 27 February 1962, 846G.46/8-460, RG 59, Box 2535, Central Decimal File, 1960–63, NARA.

49. Memo for John H. Ohly, "Preparation of Escapee Program Congressional Presentation," General – Escapee Program, ARCI, A1 1199, Box 4, Record Group 59: General Records of the Department of State, 1763–2002, NARA.

50. "A Report for OCB Examination on Effectiveness of the Escapee Program," prepared by the Office for Refugees and Migration, Foreign Operations Administration, 23 December 1953, DDE Records as President, WHCF, Confidential File Series, Box 27, Eisenhower Presidential Library.

51. See *Refugee Problem in Hong Kong and Macao.*

52. Operations Coordinating Board Minutes, 9 July 1958, Escapee Program II, 1957–60, A1 1586C, Record Group 59: General Records of the Department of State, 1763–2002, NARA.

53. 15 December 1954, Operations Coordinating Board, Escapee Program 1954, A1 1586C, Record Group 59: General Records of the Department of State, 1763–2002, NARA.

54. Frank Hunt to Esther Rhoads, 20 June 1958, [Hong Kong, Letters to Japan, 1958], AFSC Archives.

55. Frank Hunt to Esther Rhoads, 20 June 1958, "I thought Mr. Dawson's summary of the US government's attitude to the Hong Kong Refugee problem was most interesting." Hong Kong, Letters to Japan, 1958, Box: Foreign Service, 1958, AFSC Archives.

56. See Elizabeth Sinn, *Pacific Crossing: California Gold, Chinese Migration, and the Making of Hong Kong* (Hong Kong: Hong Kong University Press, 2012).

57. Judd to Dulles, 20 October 1955, Box 167, File 167.1 China File, ARCI Correspondence / General, 1954–56, ARCI, Hoover Institution Archives, Stanford University.

58. *Refugee Problem in Hong Kong and Macao: Hearings Before the United States Senate Committee on the Judiciary, Subcommittee to Investigate Problems Connected with Refugees and Escapees,* 87th Cong. 2nd Sess. 8 (1962).

59. Denis Moriarty to Frank Hunt, 5 September 1958, Box: Foreign Service, 1958, Letters: London to P, Foreign Service Section, AFSC Archives.

60. Folder, "Hong Kong—Refugees," Box 330, CARE records. Manuscripts and Archives Division. The New York Public Library. Astor, Lenox, and Tilden Foundations.

61. Folder, "Correspondence—1957," Box 568, Hong Kong 1957, CARE records. Manuscripts and Archives Division. The New York Public Library. Astor, Lenox, and Tilden Foundations.

62. Oram to Emmet, 3 January 1952, File 167.4 ARCI – Correspondence – Internal, 1951–52, Box 167, ARCI, Hoover Institution Archives, Stanford University.

63. In a 1954 report, ARCI acknowledged "openings in other parts of the world have been few: 45 persons were resettled in various parts of Southeast Asia; 17 in the US and Canada." "A Report to Our Contributors," ABMAC / ARCI Collection, Box 69 File "A Report to Our Contributors," Rare Books and Manuscripts Library, Columbia University.

64. Howard to Emmet, 23 July 1952, File: Letters from Hong Kong, Nov–Dec.52, Box 17, ARCI, Hoover Institution Archives, Stanford University.

65. Judd to McCormack, House of Representatives, 25 February 1953, File 166.3 China File, "ARCI, Correspondence / General, Jan–June 1953," Box 166, ARCI, Hoover Institution Archives, Stanford University.

66. Thomas Borstelmann, *The Cold War and the Color Line* (Harvard, MA: Harvard University Press, 2003); Mary L. Dudziak, *Cold War Civil Rights: Race and the Image of American Democracy* (Princeton, NJ: Princeton University Press, 2000).

67. Hoskins to Judd, 17 January 52, File 166.1 China File, ARCI, Correspondence / General, 1951–52, Box 166, ARCI, Hoover Institution Archives, Stanford University.

68. Judd to Hoskins, 2 January 1956, File 166.1 China File, ARCI, Correspondence / General, 1951–52, Box 166, ARCI, Hoover Institution Archives, Stanford University.

69. Jack & Janet Shepherd to William Barton et al., 2 September 1958, [Letters: London to P, Foreign Service Section], AFSC Archives.

70. Bill Channel to David Elder, 1 October 1962, [Letters to and from Hong Kong, 1962], Box: International Service Division, Refugee Program Overseas, 1962, AFSC Archives.

71. Memorandum dated 24 September 1954, File 168.3 ARCI Correspondence / Internal 1954, Box 168, ARCI, Hoover Institution Archives, Stanford University.

72. Howard to Garside, 20 March 1956, File: Jan–June.56 Letters from Hong Kong, Box 21, ARCI, Hoover Institution Archives, Stanford University.

73. Bill Channel to Marilyn Loos, 12 May 1960, File: USCR, Box: International Service Division, 1960, AFSC Archives.

74. See campaign by National Council of Churches in New Zealand, led by Revered Aland Brash, as reported in Secretary of Labor to Minister of Immigration, 25 March 1957 "Resettlement of Chinese refugees from Hong Kong and Macao," Archives New Zealand (ANZ) (Wellington).

75. Garside to Nash, 27 May 1953, File: Letters from Hong Kong, Jan–Dec.53, Box 18, ARCI, Hoover Institution Archives, Stanford University.

76. Ali, UNCHR Branch Office (Bangkok) to Hoveyasa, UNCHR (Geneva), 23 September 1953, Fonds UNHCR 11 Records of the Central Registry, Series 1, Classified Subject Files, 1951–1970, 15/2/HK, Box 262, Part 2, UNHCR Archives.

77. Statement by Dr. Yu Tsune-Chi, Sixth Regular Session of the General Assembly of the United Nations, 7 January 1952, Fonds UNHCR 11 Records of the Central Registry, Series 1, Classified Subject Files, 1951–1970 15/2/HK, Box 262, UNHCR Archives.

78. Correspondence from Lieberman to Emmanuel Freedman, Box 65, File 8, New York Times Collection. Foreign Service Desk. New York Public Library.

79. Judd to Shepardson, 17 September 1952, III.A.1. A-B, Box 6, File 5, ARCI, Carnegie Corporation of New York, Columbia University Archives.

80. See Siu-lun Wong, *Emigrant Entrepreneurs: Shanghai Industrialists in Hong Kong* (New York, NY: Oxford University Press, 1988).

81. Falling under the UNHCR's mandate meant that the High Commissioner would be "empowered to defend the interests of the refugees, to act on their behalf in respect of the British authorities in Hong Kong and, in collaboration with the British Government, to take all the necessary steps for emigration and other measures to relieve the situation." Dr. Hambro in Conversation with Governor Grantham, 30 June 1054, Fonds 23, Box 1, UNHCR Archives (Geneva). Debates over the UNHCR's mandate were bound up with debates over the legitimacy of governments in Beijing and Taiwan and whether refugees could seek protection from either regime.

82. I. H. Harris to Mr. Sidebotham, 19 October 1953, CO 1023/117, NAUK.

83. Goedhart to Ford Foundation, 7 May 1953, PA 52-90, Reel 645, Ford Foundation Archives.

84. Progress Reports to Headquarters, Fonds 23, Box 1, Jaeger to B. G. Alexander, UNCHR Geneva, 5 May 1954, UNHCR Archives.

85. Background Briefing to Advisory Committee Meeting, 1954, CO 1030 / 382 File 418/403/02, NAUK.

86. Harris to MacIntosh, 26 April 1955, CO 1030 / 382, NAUK. On Governor Grantham, see Steven Tsang, *A Modern History of Hong Kong* (London, UK: I. B. Tauris, 2007), 148.

87. Harris to MacIntosh, 26 April 1955, CO 1030 / 382, NAUK.

88. See correspondence in CO 1030 / 382 Chinese Refugees, Hong Kong (1954–1956), File 418/403/02, NAUK.

89. "Extract from notes on discussion with Sir Alexander Grantham, 12–20 July, 1954," Harris to MacIntosh, 26 April 1955, CO 1030 / 382 Chinese Refugees Hong Kong (1954–1956), File 418/403/02, NAUK.

90. Summary Record of the 1st Staff meeting, 3 May 1954, Fonds 23, Box 1, Summary Records of Staff Meetings, UNHCR Archives.

91. Hambro address to High Commissioner for Refugees Advisory Committee, Fifth Session, 6 December 1954, CO 1030 / 382 File 418/403/02, NAUK. Hambro never defined the term "political refugees." In his final survey report, he wrote, "a great number of people left the mainland

apparently either because they were opposed to the new regime or because they had lost their means of livelihood, or for fear of persecution and suppression; and a large part of these people fled to the British Colony of Hong Kong." A few paragraphs later, he wrote, "there has been a widespread belief that hundreds of thousands of Chinese people are living not only in poverty, but in misery and on the verge of starvation; and it has been suggested that a great number of them are political refugees." A chapter later, Hambro wrote, "in well-informed circles, which are naturally restricted in number, a reasonable concept prevails: there must be a political reason for the refugees leaving China or for the fact that they continue to reside outside China." It may be inferred that Hambro was thinking of political refugees as people who were opposed to the new regime or who feared persecution, but his exact meaning is unclear. Hambro, 1, 22.

92. Hambro, *Problem of People*, 69.
93. Ibid., 79.
94. Ibid., 128.
95. John Holmes for Secretary of State for External Affairs to Laval Fortier, 4 April 1956, RG 26, 3-24-12, Part 2, Vol. 110, LAC.
96. Hambro, *Problem of People*, 130.
97. Judd to Max Ascoli, 24 May 1954, File 167.1 China File, ARCI Correspondence / General, 1954–56, Box 167, ARCI, Hoover Institution Archives, Stanford University.
98. Hambro, *Problem of People*, 112.
99. It was a view shared by senior colonial administrators as well as authorities responsible for security in the colony. See Annual Report, Hong Kong Police, 1951–52, Chapter XV, "Special Problems," 46.
100. David Elder to Duncan Wood, 21 August 1963, Correspondence: Letters to and from Hong Kong, 1963, Box: International Services Division, 1963, AFSC Archives.
101. Document A/AC.79/12, referenced in Extract from the Report on the Third Session of the UNREF Executive Committee (Geneva, 26 May–1 June 1956) Document A/AC.79/41, Fonds UNHCR 11 Records of the Central Registry, Series 1, Classified Subject Files, 1951–1970 15/2/HK, Box 262, Part 3, UNHCR Archives.
102. In fact, apathy at the UN was so extensive that it was private funding that ensured publication of the mission's final report. 15/2/1 Survey of the Position of Chinese Refugees in Hong Kong (Part 3), Fonds UNHCR 11 Records of the Central Registry, Series 1, Classified Subject Files, 1951–1970 15/2/HK, Box 262, Part 6, UNHCR Archives.
103. Governor of Hong Kong to Secretary of State for the Colonies, 7 July 1955, CO 1030 / 383, NAUK.

104. Folder – "Hong Kong – Refugees" Press Release by Richard A. Shafter, Box 330, CARE records. Manuscripts and Archives Division. The New York Public Library. Astor, Lenox, and Tilden Foundations.

105. Secretary of State for the Colonies to Governor of Hong Kong, 29 May 1957, CO 1030 / 777, NAUK.

106. Correspondence between H. U. Willink, Master of Magdalene College (Cambridge) to Alan Lennox-Boyd, regarding the Oxford Famine Relief Committee's work in Hong Kong, 17 September 1956, CO 1030/384, NAUK.

107. These groups also recommended that the Chinese refugees be brought under the UN High Commissioner's mandate, that adequate funds be provided to deal with the refugee question, and that countries liberalize their immigration policies so as to alleviate the population pressures in Hong Kong. Governor of Hong Kong to Secretary of State for the Colonies, 13 August 1957, CO 1030 / 778, NAUK.

108. Governor of Hong Kong to Secretary of State for the Colonies, 27 August 1957, CO 1030 / 778, NAUK.

109. Jaeger to Alexander, 16 November 1956, Fonds UNHCR 11 Records of the Central Registry, Series 1, Classified Subject Files, 1951–1970, 15/2/ HK, Box 262, Part 3, UNHCR Archives.

110. Handwritten marginalia, correspondence, 29 May 1957, CO 1030 / 778, NAUK.

111. Governor of Hong Kong to Secretary of State for the Colonies, 3 September 1957, CO 1030 / 778, NAUK.

112. Governor of Hong Kong to Secretary of State for the Colonies, 29 August 1957, CO 1030 / 778, NAUK.

113. UNREF Executive Committee – Seventh Session, Morning Meeting, 16 January 1958, Press release No. REF/408, Press Releases, UNHCR Archives.

114. Gil Loescher, *Beyond Charity: International Cooperation and the Global Refugee Crisis* (New York, NY: Oxford University Press, 1993), 97; C. Ivor Jackson, *Refugee Concept in Group Situations* (Cambridge, MA: Kluwer Law International, 1999), 7.

115. International Affairs: Social Affairs - Refugees - Admission of Refugees to New Zealand and New Zealand Participation in World Refugee Year, ABHS 950, W4627, ANZ (Wellington).

116. Jamieson to Read, 5 March 1959, ARR88, Box 8, Country Files, "Canada," United Nations Archives, Geneva (UNAG).

117. Brief for the Australian Delegation to the First Meeting of the Special Executive Committee of the High Commissioner's Programme, Commencing on the 15th June, 1959, dated 5 June 1959, UNHCR Executive Committee - First Special Session - June 1959, A446, 1959/65585, 1957224, National Archives of Australia (NAA) (Canberra).

118. Farran to Woods, 17 April 1959, CO 1030 / 776, NAUK.

119. See correspondence in Brief for the Australian Delegation to the First Meeting of the Special Executive Committee of the High Commissioner's Programme, Commencing on the 15th June, 1959, dated 5 June 1959, UNHCR Executive Committee - First Special Session - June 1959, A446, 1959/65585, 1957224, NAA (Canberra); Refugees - General (1961-1976), AAFD, 811, W3738, 895, CAB 69/1/1, ANZ (Wellington).

120. Verbatim Statement made at the First Session of the Executive Committee of the High Commissioner's Programme, 28 January 1959, ARR, Box 37, File 65 World Refugee Year 10, UK a, UNAG.

121. Black to Wallace, 6 August 1958, CO 1030/781, NAUK.

122. Governor Grantham to Secretary of State for the Colonies, 26 September 1957, CO 1030 / 778 NAUK.

123. UKNY to Governor of Hong Kong, November 6, CO 1030/781 NAUK.

124. Statements on World Refugee Year, Meeting 871 of 13th General Assembly, ARR, Box 37, File 65 World Refugee Year 10, UK a, UNAG.

125. Even though ARCI essentially closed its operations in Hong Kong in 1959, it was concerned about the impact of its retreat on communist propaganda efforts. In April 1960, the executive committee agreed that "as long as ARCI has any funds, and as long as there is a program which would merit support both by ARCI and the Government, the name of ARCI should be kept in the picture." "Executive Committee Minutes, 14 April 1960," ABMAC Collection, ABMAC / ARCI Minutes, 1958–1969, Box 69, File Rare Books and Manuscripts Library, Columbia University. The Executive Committee minutes from 1959 to 1960 make no reference to World Refugee Year.

126. PL 85-316 redistributed unused refugee visas authorized under the Refugee Relief Act. Hsu, *The Good Immigrants,* 160.

127. All figures in US dollars.

128. Memo from Burgess to Wallace, 21 May 1960, FO 371/150430, NAUK. On government reservations about dramatic fund-raising schemes, see correspondence in File 1, Box 4, Canadian Committee for World Refugee Year Fonds, McMaster University Archives.

129. See Emma Haddad, "Danger Happens at the Border," in *Borderscapes: Hidden Geographies and Politics at Territory's Edge,* ed. Prem Kumar Rajaram and Carl Grundy-Warr (Minneapolis: University of Minnesota, 2008), 119.

130. Statements on World Refugee Year, Meeting 871 of 13th GA, ARR, Box 37, File 65 World Refugee Year 10, UK a, UNAG.

131. The South African Refugee Organization was a registered welfare organization established in the 1950s. Correspondence dated 26 August 1959. ARB, Vol.38, A153/98, The National Conference on World Refugee Year, Part 1, 1959-1960, NASA (Pretoria).

132. See correspondence in ARB, Vol.38, A153/98, The National Conference on World Refugee Year, Part 1, 1959-1960, NASA (Pretoria).

133. Ibid. See also A. J. Christopher, "Apartheid Planning in South Africa: The Case of Port Elizabeth," *The Geographical Journal* 153, no. 2 (July 1987): 195–204.

134. Ibid. The government of South Africa contributed regularly to ICEM, with half of its annual allocation being used for the transportation of migrants to South Africa.

135. "World Refugee Year and US Committee for Refugees," 27 April 1959, Box: AFSC, Minutes, 1959, AFSC Archives.

136. Peter Gatrell, *Free World? The Campaign to Save the World's Refugees, 1959–63* (Cambridge, MA: Cambridge University Press, 2011), 119.

137. *United States. Immigration. Senate. Report of the Committee on the Judiciary, United States Senate made by its subcommittee on immigration and naturalization pursuant to S. Res. 60 88th Congress, 1st session, as extended, Report 88th Congress, 2nd Session, 5* (1964).

138. Cited in Preface of *World Refugee Year, July 1959–June 1960; Report on the Participation of the United States Government* (Washington, U. S. Govt. Print. Off., 1960).

139. Ibid, 3.

140. Duncan Wood, Friends International to Richard Smith, AFSC, 20 June 1960, Box: International Service Division, 1960, AFSC Archives.

141. Tarah Brookfield, *Cold War Comforts: Canadian Women, Child Safety, and Global Insecurity* (Waterloo: Wilfrid Laurier University Press, 2012).

142. Sherene H. Razack, *Race, Space, and the Law: Unmapping a White Settler Society* (Toronto: Between the Lines, 2002), 3–4. Activists made allusions to the unpopulated space available in settler societies on numerous occasions as they sought to advance resettlement programs out of Hong Kong. See Human Rights Council of Hong Kong, 5 May 1962, HKR5545-1-23-1, Hong Kong Public Records Office (HKPRO).

143. Brief for the Australian Delegation to the First Meeting of the Special Executive Committee of the High Commissioner's Programme, Commencing on the 15th June, 1959, dated 5 June 1959, UNHCR Executive Committee - First Special Session - June 1959, A446, 1959/65585, 1957224, National Archives of Australia (NAA) (Canberra).

144. CORSO was established during the Second World War to help war-torn countries rehabilitate, and China ranked high on its list of priorities in the immediate postwar period. Tom Newnham, *New Zealand Women in China* (Auckland: Graphic Publications, 1995), 41.

145. Russell Thurlow Thompson, *New Zealand in Relief: The Story of CORSO's Twenty-One Years of Relief Service Overseas* (Wellington: New Zealand Council of Organizations for Relief Services Overseas, 1965), 82.

146. Secretary - Administrator for Australian National Committee for World Refugee Year, September 1962, Report of the Australian National

Committee for World Refugee Year for the period 1 July 1961 to 30 June 1962, Richard Donald Malcolmson Fonds, Box 2825, Folder 5, State Library of Victoria, Melbourne, Australia.

147. Correspondence, 7 July 1959, WCC, 1c WRY, 1960, 425.02.09.018 Commission of Inter-Church Aid, Refugee and World Service (CICARWS), World Council of Churches Archives, Geneva.

148. Recommendations of Executive Committee to General Committee on Allocations, United Kingdom Committee for World Refugee Year, ARR, Box 38, File 65 WRY 10, UK b, UNAG.

149. Prem Kumar Rajaram, "Humanitarianism and Representations of the Refugee," *Journal of Refugee Studies* 15, no. 3 (2002): 253.

150. On photography as representative of, and informed by, specific historical conditions and circumstances that reinforce particular conventions, see James Ryan, *Picturing Empire: Photography and the Visualization of the British Empire* (London, UK: Reaktion Books, 1997), 9.

151. Richard Donald Malcolmson Fonds, Box 2825, Folder 3, State Library of Victoria, Melbourne, Australia.

152. Duckworth-Baker to Jacobson, 26 August 1959, ARR88, Box 8, Country Files, "Canada," Verbatim record of 88th meeting of ICEM, UNAG.

153. World Council of Churches Briefs, 21 October 1959, 1b World Refugee Year, 1960, UNAG.

154. Correspondence, October 1959, CO 1030 / 782, NAUK.

155. Statement by the High Commissioner, Letter of Appeal Sent 12 February 1958, Press Releases, UNHCR Archives.

156. Governor of Hong Kong to the Secretary of State for the Colonies, 11 March 1960, CO 1030 / 1309, NAUK.

157. Correspondence in CO 1030 / 782, NAUK.

158. Gatrell, *Free World?* 3.

159. Statement by Mr. Jean J. Chenard, President of the Standing Conference of Voluntary Agencies Working for Refugees, at the Conference for World Refugee Year National Committees Convened by the ICWRY, Geneva, 16–20 January 1961. Conference documents. *Conférence de l'Année Mondiale du Réfugié* (Geneva, 1961), United Nations Library, Geneva (UNLG).

160. *Observations on Emigration as a Solution to the Chinese Problem in Hong Kong*, World Council of Churches, CO 1030/1683, NAUK.

161. Canada, for instance, limited family sponsorships for the children of Chinese Canadians to individuals under the age of twenty-one. Documents, *Année Mondiale du Réfugié*, 1959–60, 23 January 1959–5 October 1960 (Geneva: CIAMR, 1960), UNLG.

162. Press Release, REF / 613 8.10.600 "Executive Committee Concludes World Refugee Year Discussion, Hears Appeal from Chinese Delegate and Takes Note of Progress Report on Hungarian Refugees and

Report of UNHCR Mental Health Adviser," Press Releases, UNHCR Archives.

163. The greatest progress occurred in the realm of medical admissions; New Zealand admitted handicapped refugees and their families and the Canadian government supported the admission of tubercular refugees and their families.

164. The conference was organized under the auspices of the Intergovernmental Committee on European Migration (ICEM), predecessor to the International Organization of Migration (IOM). ICEM was focused on the logistics of resettling refugees and displaced persons after the Second World War.

165. Extract from a letter to H. R. E. Browne from J. M. Dutton, 27 January 1960, CO 1030 / 1309, NAUK.

166. Extract from a letter to H. R. E. Browne from R. H. Davies, 25 February 1960, CO 1030 / 1309, NAUK.

167. Extract from a letter to H. R. E. Browne from J. K Hickman, 2 January 1960, CO 1030 / 1309, NAUK.

168. Burgh (Colonial Office) to Governor Trench (Hong Kong), 29 September 1960, CO 1030 / 1310, NAUK.

169. Treating refugees as a problem was common. See, for instance, G. J. van Heuven Goedhart, *Refugee Problems and Their Solutions* (London: United Nations Association, [195-?]).

170. Statement by Mr. Jean J. Chenard, President of the Standing Conference of Voluntary Agencies Working for Refugees, at the Conference for World Refugee Year National Committees Convened by the International Committee for World Refugee Year, Geneva, 16-20 January 1961. Conference Documents. *Conférence de l'Année Mondiale du Réfugié*. (Geneva, 1961), UNLG.

4. TROUBLED TIMES

1. 2 May 1966, Chinese Case Files in Accession 1984-1985/041, LAC (additional reference details cannot be provided due to privacy agreement with LAC under Section 8(2)(j) of Canada's *Access to Information Act*, 2 February 2012).

2. Patricia Roy, *The Triumph of Citizenship: The Japanese and Chinese in Canada, 1941–1967* (Vancouver: UBC Press, 2007), 298.

3. This was theoretically possible, though family sponsorships remained an elusive reality. Canada limited the categories of eligible sponsorship for Chinese Canadians, and the People's Republic of China enforced strict emigration bans until 1973, with real reforms coming only with reforms under Deng Xiaoping in 1978.

4. General Joseph May Swing, Oral History Collection, Rare Books and Manuscripts Library, Columbia University.

5. For a full discussion, see Lisa Mar, *Brokering Belonging: Chinese in Canada's Exclusion Era, 1885–1945* (New York, NY: Oxford University Press, 2010).

6. Mae Ngai, *Impossible Subjects: Illegal Aliens and the Making of Modern America* (Princeton, NJ: Princeton University Press, 2005), 205.

7. Anna Pegler-Gordon, *In Sight of America: Photography and Development of U.S. Immigration Policy* (Berkeley: University of California Press, 2009), 36.

8. Madeleine Y. Hsu, *Dreaming of Gold, Dreaming of Home* (Stanford, CA: Stanford University Press, 2000), 88. Mae Ngai makes a similar point in *Impossible Subjects*, 204. Illegal migration has been incorporated into many studies of Chinese migration. Lisa Mar's *Brokering Belonging: Chinese in Canada's Exclusion Era, 1885–1945* explores the manner in which networks enabled the migration of people who were ineligible for entry. Erika Lee's *At America's Gates: Chinese Immigration during the Exclusion Era, 1882–1943* traces how the regimes developed in response to unwanted numbers of Chinese migrants invited additional illegality. See also Lucy Salyer, *Laws as Harsh as Tigers: Chinese Immigrants and the Shaping of Modern Immigration Law* (Chapel Hill: University of North Carolina Press, 1995). These works thoroughly document the existence of illegal migration and the manner in which migrants overcame restrictions. However, they pay little attention to the construction of the term "illegal" itself. This pursuit has fallen to legal scholars and criminal justice experts who attend to the manner in which states constructed illegality in response to the movement of people, often with larger security and control paradigms in mind. See Philippe Bourbeau, *The Securitization of Migration* (New York, NY: Routledge, 2011); S. Legomsky, "Portraits of the Undocumented Immigrant: A Dialogue," *Georgia Law Review* 44, no. 65 (2009): 1–96, Meghan G. McDowell and Nancy A. Wonders, "Keeping Migrants in Their Place: Technologies of Control and Racialized Public Space in Arizona," *Social Justice* 36, no. 2 (2009–2010): 54–72.

9. "Opium Smuggling on Our Western Coasts," *New York Herald*, 28 December 1890, 30. For discussion, see Kay Anderson, *Vancouver's Chinatown: Racial Discourse in Canada, 1875–1980* (Montreal: McGill-Queen's University Press, 1995); Peter Ward, *White Canada Forever: Popular Attitudes and Public Policy toward Orientals in British Columbia*, 3rd ed. (Montreal: McGill-Queen's University Press, 2002), 133.

10. For further context, see John Fitzgerald, *Big White Lie: Chinese Australians in White Australia* (Sydney: UNSW Press, 2007).

11. On the complex politics surrounding illegal and undocumented migrants, see Christian Joppke, "Why Liberal States Accept Unwanted Immigration," *World Politics* 50, no. 2 (January 1998): 266–293.

12. For a full discussion, see John Torpey, *Invention of the Passport: Surveillance, Citizenship, and the State* (Cambridge: Cambridge University Press, 2000).

13. Peter Nyers, *Rethinking Refugees: Beyond States of Emergency* (New York, NY: Routledge, 2005).

14. Mae Ngai, "Legacies of Exclusion: Illegal Chinese Immigration during the Cold War Years," *Journal of American Ethnic History* 18, no. 1 (1998): 6. Newspaper story by John Elfreth Watkins, "Breaking the Chinese Ring," *San Francisco Chronicle*, 21 May 1905, 5. See also "Says There Is a Conspiracy," *San Francisco Chronicle*, 3 October 1904, 12.

15. The story cast all Chinese as unscrupulous: "The lawless element is not by any means confined to the lower and poorer classes, who ordinarily constitute the criminal class, but men of wealth and influence and high social standing embark in these unlawful enterprises. . . . While the government is losing thousands of dollars every week which should be paid as duty on imported goods these men of means are becoming richer and still more influential, and they feel perfectly secure from arrest and even the slightest suspicion." See "Opium Smuggling on Our Western Coasts," *New York Herald*, 28 December 1890, 30.

16. On racialized Commonwealth discussions of refugees, see correspondence in DO 35: Dominions Office and Commonwealth Relations Office: Original Correspondence, 1943–46, NAUK.

17. Catherine Dauvergne, *Making People Illegal* (Cambridge: Cambridge University Press, 2008), 16.

18. On illegal migration to South Africa, see Clive Glaser, "White but Illegal: Undocumented Madeiran Immigration to South Africa, 1920s–1970s," *Immigrants & Minorities* 31, no. 1 (2013): 74–98; Audie Klotz, *Migration and National Identity in South Africa, 1860–2010* (Cambridge: Cambridge University Press, 2013); Andrew MacDonald, "Colonial Trespassers in the Making of South Africa's International Borders, 1900–1950," (PhD Diss., Cambridge University, 2012). On the Chinese experience specifically, see Jeremy Martens, "A Transnational History of Immigration Restriction: Natal and New South Wales, 1896–97," *The Journal of Imperial and Commonwealth History* 34, no. 3 (September 2006): 323–344. On the consequences of being a small minority community, see Karen L. Harris, "The Chinese in South Africa: A Historical Study of a Cultural Minority," *New Contree* 46 (November 1999), 89: http://dspace.nwu.ac.za/handle/10394/4969.

19. Ufrieda Ho, *Paper Sons and Daughters: Growing Up Chinese in South Africa, A Memoir* (Johannesburg: Picador Africa, 2011), 38.

20. Melanie Yap and Diane Leong Man, *Colour, Confusion, & Concessions: The History of the Chinese in South Africa* (Hong Kong: Hong Kong University Press, 1996), 351. See also position of Chinese in the Union, 1955–1961,

BTS 19/2/1, Part 3, NASA (Pretoria). On the history of the Chinese community in South Africa generally, see Yoon Jung Park, *A Matter of Honour: Being Chinese in South Africa* (Plymouth, UK: Lexington Books, 2008); Linda Human, *The Chinese People of South Africa* (Pretoria: University of South Africa, 1984).

21. Yap and Leong Man, *Colour,* 355.

22. Dauvergne, *Making People Illegal,* 16.

23. Memorandum, "Chinese Illegally Entering New Zealand," 9 February 1954, Immigration - Policy and General - Chinese, 1946-1957, ABKF, 947, W5182, 93, 22/1/115, Part 1, ANZ (Wellington).

24. Walter Judd to Paul Hoffman, Ford Foundation, 17 September 1952, PA 52-90 Reel 645, Ford Foundation Archives.

25. "Many Chinese with Illegal Certificates," *San Francisco Chronicle,* 19 September 1903, 18.

26. Glenn Nicholls observes that after the First World War, persons of Chinese and German descent were non grata in Australia, and this was reflected in their majority representation in deportation statistics, *Deported: A History of Forced Departures from Australia* (Sydney: UNSW Press, 2007), 61.

27. Fitzgerald, *Big White Lie,* 2; Klaus Neumann, *Refuge Australia: Australia's Humanitarian Record* (Sydney: UNSW Press, 2004), 98.

28. Jane Carey and Claire McLisky, eds., *Creating White Australia* (Sydney: Sydney University Press, 2009).

29. Using digital technologies, Kate Bagnall and Tim Sherratt are combing the repositories of the National Archives of Australia for visual records of non-white residents of the country pre- and post-federation in to capture the "real face of White Australia." See http://invisibleaustralians. org.

30. Most of the so-called refugees were deserting seamen who were able to gain access to Australian territory through their work on passing vessels. They were permitted to remain for the duration of the war with the understanding that they would have to leave once normal shipping routes resumed and berths became available for them. On a few exceptional occasions, wealthy Chinese merchants were able to pay their way into Australia to wait out the end of the war. However, they too were required to depart at the end of the hostilities. Telegram from Australian Legation (Chungking) to Department of External Affairs, 11 January 1942, [Re Entry of Temporary Refugees (Chinese) from Singapore], MP729/6, 67/401/67, 384550, NAA (Melbourne).

31. Sean Brawley, "Mrs. O'Keefe and the Battle for White Australia," Public Lecture for the National Archives of Australia, Presented in Canberra on 1 June 2006, www.naa.gov.au. Gwenda Tavan argues that although

the deportation controversies led to the first policy reforms in 1950, the White Australia policy was never a singular policy but rather an amalgamation of rules and regulations. It was therefore difficult to eliminate. *The Long Slow Death of White Australia* (Brunswick: Scribe Publications, 2005), 62. See also A. C. Palfreeman, *The Administration of the White Australia Policy* (London: Cambridge University Press, 1967).

32. Nicholls, *Deported*, 82.

33. James Jupp, *From White Australia to Woomera: The Story of Australian Immigration* (Cambridge: Cambridge University Press, 2002), 11. Kevin Blackburn, "Disguised Anti-Colonialism: Protest against the White Australia policy in Malaya and Singapore, 1947-1962," *Australian Journal of International Affairs* 55, no. 1 (April 2001): 101-117. Matthew Jordan, "The Reappraisal of the White Australia policy against the Background of a Changing Asia, 1945-66," (PhD Diss., University of Sydney, 2001), 259.

34. *Commonwealth Parliamentary Debates*, House of Representatives, 5 July 1949, Vol. 203, 1937 cited in Susan Hardistry, "Framing and Reframing 'Refugee': A Cultural History of the Concept in Australia from 1938 to 1951," (PhD Diss., University of Melbourne, 1999), 65.

35. Arthur Calwell, "Wartime Refugees Removals Bill, Second Reading," *Commonwealth Parliamentary Debates,* House of Representatives, 30 June 1949, No.1 1949-1950, 809.

36. KWAN Ng and Others v. The Commonwealth of Australia and Others, A10072, 1949/25, NAA (Canberra).

37. Tom Frame, *The Life and Death of Harold Holt* (Sydney: Allen & Unwin, 2005), 67, cited in Klaus Neumann and Gwenda Tavan, eds., *Does History Matter? Making and Debating Citizenship, Immigration, and Refugee Policy in Australia and New Zealand* (Canberra: ANU Press, 2009), 13, http://epress.anu.edu.au/anzsog/immigration/mobile_devices/ch01s02. html. The government also permitted 600 students and merchants to remain in Australia under "Liberal-Attitude Status Permits" after they refused to return to China following the Chinese Communist Party's rise to power. Charles Price, "Immigration Policies and Refugees in Australia," *International Migration Review* 15, no. 1/2 (Spring–Summer, 1981): 99-108.

38. "Immigration Policy" Statement by Arthur Calwell to the House of Representatives, 8 September 1949, http://www.immi.gov.au/about/anniversary/_pdf/03-statements-vol3-immigration-policy.pdf.

39. Ibid.

40. Anna Haebich, *Spinning the Dream: Assimilation in Australia 1950–1970* (Fremantle: Fremantle Press, 2008), 163. The only groups resettled from China were 13,000 White Russians and Old Believers.

41. See Nicholas Thomas, ed., *Re-Orienting Australia-China Relations: 1972 to the Present* (Aldershot, UK: Ashgate Publishing, 2004); David Walker, *Anxious Nation: Australia and the Rise of Asia, 1850–1939* (Brisbane: University of Queensland Press, 1999). See also James Curran and Stuart Ward, *The Unknown Nation: Australia after Empire* (Carlton, VIC: Melbourne University Press, 2010); Lachlan Strahan, *Australia's China: Changing Perceptions from the 1930s to the 1990s* (Cambridge: Cambridge University Press, 1996).

42. Prem Kumar Rajaram, "Disruptive Writing and a Critique of Territoriality," *Review of International Studies* 30, no. 2 (April 2004): 205.

43. Stephen Alomes et al., "The Social Context of Postwar Conservatism," in *Australia's First Cold War 1945–1953*, Vol. 1, *Society, Communism, and Culture*, ed. Ann Curthoys and John Merritt (Sydney: George Allen & Unwin, 1984).

44. Correspondence, 24 February 1950, CO 537/ 6314, NAUK.

45. "The Entry of Chinese from Hong Kong," Commonwealth Immigration Advisory Council, 26–27 July 1956, A2169, 1956, 1955269, NAA (Canberra).

46. Ibid.

47. Mr. Lang (Representative for Reid), "Aliens Bill 1947, Second Reading," *Commonwealth Parliamentary Debates,* House of Representatives, 16 March 1947, 1177.

48. Arthur Locke Chong, Shirley Fitzgerald – interviews with members of the Sydney Chinese community, 1996, Mitchell Library, MLOH 273, Sydney.

49. Memorandum to Mr. Furler, 14 November 1962, A6908, S250019, 1120263, NAA (Canberra).

50. Memo by C. H. Smith, 17 November 1954 re. Yick Chong Garden, Box 106, C3939, N1962/75101, 1052236, NAA (Sydney).

51. T. H. E. Heyes to Chief Migration Officer, New South Wales, 9 November 1959, Box 106, C3939, N1962/75101, 1052236, NAA (Sydney).

52. Memorandum to The Secretary for Immigration from H. McGinness, Assistant Secretary, 2 March 1959, Chinese and Other Asian Illegal Immigrants – Deportation Policy, A698, S250019, 1120263, NAA (Canberra).

53. This was due in part to the lack of formal diplomatic relations between the two countries, compounded by the PRC government's suspicions about Chinese whose loyalties and credentials it had not verified. For a discussion on the politics of returning overseas Chinese, see Glen Peterson, *Overseas Chinese in the People's Republic of China* (New York: Routledge, 2012).

54. "Blatant Abuse of White Australia: Chequers Chief Cops Extensions," *Truth*, 4 April 1954, Immigration – Summaries and Statistics of Activities Associated with Illegal or Prohibited Chinese Immigrants in New South Wales, Box 106, C3939, N1962/75101, 1052236, NAA (Sydney).

55. William Liu, the foremost advocate of Chinese Australian interests, consistently framed his appeals on behalf of the community in terms of the economic contributions they were making to Australian society. Representative examples include "A New Era in Australian Chinese Relations"; Liu to Dr. Tuan, 7 September 1942; Liu to Brian Penton, Editor of the *Daily Telegraph*, 24 March 1945, William Liu Papers, 6294/1, State Library of New South Wales.

56. Arthur Locke Chang, Shirley Fitzgerald – interviews with members of the Sydney Chinese community, 1996, MLOH 273, Mitchell Library. On the history of Sydney's Chinese community, see Shirley Fitzgerald, *Red Tape, Gold Scissors: The Story of Sydney's Chinese* (Sydney: State Library of New South Wales, 1996).

57. Arthur Locke Chang, Shirley Fitzgerald – interviews with members of the Sydney Chinese community, 1996, MLOH 273, Mitchell Library, Sydney.

58. "Good Farmer but Must Be a Grocer," *The Daily Telegraph,* 17 October 1949, Arthur Caldwell Manus (MS4738), Box 42, Folder: 1949, Chinese Deportees, National Library of Australia.

59. William Liu Papers, 6294/8, State Library of New South Wales.

60. Statistics Relating to Deportation of Chinese since 1 July 1953 to date by T. A. Smith, 18 April 1962, A6980, S25050, 7115768, NAA (Canberra).

61. Memo to the Minister, Deportation of Chinese Nationals to Formosa, 29 June 1954, 62/66130, 196202, NAA (Canberra).

62. Haebich, *Spinning the Dream*, 24.

63. David Lowe, *Menzies and the 'Great World Struggle': Australia's Cold War, 1948–1954* (Sydney: UNSW Press, 1999), 113.

64. H. L. Nutt to the Minister, 16 March 1954, Deportation of Chinese Nationals to Formosa, 62/6613, 1962025, NAA (Canberra).

65. Ngai, *Impossible Subjects*, 208.

66. It was also the Australian public, not politicians, who proved more inclined to liberalize the White Australia policy. Ken Rivett, *Immigration: Control or Colour Bar? The Background to "White Australia" and a Proposal for Change* (Melbourne: Melbourne University Press, 1962).

67. A. L. Nutt, Memorandum to the Minister, re. Chinese (and other Asian) Illegal Entrants – Policy as to Deportation, 4 March 1959, Chinese and Other Asian illegal immigrants – Deportation policy, A6980, S250019, 1120263, NAA (Canberra).

68. Correspondence in Deportation of Chinese Illegal Entrants – 1962 Billy Wong Case, A6980, S250503, 7115768, NAA (Canberra).

69. Memo to the Minister, Deportation of Chinese Nationals to Formosa, 29 June 1954, 62/66130, 196202, NAA (Canberra).

70. Chinese Illegal Immigrants – Policy on Deportation Procedures, A6980, S250503, 7115768, NAA (Canberra).

71. Ibid.
72. Memo, Comment on News articles, 6 April 1963, Deportation of Chinese Illegal Entrants – 1962 Billy Wong Case, A6980, S250503, 7115768, NAA (Canberra).
73. Neumann, *Refuge Australia*, 99.
74. "Reds – and Red Tape," *Sunday Telegraph*, 15 April 1962, A6980, S250503, 7115768, NAA (Canberra).
75. Memo, Comment on News articles, 16 April 1962, A6980, S250503, 7115768, NAA (Canberra).
76. Leading Editorial, *Hobart Mercury*, 17 April 1962, A6980, S250503, 7115768, NAA (Canberra).
77. "Talks on Fate of 5 Chinese," *Daily Telegraph*, 18 April 1962, A6980, S250503, 7115768, NAA (Canberra).
78. Seventeen Chinese Stowaways – One Deserter, Memo by C. H. S. Smith, 25 August 1962, NAA (Sydney).
79. Handwriting by W. R. Bickford, 20 July 1964, DO 126/4 Deportation of Chinese from Australia to Hong Kong, 1964, NAUK.
80. Ngai, "Legacies of Exclusion."
81. Ngai, *Impossible Subjects*, 206.
82. Cited in Ngai, *Impossible Subjects*, 209.
83. See correspondence in "Chinese Immigration," RG 26, File 3-33-7, Part 3, Vol. 125, LAC.
84. McLeod to Drumright, 3 March 1955, Record Group 59: General Records of the Department of State, 1763–2002, Box 19, NARA.
85. Xioajian Zhao, *Remaking Chinese America: Immigration, Family, and Community, 1940–1965* (New Brunswick, NJ: Rutgers University Press, 2002), 174.
86. Ibid., 183.
87. General Joseph May Swing, Oral History Collection, Rare Books and Manuscripts Library, Columbia University.
88. Ngai, "Legacies of Exclusion," 24.
89. Him Mark Lai, "Unfinished Business: The Confession Program," San Francisco: Chinese Historical Society of America and Asian American Studies (San Francisco State University, 1994), 47–57.
90. Zhao, *Remaking Chinese America*, 179.
91. Ngai, "Legacies of Exclusion," 26.
92. Ibid., 27.
93. "Chinese Immigration Interim Report, January 1960," RG 18, File 63, Vol. 11856, LAC.
94. Him Mark Lai, "Unfinished Business," 51.
95. Memo to James Bissett from Laval Fortier, 21 January 1960, RG 26, 3-33-7, Part 3, Vol. 125, LAC.

96. Correspondence regarding prohibited immigrants working in Chinese market gardens at Camden, SP244/2, N1950/2/16653, 7299347, NAA (Sydney).

97. Forty-five people were arrested in the initial raids. See Patricia Roy, *The Triumph of Citizenship: The Japanese and Chinese in Canada* (Vancouver: UBC Press, 2010), 278.

98. General Joseph May Swing, Oral History Collection, Rare Books and Manuscripts Library, Columbia University.

99. Governor of Hong Kong to Secretary of State for the Colonies, 3 January 1964, HKMS158-1-301, HKPRO.

100. Chinese Case Files in Accession 1984-1985/041, LAC (additional reference details cannot be provided due to privacy agreement with LAC under Section 8(2)(j) of Canada's *Access to Information Act*, 2 February 2012).

101. Roy, *Triumph of Citizenship*, 279.

102. The significance of the Status Adjustment Program has been underestimated in general immigration histories and accounts of Chinese immigration to Canada. Having first described illegal Chinese migration as a "fascinating problem," Freda Hawkins then surveys the program before assessing it as having "limited value" given the problems of investigation and enforcement. See *Canada and Immigration: Public Policy and Public Concern* (Montreal: McGill-Queen's University Press, 2002), 133. Similarly, Ninette Kelley and Michael Trebilcock describe the program as "unsuccessful" in its first two years of operations as a result of the Chinese communities' mistrust about the government's motives and guarantees. See *The Making of the Mosaic: A History of Canadian Immigration Policy* (Toronto: University of Toronto Press, 2010), 364.

103. Sid Chow Tan, interview with author, 22 October 2009, Vancouver, British Columbia.

104. Douglas Lam, interview with author, 11 July 2010, Sydney, Australia.

105. Giorgio Agamben, *Homo Sacer: Sovereign Power and Bare Life* (Stanford, CA: Stanford University Press, 1995), 121.

106. See correspondence in "Chinese Immigration," 1963, RG 26, File 3-33-7, Part 3, Vol. 125 LAC and also recollections by General Joseph May Swing, Oral History Collection, Rare Books and Manuscripts Library, Columbia University.

107. Dauvergne, *Making People Illegal*, 19.

5. COLD WAR VISUALS

1. Sharon Sliwinski, "The Childhood of Human Rights: The Kodak on the Congo," *The Journal of Visual Culture* 5 (2006): 334. The focus on a dynamic interaction between viewer and viewed has also been described

as a "visual event." See also Nicholas Mirzoeff, *An Introduction to Visual Culture* (New York, NY: Routledge, 2000), 13; and Maria Sturken and Lisa Cartwright, eds., *Practices of Looking: An Introduction to Visual Culture* (New York, NY: Oxford University Press, 2009). On media coverage and humanitarianism, see Sharon Sliwinski, "The Aesthetics of Human Rights," *Culture, Theory & Critique* 50, no. 1 (2009): 23–39; Simon Cottle and David Nolan, "Everyone was Dying for Footage: Global Humanitarianism and the Changing Aid-Media Field," *Journalism Studies* 8, no. 6 (2007): 862–878; Sue Tait, "Bearing Witness, Journalism, and Moral Responsibility," *Media, Culture & Society* 33, no. 8 (November 2011): 1220–1235.

2. For a critical discussion of Kim Phuc and the visual qualities of her experience, see Mimi Thi Nguyen, *The Gift of Freedom: War, Debt, and Other Refugee Passages* (Durham, NC: Duke University Press, 2012).

3. Prem Kumar Rajaram, "Humanitarianism and Representations of the Refugee," *Journal of Refugee Studies* 15, no. 3 (2002): 251.

4. Lisa Malkki, "Speechless Emissaries: Refugees, Humanitarianism, and Dehistoricization," *Cultural Anthropology* 11, no. 3 (1996): 378. See also Barbara Harrell-Bond, "In Search of 'Invisible' Actors: Barriers to Access in Refugee Research," *Journal of Refugee Studies*, 20, no. 2 (2007): 281–298.

5. Abigail Solomon-Godeau, *Photography at the Dock: Essays on Photographic History, Institutions, and Practices* (Minneapolis: University of Minnesota Press, 1994), 180.

6. *Refugee Problem in Hong Kong and Macao: Hearings Before the United States Senate Committee on the Judiciary, Subcommittee to Investigate Problems Connected with Refugees and Escapees,* 87th Cong. 2nd Sess. 4 (1962). See also Laura Briggs, "Mother, Child, Race, Nation: The Visual Iconography of Rescue and the Politics of Transnational and Transracial Adoption," *Gender & History* 15, no. 2 (August 2003): 179–200.

7. Melanie Yap and Dianne Leong, *Colour, Confusion, & Concessions: The History of the Chinese in South Africa* (Hong Kong: Hong Kong University Press, 1996), 350.

8. On the history of Chinese refugees in the United States, see Madeline Hsu, "The Disappearance of America's Cold War Chinese Refugees, 1948–1966," *Journal of American Ethnic History* 31, no. 4 (Summer 2012): 12–33.

9. "Troops Said Fleeing China Food Shortage," *Globe and Mail*, 12 May 1962, 2.

10. "Weird Invasion by Red Chinese: Hong Kong Baffled Over Flood of People," *New Zealand Herald*, 17 May 1962, 7.

11. "Red Refugee Flow," *Cape Argus*, 23 May 1962, 2.

12. Dave Elder to Duncan Wood, 27 August 1962, Letters to and from Hong Kong, 1962, Box: International Service Division, Refugee Program Overseas, 1962, AFSC Archives.

13. *Refugee Problem in Hong Kong and Macao*, 175.

14. Diary Entry, 20 May 1962, Diary of Captain James B. Atkinson, MSS. Eng. misc. c. 506-11, Bodleian Library, Oxford University.

15. J. P. Maunoir, Delegate of the ICRC to Paul Calderara, Delegate of the ICRC (Hong Kong), 25 May 1962, I B AG 234048-008.03 Réfugiés Chinois à Hong Kong, 15 May 1962 to 30 September 1963, International Committee of the Red Cross Archives, Geneva.

16. Description by Bishop Swanstrom of Catholic Relief Services in *Refugee Problem in Hong Kong and Macao*, 42.

17. Ibid. See also "Troops Said Fleeing China Food Shortage," *Globe and Mail*, 12 May 1962, 2.

18. "Hong Kong Bars 10,000 Refugees," *New York Times,* 13 May 1962, 7. A week later journalists were giving more credence to the possibility that the communist regime was trying to embarrass the West. "Washington Weighs Position," *New York Times*, 22 May 1962, 3.

19. Telegram from Beijing to Foreign Office, re-transmitted from Colonial Office to Hong Kong, 20 May 1962, CO 1030/1114, NAUK.

20. Harry Redl, *Exodus from China* (Hong Kong: Dragonfly Books, 1962), 2.

21. "Extract from a dispatch from the Governor of Hong Kong to the Secretary of State for the Colonies," 23 December 1956, CO 1030/384, 1954–56, NAUK.

22. Memo from Burgess to Wallace, 21 May 1960, FO 371/150430, NAUK.

23. Memo from Dalton to Wallace, 23 October 1959, CO 1030/723, NAUK.

24. Atkinson Diaries, 19 April 1962. By May 15th, of the 17,656 Chinese migrants arrested on the land frontier, 75 percent (13,411) had been returned to the mainland. Of those intercepted at sea, 93 percent were returned. Telegram from Foreign Office to UK Delegation in Geneva, 15 May 1962, CO 1030/1312, NAUK.

25. *Refugee Problem in Hong Kong and Macao*, 38.

26. Special Groups of Refugees – Chinese Refugees in Hong Kong, 15/HK/CHI, UNAG.

27. Governor of Hong Kong to Secretary of State for the Colonies, 15 May 1962, CO 1030/1312, NAUK.

28. Ibid.

29. "Hong Kong Government Policy Statement on Immigration from China and Offers of Help from Overseas," Statement by Colonial Secretary Claude Burgess in Hong Kong Legislative Council, 13 June 1962, HKR5545-1-23-1, HKPRO.

30. *Refugee Problem in Hong Kong and Macao*, 36.

31. Atkinson Diaries, 19 April 1962. Western humanitarians, including staff of the AFSC, ultimately became concerned about population control issues during their time in Hong Kong. For a discussion of various population management strategies in the postwar period, see Matthew Connelly, *Fatal Misconception: The Struggle to Control World Population* (New York, NY: Columbia University Press, 2008).

32. Atkinson Diaries, 18 May 1962.

33. Judd Correspondence, 2 January 1958, File 167.2 China File, ARCI Correspondence / General, 1957-59, ARCI Collection, Hoover Institution Archives, Stanford University.

34. Claire Chennault to Walter Judd, 11 June 1962, File 185.3 Emergency Committee for Chinese Refugees (Chinese Refugee Relief), Box 185, ARCI, Hoover Institution Archives, Stanford University.

35. In September 1962, Chenneault undertook a trip to Hong Kong to see for herself what conditions were like in the colony. US officials at the Consul reported, "she appeared not to be favorably impressed with the large resettlement estates but did not offer an alternative solution to the problem." Report, 6 September 1962, Box 2536, 846.G.49/7-462, NARA.

36. Bill Channel to Dave Elder, 18 July 1962, Letters to and from Hong Kong, 1962, American Friends Service Committee, Box ISD, 1962, AFSC Archives.

37. The Council was an affiliate of the International League for Human Rights, a United Nations Consultant Agency.

38. Human Rights Council of Hong Kong, 5 May 1962, HKR5545-1-23-1, HKPRO.

39. The 1962 Commonwealth Immigrants Act severely restricted entry to Britain from non-white sections of the Commonwealth including the Caribbean, Asia, South Asia, and Africa. On the history of race and immigration to the United Kingdom, see Kathleen Paul, *Whitewashing Britain: Race and Citizenship in the Postwar Era* (Ithaca, NY: Cornell University Press, 1997); Ian R. G. Spencer, *British Immigration Policy Since 1939: The Making of Multi-Racial Britain* (London, UK: Routledge, 1997); Dilip Hiro, *Black British / White British: A History of Race Relations in Britain*, rev. ed. (London, UK: Eyre & Spottiswoode, 1973).

40. *Refugee Problem in Hong Kong and Macao*, 15.

41. Dave Elder to Bill Channel, 20 May 1962, Letters to and from Hong Kong, 1962, Box ISD, 1962, AFSC Archives.

42. *Refugee Problem in Hong Kong and Macao*, 18.

43. In emphasizing the silence that surrounds refugees, Prem Kumar Rajaram and Lisa Malkki point to two dominant facets of refugee representation. The first is the "groupness" of refugees. Refugees were, and continue to be, consistently depicted as a mass of people in flight. Even images of refugees

in isolation are usually juxtaposed against larger group photos. Numbers testify to the scale of the problem. The second element is the anonymity of the refugee. Images erase life histories and become shorthand for the presumably desperate circumstances that lead to an individual's flight: "Humanitarianism and Representation of Refugees" and "Speechless Emissaries." See also Anna Szorenyi, "The Images Speak for Themselves? Reading Refugee Coffee Table Books," *Visual Studies* 21, no. 1 (April 2006): 36.

44. Burrows died in a helicopter crash during the Vietnam War. Ben Cosgrove, "Portrait from Hell: Larry Burrows' 'Reaching Out,' 1966," *Time*, 2 December 2014, http://time.com/3491033/life-behind-the-picture-larry-burrows-reaching-out-vietnam-1966.

45. Robert Edwin Herzstein, *Henry R. Luce, Time and the American Crusade in Asia* (Cambridge: Cambridge University Press, 2005), 9. Media outlets were well aware of their capacity to shape public opinion around life in communist China. Editors at the *New York Times* rejected a 1961 piece by Jacques Vernant on the refugee situation in Hong Kong because it lacked "local color." They asked that Vernant include tidbits about "the omnipresence of the Communists" at the border and in Hong Kong as evidenced by "shop window displays, the headquarters of the Communist union, the outlet store for Communist exports . . . ." They requested in particular "a description of one poor family in a Chinese slum" or a "refugee squatter's colony" they suggested "would do." What they wanted was to "get as close as possible to the pulse of the place" and to cast communism in a particular light. Freedman to Vernant, 16 June 1961, File 8, Box 65, New York Times Company records. Foreign Desk records. Manuscripts and Archives Division. The New York Public Library. Astor, Lenox, and Tilden Foundations.

46. *Life*, 8 June 1962, 40.

47. See contributions in Charles Ferrall, Paul Millar, and Keren Smith, eds., *East by South: China in the Australasian Imagination* (Wellington: Victoria University Press, 2005).

48. *Life*, 8 June 1962, 40.

49. Nicholas Mirzoeff describes veiled visuality as a situation where the subject is both visible and invisible, present and silenced: "On Visuality," *Journal of Visual Culture* 5, no. 53 (2006): 70.

50. See Lara Campbell, *Respectable Citizens: Gender, Family, and Unemployment in Ontario's Great Depression* (Toronto: University of Toronto Press, 2009); Elaine Tyler May, *Homeward Bound: American Families in the Cold War* (New York, NY: Basic Books, 2008).

51. Mona Gleason, *Normalizing the Ideal: Psychology, Schooling, and the Family in Postwar Canada* (Toronto: University of Toronto Press, 1999).

52. As Douglas Owram suggests, "the family was fragile in a world that had seen war and depression tear families apart. Prosperity was fragile to a

generation emerging from the war and seeking to create that house and white picket fence in the suburbs. The Cold War, especially with the outbreak of the Korean War in 1950, made the world a fragile place." *Born at the Right Time* (Toronto: University of Toronto Press, 1996), 52.

53. *New York Times*, 18 May 1962, 3.
54. Hsu, *The Good Immigrants*, 183.
55. Michael G. Davis, "Impetus for Immigration Reform: Asian Refugees and the Cold War," *The Journal of American-East Asian Relations* 7, no. 3/4 (1998): 141.
56. Donald Janson, "First Chinese Refugees Welcomed in Chicago," *New York Times*, 6 June 1962, 9. Frank Jing Eng passed away a week after his son's arrival in the United States. "Father of Chinese Refugee Admitted by Kennedy Dies," *New York Times*, 11 June 1962, 31.
57. *Refugee Problem in Hong Kong and Macao*, 93.
58. Ibid., 94.
59. Ibid., 104.
60. Ibid., 2.
61. Ibid., 49.
62. *Life*, 15 June 1962, 44C.
63. Arthur Kleinman and Joan Kleinman, "The Appeal of Experience; The Dismay of Images: Cultural Appropriations of Suffering in our Times," *Daedalus* 125, no. 1 (1996): 9.
64. *Life* Magazine, 15 June 1962, 44C.
65. Davis, 134.
66. "Hong Kong Police Take Panic Steps," *Globe and Mail*, 22 May 1962, 1.
67. Ibid.
68. Ryan M. Touhey, "Dealing in Black and White: The Diefenbaker Government and the Cold War in South Asia 1957–1963," *Canadian Historical Review* 92, no. 3 (2011): 438.
69. Ninette Kelley and Michael Trebilcock, *The Making of the Mosaic: A History of Canadian Immigration Policy* (Toronto: University of Toronto Press, 2010), 363.
70. Special Movement of Chinese Refugees from Hong Kong – Operational Control, RG 76, File 555-54-526-3, Part 1, Vol. 861, LAC.
71. Memorandum to the Minister, 10 January 1963, RG 76, File 555-54-536, Part 2, Vol. 861, LAC.
72. 1958 Brief by the Chinese Benevolent Association, RG 26, File 3-33-7, Part 3, Vol. 125, LAC.
73. In 1949, the federal government confronted the possibility that members of the Guomindang might seek asylum in Canada following their defeat at the hands of the Chinese Communist Party. Not wanting to encourage

requests for asylum from China, cabinet approved temporary entry permits for former government officials while urging private citizens to return home. A year later, the immigration department received an application from twelve Trappist monks who had fled communist China and wanted to settle in Canada temporarily. On this occasion, department officials were anxious about the kind of precedent that might be established if they permitted the monks to enter. As a result, their entry was initially refused. Petitions from Guomindang officials followed and the government eventually conceded, despite misgivings that accepting the monks would appear at best inconsistent and at worst hypocritical, given the government's ongoing refusal to expand family sponsorship opportunities for Chinese Canadians.

74. Comments on Chinese Benevolent Association Brief, RG 26, File 3-33-7, Part 2, Vol. 125, LAC.

75. Memorandum from Laval Fortier to Minister, 27 July 1955, RG 26, File 3-33-7, Part 2, Vol. 125, LAC.

76. Comments on Chinese Benevolent Association Brief, RG 26, File 3-33-7, Part 2, Vol. 125, LAC.

77. 1957 Brief by the Chinese Benevolent Association, RG 26, File 3-33-7, Part 1, Vol. 125, LAC.

78. "In Dark On Refugees – Chinese," *Toronto Star*, 2 August 1962.

79. "One of the Hundred Starts New Life Here," *Winnipeg Tribune*, 18 February 1963.

80. *Refugee Problem in Hong Kong and Macao*, 50.

81. This was all part of the "Application for Admission to Canada" questionnaire that applicants were required to complete.

82. Jim Chu, E-mail exchange with the author, 28 July 2012.

83. *Refugee Problem in Hong Kong and Macao*, 50.

84. Memo, 30 August 1962, MG 32 B1, File I-2-18 Hong Kong Refugees – Policy and Statistics, Richard Bell Fonds, Vol. 112, LAC.

85. "It's a Big, Big World," *Edmonton Journal*, 23 October 1962.

86. "Meet Mr. Kam Hung Fung; Refugee from Red China," *Winnipeg Free Press*, 13 August 1962.

87. Anna Szorenyi, "The Images Speak for Themselves?" Prem Kumar Rajaram, "Humanitarianism and Representations of the Refugee," *Journal of Refugee Studies* 15: no. 3 (2002): 251.

88. *Winnipeg Free Press*, 13 August 1962.

89. Chinese Case Files in Accession RG 76, 1984-1985/041, LAC (additional reference details cannot be provided due to privacy agreement with LAC under Section 8(2)(j) of Canada's *Access to Information Act*, 2 February 2012).

90. Memorandum regarding J. K. Abbott, 22 January 1963, MG 32 B1, Richard Bell Fonds, File I-2-18 Hong Kong Refugees – Policy and Statistics, Vol. 112, LAC.

91. Ibid.

92. Report on Private, Voluntary Action in Canada During World Refugee Year, Box 4, File 9, Canadian Committee for World Refugee Year Fonds, McMaster University Archives.

93. Acting Director of Immigration to Acting Deputy Minister, 18 October 1963, RG 26, File 3-33-7, Part 3, Vol. 125, LAC.

94. Evelyn Bark to Margaret E. Wilson, Canadian Red Cross, 16 February 1962, File 76/27(3) – Hong Kong Parcels (1961–66), British Red Cross Archives.

95. D. A. Reid to Acting Deputy Minister, 18 October 1963, RG 26, File 3-33-7, Part 3, Vol. 125, LAC.

96. Ibid.

97. Ruth Brouwer, "When Missions Became Development: Ironies of 'NGO-ization' in Mainstream Canadian Churches in the 1960s," *Canadian Historical Review* 91, no. 4 (2010): 688.

98. John Hagan, "Narrowing the Gap by Widening the Conflict: Power Politics, Symbols of Sovereignty, and the American Vietnam War Resisters' Migration to Canada," *Law & Society Review* 34, no. 3 (2000): 607–650.

99. Memorandum from General Executive Assistant to Director of Immigration, 12 June 1962, RG 26, File 3-33-7, Part 3, Vol. 125, LAC.

100. Memo to File, 10 December 1963, RG 26, File 3-33-7, Part 3, Vol. 125, LAC.

101. Memorandum to the Minister, 23 December 1968, RG 26, File 3-33-7, Part 4, Vol. 126, LAC.

102. Acting Director of Immigration to Deputy Minister, 6 March 1964, RG 26, File 3-33-7, Part 4, Vol. 126, LAC.

103. Memorandum to the Minister, 8 September 1964, RG 26, File 3-33-7, Part 4, Vol. 126, LAC.

104. Robin Galienne, "The Whole Thing Was Orchestrated" (PhD Diss., University of Auckland, 1988), 13. See also Julie Ann Robertson, "Of Scarecrows and Straw Men: Asylum in Aotearoa New Zealand" (PhD Diss., University of Otago, 2006).

105. Manying Ip, "Redefining Chinese Female Migration: From Exclusion to Transnationalism," in *Shifting Centres: Women and Migration in New Zealand History*, ed. Lyndon Fraser and Katie Pickles (Dunedin: University of Otago Press, 2002), 156.

106. Customs Department memo C33/253/M, "Asian Immigration," 29 September 1950, Labour Department, L1, 22/1/81, ANZ (Wellington). Cited in Manying Ip, "Redefining Chinese Female Migration," 156.

107. Manying Ip, "Redefining Chinese Female Migration," 156.

108. Alan Brash, *The National Council of Churches in New Zealand* (Christchurch: National Council of Churches in New Zealand, ca1955).

109. R. Thurlow Thompson, *New Zealand in Relief: The Story of CORSO's Twenty-One Years of Relief Service Overseas* (Wellington: New Zealand Council of Organizations for Relief Services Overseas, 1965), 59.

110. Resettlement of Chinese refugees from Hong Kong and Macao, Secretary of Labour to Minister of Immigration, 25 March 1957, Immigration - Policy and General - Chinese, 1946–1957, W5182, Box 93 File 22/1/115, Part 1, ANZ (Wellington).

111. Immigration - General - Refugee - International Refugee Organisation - Policy, 1961- 1962, W5182, Box 26, File 22/1/27, ANZ (Wellington).

112. Galienne, "The Whole Thing Was Orchestrated," 4.

113. Sean Brawley, "No 'White Policy' in New Zealand: Fact and Fiction in New Zealand's Immigration Record, 1946–1978," *New Zealand Journal of History* 27, no. 1 (1993): 16–36.

114. Mr. Shand, Memo for File, 29 August 1961, Immigration - General - Chinese Orphans, W5182, Box 96, File 22/1/115/1, Part 1, ANZ (Wellington).

115. Shand to Mr. G. W. Lowes, 1 June 1961, Immigration - Policy and General - Chinese, 1960–1962, W5182, Box 94, File 22/1/115, Part 3, ANZ (Wellington).

116. It is unclear from the archival record to which initiatives, exactly, Reverend Sprackett was referring. Mention of other programs may have been a rhetorical strategy more than anything else.

117. Bob Sprackett, Presbyterian Case-Work Centre, Kowloon to Mr. N. E. Kirk, House of Representatives, New Zealand, 17 August 1960, Immigration - General - Chinese Orphans, W5182, Box 96, File 22/1/115/1, Part 1, ANZ (Wellington).

118. See Tobias Hubinette, "From Orphan Trains to Babylifts: Colonial Trafficking, Empire Building, and Social Engineering," in *Outsiders Within: Writing on Transracial Adoption*, ed. Jane Jeong Trenka, Chinyere Oparah, and Sun Yung Shin (Boston, MA: South End Press, 2006), 139–149; Everett M. Ressler, Neil Boothby, and Daniel J. Steinbock, *Unaccompanied Children: Care and Protection in Wars, Natural Disasters, and Refugee Movements* (New York, NY: Oxford University Press, 1988).

119. Karen Dubinsky, *Babies without Borders: Adoption and Migration across the Americas* (Toronto: University of Toronto Press, 2010); Eleana J. Kim, *Adopted Territory: Transnational Korean Adoptees and the Politics of Belonging* (Durham, NC: Duke University Press, 2010); Veronica Strong-Boag, *Finding Families, Finding Ourselves: English Canada Encounters Adoption from the Nineteenth Century to the 1990s* (Don Mills: Oxford University Press, 2006); Ann Beaglehole, *Facing the Past: Looking Back at Refugee Childhood in New Zealand* (Sydney: Allen & Unwin, 1990).

120. L. Pycroft to Curran, 11 October 1962, Adoptions Chinese Orphans, 1962–1965 File 4/4/8, BBID 5823/107B, NAA (Auckland).

121. Letter to Mr. R. Downham, 1 December 1961, Immigration - General - Chinese Orphans, W5182, Box 96, File 22/1/115/1, Part 1, ANZ (Wellington).

122. Letter from Rev. C. R. Sprackett, Minister of St. Martins Presbyterian Church, Christchurch, to Prime Minister, 9 February 1961, Immigration - General - Chinese Orphans, W5182, Box 96, File 22/1/115/1, Part 1, ANZ (Wellington).

123. Immigration - General - Refugee - International Refugee Organisation - Policy, 1961- 1962, W5182, Box 26, File 22/1/27, ANZ (Wellington).

124. "Chinese Refugees," *Dominion,* 10 May 1962, 12.

125. "The Enigma of Chinese Refugees," *New Zealand Herald,* 25 May 1962, 4.

126. Chinese Refugees in Hong Kong, RG 76, File 555-54-536, Part 2, Vol. 861, LAC.

127. Mr. Shand, Minister of Immigration, to Mr. Hallyburton Johnstone, 3 August 1962, Immigration - General - Chinese Orphans, W5182, Box 96, File 22/1/115/1, Part 1, ANZ (Wellington).

128. External Affairs to High Commissioner for New Zealand, Canberra, 12 June 1962, Immigration - General - Chinese Orphans, W5182, Box 96, File 22/1/115/1, Part 1, ANZ (Wellington).

129. Mr. Shand, Minister of Immigration, to Mr. Hallyburton Johnstone, 3 August 1962, Immigration - General - Chinese Orphans, W5182, Box 96, File 22/1/115/1, Part 1, ANZ (Wellington).

130. New Zealand Chinese Association to Prime Minister, 6 June 1962, Immigration - General - Chinese Orphans W5182, Box 96, File 22/1/115/1, Part 1, ANZ (Wellington).

131. Mr. Shand to W. S. Goosman, 26 July 1962, Immigration - General - Chinese Orphans, W5182, Box 96, File 22/1/115/1, Part 2, ANZ (Wellington).

132. J. P. Costello, Trade Commissioner to Director of Labour, 27 July 1962, Immigration - General - Chinese Orphans, W5182, Box 96, File 22/1/115/1, Part 1, ANZ (Wellington).

133. On the work of the ISS, see Tara Zahra, *The Lost Children: Reconstructing Europe's Families after World War II* (Boston, MA: Harvard University Press, 2011). In 1958, with financial support from the American government, the ISS initiated a program to match prospective American parents with Chinese orphans. It resettled 500 children from Hong Kong in three years.

134. Years later, in a profile article in a national newspaper, adoptee Kim Makae talked about how isolating it was to grow up Chinese in New Zealand, "Search Reunites Chinese Orphans," *Dominion,* 11 December 1999.

135. Department of Labour to Immigration, 16 September 1960, Immigration - General - Chinese Orphans, W5182, Box 96, File 22/1/115/1, Part 1, ANZ (Wellington).

136. Circular Memo No.1962/1951, 14 September 1962, Adoptions Chinese Orphans, 1962–1965 File 4/4/8, BBID 5823/107B, ANZ (Auckland).

137. Flint to Curran, 2 August 1962, Adoptions Chinese Orphans, 1962–1965 File 4/4/8, BBID 5823/107B, ANZ (Auckland).

138. Pycroft to Curran, 11 October 1962, Adoptions Chinese Orphans, 1962–1965 File 4/4/8, BBID 5823/107B, ANZ (Auckland).

139. Adoptions Chinese Orphans, 1962–1965 File 4/4/8, BBID 5823/107B, ANZ (Auckland).

140. Movement of Chinese Refugees from Hong Kong, RG 76, File 555-54-526-3, Vol. 861, LAC.

141. Draft Statement, RG 26, File 3-33-7, Part 4, Vol. 126, LAC.

142. For a description of events, see Timothy Brook, *Quelling the People: The Military Suppression of the Beijing Democracy Movement* (Stanford, CA: Stanford University Press, 1998).

143. Jan Wong, *Jan Wong's China: Reports from a Not-So-Foreign Correspondent* (Toronto: Doubleday Canada, 1999), 15.

6. NAVIGATING CHANGE

1. Registrations, ABMAC / ARCI – Case I, Box 67, ARCI Collection, Columbia University Archives.

2. Ibid.

3. There was considerable ambivalence globally about how the protocol should be structured. Sara E. Davies, "Redundant or Essential? How Politics Shaped the Outcome of the 1967 Protocol," *International Journal of Refugee Law* 19, no. 4 (2007): 703–728.

4. The United States never signed the convention, preferring to define refugees in domestic legislation such as the 1953 Refugee Relief Act and the 1980 Refugee Act.

5. David Palmer has studied the limited humanitarianism in Australia's ratification of the convention. In his assessment, "the intention was less to avoid granting refuge to non-Europeans, than to ensure Australia had the power to remove them when they were no longer in need of protection, and so avoid a grant of asylum being automatically equated with permanent residence." See "The Quest for 'Wriggle Room': Australia and the Refugees Convention, 1951–73," *Australian Journal of International Affairs* 63, no. 2 (2009): 305.

6. On the history of refugee policy in South Africa, see Jonathan Crush, ed., *Beyond Control: Immigration and Human Rights in a Democratic South Africa*

(Cape Town: IDASA and Queen's University, Canada, 1998); Timothy Robin Smith, "Making of the 1998 Refugees Act: Consultation, Compromise, and Controversy" (MA Thesis, University of Witwatersrand, 2003).

7. Sean Brawley, "No 'White Policy' in New Zealand: Fact and Fiction in New Zealand's Asian Immigration Record, 1946–1978," *Journal of New Zealand History* 27, no. 1 (1993): 19.

8. Cited in Brawley, "No 'White Policy' in New Zealand," 63.

9. Nigel Murphy, *Guide to Laws and Policies Relating to the Chinese in New Zealand 1871–1997* (Wellington: New Zealand Chinese Association, 2008), 336.

10. The Labor portfolio included responsibilities for immigration.

11. Shand to Minister of Defence, Immigration Policy – Hong Kong Residents, 14 March 1966, Immigration - Policy and General - Chinese, 1966–1970, ABKF, 947, W5182, 94, 22/1/115, Part 5, NAA (Canberra).

12. Shand to Ngan, 7 July 1964, Immigration - Policy and General - Chinese, 1963–1966, ABKF, 947, W5182, 94, 22/1/115, Part 4, ANZ (Wellington).

13. President Eisenhower's handling of the Little Rock school crisis in 1954 drew international attention as did the violent Sharpeville massacre in 1960. Both of these events sounded alarm bells for countries concerned about their own domestic race relations. On Little Rock and Sharpeville, see Mary L. Dudziak, *Cold War Civil Rights: Race and the Image of American Democracy* (Princeton, NJ: Princeton University Press, 2000) and Peter Gatrell, *Free World? The Campaign to Save the World's Refugees, 1956–1963* (Cambridge: Cambridge University Press, 2011).

14. http://www.stats.govt.nz/browse_for_stats/population/estimates_and_projections/historical-population-tables.aspx.

15. Brawley, "No 'White Policy' in New Zealand," 30.

16. Shand to Brash, 30 July 1962, regarding visit to Hong Kong and discussions with Mr. Sedgwick, Commissioner of Labour and Immigration in Hong Kong, Immigration - Policy and General - Chinese, 1960–1962, ABKF, 947, W5182, 94, 22/1/115, Part 3, ANZ (Wellington).

17. New Zealand Chinese Association to Prime Minister, 6 June 1962, Immigration - General - Chinese Orphans, W5182, Box 96, File22/1/115/1, Part 1, ANZ (Wellington).

18. Handwritten notes, 13 March 1957, Immigration – Policy and General – Chinese, 1946–1957, W5182, Box 93, File 22/1/115, Part 1, ANZ (Wellington).

19. Mr. Thompson to Mr. Parsonage, 23 April 1957, Immigration - Policy and General - Chinese, 1946–1957, W5182, Box 93, File 22/1/115, Part 1, ANZ (Wellington).

20. Immigration – Policy and General – Chinese, 1946–1957, W5182, Box 93, File 22/1/115, Part 1, ANZ (Wellington).

21. Ibid.

22. Rev. Brash to Mr. Shand, 26 July 1963, Immigration - General - Chinese Orphans, W5182, Box 96, File 22/1/115/1, Part 2, ANZ (Wellington).

23. Mr. Moohan (Petone), 26 June 1957, *Parliamentary Debates (Hansard)* (Wellington, NZ: Government Printer, 1957).

24. The position later became permanent and was filled by Reverend O'Grady for many years.

25. For details on the operations of the NCC in the field of refugee resettlement, see Gerald Fitzgerald, "Refugees and Migrant Resettlement & Adjustment in New Zealand, 1964–1976" (MA Thesis, University of Otago, 1982).

26. Sponsorship by the National Council of Churches of Migrants Including Refugees, 10 February 1966, Refugees - General (1961–1976), AAFD, 811, W3738, 8, 95, CAB 69/1/1, ANZ (Wellington).

27. Ibid.

28. Ibid.

29. Ibid.

30. Immigration - General - International Refugees Organization - Chinese in Hong Kong 1967–1984, ABKF, 947, W5182, 33, 22/1/27/17, Part 1, ANZ (Wellington).

31. Neugebauer to Crawford, 9 August 1971, Immigration - General - International Refugees Organization - Chinese in Hong Kong 1967–1984, ABKF, 947, W5182, 33, 22/1/27/17, Part 1, ANZ (Wellington).

32. External Affairs to Crawford, 30 August 1971, Immigration - General - International Refugees Organization - Chinese in Hong Kong 1967–1984, ABKF, 947, W5182, 33, 22/1/27/17, Part 1, ANZ (Wellington).

33. Ibid.

34. Labour to Crawford, 15 December 1971, External Affairs to Crawford, 30 August 1971, Immigration - General - International Refugees Organization - Chinese in Hong Kong 1967–1984, ABKF, 947, W5182, 33, 22/1/27/17, Part 1, ANZ (Wellington).

35. This intervention was warmly received. The Minister of Labour annotated the memorandum with the following comment: "I couldn't agree more. I have long felt sure that there must be more deserving cases in Hong Kong than the type of case usually put forward by Rev. O'Grady, 23 August 1971." External Affairs to Crawford, 30 August 1971, Immigration - General - International Refugees Organization - Chinese in Hong Kong 1967–1984, ABKF, 947, W5182, 33, 22/1/27/17, Part 1, ANZ (Wellington).

36. See Immigration - General - International Refugees Organization - Chinese in Hong Kong 1967–1984, ABKF, 947, W5182, 33, 22/1/27/17, Part 1, ANZ (Wellington).

37. Labour to O'Grady, 18 July 1969, Immigration - General - International Refugees Organization - Chinese in Hong Kong 1967–1984, ABKF, 947, W5182, 33, 22/1/27/17, Part 1, ANZ (Wellington).

38. Neugebauer to Crawford, 26 February 1971, External Affairs to Crawford, 30 August 1971, Immigration - General - International Refugees Organization - Chinese in Hong Kong 1967–1984, ABKF, 947, W5182, 33, 22/1/27/17, Part 1, ANZ (Wellington).

39. External Affairs to Crawford, 30 August 1971, Immigration - General - International Refugees Organization - Chinese in Hong Kong 1967–1984, ABKF, 947, W5182, 33, 22/1/27/17, Part 1, ANZ (Wellington).

40. Neugebauer to O'Grady, 10 May 1972; External Affairs to Crawford, 30 August 1971, Immigration - General - International Refugees Organization - Chinese in Hong Kong 1967–1984, ABKF, 947, W5182, 33, 22/1/27/17, Part 1, ANZ (Wellington).

41. Coveny for Secretary of Labour to Crawford, 29 July 1971, External Affairs to Crawford, 30 August 1971, Immigration - General - International Refugees Organization - Chinese in Hong Kong 1967–1984, ABKF, 947, W5182, 33, 22/1/27/17, Part 1, ANZ (wellington).

42. The government preserved news clippings on illegal migration from China. See HKR5545-1-23-1, HKPRO.

43. James Mitchell, "Immigration and National Identity in 1970s New Zealand" (Unpublished PhD Thesis, University of Otago, 2010), 14.

44. Murphy, *Guide to Laws and Policies Relating to the Chinese in New Zealand 1871–1997*, 290.

45. Political scientist William Joseph describes the Cultural Revolution as "an enormously complex" series of events. He identifies three distinct stages to the revolution: the mass phase from 1966–1969, the military phase (1969), and the secession phase. "Foreword" to Yuan Gao, *Born Red: A Chronicle of the Cultural Revolution* (Stanford, CA: Stanford University Press, 1987), 16; Yan Jiaqi, trans. D. W. Kwok, *Turbulent Decade: A History of the Cultural Revolution* (Honolulu: University of Hawai'i Press, 1996), 2; Roderick MacFarquhar and Michael Schoenhals, *Mao's Last Revolution* (Cambridge, MA: The Belknap Press of Harvard University Press, 2006), 1.

46. Bernard Frolic, *Mao's People: Sixteen Portraits of Life in Revolutionary China* (Cambridge, MA: Harvard University Press, 1980), 42.

47. Lynn T. White and Kam-Yee Law, "Explanations for China's Revolution at Its Peak," and Hong Yung Lee, "Historical Reflections on the Cultural Revolution as a Political Movement," in *The Chinese Cultural Revolution Reconsidered*, ed. Kam-Yee Law (New York, NY: Palgrave Macmillan, 2003).

48. MacFarquhar and Schoenhals, *Mao's Last Revolution*, 124.

49. Ibid., 125.

50. Ibid.

51. Frolic, *Mao's People*, 42.

52. Hong Yung Lee, "Historical Reflections on the Cultural Revolution as a Political Movement," in *The Chinese Cultural Revolution Reconsidered*, ed. Kam-Yee Law (New York, NY: Palgrave Macmillan, 2003), 93.

53. Frolic, *Mao's People*, 192.

54. Ibid., 4.

55. Robert Bickers and Ray Yep, "Studying the 1967 Riots," in *May Days in Hong Kong: Riots and Emergency in 1967*, ed. Robert Bickers and Ray Yep (Hong Kong: Hong Kong University Press, 2009), 1. See also Ray Yep, "Cultural Revolution in Hong Kong: Emergency Powers, Administration of Justice, and the Turbulent Year of 1967," *Modern Asian Studies* 46, no. 4 (2012): 1007–1032; John Cooper, *Colony in Conflict: The Hong Kong Disturbances, May 1967–January 1968* (Hong Kong: Swindon, 1970).

56. "World Survey – 1967–1968, Asia," *International Review of Missions* 58, no. 229 (1969): 10.

57. Bickers and Yep, "Studying the 1967 Riots," 9.

58. These occurred most obviously at three-year intervals between 1973 and 1979. In 1973, when there was an initial surge, the governor of Hong Kong immediately introduced new restrictions on illegal entries on the grounds that the colony needed to "defend against possible disturbances on the border and possibly within the colony." Stuart to Youde, 7 November 1973, FCO 40/812, NAUK.

59. Arnold to Scholar, 27 July 1967, T 225/3778, NAUK.

60. See Alan Smart, "Unreliable Chinese: Internal Security and the Devaluation and Expansion of Citizenship in Postwar Hong Kong," in *War, Citizenship, Territory*, ed. Deborah Cowen and Emily Gilbert (New York, NY: Routledge, 2008), 219–240; Agnes Ku, "Immigration Policies, Discourses, and the Politics of Local Belonging in Hong Kong (1950–1980)," *Modern China* 30, no. 3 (2004): 326–360.

61. Ku, "Immigration Policies," 329.

62. Xiao-Feng Liu and Glen Norcliffe, "Closed Windows, Open Doors: Geopolitics and Post-1949 Mainland Chinese Immigration to Canada," *The Canadian Geographer* 40, no. 4 (1996): 310. Johannes M. M. Chan, "Immigration Policies and Human Resources Planning," in *Hong Kong Mobile: Making a Global Population*, ed. Helen F. Siu and Agnes Ku (Hong Kong: Hong Kong University Press, 2008), 159. For a related discussion on perceptions of migrants in the Canadian context, see David Ley, "Seeking Homo Economicus: The Canadian State and the Strange Story of the Business Immigration Program," *Annals of the Association of American Geographers* 93, no. 2 (2003): 426–441.

63. Cheung Tak-Wai, "Illegal Immigrants in Hong Kong: A Study of the Government's Policy and Control" (MPA Thesis, University of Hong Kong, 1995), 41.

64. Frolic, *Mao's People*, 119.

65. *Hong Kong Standard*, 18 November 1974, cited in Cheung Tak-Wai, "Illegal Immigrants in Hong Kong," 42. See also Frolic, *Mao's People*, 42.

66. John Burns, "Immigration from China and the Future of Hong Kong," *Asian Survey* 27, no. 6 (June 1987): 665.

67. See Carol Jones and Jon Vagg, *Criminal Justice in Hong Kong* (New York, NY: Routledge-Cavendish, 2007); Chung-Kwong Wong, "Chinese Illegal Immigrants: Their Effects on the Social and Public Order in Hong Kong" (MA Thesis, University of Leicester, 1995); Jon Vagg, "Sometimes a Crime: Illegal Immigration and Hong Kong," *Crime & Delinquency* 39 (1993): 355–372.

68. See correspondence in CO 1030 / 384, NAUK.

69. Raph Girard, interview with author, 9 January 2012, Ottawa, Ontario.

70. See correspondence in Selection and Processing – China, RG 76, File 5855-1-526, Part 6, Vol. 1277, LAC.

71. The repeal of the Chinese Immigration Act in 1947 was followed shortly by the PRC government's imposition of exit controls in 1951, which meant that the family reunification agreement facilitated the most open movement between the two countries since 1885.

72. Text of agreement in RG25, File 80-3-1-PRC, Part 2, Vol. 11050, LAC.

73. Pierre Trudeau had visited China in 1960 and wrote about it with Jacques Hébert in *Two Innocents in China* (Toronto: Douglas & McIntyre, 1968).

74. For press coverage, see *Globe and Mail*, 5–11 October 1973.

75. See correspondence in RG76, File 5855-1-526, Part 8, Vol, 1277, LAC.

76. On gatekeeping as a foundational principle of national immigration services, see Allison Mountz, *Seeking Asylum: Human Smuggling and Bureaucracy at the Border* (Minneapolis: University of Minnesota Press, 2010); Franca Iacovetta, *Gatekeepers: Reshaping Immigrant Lives in Cold War Canada* (Toronto: Between the Lines Press, 2006).

77. Don Cameron, interview with author, 8 December 2013, Steveston, British Columbia.

78. Kirk Bell to Jean Edmonds, 7 November 1974, RG76, File 5855-1-526, Part 9, Vol. 1277, LAC.

79. Gerry Campbell, e-mail correspondence with author, 18 April 2012.

80. "Family Reunification," provided to Deputy Minister of Manpower and Immigration, 4 November 1974, RG76, File 5855-1-526, Part 8, Vol. 1277, LAC.

81. Ibid.

82. Ibid.

83. Much of the debate was over the 1974 Green Paper, which suggested potential negative impacts if the Canadian state admitted too many

migrants. Ninette Kelley and Michael Trebilcock, *The Making of the Mosaic: A History of Canadian Immigration Policy* (Toronto: University of Toronto Press, 2010), 389.

84. The government was acutely aware of public opinion as a result of a white paper consultation process initiated in 1974.

85. Mike Molloy, e-mail correspondence with author, 17 April 2012.

86. Raph Girard, interview with author, 9 January 2012, Ottawa, Ontario.

87. Memo to the Minister re. Refugee Sponsorship, 18 June 1979, RG 76, File 8630-6C, Part 2, Vol. 1832, LAC.

88. Human Rights Consultation, 1974 - constitution and bylaws, MG 28 I37, File 8, Vol. 185, Canadian Council of Churches Fonds, LAC.

89. Raph Girard, interview with author, 9 January 2012, Ottawa, Ontario. For a discussion of how racial hierarchies and structural discrimination perpetuated legacies of white supremacy in international relations, see John Price, *Orienting Canada: Race, Empire, and the Transpacific* (Vancouver: UBC Press, 2011), 317; Sean Brawley, *The White Peril: Foreign Relations and Asian Immigration to Australasia and North America, 1919–1978* (Sydney: University of New South Wales Press, 1995), 3.

90. Prior to RSAC, applicants who were refused admission to Canada could appeal to the Immigration Appeal Board, established in 1952, on the basis that they were convention refugees. Failed claims at the Immigration Appeal Board were then heard either by the immigration minister or the Federal Court. This process was described as an "ad hoc system of refugee protection." In 1973, the government amended the 1967 Immigration Appeal Board to create the first statutory basis for refugee admissions in Canada. See Preliminary Report - H. G. Plaut, RG 82, 1995/96-137, Box 2, LAC. See also Ian Hunter, *The Immigration Appeal Board: A Study* (Toronto: Law Reform Commission of Canada, 1976).

91. Of the thousands of Chinese migrants who came to Canada in the period under study, only two cases survive in sufficiently substantial form to determine that the issue at stake in their appearance before the Immigration Appeal Board was one of refugee status. The story of other refugee claimants from the People's Republic of China has been lost. The legacy of RSAC's operations is to be found in fourteen thousand unmarked boxes of case file records presently stored in several Toronto warehouses. The contents of the boxes are a mystery. There are no surviving file lists nor did RSAC track the demographics of the cases it considered. The available statistics demonstrate approval rate by geographic region in Canada, demonstrating the preoccupations with processing efficiency that have characterized refugee determination systems in Canada since they were first established in 1973. The loss of intellectual

control over these records means that there is no way of identifying the contents of the files, short of physically sorting through the boxes. The only way to document the appearance of Chinese migrants in the refugee determination process, one which amounts to a very poor substitute, is to consult the checkered records documenting cases initially refused by RSAC, which were later heard by the Immigration Appeal Board. Under the process established by the 1976 Immigration Act, a senior immigration officer first interviewed in-country applicants under oath. The transcript of this interview was then forwarded to the minister and the claimant. RSAC reviewed the transcript and advised the minister of its decision. Under the terms of the act, an appeal could be made to the Immigration Appeal Board. The board reserved the right to determine if there were grounds for believing that a claim could be established before proceeding to a full hearing, where necessary. As a final step, an appeal to the courts might be made. Details about the boxes were acquired as a result of an Access to Information Request to Immigration and Refugee Board on 28 July 2011.

92. Decisions, 25 April 1979, *Notes of Recent Decisions Rendered by the Immigration Appeal Board* (Ottawa: Canadian Law Information Council, 1979–1989).

93. No. 108 March 1988, 108.14 Hua Kien Hui, *A Review of Operations, 1967–1970* (Ottawa: Immigration Appeal Board, 1971).

94. David Haines, *Refugees as Immigrants: Cambodians, Laotians, and Vietnamese in America* (New York, NY: Rowman & Littlefield, 1989).

7. HUMANITARIANISM IN MYTH AND PRACTICE

1. http://www.archives.gov/research/military/vietnam-war/casualty-statistics.html.

2. There is a popular theory that because the United States lost the war, the conflict has been mythologized more than any other in America's history, with the exception of the Civil War. Jerry Lembcke, *The Spitting Image: Myth, Memory, and the Legacy of Vietnam* (New York, NY: New York University Press, 1998), 10. See also Yen Le Espiritu, "The 'We-Win-Even-When-We-Lose' Syndrome: U.S. Press Coverage of the Twenty-Fifth Anniversary of the 'Fall of Saigon,'" *American Quarterly* 58 , no. 2 (June 2006): 339; Marita Sturken, *Tangled Memories: The Vietnam War, the AIDS Epidemic, and the Politics of Remembering* (Berkeley: University of California Press, 1997); and John Hellman, *American Myth and the Legacy of Vietnam* (New York, NY: Columbia University Press, 1986). Mythologizing the Vietnam War is not unique to American history. See Jeffrey Grey and Jeff Doyle, eds., *Vietnam: War, Myth,*

and Memory - Comparative Perspectives on Australia's War in Vietnam (Sydney: Allen & Unwin, 1992).

3. Mary Terrell Cargill and Jade Quang Huynh, *Voices of Vietnamese Boat People: Nineteen Narratives of Escape and Survival* (Jefferson, NC: McFarland & Company, 2000); John Chr. Knudsen, "Prisoners of International Politics: Vietnamese Refugees Coping with Transit Life," *Southeast Asian Journal of Social Science* 18, no. 1 (1990): 153–165.

4. Audie Klotz attributes this failure to the debates over the refusal of Jewish refugees during the Second World War and the subsequent "treatment of white refugees as ordinary immigrants" as this perpetuated the "historical dearth of advocates and their lack of political allies." *Identity in South Africa, 1860–2010* (Cambridge: Cambridge University Press, 2015), 172.

5. Speaking notes for The Honorable Jason Kenney, P. C., M. P. Minister of Citizenship, Immigration and Multiculturalism, Address to the Montreal Council on Foreign Relations, 20 April 2012. See http://www.cic.gc.ca/english/department/media/speeches/2012/2012-04-20.asp.

6. Murdoch Stephens, "No defence for keeping NZ's refugee quota so small," *The Dominion Post*, 28 August 2015, http://www.stuff.co.nz/dominion-post/comment/71494488/opinion-no-defence-for-keeping-nzs-refugee-quota-so-small.

7. Robert Manne, "Asylum Seekers," *The Monthly*, http://www.themonthly.com.au/issue/2010/september/1354143949/robert-manne/comment.

8. "Humanitarian Program Information Paper," at http://www.border.gov.au/Refugeeandhumanitarian/Documents/humanitarian-program-information-paper-14-15.pdf .

9. Mimi Thi Nguyen, *Gift of Freedom: War, Debt, and Other Refugee Passages* (Durham, NC: Duke University Press, 2012), 5; Nguyen offers a highly critical analysis of refugee assistance, which she frames as an outreach of liberal empire building. More innocuously but equally significant, the phrase "gift of freedom" has also been used to describe the history of resettlement efforts in Canada. See Brian Buckley, *Gift of Freedom: How Ottawa Welcomed the Vietnamese, Cambodian, and Laotian Refugees* (Renfrew: General Store Publishing House, 2008); Rene Pappone, *The Hai Hong: Profit, Tears, and Joy* (Ottawa: Employment and Immigration Canada, 1982), 4.

10. Kristen Grim Hughes, "Closed Camps: Vietnamese Refugee Policy in Hong Kong" (PhD Diss., University of California, Berkeley, 1985), 74.

11. W. T. Delworth, "Vietnamese Refugee Crisis 1954/55," in *The Indochinese Refugee Movement: The Canadian Experience*, ed. Howard Adelman (Toronto: Operation Lifeline, 1980), 62.

12. Carl Bon Tempo, *Americans at the Gate: The United States and Refugees during the Cold War* (Princeton, NJ: Princeton University Press, 2008), 145.

13. Charles Keely, "The International Refugee Regime(s): The End of the Cold War Matters," *International Migration Review* 35, no. 1 (2001): 309.

14. Anton Binzegger, *New Zealand's Policy on Refugees* (Wellington: New Zealand Institute of International Affairs, 1980), 57.

15. Paul J. Strand and Woodrow Jones Jr. *Indochinese Refugees in America: Problems of Adaptation and Assimilation* (Durham, NC: Duke University Press, 1985), 32.

16. Keely, "The International Refugee Regime(s)," 309.

17. Hughes, "Closed Camps," 50.

18. Imperial networks, such as those established through shared educational experiences and commercial ventures, endured long after the formal end of the empire. Significantly, the mythology around Indochinese refugees to France has many parallels with the American story. See Claude Gilles, *De L'Enfer à la Liberté: Cambodge – Laos – Vietnam* (Paris: L'Harmattan, 2000).

19. Australia sent troops to Vietnam to support American forces beginning in 1965. Jeff Doyle, Jeffrey Grey, and Peter Pierce, eds., *Australia's Vietnam War* (College Station: Texas A&M University Press, 2002). Canada did not participate militarily but did support the US effort through the sale of *matériel*. On Australian efforts regarding Indochinese refugees, see Nancy Vivani, *The Long Journey: Vietnamese Migration and Settlement in Australia* (Carlton: Melbourne University Press, 1984); Nancy Vivani, *Australian Government Policies on the Entry of Vietnamese: Record and Responsibility* (Griffith University: Centre for the Study of Australian – Asian Relations, 1982).

20. Copy of US White Paper: Indochinese Refugees, 20 July 1979, RG 25, MF-NUM 3627, Vol. 9780, LAC.

21. Hughes, "Closed Camps," 61.

22. Ibid.

23. Courtland Robinson, *Terms of Refuge: The Indochinese Exodus and the International Response* (London, UK: Zed Books, 1998), 50.

24. Hughes, "Closed Camps," 51. Larry Clinton Thompson embraces a more conservative estimate at 10 to 50 percent. He maintains, "it will never be known how many of the Vietnamese boat people died at sea of hunger, thirst, shipwreck and pirates." He observes that even at 10 percent, it still means close to 50,000 people perished in their flight from Indochina. See *Refugee Workers in the Indochina Exodus, 1975–1982* (Jefferson, NC: McFarland & Company, 2010), 169.

25. Cabinet Minute, 5 May 1978, Submission No 2173: Indo-Chinese refugees (see also Paper No 398: Indo-Chinese Refugees & Paper No 418: Social Security Payments to Indo-Chinese Refugees) - Programme for 1978–79 - Decisions 5258, 5372 and 5474, NAA (online).

26. Cabinet Minute, 5 May 1978, Submission No 2173: Indo-Chinese refugees (see also Paper No 398: Indo-Chinese Refugees & Paper No 418: Social Security Payments to Indo-Chinese Refugees) - Programme for 1978–79 - Decisions 5258, 5372 and 5474, NAA (online).

27. Bruce Grant, *The Boat People: An 'Age' Investigation* (New York, NY: Penguin Books, 1979), 185.

28. Cabinet Minute, 5 May 1978, Submission No 2173: Indo-Chinese refugees (see also Paper No 398: Indo-Chinese Refugees & Paper No 418: Social Security Payments to Indo-Chinese Refugees) - Programme for 1978–79 - Decisions 5258, 5372 and 5474, NAA (online).

29. Ibid.

30. Refugee Vessel – Hai Hong, A6980, S251099, Part 1, NAA (Canberra).

31. Cabinet Minute, 5 May 1978, Submission No 2173: Indo-Chinese refugees (see also Paper No 398: Indo-Chinese Refugees & Paper No 418: Social Security Payments to Indo-Chinese Refugees) - Programme for 1978–79 - Decisions 5258, 5372 and 5474, NAA (online).

32. Cabinet Memorandum 380, 13 July 1979, Refugee Policy A10756, LC1366, Part 3, NAA (Canberra).

33. Pappone, *The Hai Hong,* 11.

34. Pappone, *The Hai Hong,* 11.

35. Linda Hitchcox, *Vietnamese Refugees in Southeast Asian Camps* (London, UK: Macmillan Academic and Professional, 1990).

36. Ronald Skeldon, "Hong Kong's Response to the Indochinese Influx, 1975–93," *The Annals of the American Academy of Political and Social Science* 534, no. 1 (1995): 104. .

37. Brian Eads, "Boat Ride to Death," *Observer,* 25 November 1978.

38. "900 Troops Going to Hong Kong: Refugee Controls to be Tightened," *Telegraph,* 26 June 1979, 1.

39. "Hong Kong Authorities Open Fire on Refugees," 7 December 1979 in File 325-11, HKPRO.

40. Hughes, "Closed Camps," 195.

41. Ibid., 181.

42. Kwok Bun Chan, "Hong Kong's Response to the Vietnamese Refugees: A Study in Humanitarianism, Ambivalence, and Hostility," *Southeast Asian Journal of Social Science* 18, no. 1 (1990): 95.

43. Skeldon, "Hong Kong's Response," 91; John Knudsen, *Boat People in Transit: Vietnamese in Refugee Camps in the Philippines, Hong Kong, and Japan* (New York, NY: Lilian Barber Press, 1985), 67. See also Leonard Davis, *Hong Kong and the Asylum-Seekers from Vietnam* (London, UK: McMillan Academic and Professional, 1991).

44. Hughes, "Closed Camps," 185.

45. Kwok Bun Chan, "Hong Kong's Response to the Vietnamese Refugees," 95.

46. The UNHCR's insistence on complicated screening procedures later hampered the government of Hong Kong's efforts to repatriate refugees after 1988. In an interview with Gordon Chu, a former immigration officer in Hong Kong, he recalled a very collegial working relationship with social service agencies in the camps. However, he was critical of the UNHCR's deficiencies. Gordon Chu, telephone interview with author, 18 April 2012.

47. S. J. Chan, "Caritas – Hong Kong and the Vietnamese Refugees," in *They Sojourned in Our Land: The Vietnamese in Hong Kong, 1975–2000*, ed. Joyce Chang et al. (CARITAS – Hong Kong: Social Work Services Division, 2003), 30.

48. Roda Mushkat, "Refuge in Hong Kong," *International Journal of Refugee Law* 1, no. 4 (1989): 449.

49. Ibid., 450.

50. Skeldon, "Hong Kong's Response," 104.

51. Indochinese Refugees – Discussions Between Australian Immigration and US Department of State Officers, 26–27 April 1978, Submission No 2906: Review of Indo-Chinese Refugee Situation - Decision No 7510, A12909, 2906, NAA (Canberra).

52. VIETNAM. Vietnamese Refugees in Hong Kong; Resettlement in UK, Part 1–2, PREM 19/130, NAUK.

53. Ibid.

54. Cabinet Memorandum 380, 13 July 1979, Refugee Policy, A10756, LC1366, Part 3, NAA (Canberra).

55. Ibid.

56. Copy of US White Paper: Indochinese Refugees, 20 July 1979, MFNUM 3627, RG 25, Vol. 9780, LAC.

57. Sokeary Pheng, "La politique d'accueil des réfugiés de la Nouvelle-Zélande: Entre obligations internationales et intérêts nationaux, 1944–2006" (PhD Diss., l'Université d'Avignon et des Pays de Vaucluse, 2006); Freda Hawkins, *Critical Years in Immigration: Canada and Australia Compared* (Montreal: McGill-Queen's University Press, 1992).

58. Kenneth Rivett, "Towards a Policy on Refugees," *Australian Outlook* 33, no. 2 (1979): 138.

59. Ibid., 153.

60. Van Thi-The Huynh interviewed by Ann-Mari Jordens [sound recording], Petherick Reading Room (Oral History) OH ORAL TRC 5817, National Library of Australia.

61. Selection and Assessment Report, PB 221026, Bidong, Malaysia, Indochinese Refugees – Selection Documents / Interview Reports, A446, 1984/77610, NAA (Canberra).

62. The regulation of migrants through the selection and screening process also occurred in other white settler societies. See Aihwa Ong, *Buddha is Hiding: Refugees, Citizenship, the New America* (Berkeley: University of California Press, 2003).

63. Grant, *The Boat People*, 186.

64. Cited in James Mitchell, "Immigration and National Identity in 1970s New Zealand." (PhD Diss., University of Otago, 2010) 46.

65. Robin Galienne, "The Whole Thing Was Orchestrated" (PhD Diss., University of Auckland, 1988), 201–202.

66. Grant, *The Boat People*, 185.

67. The impulse to assist was pronounced and generated ambitious, creative ideas about how to resolve the situation. One senior manager suggested securing a large boat to bring refugees from the camps in Southeast Asia to Canada. The idea was that over the course of their long journey they would be instructed on Canadian life and receive language lessons so that much of the "settlement work" would be done by the time they arrived. Officials never secured an appropriately large boat. On another occasion, Canadian officials heard rumors of Greek vessels refusing to rescue people at sea. Dismayed, Raph Girard suggested to the Greek delegation at the UNHCR that if their boats would pick up people at sea, the Canadian state would ensure that all of the refugees were resettled. The Greek government never replied to this offer. Interviews with Gordon Barnett, 11 April 2012 (Ottawa, Ontario) and Raph Girard, 18 April 2012 (telephone).

68. "Indochina Refugees: Future Canadian Policy," RG 76, 8700-0, Vol. 1835, LAC.

69. Grant, *The Boat People*, 185. See also Binzegger, 60 and Galienne, 203.

70. Ron Atkey, telephone interview with author, 23 December 2013.

71. This number was later increased to 60,000 due to the optics of resettling 50,000 people at the same time that 50,000 people were being laid off from the civil service. Ron Atkey, telephone interview with author, 23 December 2013.

72. Memo to the Minister re. Refugee Sponsorship, 18 June 1979, RG 76, File 8630-6C, Part 2, Vol. 1832, LAC.

73. Ibid.

74. Gordon Barnett, interview with author, 11 April 2012, Ottawa, Ontario.

75. Howard Adelman, telephone interview with author, 18 April 2012.

76. Gordon Barnett, interview with author, 11 April 2012, Ottawa, Ontario.

77. The MCC was also active in the United States. The organization's intervention was therefore particularly important because the subject of the Vietnam War had been the focus of much internal discussion.

78. Bill Janzen, interview with author, 16 April 2012, Ottawa, Ontario.

79. Gordon Barnett, interview with author, 11 April 2012, Ottawa, Ontario.

80. Bill Janzen, interview with author, 16 April 2012, Ottawa Ontario.

81. Howard Adelman, *Canada and the Indochinese Refugees* (Regina: L. A. Weigl Education Associates, 1982), 123.

82. Canada's Refugee Strategy, RG 76, File 8700-0, Part 1, Vol. 1835, LAC.

83. Memorandum from Bell to Molloy, 16 November 1979, RG 76, File 8703-1, Part 2, Vol. 1839, LAC.

84. Ibid.

85. Correspondence dated 5 April, 1975, A1838, 1634/70/2 PART 2, Australian immigration policy and relations with other countries - South Vietnam political refugees – General, 1975–1975, 1872884, NAA (Canberra).

86. Ron Atkey, telephone interview with author, 23 December 2013.

87. Ibid.

88. Mike Molloy, interview with author, 13 April 2012, Ottawa, Ontario.

89. Gerry Campbell, telephone interview with author, 14 April 2012.

90. Bill Janzen cited the MCC report "Welcoming Strangers" during interview with author, 16 April 2012, Ottawa, Ontario.

91. Knudsen, *Boat People in Transit*, 74.

92. Ibid., 76.

93. Memorandum to the Minister re. Indochinese Refugees Program, 10 October 1979, RG 76, File 8703-1, Part 2, Vol. 1839, LAC.

94. Memorandum to Cabinet, 1 November 1979, RG 76, File 8703-1, Part 2, Vol. 1839, LAC. Robin Galienne argues that the outpouring of public support for the Indochinese refugees similarly came as a surprise to the New Zealand government. He suggests that New Zealand might have accepted many more refugees had the government not been so "conservative and cautious." See "The Whole Thing was Orchestrated," 201.

95. Handwriting on Memorandum to the Minister re. Indochinese Refugees Program, 10 October 1979, RG 76, File 8703-1, Part 2, Vol. 1839, LAC.

96. Memorandum, 6 December 1979, RG 76, File 8700-1, Part 2, Vol. 1835, LAC.

97. As recalled by Mike Molloy, interview with author, 13 April 2012, Ottawa, Ontario. Molloy attended the meeting along with Kirk Bell and the Director of Refugee Policy, Doug Hill. They bore the brunt of the room's displeasure following the ministers' abrupt departure.

98. Memorandum to the Minister, 10 December 1979, RG 76, File 8703-1, Part 2, Vol. 1839, LAC. When Joe Clark's Conservative government fell and Trudeau's Liberals returned later in 1979, the new Immigration Minister, Lloyd Axworthy, "corrected" the Conservative mistake of walking away from the matching agreement. The resettlement target was increased by 10,000 people, all of whom were to be government sponsored.

99. Refugee and Special Humanitarian Programs, 1981–82, Cabinet Submission 5039, Refugee Policy A10756, LC1366, Part 3, NAA (Canberra).

100. In 1981, the United States announced that it was decreasing its resettlement quota from 140,000 to 100,000, a move that Kristen Grim Hughes calls "indicative of a new mood" amongst all the resettlement countries. See Hughes, "Closed Camps," 85.

101. Knudsen, *Boat People in Transit*, 71–72.

102. Cited in Knudsen, 73.

103. OXFAM, *How Hong Kong Cares for Vietnamese Refugees* (Hong Kong: OX-FAM, April 1986), 5.

104. Hughes, "Closed Camps," 223.

105. OXFAM, *How Hong Kong Cares for Vietnamese Refugees*, 10.

106. Ibid.

107. Hughes, "Closed Camps," 274.

108. Chan Kwok Bun, "Hong Kong's Response to the Vietnamese Refugees," 106.

109. Memorandum, 9 November 1988, RG 25, File 85-29-4 INDOCHINA, Part 3, Vol. 12498, LAC.

110. Chan Kwok Bun, "Hong Kong's Response to the Vietnamese Refugees," 99.

111. Ibid.

112. Ibid., 96.

113. Ibid.

114. Yuk Wah Chan, *The Chinese / Vietnamese Diaspora: Revisiting the Boat People* (London, UK: Routledge, 2013), 7.

115. Chan Kwok Bun, "Hong Kong's Response to the Vietnamese Refugees," 95.

116. US Embassy Memorandum: Talking Points for US Approach to Canada, Australia, New Zealand and Japan, 28 June 1988, RG 25, File 85-29-4 INDOCH, Part 15, Vol. 12489, LAC.

117. Briefing materials, RG 25, Files 47-4-ICIR 9371 and 47-4-ICR MF9371, Vol. 25391, LAC.

118. See Ottawa Consultations, 7–8 April 1988, RG 25, File 47-4-UN-HCR-1-INDOCHIN, Vol. 26038, LAC.

119. Mike Molloy, interview with author, 13 April 2012, Ottawa, Ontario.

120. Ibid.

121. Indochina Refugees: Future Canadian Policy, RG 76, File 8700-0, Vol. 1835, LAC.

122. OM IS 434 Changes to IC DC Regulations, 20 April 1990, RG 25, File 47-1-1-17, Part 1, Vol. 12350, LAC.

123. Ibid.

124. This accusation apparently came from Rick Berube, an MCC worker in Vietnam. See Memo to the Minister, 7 March 1990, RG 76, File 8700-15, Vol. 2010, LAC.

125. Memo to the Minister, 7 March 1990, RG 76, File 8700-15, Vol. 2010, LAC.

126. Ibid. This is a sentiment echoed in the literature on the history of global humanitarianism. See Gary J. Bass, *Freedom's Battle: The Origins of Humanitarian Intervention* (New York, NY: Knopf, 2008); David Rieff, *A Bed for the Night: Humanitarianism in Crisis* (New York, NY: Simon & Schuster, 2002); Tony Vaux, *The Selfish Altruist: Relief Work in Famine and War* (London, UK: Earthscan, 2001); Jennifer Hyndman, *Managing Displacement: Refugees and the Politics of Humanitarianism* (Minneapolis: University of Minnesota Press, 2000). By contrast, Michael Ignatieff in *The Needs of Strangers* (New York, NY: Picador Press, 2002) tends to be more celebratory about the capacity for humanitarian good since the end of the Second World War.

127. Making sure that the planes were sufficiently full also became a priority for selection officials. Empty charters landing in Canada generated bad press. E-mail correspondence with Mike Molloy, 29 April 2012. Telephone interview with Gerry Campbell, 14 April 2012.

EPILOGUE

1. Jim Chu, e-mail to author, 28 July 2012.

2. Ibid.

3. See, for instance, Emma Haddad, *The Refugee in International Society: Between Sovereigns* (Cambridge: Cambridge University Press, 2008).

4. Peter Gatrell, *The Making of the Modern Refugee* (Cambridge: Cambridge University Press, 2012), 1.

5. Franca Iacovetta, *Gatekeepers: Reshaping Immigrant Lives in Cold War Canada* (Toronto: Between the Lines, 2006), 47, 50.

6. Raph Girard, interview with author, 9 January 2012.

7. See general discussion in Caroline Andrew et al., eds., *Electing a Diverse Canada: The Representation of Immigrants, Minorities, and Women* (Vancouver: UBC Press, 2008).

8. "Story of ARCI Intellectual, ARCR Reg. No. 8703, Nieh Chih Fong" and "Story of Siou Wee-min, ARCI Reg. No. 17135 by Peiling Liang," respectively. Box 67, File Case Histories – Vol. 2, ARCI / ABMAC Collection at Columbia University Archives.

9. Tony Enns, telephone interview with author, 29 August 2013.

10. On accounting for the historical past, see Paulette Regan, *Unsettling the Settler Within: Indian Residential Schools, Truth Telling, and Reconciliation in Canada* (Vancouver: UBC Press, 2010).

11. Bonita Lawrence and Enakshi Dua, "Decolonizing Antiracism," *Social Justice* 32, no. 4 (2005): 120–143.

BIBLIOGRAPHY

NEWSPAPERS AND MEDIA

Cape Argus (South Africa)
Daily Telegraph (Australia)
Dominion (New Zealand)
Edmonton Journal (Canada)
Globe and Mail (Canada)
Hong Kong Standard (Hong Kong)
Life (United States)
New York Herald (United States)
New York Times (United States)
New Zealand Herald (New Zealand)
Observer (United Kingdom)
San Francisco Chronicle (United States)
Telegraph (United Kingdom)
Truth (Australia)
Winnipeg Free Press (Canada)

INTERVIEWS

Howard Adelman, Toronto, Ontario, telephone interview, 18 April 2012.
Ron Atkey, Toronto, Ontario, telephone interview, 22 December 2013.
Gordon Barnett, Ottawa, Ontario, 11 April 2012.

Don Cameron, Steveston, British Columbia, 8 December 2013.

Gerry Campbell, Vancouver, British Columbia, 26 March 2011 (with subsequent e-mail correspondence and telephone interview on 14 April 2012).

Gordon Chu, Vancouver, British Columbia, 14 October 2009 and telephone interview on 18 April 2012.

Tony Enns, Winnipeg, Manitoba, telephone and e-mail interviews, August 2013.

Raph Girard, Ottawa, Ontario, 30 January 2012.

Maggie Ip, Vancouver, British Columbia, 27 October 2009.

Bill Janzen, Ottawa, Ontario, 16 April 2012.

Douglas Lam, Sydney, Australia, 11 July 2010.

Mike Molloy, Ottawa, Ontario, 29 July 2011 (with subsequent e-mail correspondence and additional interview on 13 April 2012).

Sid Chow Tan, Vancouver, British Columbia, 22 October 2009.

ARCHIVAL AND LIBRARY COLLECTIONS

Alexander Turnbull Library (National Library of New Zealand), Wellington, New Zealand.

American Friends Service Committee Archives, Philadelphia, United States.

Anglican Church of Canada Archives, Toronto, Ontario.

Bodleian Library, Oxford, England.

Columbia University Archives, New York, United States.

Eisenhower Presidential Library, Abilene, Kansas, United States.

Hong Kong Public Records Office, Hong Kong.

Hoover Institution Archives, Stanford University, Stanford, United States.

Library and Archives Canada, Ottawa, Canada.

Library of Congress, Washington, DC, United States.

Lutheran World Federation, Geneva, Switzerland.

McMaster University Archives, Hamilton, Ontario, Canada.

Mitchell Library, Sydney, Australia.

National Archives and Records Administration, Washington, DC, United States.

National Archives of Australia, Canberra, Sydney, Melbourne, Australia.

National Archives of New Zealand, Auckland and Wellington, New Zealand.

National Archives of South Africa, Pretoria, South Africa.

National Archives of the United Kingdom, London, England.

National Library of Australia, Canberra, Australia.

New York Public Library, New York, United States.

Rockefeller and Ford Foundation Archives, New York, United States.

State Library of Victoria, Melbourne, Australia.

United Church of Canada Archives, Toronto, Ontario.

United Nations Archives, Geneva, Switzerland

United Nations High Commissioner for Refugees, Geneva, Switzerland.

United Nations Library, Geneva, Switzerland.

University of Melbourne Library (Special Collections), Melbourne, Australia.

World Council of Churches, Geneva, Switzerland.

SECONDARY SOURCES

Abella, Irving, and Harold Troper. *None Is Too Many: Canada and the Jews of Europe, 1933–1948*. Toronto: University of Toronto Press, 1983, reprinted in 2013.

Adelman, Howard. *Canada and the Indochinese Refugees*. Regina: L. A. Weigl Education Associates, 1982.

Agamben, Giorgio. *Homo Sacer: Sovereign Power and Bare Life*. Stanford, CA: Stanford University Press, 1995.

Aleinikoff, T. Alexander. "State-Centred Refugee Law: From Resettlement to Containment." In *Mistrusting Refugees*, edited by Daniel E. Valentine and John Chr. Knudsen, 257–278. Berkeley: University of California Press, 1995.

Alomes, Stephen, Mark Dober, and Donna Hellier. "The Social Context of Postwar Conservatism." In *Australia's First Cold War*, Vol. 1, *Society, Communism, and Culture*, edited by Ann Curthoys and John Merritt, 1–28. Sydney: George Allen & Unwin, 1984.

Amrith, Sunil S. *Migration and Diaspora in Modern Asia*. Cambridge, UK: Cambridge University Press, 2011.

———. *Crossing the Bay of Bengal: The Furies of Nature and the Fortunes of Migrants*. Cambridge, MA: Harvard University Press, 2013.

Anderson, Kay. *Vancouver's Chinatown: Racial Discourse in Canada, 1875–1980*. Montreal: McGill-Queen's University Press, 1995.

Andrew, Caroline, John Biles, Myer Siemiatycki, and Erin Tolley, eds. *Electing a Diverse Canada: The Representation of Immigrants, Minorities, and Women*. Vancouver: UBC Press, 2008.

Arendt, Hannah. "Race-Thinking before Racism." *Review of Politics* 6, no. 1 (1944): 36–73.

———. *Origins of Totalitarianism*. San Diego, CA: Harcourt, Brace, 1979.

Austin, Alvyn. *Saving China: Canadian Missionaries in the Middle Kingdom, 1888–1959*. Toronto: University of Toronto Press, 1986.

———. *China's Millions: The China Inland Mission and Late Qing Society, 1832–1905*. Grand Rapids, MI: William B. Eerdmans, 2007.

———, and Jamie S. Scott. *Canadian Missionaries, Indigenous Peoples: Representing Religion at Hone Home and Abroad*. Toronto: University of Toronto Press, 2005.

Australia. Parliament. House of Representatives. *Parliamentary Debates (Hansard)*. Canberra: Commonwealth Government Printer, 1957.

Australian Council of Churches. *Strangers in Our Midst: Guidelines and Suggestions for Helping Refugees*. Migration and Ethnic Affairs: A Review of the Work of the Australian Council of Churches. Sydney: Australian Council of Churches, 1979.

Bagnall, Kate, and Tim Sherratt. "Invisible Australians." http://invisibleaustralians.org.

Bakewell, Oliver. "Research Beyond the Categories: The Importance of Policy Irrelevant Research into Forced Migration." *Journal of Refugee Studies* 21, no. (4) (2008): 432–453.

Ballantyne, Tony. *Orientalism and Race: Aryanism in the British Empire*. Cambridge, UK: Cambridge Imperial and Post-Colonial Studies Series, Palgrave, 2001.

———. "Writing Out Asia: Race, Colonialism, and Chinese Migration in New Zealand History." in In *East by South: China in the Australasian Imagination*, edited by Charles Ferrall, Paul Millar, and Keren Smith, 87–109. Wellington: Victoria University Press, 2005.

———. *Webs of Empire: Locating New Zealand's Colonial Past*. Vancouver: UBC Press, 2014.

Barnett, Michael. *Empire of Humanity: A History of Humanitarianism*. Ithaca, NY: Cornell University Press, 2010.

Bashford, Alison. "At the Border: Contagion, Immigration, Nation." *Australian Historical Studies* 33, no. 120 (2002): 344–358.

Bass, Gary J. *Freedom's Battle: The Origins of Humanitarian Intervention*. New York, NY: Knopf, 2008.

Beaglehole, Ann. *Facing the Past: Looking Back at Refugee Childhood in New Zealand*. Sydney: Allen & Unwin, 1990.

Belich, James. *Paradise Reforged: A History of the New Zealanders from the 1880s to the Year 2000*. Honolulu: University of Hawai'i Press, 2001.

———Belich, James. *Replenishing the Earth: The Settler Revolution and the Rise of the Angloworld*. Oxford, UK: Oxford University Press, 2009.

Bernkopf Tucker, Nancy. *Taiwan, Hong Kong, and the United States, 1945–1992*. New York, NY: Twayne Publishers: Maxwell Macmillan International, 1994.

Beyer, Gunther. "The Political Refugee: 35 Years Later." *International Migration Review* 15, no. (1/2) (Spring–Summer 1981): 26–34.

Bickers, Robert, and Ray Yep, eds. *May Days in Hong Kong: Riots and Emergency in 1967*. Hong Kong: Hong Kong University Press, 2009.

Binzegger, Anton. *New Zealand's Policy on Refugees*. Wellington: New Zealand Institute of International Affairs, 1980.

Black, Maggie. *A Cause for Our Times: OXFAM, The First Fifty Years*. Oxford, UK: Oxfam Professional, 1992.

Blackburn, Kevin. "Disguised Anti-Colonialism: Protest Against against the White Australia Policy in Malaya and Singapore, 1947-1962." *Australian Journal of International Affairs* 55, no. 1 (April 2001): 101–117.

Blay, Sam. "Regional Developments: Asia.," in In *The 1951 Convention Relating to the Status of Refugees and its Its 1967 Protocol,* edited by Andreas Zimmerman, 145–184. Oxford, UK: Oxford University Press, 2011.

Bon Tempo, Carl. *Americans at the Gate: The United States and Refugees during the Cold War.* Princeton, NJ: Princeton University Press, 2008.

Borstelmann, Thomas. *The Cold War and the Color Line.* Cambridge, MA: Harvard University Press, 2003.

Bothwell, Robert. *Alliance and Illusion: Canada and the World, 1945–1984.* Vancouver: UBC Press, 2007.

Bourbeau, Philippe. *The Securitization of Migration.* New York, NY: Routledge, 2011.

Bradley, Mark Philip, and Marilyn B. Young. *Making Sense of the Vietnam Wars: Local, National, and Transnational Perspectives.* Oxford, UK: Oxford University Press, 2008.

Brash, Alan. *The National Council of Churches in New Zealand.* Christchurch: National Council of Churches in New Zealand, ca1955.

Brawley, Sean. "No 'White Policy' in New Zealand: Fact and Fiction in New Zealand's Immigration Record, 1946–1978." *New Zealand Journal of History* 27, no. 1 (1993): 16–36.

———. *The White Peril: Foreign Relations and Asian Immigration to Australasia and North America, 1919–1978.* Sydney: University of New South Wales Press, 1995.

———. "Mrs. O'Keefe and the Battle for White Australia." Public lecture for the National Archives of Australia, presented in Canberra, 1 June 2006. www.naa.gov.au.

Briggs, Laura. "Mother, Child, Race, Nation: The Visual Iconography of Rescue and the Politics of Transnational and Transracial Adoption." *Gender & History* 15, no. 2 (August 2003): 179–200.

Brook, Timothy. *Quelling the People: The Military Suppression of the Beijing Democracy Movement.* Stanford, CA: Stanford University Press, 1998.

Brookfield, Tarah. *Cold War Comforts: Canadian Women, Child Safety, and Global Insecurity.* Waterloo: Wilfrid Laurier University Press, 2012.

Brouwer, Ruth. "When Missions Became Development: Ironies of 'NGO-ization' in Mainstream Canadian Churches in the 1960s." *Canadian Historical Review* 91, no. 4 (2010): 661–693.

Buckley, Brian. *Gift of Freedom: How Ottawa Welcomed the Vietnamese, Cambodian, and Laotian Refugees.* Renfrew: General Store Publishing House, 2008.

Burns, John. "Immigration from China and the Future of Hong Kong." *Asian Survey* 27, no. 6 (June 1987): 661–682.

Campbell, Lara. *Respectable Citizens: Gender, Family, and Unemployment in Ontario's Great Depression.* Toronto: University of Toronto Press, 2009.

Canada. House of Commons. *Parliamentary Debates (Hansard).* Ottawa: Queen's Printer, 1947 and 1969.

Canadian Law Information Council. *Notes of Recent Decisions Rendered by the Immigration Appeal Board.* Ottawa: Canadian Law Information Council, 1979–1989.

Carey, Jane, and Claire McLisky, eds. *Creating White Australia.* Sydney: Sydney University Press, 2009.

Cargill, Mary Terrell, and Jade Quang Huynh. *Voices of Vietnamese Boat People: Nineteen Narratives of Escape and Survival.* Jefferson, NC: McFarland & Company, 2000.

Carroll, John. "Colonialism and Collaboration: Chinese Subjects and the Making of British Hong Kong." *China Information* 12, no. 12 (1997): 12–35.

———. *Edge of Empires: Chinese Elites and British Colonials in Hong Kong.* Cambridge, MA: Harvard University Press, 2005.

Carruthers, Susan. "Between Camps: Eastern Bloc 'Escapees' and Cold War Borderlands." *American Quarterly* 57, no. 3 (2005): 911–942.

———. *Cold War Captives: Imprisonment, Escape, and Brainwashing.* Berkeley: University of California Press, 2009.

Castles, Stephen. "Guestworkers in Europe: A Resurrection?" *International Migration Review* 40, no. 4 (December 2006): 741–766.

Chan, Johannes M. M. "Immigration Policies and Human Resources Planning." In *Hong Kong Mobile: Making a Global Population,* edited by Helen F. Siu and Agnes Ku, 149–200. Hong Kong: Hong Kong University Press, 2008.

Chan, Kwok Bun. "Hong Kong's Response to the Vietnamese Refugees: A Study in Humanitarianism, Ambivalence, and Hostility." *Southeast Asian Journal of Social Science* 18, no. 1 (1990): 94–110.

Chan, Ming K, ed., with collaboration from John Young. *Precarious Balance: Hong Kong between China and Britain, 1842–1992.* Armonk, NY: M. E. Sharpe, 1994.

———. "The Legacy of the British Administration of Hong Kong: A View from Hong Kong." *The China Quarterly* 151 (1997): 567–582.

Chan, S. J. "Caritas—Hong Kong and the Vietnamese Refugees." In *They Sojourned in Our Land: The Vietnamese in Hong Kong, 1975–2000,* edited by Joyce Chang. CARITAS—Hong Kong: Social Work Services Division, 2003.

Chan, Yuk Wah, ed. *The Chinese / Vietnamese Diaspora: Revisiting the Boat People.* London, UK: Routledge, 2011.

Chang, Wen-Chin. "From War Refugees to Immigrants: The Case of the KMT Yunnanese Chinese in Northern Thailand." *International Migration Review* 35, no. 4 (Winter, 2001): 1086–1105.

Chataway, Christopher, Colin Jones, Trevor Philpott, and Timothy Raison. "Wanted: A World Refugee Year." *Crossbow* (Spring, 1958).

Cheung, Tak-Wai. "Illegal Immigrants in Hong Kong: A Study of the Government's Policy and Control." MPA Thesis, University of Hong Kong, 1995.

Chimni, B. S. "The Geopolitics of Refugee Studies: A View from the South." *Journal of Refugee Studies* 11, no. 4 (1998): 350–375.

———. "Globalisation, Humanitarianism, and the Erosion of Refugee Protection." *Journal of Refugee Studies* 13, no. 3 (2000): 243–263.

———. "From Resettlement to Involuntary Repatriation: Towards a Critical History of Durable Solutions to Refugee Problems." *Refugee Survey Quarterly* 23, no. 3 (2004): 55–73.

Christopher, A. J. "Apartheid Planning in South Africa: The Case of Port Elizabeth." *The Geographical Journal* 153, no. 2 (July 1987): 195–204.

Chu, Cindy Yik-yi, ed., *Diaries of the Maryknoll Sisters in Hong Kong.* London, UK: Palgrave Macmillan, 2007.

Chung, Wong Yiu. "The Policies of the Hong Kong Government Toward the Chinese Refugee Problem, 1945–1962." PhD Diss., Hong Kong Baptist University, 2008.

Cohen, Daniel. *In War's Wake: Europe's Displaced Persons in the Postwar Order.* New York, NY: Oxford University Press, 2011.

Connelly, Matthew. *Fatal Misconception: The Struggle to Control World Population.* New York, NY: Columbia University Press, 2008.

Conway-Lanz, Sahr. "Beyond No Gun Ri: Refugees and the United States Military in the Korean War." *Diplomatic History* 29, no. 1 (2005): 49–81.

Coombes, Annie E., ed. *Rethinking Settler Colonialism: History and Memory in Australia, Canada, Aoetearoa New Zealand, and South Africa.* Manchester, UK: Manchester University Press, 2006.

Cooper, John. *Colony in Conflict: The Hong Kong Disturbances, May 1967–January 1968.* Hong Kong: Swindon, 1970.

Cosgrove, Ben. "Portrait from Hell: Larry Burrows' 'Reaching Out,' 1966." *Time,* 2 December 2014. http://time.com/3491033/life-behind-the-picture-larry-burrows-reaching-out-vietnam-1966.

Cottle, Simon, and David Nolan. "Everyone Was Dying for Footage: Global Humanitarianism and the Changing Aid-Media Field." *Journalism Studies* 8, no. 6 (2007): 862–878.

Cribb, Robert, and Li Narangoa., "Orphans of Empire: Divided Peoples, Dilemmas of Identity, and Old Imperial Borders in East and Southeast Asia.," *Comparative Studies in Society and History* 46, no. 1 (January 2004): 164–187.

Cronin, K. "A Culture of Control: An Overview of Immigration Policy-Making." In *The Politics of Australian Immigration,* edited by James Jupp and Maria Kabala, 83–104. Canberra: Australian Government Publishing Service, 1993.

Crush, Jonathan, ed. *Beyond Control: Immigration and Human Rights in a Democratic South Africa*. Cape Town: IDASA and Queen's University, Canada, 1998.

Curran, James, and Stuart Ward. *The Unknown Nation: Australia after Empire*. Carlton: Melbourne University Press, 2010.

Curthoys, Ann, and John Merritt, eds. *Australia's First Cold War, 1945–1953*. Vol. 1, *Society, Communism, and Culture*. Sydney: George Allen & Unwin, 1984.

Darwin, John. "Hong Kong in British Decolonisation." In *Hong Kong's Transitions 1842–1997*, edited by Judith Brown and Rosemary Foot. New York, NY: St. Martin's Press, 1997.

Dauvergne, Catherine. *Humanitarianism, Identity, and Nation: Migration Laws in Canada and Australia*. Vancouver: UBC Press, 2005.

———. *Making People Illegal: What Globalization Means for Migration and Law*. Cambridge, UK: Cambridge University Press, 2008.

Davies, Sara E. "Redundant or Essential? How Politics Shaped the Outcome of the 1967 Protocol." *International Journal of Refugee Law* 19, no. 4 (2007): 703–728.

Davis, Leonard. *Hong Kong and the Asylum-Seekers from Vietnam*. London, UK: McMillan Academic and Professional, 1991.

Davis, Michael G. "Impetus for Immigration Reform: Asian Refugees and the Cold War." *The Journal of American-East Asian Relations* 7, no. 3/4 (1998): 127–156.

Delworth, W. T. "Vietnamese Refugee Crisis 1954/55." In *The Indochinese Refugee Movement: The Canadian Experience*, edited by Howard Adelman. Toronto: Operation Lifeline, 1980.

Dirks, Gerald. *Canada's Refugee Policy: Indifference or Opportunism?* Montreal: McGill-Queen's University Press, 1977.

Doty, Roxanne. *Anti-Immigrantism in Western Democracies: Statecraft, Desire, and the Politics of Exclusion*. London, UK: Routledge, 2003.

Dowty, Alan. *Closed Borders: The Contemporary Assault on Freedom of Movement*. New Haven, CT: Yale University Press, 1987.

Doyle, Jeff, Jeffrey Grey, and Peter Pierce, eds. *Australia's Vietnam War*. College Station: Texas A&M University Press, 2002.

Drakakis-Smith, David. *High Society: Housing Provision in Metropolitan Hong Kong, 1954 to 1979: A Jubilee Critique*. Hong Kong: Centre of Asian Studies, University of Hong Kong, 1979.

Dubinsky, Karen. *Babies without Borders: Adoption and Migration across the Americas*. Toronto: University of Toronto Press, 2010.

Duchesne, Père Paul. "Activités Catholiques à Hong Kong." Mission Bulletin 7, no. 4 (April 1955).

Dudziak, Mary L. *Cold War Civil Rights: Race and the Image of American Democracy*. Princeton, NJ: Princeton University Press, 2000.

Dwork, Deborah. *Flight from the Reich: Refugee Jews, 1933–1946*. New York, NY: W. W. Norton, 2009.

Einarsen, Terje. "Drafting History of the 1951 Convention and the 1967 Protocol." In *The 1951 Convention Relating to the Status of Refugees and Its 1967 Protocol*, edited by Andreas Zimmerman, 37–74. Oxford, UK: Oxford University Press, 2011.

Elkins, Caroline, and Susan Pedersen, eds. *Settler Colonialism in the Twentieth Century*. New York, NY: Routledge, 2005.

Le Espiritu, Yen. "The 'We-Win-Even-When-We-Lose' Syndrome: U.S. Press Coverage of the Twenty-Fifth Anniversary of the Fall of Saigon," *American Quarterly* 58, no. 2 (June 2006): 329–352.

———. *Body Counts: The Vietnam War and Militarized Refugees*. Berkeley: University of California Press, 2014.

Ettinger, Patrick. *Imaginary Lines: Border Enforcement and the Origins of Undocumented Immigration, 1882–1930*. Austin: University of Texas Press, 2009.

Evangelical Lutheran Church of Hong Kong. *The Church Doth Stand: A Report of the Work of the Evangelical Lutheran Church of Hong Kong*. [Kowloon: The Church, 1958?].

Fan, Joshua. *China's Homeless Generation: Voices from the Veterans of the Chinese Civil War, 1940s–1990s*. New York, NY: Routledge, 2011.

Fan, Shu Shing. *The Population of Hong Kong*. United Nations: The Committee for International Coordination of National Research in Demography, 1974.

Ferrall, Charles, Paul Millar, and Keren Smith, eds. *East by South: China in the Australasian Imagination*. Wellington: Victoria University Press, 2005.

Fitzgerald, Gerald. "Refugees and Migrant Resettlement & Adjustment in New Zealand, 1964–1976." MA Thesis, University of Otago, 1982.

Fitzgerald, John. *Big White Lie: Chinese Australians in White Australia*. Sydney: University of New South Wales Press, 2007.

Fitzgerald, Shirley. *Red Tape, Gold Scissors: The Story of Sydney's Chinese*. Sydney: State Library of New South Wales, 1996.

Frame, Tom. *The Life and Death of Harold Holt*. Sydney: Allen & Unwin, 2005.

Frolic, B. Michael. *Mao's People: Sixteen Portraits of Life in Revolutionary China*. Cambridge, MA: Harvard University Press, 1980.

Gagan, Rosemary. *A Sensitive Independence: Canadian Methodist Missionaries in Canada and the Orient, 1881–1925*. Montreal: McGill-Queen's University Press, 1992.

Galienne, Robin. "The Whole Thing Was Orchestrated." PhD Diss., University of Auckland, 1988.

Gallagher, Dennis. "The Evolution of the International Refugee System." *International Migration Review* 23, no. 3 (Autumn 1989): 579–598.

Gao, Yuan. *Born Red: A Chronicle of the Cultural Revolution*. Stanford, CA: Stanford University Press, 1987.

Garland, Libby. *After They Closed the Gates: Jewish Illegal Immigration to the United States, 1921–1965*. Chicago, IL: University of Chicago Press, 2014.

Gatrell, Peter. *Free World? The Campaign to Save the World's Refugees, 1959–63*. Cambridge, UK: Cambridge University Press, 2011.

———. *The Making of the Modern Refugee*. Cambridge, UK: Cambridge University Press, 2013.

Gibney, Matthew. *The Ethics and Politics of Asylum: Liberal Democracy and the Response to Refugees*. Cambridge, UK: Cambridge University Press, 2004.

Gill, Rebecca. *Calculating Compassion: Humanity and Relief in War, Britain, 1870–1914*. Cambridge, UK: Cambridge University Press, 2013.

Gilles, Claude. *De L'Enfer à la Liberté: Cambodge—Laos—Vietnam*. Paris: L'Harmattan, 2000.

Gilroy, Paul. *Against Race: Imagining Political Culture beyond the Color Line*. Cambridge, MA: Belknap Press of Harvard University Press, 2000.

Glaser, Clive. "White but Illegal: Undocumented Madeiran Immigration to South Africa, 1920s–1970s." *Immigrants & Minorities* 31, no. 1 (2013): 74–98.

Gleason, Mona. *Normalizing the Ideal: Psychology, Schooling, and the Family in Postwar Canada*. Toronto: University of Toronto Press, 1999.

Glick Schiller, Nina, Linda Basch, and Cristina Szanton Blanc. "From Immigrant to Transmigrant: Theorizing Transnational Migration." *Anthropological Quarterly* 68, no. 1 (January 1995): 48–63.

Glynn, Irial. "The Genesis and Development of Article 1 of the 1951 Refugee Convention." *Journal of Refugee Studies* 25, no. 1 (December 2011): 134–148.

Goedhart, G. J. van Heuven. *Refugee Problems and Their Solutions*. London, UK: United Nations Association, [195-?].

Goldstein, Alyosha. "Where the Nation Takes Place: Proprietary Regimes, Antistatism, and U.S. Settler Colonialism." In *Settler Colonialism, The South Atlantic Quarterly*, edited by Alyosha Goldstein and Alex Lubin, 833–861. Durham, NC: Duke University Press, 2008.

Goutor, David. "Constructing the 'Great Menace': Canadian Labour's Opposition to Asian Immigration, 1880–1915." *The Canadian Historical Review* 88, no. 4 (December 2007): 549–576.

Grant, Bruce. *The Boat People: An 'Age' Investigation*. New York, NY: Penguin Books, 1979.

Great Britain. House of Commons. *Parliamentary Debates (Hansard)*. London, UK: H.M.S.O., 1964.

Greene, Bonnie, ed. *Canadian Churches and Foreign Policy*. Toronto: James Lorimer & Company Limited, 1990.

Grey, Jeffrey, and Jeff Doyle, eds. *Vietnam: War, Myth and Memory—Comparative Perspectives on Australia's War in Vietnam*. Sydney: Allen & Unwin, 1992.

Gungwu, Wang. *The Chinese Overseas: From Earthbound China to the Quest for Autonomy*. Cambridge, MA: Harvard University Press, 2000.

———. *Don't Leave Home: Migration and the Chinese*. Singapore: Eastern Universities Press, 2001.

Haddad, Emma. "Danger Happens at the Border." In *Borderscapes: Hidden Geographies and Politics at Territory's Edge*, edited by Prem Kumar Rajaram and Carl Grundy-Warr, 119–136. Minneapolis: University of Minnesota, 2008.

———. *The Refugee in International Society: Between Sovereigns*. Cambridge, UK: Cambridge University Press, 2008.

Haebich, Anna. *Spinning the Dream: Assimilation in Australia 1950–1970*. North Fremantle, WA: Fremantle Press, 2008.

Hagan, John. "Narrowing the Gap by Widening the Conflict: Power Politics, Symbols of Sovereignty, and the American Vietnam War Resisters' Migration to Canada." *Law & Society Review* 34, no. 3 (2000): 607–650.

Haines, David. *Refugees as Immigrants: Cambodians, Laotians, and Vietnamese in America*. New York, NY: Rowman & Littlefield Publishers, Inc., 1989.

Hall, Catherine, and Keith McLelland, eds. *Race, Nation, and Empire: Making Histories, 1750 to the Present*. Manchester, UK: Manchester University Press, 2007.

Hall, Ronald O. *Hong Kong: What of the Church?* London, UK: Edinburgh House Press, 1952.

Hambro, Edward. *The Problem of Chinese Refugees in Hong Kong: Report Submitted to the United Nations High Commissioner for Refugees*. Leiden, NL: A. W. Sijthoff, 1955.

Hardistry, Susan. "Framing and Reframing 'Refugee': A Cultural History of the Concept in Australia from 1938 to 1951." PhD Diss., University of Melbourne, 1999.

Harper, Francis, ed. *Out of China: A Collection of Interviews with Refugees from China*. Hong Kong: Dragonfly Books, 1964.

Harrell-Bond, Barbara. "In Search of 'Invisible' Actors: Barriers to Access in Refugee Research." *Journal of Refugee Studies,* 20, no. 2 (2007): 281–298.

Harris, Karen L. "The Chinese in South Africa: A Historical Study of a Cultural Minority." *New Contree* 46 (November 1999): 82–95.

———. "Scattered and Silent Sources: Researching the Chinese in South Africa," in *Chinese Overseas: Migration, Research, and Documentation*, ed. Tan Chee-Beng, Colin Storey, and Julia Zimmerman, 139–165. Hong Kong: The Chinese University Press of Hong Kong, 2003.

Hathaway, James. "The Evolution of Refugee Status in International Law: 1920–1950." *International and Comparative Law Quarterly* 33, no. 2 (1984): 348–380.

Hawkins, Freda. *Critical Years in Immigration: Canada and Australia Compared*. Montreal: McGill-Queen's University Press, 1991.

————. *Canada and Immigration: Public Policy and Public Concern*. Montreal: McGill-Queen's University Press, 2002.

Hellman, John. *American Myth and the Legacy of Vietnam*. New York, NY: Columbia University Press, 1986.

Herzstein, Robert Edwin. *Henry R. Luce, Time, and The American Crusade in Asia*. Cambridge, UK: Cambridge University Press, 2005.

Hiro, Dilip. *Black British / White British: A History of Race Relations in Britain*. Rev. ed. London, UK: Eyre & Spottiswoode, 1973.

Historical Population Estimates Table. http://www.stats.govt.nz/browse_for_stats/population/estimates_and_projections/historical-population-tables.aspx.

Hitchcox, Linda. *Vietnamese Refugees in Southeast Asian Camps*. London, UK: Macmillan Academic and Professional, 1990.

Ho, Ufrieda. *Paper Sons and Daughters: Growing Up Chinese in South Africa*. Johannesburg: Picador Africa, 2011.

Hoerder, Dirk. *Cultures in Contact: World Migrations in the Second Millenium*. Durham, NC: Duke University Press, 2002.

Holborn, Louise. *The International Refugee Organization, A Specialized Agency of the United Nations: Its History and Work, 1946–1952*. New York, NY: Oxford University Press, 1956.

Hong Kong Council of Social Services. *Working Together: A Survey of the Work of Voluntary and Government Social Service Organizations in Hong Kong*. Hong Kong: Hong Kong Council of Social Services, 1958.

————. *Hong Kong Council of Social Services—40th Anniversary: A Commemorative Issue*. Hong Kong: Hong Kong Council of Social Services, 1988.

Hopkins, Keith. *Hong Kong: The Industrial Colony: A Political, Social, and Economic Survey*. Oxford, UK: Oxford University Press, 1971.

Hsu, Madeline. *Dreaming of Gold, Dreaming of Home: Transnationalism and Migration between the United States and South China, 1882–1943*. Stanford, CA: Stanford University Press, 2000.

————. "The Disappearance of America's Cold War Chinese Refugees, 1948–1966." *Journal of American Ethnic History* 31, no. 4 (Summer 2012): 12–33.

————. *The Good Immigrants: How the Yellow Peril became the Model Minority*. Princeton, NJ: Princeton University Press, 2015.

Hubinette, Tobias. "From Orphan Trains to Babylifts: Colonial Trafficking, Empire Building, and Social Engineering." In *Outsiders within: Writing on Transracial Adoption*, edited by Jane Jeong Trenka, Chinyere Oparah, and Sun Yung Shin, 139–149. Boston, MA: South End Press, 2006.

Hughes, Kristen Grim. "Closed Camps: Vietnamese Refugee Policy in Hong Kong." PhD Diss., University of California, Berkeley, 1985.

Hughes, Richard. "Hong Kong: An Urban Study." *The Geographical Journal* 117, no. 1 (1951): 1–23.

Human, Linda. *The Chinese People of South Africa*. Pretoria: University of South Africa, 1984.

Humanitarian Program Information Paper. http://www.immi.gov.au/media/publications/pdf/hp-client-info-paper.pdf.

Hunter, Ian. *The Immigration Appeal Board: A Study*. Toronto: Law Reform Commission of Canada, 1976.

Huttenbach, R. A. "The British Empire as a 'White Man's Country': Racial Attitudes and Immigration Legislation in the Colonies of White Settlement." *Journal of British Studies* 13, no. 1 (November 1973): 108–137.

Hyndman, Jennifer. *Managing Displacement: Refugees and the Politics of Humanitarianism*. Minneapolis: University of Minnesota Press, 2000.

Iacovetta, Franca. *Gatekeepers: Reshaping Immigrant Lives in Cold War Canada*. Toronto: Between the Lines, 2006.

Ignatieff, Michael. *The Needs of Strangers*. New York, NY: Picador Press, 2002.

Ignatiev, Noel. *How the Irish Became White*. London, UK: Routledge, 1996.

Ingrams, Harold. *Hong Kong*. London, UK: Her Majesty's Stationery Office, 1952.

Ip, Manying. "Redefining Chinese Female Migration: From Exclusion to Transnationalism." In *Shifting Centres: Women and Migration in New Zealand History*, edited by Lyndon Fraser and Katie Pickles, 149–166. Dunedin: University of Otago Press, 2002.

———. *Unfolding History, Evolving Identity: The Chinese in New Zealand*. Auckland: Auckland University Press, 2003.

Iriye, Akira. *The Cold War in Asia: A Historical Introduction*. Englewood Cliffs, NJ: Prentice-Hall, 1974.

———. *Global Community: The Role of International Organizations in the Making of the Contemporary World*. Berkeley: University of California Press, 2002.

———. *Global and Transnational History: The Past, Present, and Future*. London, UK: Palgrave, 2012.

Jackson, Ivor C. *The Refugee Concept in Group Situations*. Cambridge, MA: Kluwer Law International, 1999.

Jakubowicz, Andrew. "Chinese Walls: Australian Multiculturalism and the Necessity for Human Rights." *Journal of Intercultural Studies* 2, no. 6 (December 2011): 691–706.

Jian, Chen. *Mao's China and the Cold War*. Chapel Hill: University of North Carolina Press, 2001.

Jones, Carol, and Jon Vagg. *Criminal Justice in Hong Kong*. New York, NY: Routlege-Cavendish, 2007.

Joppke, Christian. "Why Liberal States Accept Unwanted Immigration." *World Politics* 50, no. 2 (January 1998): 266–293.

Jordan, Matthew. "The Reappraisal of the White Australia Policy Against the Background of a Changing Asia, 1945–66." PhD Diss., University of Sydney, 2001.

Joseph, William. Foreword to *Born Red: A Chronicle of the Cultural Revolution*, by Yuan Gao. Stanford, CA: Stanford University Press, 1987.

Jupp, James. *Exile or Refuge? The Settlement of Refugee, Humanitarian, and Displaced Immigrants*. Canberra: Australian Government Publishing Service, 1994.

———. *From White Australia to Woomera: The Story of Australian Immigration*. Cambridge, UK: Cambridge University Press, 2002.

Kaprielian-Churchill, Isabel. "'Misfits': Canada and the Nansen Passport." *International Migration Review* 28, no. 2 (Summer 1994): 281–306.

Kearney, Michael. "The Classifying and Value-Filtering Missions of Borders." *Anthropological Theory* 4, no. 2 (2004): 131–156.

Keely, Charles. "The International Refugee Regime(s): The End of the Cold War Matters." *International Migration Review* 35, no. 1 (2001): 303–314.

Kelley, Ninette, and Michael Trebilcock. *The Making of the Mosaic: A History of Canadian Immigration Policy*. Toronto: University of Toronto Press, 2010.

Kim, Eleana J. *Adopted Territory: Transnational Korean Adoptees and the Politics of Belonging*. Durham, NC: Duke University Press, 2010.

Klein, Christina. *Cold War Orientalism: Asia in the Middlebrow Imagination, 1945–1961*. Berkeley: University of California Press, 2003.

Kleinman, Arthur, and Joan Kleinman. "The Appeal of Experience; the Dismay of Images: Cultural Appropriations of Suffering in our Times." *Daedalus* 125, no. 1 (1996): 1–23.

Klotz, Audie. *Migration and National Identity in South Africa, 1860–2010*. Cambridge, UK: Cambridge University Press, 2013.

Kneebone, Susan, ed. *Refugees, Asylum Seekers, and the Rule of Law: Comparative Perspectives*. Cambridge, UK: Cambridge University Press, 2009.

Knudsen, John Chr. *Boat People in Transit: Vietnamese in Refugee Camps in the Philippines, Hong Kong, and Japan*. New York, NY: Lilian Barber Press, 1985.

———. "Prisoners of International Politics: Vietnamese Refugees Coping with Transit Life." *Southeast Asian Journal of Social Science* 18, no. 1 (1990): 153–165.

Koser, Khalid. "Social Networks and the Asylum Cycle: The Case of Iranians in the Netherlands." *International Migration Review* 31, no. 3 (1997): 591–611.

———, and Charles Pinkerton. "The Social Networks of Asylum Seekers and the Dissemination of Information about Countries of Asylum." London: Home Office, 2002. http://library.npia.police.uk/docs/hordsolr/social-network.pdf.

Ku, Agnes. "Immigration Policies, Discourses, and the Politics of Local Belonging in Hong Kong (1950–1980)." *Modern China* 30, no. 3 (2004): 326–360.

———, and Helen Tsui, with C. Tsui. *Hong Kong Mobile: Making a Global Population*. Hong Kong: Hong Kong University Press, 2008.

Kulischer, Eugene M. "Displaced Persons in the Modern World." *Annals of the American Academy of Political and Social Science*, 262 (March 1949): 166–177.

Kunz, E. F. "The Refugee in Flight: Kinetic Models and Forms of Displacement." *International Migration Review* 7, no. 2 (Summer 1973): 125–146.

Labman, Shauna. "Invisibles: An Examination of Refugee Resettlement." MLaw Thesis, University of British Columbia, 2007.

Lai, Him Mark. "Unfinished Business: The Confession Program." San Francisco, CA: Chinese Historical Society of America and Asian American Studies, San Francisco State University, 1994.

Lanphier, C. Michael. "Canada's Response to Refugees." *International Migration Review* 15, no. 1/2 (1981): 113–129.

Law, Kam-Yee, ed. *The Chinese Cultural Revolution Reconsidered.* New York, NY: Palgrave Macmillan, 2003.

Lawrence, Bonita, and Enakshi Dua. "Decolonizing Antiracism." *Social Justice* 32, no. 4 (2005): 120–143.

Lee, Christopher. "Humanitarian Assistance as Containment: New Codes for a New Order." Working Paper No. 72. Oxford, UK: Refugee Studies Centre, 2010. http://www.rsc.ox.ac.uk/publications/working-papers-folder_contents/RSCworkingpaper72.pdf.

Lee, Eliza W. Y. "Nonprofit Development in Hong Kong: The Case of a Statist-Corporatist Regime." *Voluntas: International Journal of Voluntary and Nonprofit Organizations* 16, no. 1 (2005): 51–68.

Lee, Erika. *At America's Gates: Chinese Immigration during the Exclusion Era, 1882–1943.* Chapel Hill: University of North Carolina Press, 2003.

Lee, Steven. "The United States, the United Nations, and the Second Occupation of Korea, 1950–1951." *The Asia-Pacific Journal* 7, (2009): 1–9.

Leffler, Melvyn P. *A Preponderance of Power: National Security, the Truman Administration, and the Cold War.* Stanford, CA: Stanford University Press, 1992.

Legomsky, S. "Portraits of the Undocumented Immigrant: A Dialogue." *Georgia Law Review* 44, no. 65 (2009): 1–96.

Lembcke, Jerry. *The Spitting Image: Myth, Memory, and the Legacy of Vietnam.* New York: New York University Press, 1998.

Lester, Alan. "Imperial Circuits and Networks: Geographies of the British Empire." *History Compass* 4, no. 1 (2006): 124–141.

Leung, Beatrice. *Sino-Vatican Relations: Problems in Conflicting Authority, 1976–1986.* Cambridge, UK: Cambridge University Press, 1992.

———, and Shun-hing Chan. *Changing Church and State Relations in Hong Kong, 1950–2000.* Hong Kong: Hong Kong University Press, 2003.

Ley, David. "Seeking Homo Economicus: The Canadian State and the Strange Story of the Business Immigration Program." *Annals of the Association of American Geographers* 93, no. 2 (2003): 426–441.

Link, Eugene Perry. *Refugees in Hong Kong* [n.p.: s.n., 1976?]. Photocopy from Harvard University. East Asian Research Centre. Papers on China, v.22B, Dec. 1969, p. 1–19.

Liu, Xiao-Feng, and Glen Norcliffe. "Closed Windows, Open Doors: Geopolitics and Post-1949 Mainland Chinese Immigration to Canada." *The Canadian Geographer* 40, no. 4 (1996): 306–319.

Loescher, Gil. *Beyond Charity: International Cooperation and the Global Refugee Crisis.* New York, NY: Oxford University Press, 1993.

———. *The UNHCR and World Politics: Perilous Path.* Oxford, UK: Oxford University Press, 2001.

———, with Jon Scanlan. *Calculated Kindness: Refugees and America's Half-Open Door, 1945 to the Present.* New York, NY: Simon and Schuster, 1998.

Lowe, David. *Menzies and the Great World Struggle: Australia's Cold War, 1948–1954.* Sydney: University of New South Wales Press, 1999.

Lüthi, Lorenz. *Sino-Soviet Split: Cold War in the Communist World.* Princeton, NJ: Princeton University Press, 2008.

MacDonald, Andrew. "Colonial Trespassers in the Making of South Africa's International Borders, 1900–1950." PhD Diss., Cambridge University, 2012.

MacFarquhar, Roderick, and Michael Schoenhals. *Mao's Last Revolution.* Cambridge, MA: The Belknap Press of Harvard University Press, 2006.

MacKinnon, Stephen. *Wuhan, 1938: War, Refugees, and the Making of Modern China.* Berkeley: University of California Press, 2008.

Malkki, Lisa. "Speechless Emissaries: Refugees, Humanitarianism, and Dehistoricization." *Cultural Anthropology* 11, no. 3 (August 1996): 377–404.

Manne, Robert. "Asylum Seekers," *The Monthly,* http://www.themonthly.com.au/issue/2010/september/1354143949/robert-manne/comment.

Mar, Lisa. *Brokering Belonging: Chinese in Canada's Exclusion Era, 1885–1945.* New York: Oxford University Press, 2010.

Mark, Chi-Kwan. *Hong Kong and the Cold War: Anglo-American Relations 1949–1957.* Oxford, UK: Oxford University Press, 2004.

———. "The 'Problem of People': British Colonials, Cold War Powers, and the Chinese Refugees in Hong Kong, 1949–62." *Modern Asian Studies* 41, no. 6 (2007): 1–37.

Marrus, Michael. *The Unwanted: European Refugees in the Twentieth Century.* Philadelphia, PA: Temple University Press, 2002.

Martens, Jeremy. "A Transnational History of Immigration Restriction: Natal and New South Wales, 1896–97." *The Journal of Imperial and Commonwealth History* 34, no. 3 (September 2006): 323–344.

May, Elaine Tyler. *Homeward Bound: American Families in the Cold War.* New York, NY: Basic Books, 2008.

McCleary, Rachel M. *Global Compassion: Private Voluntary Organizations and U.S. Foreign Policy since 1939.* Oxford, UK: Oxford University Press, 2009.

McDowell, Meghan G., and Nancy A. Wonders. "Keeping Migrants in Their Place: Technologies of Control and Racialized Public Space in Arizona." *Social Justice* 36, no. 2 (2009-2010): 54–72.

McKeown, Adam. *Chinese Migrant Networks and Cultural Change: Peru, Chicago, Hawaii, 1900–1936*. Chicago, IL: University of Chicago Press, 2001.

————. *Melancholy Order: Asian Migration and the Globalization of Borders*. New York, NY: Columbia University Press, 2008.

Mirzoeff, Nicholas. *An Introduction to Visual Culture*. New York, NY: Routledge, 2000.

————. "On Visuality." *Journal of Visual Culture* 5, no. 53 (2006): 53–79.

Mitchell, James. "Immigration and National Identity in 1970s New Zealand." PhD Diss., University of Otago, 2010.

Mitchell, Robert Edward. *Velvet Colonialism's Legacy to Hong Kong, 1967 and 1997*. Hong Kong: Hong Kong Institute of Asia-Pacific Studies, 1998.

Mohanram, Radhika. *Imperial White: Race, Diaspora, and the British Empire*. Minneapolis: University of Minnesota Press, 2007.

Moore, Bob, and Frank Caestecker, eds. *Refugees from Nazi Germany and the Liberal European States*. New York, NY: Berghahn Books, 2010.

Mountz, Allison. *Seeking Asylum: Human Smuggling and Bureaucracy at the Border*. Minneapolis: University of Minnesota Press, 2010.

Moyn, Samuel. *The Last Utopia: Human Rights in History*. Cambridge, MA: Harvard University Press, 2010.

Murphy, Nigel. *Guide to Laws and Policies Relating to the Chinese in New Zealand 1871–1997*. Wellington: New Zealand Chinese Association, 2008.

Mushkat, Roda. "Refuge in Hong Kong." *International Journal of Refugee Law* 1, no. 4 (1989): 449–480.

National Catholic Welfare Conference Administrative Board in the Name of the Bishops of the United States. *People on the Move: A Compendium of Church Documents on the Pastoral Concern for Migrants and Refugees*. Bishops' Committee on Priestly Formation: Bishops' Committee on Migration, National Conference of Catholic Bishops, 1988.

Nawyn, Stephanie. "Making a Place to Call Home: Refugee Resettlement Organizations, Religion, and the State." PhD Diss., University of Southern California, 2006.

Neumann, Klaus. *Refuge Australia: Australian's Humanitarian Record*. Sydney: University of New South Wales Press, 2004.

————, and Gwenda Tavan, eds. *Does History Matter? Making and Debating Citizenship, Immigration, and Refugee Policy in Australia and New Zealand*. Canberra: Australian National University Press, 2009.

Newnham, Tom. *New Zealand Women in China*. Auckland: Graphic Publications, 1995.

Ngai, Mae. "Legacies of Exclusion: Illegal Chinese Immigration during the Cold War Years." *Journal of American Ethnic History* 18, no. 1 (1998): 3–35.

——. *Impossible Subjects: Illegal Aliens and the Making of Modern America.* Princeton, NJ: Princeton University Press, 2005.

Nguyen, Mimi. *The Gift of Freedom: War, Debt, and Other Refugee Passages.* Durham, NC: Duke University Press, 2012.

Nicholls, Glenn. *Deported: A History of Forced Departures from Australia.* Sydney: University of New South Wales Press, 2007.

Nyers, Peter. *Rethinking Refugees: Beyond States of Emergency.* London, UK: Routledge, 2005.

On Wai Lan, Kenneth. "Rennie's Mill: The Origin and Evolution of a Special Enclave in Hong Kong." PhD Diss., University of Hong Kong, 2006.

Ong, Aihwa. *Buddha is Hiding: Refugees, Citizenship, the New America.* Berkeley: University of California Press, 2003.

Owram, Douglas. *Born at the Right Time.* Toronto: University of Toronto Press, 1996.

OXFAM. *How Hong Kong Cares for Vietnamese Refugees.* Hong Kong: OXFAM, April 1986.

Oyen, Meredith. *The Diplomacy of Migration: Transnational Lives and the Making of U.S.-Chinese relations in the Cold War.* Ithaca, NY: Cornell University Press, 2015.

——. "The Right of Return: Chinese Displaced Persons and the International Refugee Organization, 1947-56," *Modern Asian Studies* 49, no. 2 (2015): 546–571.

Page, Don. "The Representation of China in the United Nations: Canadian Perspectives and Initiatives, 1949–1971." In *Reluctant Adversaries: Canada and the People's Republic of China, 1949–1970*, edited by Paul Evans and B. Michael Frolic, 73–84. Toronto: University of Toronto Press, 1991.

Palfreeman, A. C. *The Administration of the White Australia Policy.* Cambridge, UK: Cambridge University Press, 1967.

Palmer, David. "The Quest for 'Wriggle Room': Australia and the Refugees Convention, 1951-73." *Australian Journal of International Affairs* 63, no. 2 (2009).

Pappone, Rene. *The Hai Hong: Profit, Tears, and Joy.* Ottawa: Employment and Immigration Canada, 1982.

Park, Yoon Jung. *A Matter of Honour: Being Chinese in South Africa.* Plymouth, UK: Lexington Books, 2008.

Paul, Kathleen. *Whitewashing Britain: Race and Citizenship in the Postwar Era.* Ithaca, NY: Cornell University Press, 1997.

Pearson, David. *The Politics of Ethnicity in Settler Societies: States of Unease.* New York, NY: Palgrave, 2001.

————, and Patrick Ongley. "Post-1945 International Migration: New Zealand, Australia and Canada Compared." *International Migration Review* 29, no. 3 (1995): 765–793.

Peberdy, Sally. *Selecting Immigrants National Identity and South Africa's Immigration Policies, 1910–2005*. Johannesburg: Wits University Press, 2009.

Pegler-Gordon, Anna. *In Sight of America: Photography and Development of U.S. Immigration Policy*. Berkeley: University of California Press, 2009.

Pendakur, Ravi. *Immigrants and the Labour Force: Policy, Regulation, and Impact*. Montreal: McGill-Queen's University Press, 2001.

Perin, Roberto. "Churches and Immigrant Integration in Toronto, 1947–65." In *The Churches and Social Order in Nineteenth- and Twentieth-Century Canada*, edited by Michael Gauvreau and Olivier Hubert, 274–291. Montreal: McGill-Queen's University Press, 2006.

Perry, Adele. *On the Edge of Empire: Gender, Race, and the Making of British Columbia, 1849–1871*. Toronto: University of Toronto Press, 1994.

Peterson, Glen. "To Be or Not to Be a Refugee: The International Politics of the Hong Kong Refugee Crisis, 1949–1955." *The Journal of Imperial and Commonwealth History* 36, no. 2 (2008): 171–195.

————. *Overseas Chinese in the People's Republic of China*. New York, NY: Routledge, 2012.

Pheng, Sokeary. "La politique d'accueil des réfugiés de la Nouvelle-Zélande: Entre obligations internationales et intérêts nationaux, 1944-2006." PhD Diss., l'Université d'Avignon et des Pays de Vaucluse, 2006.

Poston, Dudley L., Jr., and Mei-Yu Yu. "The Distribution of the Overseas Chinese in the Contemporary World." *International Migration Review*, 24, no. 3 (1990): 480–508.

Price, Charles A. *The Great White Walls Are Built: Restrictive Immigration to North America and Australasia, 1836–1888*. Canberra: Australian Institute of International Affairs in association with Australian National University Press, 1974.

————. "Immigration Policies and Refugees in Australia." *International Migration Review* 15, no. 1–2 (Spring–Summer, 1981): 99–108.

Price, John. *Orienting Canada: Race, Empire, and the Transpacific*. Vancouver: UBC Press, 2011.

Ptolemy, Kathleen. "Ministering to the Uprooted." In *Hope in the Desert: The Churches' United Response to Human Need, 1944–1984*, edited by Kenneth Slack, 107–118. Geneva: World Council of Churches, 1986.

Rajaram, Prem Kumar. "Humanitarianism and Representations of the Refugee." *Journal of Refugee Studies* 15, no. 3 (2002): 247–264.

————, and Carl-Grundy Warr, Eds. *Borderscapes: Hidden Geographies and Politics at Territory's Edge*. Minneapolis: University of Minnesota Press, 2007.

Razack, Sherene H. *Race, Space, and the Law: Unmapping a White Settler Society.* Toronto: Between the Lines, 2002.

———. *Casting Out: The Eviction of Muslims from Western Law & Politics.* Toronto: Toronto University Press, 2008.

Redl, Harry. *Exodus from China.* Hong Kong: Dragonfly Books, 1962.

Regan, Paulette. *Unsettling the Settler Within: Indian Residential Schools, Truth Telling, and Reconciliation in Canada.* Vancouver: UBC Press, 2010.

Reid, Nicholas. "Struggle for Souls: Catholicism and Communism in Twentieth Century New Zealand." *Australian Historical Studies* 128 (2006): 72–88.

Ressler, Everett M., Neil Boothby, and Daniel J. Steinbock. *Unaccompanied Children: Care and Protection in Wars, Natural Disasters, and Refugee Movements.* New York, NY: Oxford University Press, 1988.

Richards, Eric. *Destination Australia: Migration to Australia since 1901.* Sydney: University of New South Wales Press, 2008.

Richmond, Anthony. *Global Apartheid: Refugees, Racism, and the New World Order.* Toronto, ON: Oxford University Press, 1994.

Rieff, David. *A Bed for the Night: Humanitarianism in Crisis.* New York, NY: Simon & Schuster, 2002.

Rivett, Kenneth. *Immigration: Control or Colour Bar? The Background to "White Australia" and a Proposal for Change.* Melbourne: Melbourne University Press, 1962.

———. "Towards a Policy on Refugees." *Australian Outlook* 33, no. 2 (1979): 137–156.

Robertson, Julie Ann. "Of Scarecrows and Straw Men: Asylum in Aotearoa New Zealand." PhD Diss., University of Otago, 2006.

Robinson, W. Courtland. *Terms of Refuge: The Indochinese Exodus and the International Response.* London, UK: Zed Books, 1998.

Roy, Anjali Gera, and Nandi Bhatia, eds. *Partitioned Lives: Narratives of Home, Displacement, and Resettlement.* New Delhi, India: Dorling Kindersley, 2008.

Roy, Patricia. *Oriental Question: Consolidating a White Man's Province, 1914–1941.* Vancouver: University of British Columbia Press, 2003.

———. *The Triumph of Citizenship: The Japanese and Chinese in Canada.* Vancouver: UBC Press, 2010.

Royal Hong Kong Police. *Annual Review / Commissioner of Police, Hong Kong.* Hong Kong: Government Printer, 1949–1950.

Ryan, James. *Picturing Empire: Photography and the Visualization of the British Empire.* London, UK: Reaktion Books, 1997.

Salomon, Kim. *Refugees in the Cold War: Toward a New International Refugee Regime in the Early Postwar Era.* Lund, Sweden: Lund University Press, 1991.

Salyer, Lucy. *Laws as Harsh as Tigers: Chinese Immigrants and the Shaping of Modern Immigration Law.* Chapel Hill: University of North Carolina Press, 1995.

Satsiulis, Daiva, and Nira Yuval-Davis, eds. *Unsettling Settler Societies: Articulations of Gender, Race, Ethnicity, and Class*. London, UK: SAGE Publications, 1995.

Shacknove, Andrew. "Who Is a Refugee?" *Ethics* 85, no. 2 (1985): 274–284.

Shah, Nayan. *Contagious Divides: Epidemics and Race in San Francisco's Chinatown*. Berkeley: University of California Press, 2001.

Shah, Prakash A. *Refugees, Race, and the Legal Concept of Asylum in Britain*. London, UK: Cavendish, 2000.

Sharma, Nandita. *Home Economics: Nationalism and the Making of 'Migrant Workers' in Canada*. Toronto: University of Toronto Press, 2006.

Sicakkan, Hakan. "The Modern State, the Citizen, and the Perilous Refugee." *Journal of Human Rights* 3, no. 4 (2004): 445–463.

Simmons, Alan B., and Keiran Keohane. "Shifts in Canadian Immigration Policy: State Strategies and the Quest for Legitimacy." *Canadian Review of Anthropology and Sociology* 29, no. 4 (1990): 421–452.

Sinn, Elizabeth, ed. *Hong Kong, British Crown Colony, Revisited*. Centre of Asian Studies: University of Hong Kong, 2001.

———. *Power and Charity: A Chinese Merchant Elite in Colonial Hong Kong*. Hong Kong: Hong Kong University Press, 2003.

———. *Pacific Crossing: California Gold, Chinese Migration, and the Making of Hong Kong*. Hong Kong: Hong Kong University Press, 2012.

Skeldon, Ronald. "Hong Kong's Response to the Indochinese Influx, 1975–1993." *The Annals of the American Academy of Political and Social Science* 534 (1994): 91–105.

———. "Migration from China." *Journal of International Affairs*, 49, no. 2 (1996): 43–65.

Skran, Claudena M. *Refugees in Inter-War Europe: The Emergence of a Regime*. London, UK: Clarendon Press, 1995.

Sliwinksi, Sharon. "The Childhood of Human Rights: The Kodak on the Congo." *The Journal of Visual Culture* 5 (2006): 333–363.

———. "The Aesthetics of Human Rights." *Culture, Theory & Critique* 50, no. 1 (2009): 23–39.

Smart, Alan. *The Shek Kip Mei Myth: Squatters, Fires, and Colonial Rulers in Hong Kong*. Hong Kong: Hong Kong Press, 2006.

———. "Unreliable Chinese: Internal Security and the Devaluation and Expansion of Citizenship in Postwar Hong Kong." In *War, Citizenship, Territory*, edited by Deborah Cowen and Emily Gilbert, 219–240. New York, NY: Routledge, 2008.

———, and Josephine Smart. "Time-Space Punctuation: Hong Kong's Border Regime and Limits on Mobility." *Pacific Affairs* 81, no. 2 (2008): 175–193.

Smith, Timothy Robin. "Making of the 1998 Refugees Act: Consultation, Compromise, and Controversy." MA Thesis, University of Witwatersrand, 2003.

Soguk, Nevzat. *States and Strangers: Refugees and Displacement of Statecraft*. Minneapolis: University of Minnesota Press, 1999.

Solomon-Godeau, Abigail. *Photography at the Dock: Essays on Photographic History, Institutions, and Practices*. Minneapolis: University of Minnesota Press, 1994.

Sovik, Ruth. *Mission in Formosa and Hong Kong: Studies in the Beginning and Development of the Indigenous Lutheran Church in Formosa and Hong Kong*. Minneapolis, MN: Augsburg Publishing House, 1957.

Spalding, Elizabeth Edwards. *The First Cold Warrior: Harry Truman, Containment, and the Remaking of Liberal Internationalism*. Lexington: University Press of Kentucky, 2006.

Speaking notes for The Honorable Jason Kenney, P. C., M. P. Minister of Citizenship, Immigration, and Multiculturalism, Address to the Montreal Council on Foreign Relations, 20 April 2012. See http://www.cic.gc.ca/english/department/media/speeches/2012/2012-04-20.asp.

Spencer, Ian R. G. *British Immigration Policy since 1939: The Making of Multi-Racial Britain*. London, UK: Routledge, 1997.

Stephens, Murdoch. "No Defence for Keeping NZ's Refugee Quota so Small." *The Dominion Post*, 28 August 2015. http://www.stuff.co.nz/dominion-post/comment/71494488/opinion-no-defence-for-keeping-nzs-refugee-quota-so-small.

Stoessinger, John. *The Refugee and the World Community*. Minneapolis: University of Minnesota Press, 1957.

Stoler, Ann Laura. *Carnal Knowledge and Imperial Power: Race and the Intimate in Colonial Rule*. Berkeley: University of California Press, 2002.

———. *Along the Archival Grain: Epistemic Anxieties and Colonial Common Sense*. Princeton, NJ: Princeton University Press, 2009.

Strahan, Lachlan. *Australia's China: Changing Perceptions from the 1930s to the 1990s*. Cambridge, UK: Cambridge University Press, 1996.

Strand, Paul J., and Woodrow Jones, Jr. *Indochinese Refugees in America: Problems of Adaptation and Assimilation*. Durham, NC: Duke University Press, 1985.

Strong-Boag, Veronica. *Finding Families, Finding Ourselves: English Canada Encounters Adoption from the Nineteenth Century to the 1990s*. Don Mills: Oxford University Press, 2006.

Sturken, Maria. *Tangled Memories: The Vietnam War, the AIDS Epidemic, and the Politics of Remembering*. Berkeley: University of California Press, 1997.

———, with Lisa Cartwright, eds. *Practices of Looking: An Introduction to Visual Culture*. New York, NY: Oxford University Press, 2009.

Szorenyi, Anna. "The Images Speak for Themselves? Reading Refugee Coffee Table Books." *Visual Studies* 21, no. 1 (April 2006): 24–41.

Tabori, Paul. *The Anatomy of Exile: A Semantic and Historical Study.* London, UK: George G. Harrap, 1972.

Tait, Sue. "Bearing Witness, Journalism and Moral Responsibility." *Media, Culture & Society* 33, no. 8 (November 2011): 1220–1235.

Tavan, Gwenda. *The Long Slow Death of White Australia.* Brunswick: Scribe Publications, 2005.

Thomas, Nicholas. *Democracy Denied: Identity, Civil Society, and Illiberal Democracy in Hong Kong.* London, UK: 1999.

———, ed. *Re-Orienting Australia-China Relations: 1972 to the Present.* Aldershot, UK: Ashgate Publishing, 2004.

Thompson, Andrew S. *In Defence of Principles: NGOs and Human Rights in Canada.* Vancouver: UBC Press, 2010.

———, and Stephanie Bangarth. "Transnational Christian Charity: The Canadian Council of Churches, the World Council of Churches, and the Hungarian Refugee Crisis, 1956–1957." *American Review of Canadian Studies* 38, no. 3 (2008): 295–316.

Thompson, Larry Clinton. *Refugee Workers in the Indochina Exodus, 1975–1982.* Jefferson, NC: McFarland & Company, 2010.

Thompson, Russell Thurlow. *New Zealand in Relief: The Story of CORSO's Twenty-One Years of Relief Service Overseas.* Wellington: New Zealand Council of Organisations for Relief Services Overseas, 1965.

Torpey, John. *Invention of the Passport: Surveillance, Citizenship, and the State.* Cambridge: Cambridge University Press, 2000.

Touhey, Ryan M. "Dealing in Black and White: The Diefenbaker Government and the Cold War in South Asia, 1957–1963." *Canadian Historical Review* 92, no. 3 (2011): 429–454.

Trenka, Jane Jeong, Chinyere Oparah, and Sun Yung Shin, eds. *Outsiders Within: Writing on Transracial Adoption.* Boston, MA: South End Press, 2006.

Trudeau, Pierre, and Jaques Hébert. *Two Innocents in Red China.* Toronto: Oxford University Press, 1968.

Tsang, Steven. *A Modern History of Hong Kong.* London, UK: I. B. Tauris, 2004.

United Nations. *Conférence de l'Année Mondiale du Réfugié.* Geneva: United Nations, 1961.

UN Relief and Rehabilitation Administration. "Agreement for UNRRA." 9 November 1943. http://www.ibiblio.org/pha/policy/1943/431109a.html.

United States. Congress. House of Representatives. Report of a Special Subcommittee of the Committee on the Judiciary. *Refugee Problem in Hong Kong.* Washington : U.S.G.P.O., 1962.

United States. Congress. Senate. Committee on the Judiciary. Subcommittee to Investigate Problems Connected with Refugees and Escapees. *Refugee Problem in Hong Kong and Macao: Hearings Before the United States Senate Committee on the Judiciary, Subcommittee to Investigate Problems Connected with Refugees and Escapees,* 87th Cong., 2nd Sess., on May 29, June 7, 8, 28, July 10, 1962. Washington: U.S.G.P.O., 1962.

United States. *World Refugee Year, July 1959–June 1960; Report on the Participation of the United States Government.* Washington, DC: U.S. Govt. Print. Off., 1960.

United States. Senate. *Report of the Committee on the Judiciary, United States Senate made by its subcommittee on immigration and naturalization pursuant to S. Res. 60 88th Congress, 1st session, as extended, Report 88th Congress, 2nd Session, 5.* Washington: U.S.G.P.O (1964).

Vagg, Jon. "Sometimes a Crime: Illegal Immigration and Hong Kong." *Crime & Delinquency* 39 (1993): 355–372.

van Dok, Geert, Christian Varga, and Romain Schroeder. "Humanitarian Challenges: The Political Dilemmas of Emergency Aid." Caritas Switzerland: Position Paper 11, Caritas Luxembourg: LES CAHIERS CARITAS No 3. Lucerne/Luxembourg, November 2005.

Vaux, Tony. *The Selfish Altruist: Relief Work in Famine and War.* London, UK: Earthscan, 2001.

Veracini, Lorenzo. *Settler Colonialism: A Theoretical Overview.* New York, NY: Palgrave Macmillan, 2010.

Vernant, Jacques. *The Refugee in the Post-War World.* New Haven, CT: Yale University Press, 1953.

Viviani, Nancy. *Australian Government Policies on the Entry of Vietnamese: Record and Responsibility.* Queensland: Griffith University, Centre for the Study of Australian–Asian Relations, 1982.

———. *The Long Journey: Vietnamese Migration and Settlement in Australia.* Carlton: Melbourne University Press, 1984.

Walker, David. *Anxious Nation: Australia and the Rise of Asia, 1850–1939.* Brisbane: University of Queensland Press, 1999.

Ward, Peter. "The Oriental Immigrant and Canada's Protestant Clergy." *BC Studies* 22 (Summer 1974): 40–55.

———. *White Canada Forever: Popular Attitudes and Public Policy toward Orientals in British Columbia.* 3rd ed. Montreal: McGill–Queen's University Press, 2002.

Watenpaugh, Keith David. "The League of Nations' Rescue of Armenian Genocide Survivors and the Making of Modern Humanitarianism, 1920–1927." *The American Historical Review* 115, no. 5 (2010): 1315–1339.

Weiner, Myron. "Bad Neighbors, Bad Neighborhoods: An Inquiry into the Causes of Refugee Flows." *International Security* 21, no. 1 (1996): 5–42.

Weis, Paul. "The International Protection of Refugees." *The American Journal of International Law* 48, no. 2 (April 1954): 193–221.

Whitaker, Reg. *Double Standard: The Secret History of Canadian Immigration.* Toronto: Lester & Orpen Dennys Publishers, 1987.

White, Lynn T., and Kam-Yee Law. "Explanations for China's Revolution at its Peak." In *The Chinese Cultural Revolution Reconsidered*, edited by Kam-Yee Law, 1–25. New York: Palgrave Macmillan, 2003.

Wolfe, Patrick. *Settler Colonialism and the Transformation of Anthropology*. London, UK: Cassell, 1999.

Wong, Chung-Kwong. "Chinese Illegal Immigrants: Their Effects on the Social and Public Order in Hong Kong." MA Thesis, University of Leicester, 1995.

Wong, Jan. *Jan Wong's China: Reports from a Not-So-Foreign Correspondent*. Toronto: Doubleday Canada, 1999.

Wong, Siu-Lun. *Emigrant Entrepreneurs: Shanghai Industrialists in Hong Kong*. New York, NY: Oxford University Press, 1988.

Wright, Robert. *A World Mission: Canadian Protestantism and the Quest for a New International Order, 1918–1939*. Montreal: McGill-Queen's University Press, 1991.

Wu, Tuong, and Wasana Wongsurawat, eds. *Dynamics of the Cold War in Asia: Ideology, Identity, and Culture*. New York, NY: Palgrave Macmillan, 2009.

Yan, Jiaqi. *Turbulent Decade: A History of the Cultural Revolution*. Translated by D. W. Kwok. Honolulu: University of Hawaii Press, 1996.

Yang, Meng-Hsuan. "The Great Exodus: Chinese Mainlanders in Taiwan." Paper Prepared for the Canadian Asian Studies Association Conference, November 13–16, 2008.

Yangwen, Zheng, Hong Liu, and Michael Szonyi, eds. *The Cold War in Asia: The Battle for Hearts and Minds*. Leiden: Brill, 2010.

Yap, Melanie, and Dianne Leong Man. *Colour, Confusion, & Concessions: The History of the Chinese in South Africa*. Hong Kong: Hong Kong University Press, 1996.

Yep, Ray. "Cultural Revolution in Hong Kong: Emergency Powers, Administration of Justice, and the Turbulent Year of 1967." *Modern Asian Studies* 46, no. 4 (2012): 1007–1032.

Zahra, Tara. *The Lost Children: Reconstructing Europe's Families after World War II*. Cambridge, MA: Harvard University Press, 2011.

Zamindar, Vazira Fazila-Yacoobali. *The Long Partition and the Making of Modern South Asia*. New York, NY: Columbia University Press, 2010.

Zetter, Roger. "Labelling Refugees: Forming and Transforming a Bureaucratic Identity." *Journal of Refugee Studies* 4, no. 1 (1991): 39–62.

———. "More Labels, Fewer Refugees: Remaking the Refugee Label in an Era of Globalization." *Journal of Refugee Studies* 20, no. 2 (2007): 172–192.

Zolberg, Aristide, Astri Suhrke, and Sergio Aguayo. "International Factors in the Formation of Refugee Movements." *International Migration Review* 20, no. 2 (1986): 151–169.

ACKNOWLEDGMENTS

I OWE so much to so many. This book has been a labor of love; one that has been sustained by a rich community of family, friends, and colleagues. I am profoundly grateful.

First thanks go to my editor, Andrew Kinney, who saw early promise in this project and worked his magic to see it through to fruition.

This project emerged from my work at the University of British Columbia, which was supported by funding from the Social Sciences and Humanities Research Council of Canada and the Pierre Elliot Trudeau Foundation. Henry Yu pushed me to interrogate any and all received wisdom and to stretch my intellectual limits as far as I could, and then some. Steve Lee provided invaluable moral support and counsel. So, too, did other members of the wonderful community of scholars I discovered in Vancouver: Gabriela Aceves, Kelly Cairns, Catherine Dauvergne, Michel Ducharme, Jan Friedrichs, Noa Grass, Dan Hiebert, Chelsea Horton, Laura Ishiguro, Asha Kaushal, Shauna Labman, Tina Loo, Ruth Mandajuano, Birga Meyer, Tamara Myers, Glen Peterson, Lawrence Santiago, Jamie Sedgwick, Patrick Slaney, Coll Thrush, Phil Van Huizen, Cameron Whitehead, and Brendan Wright.

A number of scholars have been the source of great intellectual stimulation as well as models of generosity. For this, I give thanks to

Emily Andrew, Carl Bon Tempo, May Chazan, Tina Chen, Lisa Chilton, Greg Donaghy, Jérôme Élie, Marlene Epp, Peter Gatrell, Julie Gilmour, Elaine Ho, Madeline Hsu, Teresa Iacobelli, Franca Iacovetta, Valerie Knowles, Leah Levac, Dominique Marshall, Francine McKenzie, Sean Mills, Mae Ngai, Adele Perry, John Price, Beth Robertson, Patricia Roy, Daniel Rück, Jordan Stanger-Ross, Will Tait, Erin Tolley, Ryan Touhey, James Walker, and David Webster.

On a number of occasions I had the opportunity to present my work among the growing community of scholars researching the history of refugees. I am especially grateful to Anna Holian for the invitation to participate the Refugee in the Postwar World conference at Arizona State University. I am also grateful to the editors and anonymous reviewers for *Modern Asian Studies* and the *Journal of Refugee Studies* for allowing me to develop my ideas about the refugee situation in Hong Kong in "Surveying Hong Kong in the 1950s: Western Humanitarians and the 'Problem' of Chinese Refugees," *Modern Asian Studies* 49 No. 2 (2014): 493–524 and "Borders Transformed: Sovereign Concerns, Population Movements and the Making of Territorial Frontiers in Hong Kong, 1949–1967," *Journal of Refugee Studies* 25, no. 3 (2012): 407–427.

Many archivists and librarians gave generously of their time and expertise to assist me with the research for this book. I am particularly grateful to Bernard Hui at the Public Records Office in Hong Kong, Roger Kershaw and Mark Pearsall at the National Archives of the United Kingdom, Lucy McCann at the Rhodes House Library in Oxford, Kim Brenner and Patricia Fluckinger-Livingstone at the UNHCR, Graham Langston at Archives New Zealand and Karan Oberoi at the National Archives of Australia. Additional thanks to the staff at Library and Archives Canada, especially Alix McEwen, who provided invaluable references services, and to Don Davis of the American Friends Service Committee Archives in Philadelphia. I would also like to acknowledge the assistance of staff at the National Archives of South Africa, the Library of Congress and the National Archives and Records Administration in Washington, the New York Public Library, Columbia University Archives, the Ford and Rockefeller Foundation Archives, and the Hoover Institution Archives.

I want to express my deep gratitude to the people whom I interviewed for this project, some of whose words appear in print and others who provided much in the way of food for thought and who ultimately shaped the book's core trajectory: Ron Atkey, Kate Bangarth, Sean Brawley, Timothy Brook, Jocelyn Chey, Gordon Chu, Jim Chu, Joanne Chu, Sophie Couchman, Janet Dench, Dave Elder, Tony Enns, Harry Fan, King Fong, Collen French, Michael Frolic, Karen Harris, Maggie and Kelly Ip, Manying Ip, Bill Janzen, Daphne Lowe Kelley, Andrew Lai, Peggy Lai, Douglas Lam, Art Lee, Robert Lee, Dianne Leong, Paul Liu, Jaqueline Lo, Kai Luey, James Ng, Dora Nipp, Sid Chow Tan, Hayne Wai, Sandra Wilking, and Melanie Yap. Special thanks to Mike Molloy of the Canadian Immigration Historical Society, as well as society members Don Cameron, James Bissett, Gerry Van Kessel, Ron Button, Gerry Campbell, Raph Girard, Lloyd Champoux, and Gordon Barnett. Thanks to Russell Burrows for conversations as well as for supplying reproductions of images taken by his father in Hong Kong in 1962.

At McGill, and in Montreal, thanks are owed to Megan Bradley, Kate Desbarats, Allan Downey, Elizabeth Elbourne, Shanon Fitzpatrick, Stephan Gervais, Elsbeth Heaman, Lynn Kozak, Catherine Lu, Lorenz Lüthi, David Meren, Sue Morton, Mireille Pacquet, Laila Parsons, Mary Anne Poutanen, Sonya Roy, Jarrett Rudy, Jon Soske, Gavin Walker, David Wright, and John Zucchi.

Further acknowledgments go to those who have been a source of inspiration above and beyond the writing of this book. For their friendship, I thank Christine Barrass, Miriam Beauchamp, Andre Bernier, Jana Buhlmann, Karine Burger, Marnie Burnham, Jill Delaney, Elizabeth Doyle, Ginette Fisher, Jay Gilbert, Marsha Khan, Omar Khan, Kayley Kimball, Carrie Lepage, Duncan McGregor, April Miller, Johanna Mizgala, Élizabeth Mongrain, Mary Ocampo-Gauthier, Amanda Potts, Dara Price, Kathryn Reynolds, Johanna Smith, Amy Tector, and Bob Zavitz, as well as Bronwen Keddie and her delightful gang.

To my family, namely the extended Madokoro, Kimoto, Rothfels, and Manning clans, thank you for your unwavering support and for nourishing me with stories. Along with thousands of other Japanese Canadian families, the Madokoros and Kimotos were interned during the Second World War. My maternal grandfather moved to Canada as a Jewish refugee from Germany. This dual history has been an important influence on my work and life, although by no means a defining one.

More thanks: to my dad, who passed too soon, but who has been with me in spirit every step of the way; to my mom, for daily lessons in living a life of grace and kindness; and to my brothers Mike and Dave, for keeping it real, making me laugh, and imparting much needed wisdom and perspective.

This book is seeing the light of day because it comes from a place of caring and compassion. For this, I am grateful to Tom, who challenges and inspires me in everything I do with his curiosity, irreverence, and generosity of spirit. And to Eli and Hanako, who have filled our home with joy and laughter, as well as a magical sense of wonder.

INDEX

Australia (*continued*): response to 1962 grain shortage refugees, 129; response to Vietnamese boat people, 188, 190, 191–193, 197–198, 206, 209; response to World Refugee Year, 82, 84, 88–89, 90; signs UN Convention and protocol on refugees, 164; view of Hong Kong Chinese resettlement, 88, 93

Barnett, Gord, 202, 203
Best, Cal, 202
Bien, Paul B., 162–163
Black, Robin, 42, 48, 83, 91, 119–120, 132
Brash, Alan, 153, 156, 167
British Friends Service Committee, 73
Brown, Richard, 68, 136
Brynner, Yul, 84
Burgess, Claude, 90, 131, 133–134
Burgmann, Bishop, 110
Burrows, Larry, 124, 126–127, 136, 138

Calwell, Arthur, 105–106, 107
Cameron, Don, 179, 180
Campbell, Gerry, 180
Canada: confusion over difference between migrants and refugees, 181; and Convention Relating to the Status of Refugees, 26, 28, 164; defines a refugee in law, 164; family reunification plan with PRC, 120, 178–181; and humanitarian approach to immigration, 181–186, 204; illegal Chinese immigration, 96–97, 118–120, 149, 204; Immigration Act of 1976, 181–184; meeting of refugees and Indigenous peoples, 219–220; present day refugee system, 18; race-based immigration restrictions in, 99, 145; resettlement of Hong Kong Chinese refugees, 78, 93, 118–121, 122, 142–152, 177; resettlement of Vietnamese

boat people, 188, 190, 200–206, 209–210, 212; response to 1962 grain shortage refugees, 129; response to World Refugee Year, 82, 84, 87, 90; and Syrian refugees, 18
Canadian Council of Churches, 150, 202
CARE, 43, 51, 68, 70, 71, 79–80
Caritas, 195
Chan, Kin Yip Peter, 172
Chance, Leslie, 26
Channel, Bill, 63–64, 74
Channel, Roberta, 63–64
Chen, Helen, 64
Chenard, Jean J., 91–92, 94
Cheng Pao-Nan, 79
Chennault, Anna, 135, 140, 141
Chennault, Claire, 135
Cheung Jut Wong, 183–184
"chicken farmer" story, 180
Chilean refugees, 182, 202
China, 2–3, 4, 26. *See also* People's Republic of China (PRC); Republic of China (ROC)
Chinese Benevolent Association, 74, 118
Chinese Confession Program (US), 115, 116–118, 120–122
Chinese Consolidated Benevolent Association, 116
Chinese Refugee Committee, 141
Chinese Refugee Program (Canada), 143–147
Chinese Refugee Relief, 135
Ching Ma, 179
Christian Reformed Church, 203
Chu, Deanna, 141–142
Chu, Jim, 146, 214–216
Chu, Joanne, 215–216
Chu, Show Hwa, 146
Chu, Ton-Son, 146, 147, 215
Civic Association, 80
Cold War: and debate over illegal immigration, 99–100; and D. Lam, 35; effect on immigration in

Hart, Philip, 140–141

Heyes, Tasman, 30, 113

Hickman, Baden, 90

Ho, Ufrieda, 102

Hoare, Samuel, 28

Hoffman, Paul, 70

Holyoake, Keith J., 156

Hong Kong: after Japanese occupation, 4, 42; ARCI survey of, 65–67; attempt to calculate number of refugees from PRC in, 1–2; background to humanitarian groups in, 55–61; and Convention Relating to the Status of Refugees, 33; effect of Cultural Revolution on, 174–175; effect of PRC emigration ban on, 40–41; Guomindang-Communist violence in, 51–52; Guomindang in, 45–46; history of migration pressures on, 35–36, 37; Immigration Ordinance of 1971, 176; lack of resettlement outlets for, 47–48; life of postwar migrant in, 34–35; migration from PRC to, 4–6, 37, 174–175, 193–194, 208; recipient of political aid, 49–50; reluctance of Chinese migrants to identify as refugees, 6–7; response to Vietnamese boat people, 189, 193–195, 212; squatter problem of, 37, 41–42, 43, 44–45, 48–49; traditional relationship with mainland China, 2–3, 4; US aid to, 43, 57, 81, 91; views on resettlement of its refugees, 58

Hong Kong colonial government: agreement with Canadian government over illegal migrants, 119–120; attitude toward humanitarian aid, 43–44, 57, 61, 74–75; categorizing of residents in, 163–164; change of attitude toward refugees, 48–49; denying relief for squatters, 41–42, 44–45, 48–49; management of population pressures, 4–5, 35, 37–40, 45, 48, 52–54, 61, 160, 176–177, 193–194, 208; reaction to Guomindang, 45; and refugees from 1962 grain shortage, 124, 131–132; relations with PRC, 49–51, 52, 81; response to fires, 42–43; response to violence due to Cultural Revolution, 175–176; response to World Refugee Year, 90–91, 93; setting up Rennie's Mill Camp, 45–47; and Vietnamese boat people, 189, 193–195, 206–209; view of 1953 refugee survey, 76–77, 78–79; view of UN refugee fund, 81

Hoskins, Lewis, 66, 72–73

Howard, Bill, 74

Huey Fong (ship), 194

Hughes, Kent, 114

Hui, Bernard, 172

Hui Hua Kien, 184

humanitarian groups: background to in Hong Kong, 55–61; and Cold War, 43–44, 58, 135; competition for endorsing agency status, 74; complicated messaging of, 14–15; criticism of governments' attitude towards resettlement, 91–93; effect on white settler society immigration systems, 13–15; fundraising for, 61–62, 65–66, 68–70, 74, 89–90; and Hambro report, 78, 79–80; Hong Kong government attitude toward, 43–44, 57, 61, 74–75; and Hong Kong refugee resettlement in Canada, 150–152; and Hong Kong refugee resettlement in New Zealand, 152–153, 154, 155–156; and Hong Kong squatters, 41, 42, 43; media effect on, 159; move to Hong Kong from PRC, 5–6; and 1962 grain shortage refugees, 129–130, 135; personality conflicts between, 74, 75; public appeals of, 63–67; and rebuilding Hong

Kong after Japanese occupation, 42; rejection of British position on 1962 refugees, 132, 133, 134; and Rennie's Mill Camp, 46, 47; shaping of international community's interest in Hong Kong, 57–58, 63, 80; and Vietnamese boat people, 187–189, 195, 201–205, 206; view of resettlement, 56, 57, 58, 60, 70–71; and World Refugee Year, 84–85, 89–90. *See also* Aid Refugee Chinese Intellectuals (ARCI); American Friends Service Committee (AFSC)

Human Rights Council of Hong Kong, 135

Hunt, Frank, 69

illegal immigration: association with criminality, 99, 100–101; in Australia, 104–115, 122–123; to Canada, 96–97, 118–120, 204; claims of about Vietnamese boat people, 189, 192–193, 204; and Cold War, 99–100; during Cultural Revolution, 175; and deportation, 103–115; as economic blight, 101; to Hong Kong, 160, 176–177, 193–194, 208; in New Zealand, 103, 154, 168; and paper son schemes, 97–98, 116–117, 118, 119, 121; and refugees from 1962 grain shortage, 133–134; South African restrictions against, 101–103; as strategy to target unwanted migrants, 122–123, 160

Immigrant Controls Ordinance, 38

India, 23

Indigenous peoples, 219–220

International Refugee Organization (IRO), 21–22

International Social Service (ISS), 157

Italy, 28–29

Ivy, James, 65, 66

Jack, Dave, 74

Janson, Donald, 140

Janzen, Bill, 203, 211

Jewish Immigrant Aid Services, 203

Jewish refugees, 20

Johnson, Lyndon, 16, 17

Judd, Walter, 55, 59, 63, 72–73, 78, 135

Keating, Kenneth, 128

Kennedy, Robert, 139

Kirk, Norman, 155, 173

Korean War, 9, 24–25, 99

Kwan Ng, 106

Lai, Kwong-Chun, 168

Lam, Douglas, 34–35, 51, 121

Lau, Wui Shun, 145

League of Nations, 20

Lehman, Herbert, 86

Lieberman, Henry, 75

Life (magazine), 124, 126–127, 136–138

Lilly Endowment, Inc., 70

Lindt, Auguste, 81

Liu, William, 110, 111

Locke Chang, Arthur, 108

Long, Ernest E., 151

Luce, Henry, 59, 136

Lutheran Church, 57

Lutheran World Federation, 55, 60–61, 64

Lutheran World Service, 41, 43

MacKellar, Michael, 192

Mainland Refugee General Relief Association of Taiwan, 47

Malaysia, 193

Manion, Jack, 201

Mao Zedong, 174, 179

Marchand, Jean, 120

Marks, Edward, 86

Maryknoll Sisters, 56, 68

Massey, William F., 165–166

McDonald, Flora, 201

McGinness, H., 109

McGuire, Frederick A., 65, 66

immigration, 8–13, 28, 99, 104, 111, 163; as point of contention among humanitarian assistance, 75; and resettlement of Hong Kong migrants, 71; and South African immigration, 16, 99, 101–103

race-thinking, 11–13

Red Cross, 47, 92, 156, 195

Redl, Harry, 131

Rees, Elfan, 80

Refugee Relief Act (US), 67, 69

Refugee Status Advisory Committee (RSAC) (Canada), 183–184, 186

refugee stigma, 215–218

Registration of Persons Ordinance (Hong Kong), 38

Rennie's Mill Camp, 45–47, 91

Republic of China (ROC): and Convention Relating to the Status of Refugees, 26, 27; and delegate on UNHCR, 83; establishment of, 4; helping Hong Kong refugees, 5, 49, 62–63, 80, 81, 133; and refugee survey, 76; resettlement of Hong Kong refugees, 47, 68; setting up of FCRA, 46; and UN problem with two Chinas, 29–30. *See also* Guomindang

rice refugees, 2, 13, 199

Rivett, Kenneth, 197–198

Robinson, Jacob, 29, 30

Rochefort, Robert, 28, 31

Roman Catholic Church, 57, 132

Romaniello, John, 56

Royal Canadian Mounted Police (RCMP), 118, 119, 149

Savage, Michael, 152

Savre, Francis B., 86

Shaefter, Richard, 80

Shand, T. S., 154, 157, 166, 167, 169

Shaw, Mark, 60

Shaw, Patrick, 30

Shek Kip Mei fire, 48

Shepherd, Jack, 73

Shepherd, Janet, 73

South Africa: defines a refugee in law, 164; immigration restrictions in, 16, 99, 101–103; response to 1962 grain shortage refugees, 128–129; signs UN Convention and protocol on refugees, 164; and Vietnamese refugees, 187–188; and World Refugee Year, 85–86

South Korea, 9, 24–25

Soviet Union, 21, 50

Sprackett, Robert, 155–157

Status Adjustment Program (Canada), 119–121, 122, 143

St. Louis (ship), 20, 201

Stumpf, Reverend, 56, 94

Swanstrom, Bishop, 132, 134

Swing, Joseph May, 117, 119

Syrian refugees, 18, 218

Szeto, Kuen, 148

Taiwan, 46, 71, 111

Taiyuan incident, 112

Tan, Sid Chow, 121

Thatcher, Margaret, 196

Thompson, H. C. J., 168

Tiananmen Square refugees, 160–161

Tremblay, René, 160

Trench, David, 42

Trudeau, Pierre, 179, 201

United Church, 151, 201, 204

United Nations Association of Hong Kong, 80

United Nations High Commissioner for Refugees (UNHCR): accepts Hong Kong Chinese as refugees, 84; and advisory role in RSAC, 183; criticized on Hong Kong refugees, 75; established, 22; at Geneva Conference on Indochinese refugees, 196, 197; and 1953 refugee survey, 76–80; and 1962 grain shortage refugees, 133;

17, 187–189; response to World Refugee Year, 82, 85–89, 94; shared immigration practices of, 15–16. *see also* Australia; Canada; New Zealand; South Africa; United States

Wong, Willie, 113–114, 115, 123

Wong, Foon Sien, 143–144

Wong, Jap Kuan, 109

Wong, Yew, 112–113

Wood, Duncan, 87

World Council of Churches (WCC): and Cultural Revolution, 175; and Hong Kong squatters, 47; and 1962 grain shortage refugees, 130; reaction to Hambro report, 80; and resettlement of Chinese in New Zealand, 167–168, 169, 170, 171, 172; sponsoring Hong Kong Chinese, 74; view of resettlement, 92; and World Refugee Year, 89, 90

World Refugee Year: Hong Kong government response to, 90–91, 93; humanitarian groups response to, 84–85, 89–90; idea for, 81–82; international response to, 58, 83–85, 150; New Zealand response to, 84, 88, 153, 155; and resettlement issue, 86–88, 91–93; success of, 93, 94; white settler society response to, 82, 84, 85–89, 90, 94

World Vision, 203–204

You, Ng Chuck, 110

Yu, Tsune-Chi, 75

Zhou Enlai, 51–52